B-24 NOSE NAME DIRECTORY

INCLUDES GROUP, SQUADRON AND AIRCRAFT SERIAL NUMBERS AND PHOTO AVAILABILITY

BY

WALLACE R. FORMAN

SPECIALTY PRESS

ISBN: 1-58007-003-5

Library of Congress Catalog Card Number: 97-61943

Text by Wallace R. Forman

Published by:
  Specialty Press Publishers and Wholesalers
  11481 Kost Dam Road
  North Branch, MN 55056
  1-800-895-4585

Printed in the United States of America

PREFACE

This directory is the product of years of statistical research by the author. It is not drawn from "official" records, as no single document contains this information. Incomplete data on aircraft names and serial numbers is scattered through unit records, missing air crew reports, etc. but is not consolidated in any archives. Nor does this directory purport to be all inclusive. It does however, list over **7,800** Consolidated B-24s in all their variations from the World War II era on which some sort of **name** identification was obtained, showing name and, where available, group, squadron and serial number.

The first volume in the series, B-17 Nose Art Name Directory, may be obtained from this publisher.

PHOTO AND TEXT CREDITS

Many of the photos in this work came from the author's collection and the collection of Jack Lambert. A very large percentage were loaned by "Mr. B-24", John R. Beitling who served with a B-24 outfit, the 564th Bomb Squadron and has been an historian and archivist for the Liberator.

As always, Ed Kueppers of the Eighth Air Force Historical Society was most helpful on photos from that source. A number of other people helped in various ways and the order of their listing is not indicative of their degree of cooperation. They are: Hill Goodspeed, National Museum of Naval Aviation (Pensacola); Fred Johnsen, author of fine aviation history and expert on the B-24; and Stephen Hutton, who led us to some of those obscure special units of the Eighth Air Force. Generations to come are in their debt for having preserved so much World War II history.

FRONT COVER: The slab sided fuselage of the Liberator allowed artists and crews to give full expression to their sense of fantasy, audacity and humor. FLAK MAGNET was an Eighth Air Force B-24H serving with the 753rd Sq., 458th Bomb Group. The Emerson A-15 nose turret is nicely displayed. The armor plate under the pilot's window was a field modification. It saved the pilot but not FLAK MAGNET, who lived up to her name. She was set afire by AA and fighters over Germany in April 1944. The crew parachuted and were made Prisoners of War. (Beitling)

BACK COVER: Here the Brooks' crew of TEPEE TIME GAL (variation on a popular tune of the day "Sleepy Time Gal") continued to display the operational record of this 741st Sq., 455th Bomb Group Liberator. This Fifteenth Air Force B-24H brought several crews back after 100 missions. The four Swastikas are claims for German fighters. (Beitling)

INTRODUCTION

This list is called a "consolidation listing"; an unusual term but accurately descriptive. This compilation is not the result of one man's work but of several. What I did was to consolidate their collective but independent efforts.

Paul M. Andrews and William H. Adams have led the way for years putting together the Eighth Air Force Historical Society's "Bits & Pieces" lists of B-17s and B-24s which get bigger and more accurate every time they are reissued. Rhodes F. Arnold in his book *The B-24/PB4Y in Combat* provided a marvelous data list for B-24s. William H. Greenhalgh and Alwyn Lloyd at different times provided B-24 lists to the Journal of the American Aviation Historical Society. I had developed considerable lists on my own for both B-17s and B-24s, with great help on the B-24 list from John R. Beitling, "Mr. B-24", whose knowledge and records are fantastic. All of their inputs, and help from many others, made this venture feasible.

Each of these sources was most helpful. Yet when someone called on the phone with a question, it was a scramble to know which list to look at for an answer. One might have to wade through all of them before finding it. I thought, "Wouldn't it be nice to have a single big list containing all of this data so I'd only have to look just one place to see if there's an answer." I tried to create such a list by consolidating the other men's lists first with each other's and then with my own file.

Months of effort followed, eliminating errors and digging out duplications. Also there were decisions on how many variations to show where old crewmen's memories disagreed on spelling and punctuation of names, accuracy of numbers, etc.

Finally, on May 19, 1993 the resulting consolidation list was sent to all the above mentioned men asking for their comments, and if they had any objection to my using it as a reference or sharing it with some other serious aviation history buffs. There were no negative comments, and a couple of them even expressed gratefulness for my trying something new.

Since then, the lists have been seen by knowledgeable people and a lot of correcting and improving has taken place. In fact this is actually the fifth generation of the list. I continue updating and correcting it almost daily, but it is such a big job that reprinting just isn't a very frequent probability.

What motivates one to get involved in a venture like this?

As a new hobby, started in 1969, I set an objective to get a picture of every make and model of airplane ever built, anywhere in the world, either commercial or military. I had no idea how many this might be, but after twenty-five years , in 1994, I estimated the collection contained some 750,000 pictures of 35,000 different makes and models.

While building this collection, there were two categories which got thrown into boxes rather than getting sorted out at the time. Maybe later. The two categories were home built aircraft and military nose art. On a rainy day I did sort out the nose art by type of plane. There were 1,300 from B-24s and 700 from B-17s. Today there are 3,800 from B-24s and 1,900 from B-17s, with lesser numbers from most other key type WW II combat planes.

The assembling of data lists showing name, group, squadron and serial number of planes already pictured in my nose art collection was a real challenge, and most fascinating. Soon there was also a push in the direction of getting the same data for planes known to have been named, but not yet pictured, in my collection. My own inquisitiveness regarding this resulted in the list before you now.

The nose art aspect of my hobby continues to intrigue me. I believe that nose art in WW II was a very unique piece of Americana. When I pass on, I want to leave behind me, to some institution, a big enough collection of nose art that future generations can look at it and know that art form. Every day veterans are passing on, and widows and children are tossing out one of a kind nose art pictures, unaware of their uniqueness and significance; thus my effort to get them into my collection while the vets are still around. I think they might be glad to see their nose art pictures preserved for posterity.

Some tell me it's a shame not to also get data on unnamed planes. Maybe so, but to me when someone bestowed a name to an aircraft, they also gave it a personality of sorts, which made it quite unique and special, whereas a plane with only a number is just that.

As you can tell from this explanation, I better be better at researching than I am at writing. But the creation of this list has been helpful to me and I hope it will be useful to others. If not useful, at least it may be entertaining as you look at some of the very creative and expressive names GIs coined during World War II.

Inquiries regarding listings and pictures in the directory or donations of nose art pictures are welcomed and can be addressed to:

Wallace R. Forman
2161 W. County Road B
St. Paul, MN 55113-5333
E-Mail: Avibuff@AOL.Com

GLOSSARY

AD	Air Division Depot
AF	Air Force (numbered)
APH	Aphrodite Project (radio-controlled drone bombers)
AS	Anti-Submarine
ASR	Air-Sea Rescue
ATC	Air Transport Command
Aust	Australia
AZON	Steerable Bomb Project
CCR	Combat Crew Replacement Center
CM	Combat Mapping
GRP	Bomb Group
HALP	Halpro Project – Initial Ploesti Raid
Misc	Miscellaneous
Navy	U.S. Navy, unit unknown
NLS	Night Leaflet Squadron
PC	Photo Composite
PIC	'Yes', means picture exists in Forman collection.
PR	Photo Recon
RAF	Royal Air Force (English)
RCAF	Royal Canadian Air Force
RCM	Radio Counter Measures
REC	Reconnaissance
RNavy	British Royal Navy
SCA	Southern Cross Airways
SOP	Secret Operations
SQ	Squadron
VB	U.S. Navy – Bomber Squadron
VD	U.S. Navy – Recon Squadron
VP	U.S. Navy – Patrol Squadron
VPB	U.S. Navy – Patrol-Bomber Squadron
W or WEA	Weather Intelligence

AIRCRAFT NAMES IN ALPHABETICAL ORDER

Name	Grp.	Sq.	Serial	Pic.	Name	Grp.	Sq.	Serial	Pic.
$64 Question	93	330	42-64437	yes	Agony Wagon	465	780	42-52726	no
$64 Question	445	701		no	Agony Wagon	489	846	42-94914	yes
108 Missions	380	531	44-40189	yes	Agony Wagon				yes
21 Special	RCM	36	44-10609	no	Agony Wagon				yes
2nd Ave. El	448			no	Agony Wagon				yes
4-F		4PC		no	Ain't Bluffin'	491	854	44-40246	no
4F	ZI			yes	Ain't Misbehavin'	466	784	42-52509	yes
663	453	735	42-52240	no	Ain't Misbehavin' Minnie	464	776	42-52540	no
A & G Fish Shoppe	458			yes	Ain't Miss Behavin'				no
A - Abel	446	707	44-48838	no	Ain't She Sweet				no
A Drupe				no	Aincha Sorry	90		41-23824	yes
A Run on Sugar				yes	Air Lobe	98	345	42-40312	yes
A Tisket A Tasket...			41-23757	yes	Air Pocket	90	319	44-49479	yes
A Token for Tokio				yes	Air Tramp	479		42-40618	yes
A Train (The)	451	726	42-52082	yes	Air Wac (The)				yes
A Wing and Ten Prayers	380	528	44-42378	yes	Airborn Angel	491	852	42-51294	no
A+	307		41-23919	no	Al's Youth	458			no
A+	90		41-23919	no	Alabama Exterminator	448			no
A-1	34	18	42-94879	no	Alamagordo	2AD			no
A-Broad Abroad	484	827	42-51993	yes	Alda M.	489	844	42-50320	yes
A-Tease	Navy			yes	Alexander's Rag Time Band	460	763	41-29320	no
A-vailable			42-40980	yes	Alfred	392	578	42-7485	no
A-Vailable	30	27	42-72979	yes	Alfred II	392	577	42-7546	yes
A. W. O. L.	30	38	42-72970	no	Alfred III	392			no
Abie's Irish Rose	448	714	41-28606	no	Alfred IV	392	579	42-94961	yes
Abie's Irish Rose	448	714	42-7606	no	Alfred V	392	577	42-95118	no
Able Mabel				yes	Algy	RCAF			yes
Able Mabel	93	328	42-110081	yes	Ali Baba and His Nine Wolves				no
Able Mabel	392	578	42-52544	yes	Alice	467		44-40140	no
About Average	5	23	42-72777	yes	Alice	456	747	42-94777	no
Abroad for Action	VPB	121	Bu59450	yes	Alice	492	857	44-40140	yes
Accentuate the Positive	VPB	108	Bu59441	yes	Alice of Dallas	464			no
Ace of Spades	467		41-28976	no	Alice the Goon	11	26	41-23868	yes
Ace of Spades	43	63	42-40945	no	Alice the Goon	98	344	41-11786	yes
Ace of Spades	489	844	41-28976	no	All 'er Nothin'			42-98017	no
Achtung, Moon Balloon	448		44-50540	yes	All American	448			no
Acme Beer Barrel	308		42-100249	no	All American	461	765	42-78444	yes
Adelaide Fever	380	531	42-41247	yes	All American	ZI	rest.		yes
Admirable Character	458			no	All Meat, No Potatoes	464	777	42-78318	yes
Admirable Little Character	458	754	42-52335	yes	All Mine				no
Adolph and Tojo	451	724	42-7725	no	Alley Oop	6	3	42-63793	yes
Adorable Angie				yes	Alley Oop	380	530	41-24248	yes
After Hours				yes	Alley Oop	465	780		yes
Agony Wagon	392	578	44-50542	no	Alma-Mi-Amor	461	765		yes
Agony Wagon	456	746	44-50436	no	Also Ran	467	790	41-29445	no
Agony Wagon	460	763	42-52355	yes	Amacraw Lou	454	737	42-78395	no
Agony Wagon	465	780	42-52376	no					

Name	Grp.	Sq.	Serial	Pic.
Amapola	93	328	42-40269	no
Amblin' Okie	392	577	41-29174	no
Amblin' Okie	44	67	41-29174	no
Ambrose	93	330	41-23712	yes
Ambrose #2	93	330	41-23909	no
Ambrose III	93	330		no
American Beauty	6PR	20CM	42-73045	yes
American Beauty	308	375	44-41251	yes
American Beauty	392	578	42-95293	no
American Beauty	451	724	41-29530	no
American Beauty	484	827	41-29530	no
American Beauty	486	834	42-98008	no
American Beauty (F7A)	5		42-73065	no
American Lady	489		42-50384	yes
American Maid	451	724	42-78276	no
Anchors Away	VPB	121	Bu59483	yes
Ancient and Honorable Artillery Company of Massachussetts	454	737	42-52264	yes
Andy's Angels	486	833	42-52732	no
Angel				yes
Angel	467	790	42-95057	yes
Angel				yes
Angel Ann	389			no
Angel Face	11	98	42-40960	no
Angel Face 3rd	11	98		no
Angel Face II	30	819		no
Angel Face the 2nd	11		42-73217	no
Angel Face the 2nd	11	98	42-100217	yes
Angel Face the 3rd	11	98	42-109949	yes
Angel in de Skies	380	528	42-73464	yes
Angel of the Sky	460		42-52365	yes
Angel of the Sky	465	781	42-51254	yes
Angel of the Sky	465	781	42-52365	yes
Angel of the Sky	465	781	42-52365	yes
Angela	11	42	44-40498	yes
Angie the Ox	376	515	41-24031	yes
Angry Angel (The)	308	374	42-73436	yes
Anita Lynn (The)	456	744	42-52276	no
Ann	34		42-51190	no
Ann	445	701	42-7622	no
Annie	30	392	42-72958	yes
Annie Fay	307		41-24096	yes
Annie Oakley Crack Shot	44	67	42-40126	yes
Annie's Cousin Mamie	93			no
Any Gum Chum?	44	68	42-110035	yes
Ape	451	727	42-95239	no
Apocalypse	7	436	41-23879	no
Apocalypse	487	836	41-23879	no
Appassionata	489	846	42-50437	yes
Aquaria	486	834	42-52545	yes
Aquarius	486	834	xx-xx650	no
Aquina	376		40-698	no
Arabian Nights			40-2370	no
Archibald	453	735	41-28591	no
Aries				no
Aries	486	834	xx-xx545	yes
Aries II	486	834	42-52693	yes
Aries the 1st	486	834	42-52765	yes
Arise My Love and Come With Me	458	754	42-50768	yes
Ark Angel	491	853	44-40073	yes
Ark Angel	491	854	44-40271	no
Arkansas Bobo				no
Arkansas Joe	455	741	42-64456	no
Arkansas Joe	456	746	42-78594	no
Arkansas Traveler	445		42-50618	no
Arkansas Traveler	376	515	41-11616	yes
Arkansas Traveler II	98	345	41-23781	yes
Arkansas Traveller	98	345	41-11809	yes
Arlene the Lincoln Queen	376			yes
Armed Venus	494	867	44-40740	yes
Armored Angel	308	374	44-49624	yes
Arrowhead	44	68	42-51108	no
Arrowhead	453	734	42-51108	yes
Arsenal (The)	392	577	42-109826	no
Arsenic & Old Lace	461	765	42-52025	no
Art's Cart	43	63	42-40896	yes
As You Like It	93	409	41-23748	no
As You See It	93			no
As-cend Charlie	11	98	42-73009	yes
Asbestos Alice	445			no
Ash Can Annie	480		41-24021	no
Ashcan Charlie	460	763	42-99798	no
Assam Wagon	308	374		no
Assender				no
Assender II	93			no
Assole	466	787	42-52518	no
Asterperious Special	90	319	42-73493	yes
At Ease	43	63	42-40955	no
Atchison, Topeka & Santa Fe	28	404	44-49807	yes
Atom Smasher	380	530	42-64045	yes
Atomic Blonde	380	531	41-51414	yes
Atomic Blonde	380	531	44-42414	no
Attitude Adjustment	446			no
Augusta P.	450	721	42-78455	no
Available	307	370	42-40980	yes
Available	308	375	42-100269	yes
Available Jones	44	67	42-40780	yes
Avenger				yes
Avenger	44	68	41-23788	yes
Avenger II	44	66	42-40130	no
Avenger of Agony Wagon	460	763	42-78301	no
Awkward Angel	484	825	41-29502	yes
Axis Ex-Lax	445	702	42-94820	no
Axis Ex-Lax	490	848	42-94820	no
Axis ExLax	490	848	41-28870	no
Axis Grinder	392	577	42-7495	yes
Axis Nightmare	308	373	41-24138	yes
Aye's Dynamiters	467	789	42-50515	no

Name	Grp.	Sq.	Serial	Pic.	Name	Grp.	Sq.	Serial	Pic.
Azza	459	757		no	Back Sheesh Bessie				no
B-23 1/2	ZI			yes	Back to the Sack			42-7563	no
B. O. II			42-95177	no	Back to the Sack	448	713	42-51288	yes
B. T. O.	446		44-40072	no	Back to the Sack	448	713	42-51291	no
B. T. O.	448		42-73193	no	Back to the Sack	491	854	44-40249	yes
B. T. O.	455			yes	Bad Boy	486	835	41-29472	no
B. T. O.	466		44-40072	no	Bad Girl	AZON		44-40288	yes
B. T. O.	98	344	41-24040	no	Bad Girl	458	753	44-40288	yes
B. T. O.	392	578	42-99981	yes	Bad Penny	34		42-94764	no
B. T. O.	445	702	42-7627	no	Bad Penny	448			no
B. T. O.	448	714	42-50678	no	Bad Penny	90	321	44-41314	yes
B. T. O.	454	738	42-78504	yes	Bad Penny	44	67	42-7650	no
B. T. O.	459	758	42-52326	yes	Bad Penny				yes
B. T. O.	489	846	44-40072	yes	Bad Penny (The)				no
B. T. O.	491	855	42-50678	no	Bad Penny (The)	307	370	41-23899	yes
B. T. O.	492	857	44-40072	yes	Bad Penny (The)	308	375	41-24238	yes
Bab King Kong	445			no	Bad Penny (The)	389	564	42-40767	no
Babby Maggy	93			no	Bad Penny (The)	451	726	42-51321	yes
Babe	451	727	42-95359	no	Bad Penny (The)	464	779	42-78488	yes
Babe in Arms	450	720	42-78234	yes	Bad Penny Always Comes Back	490			no
Babe the Big Blue Ox	376	515	41-11602	no	Bad Penny II	34			no
Babes in Arms	307	370	42-73263	yes	Bad Penny II	493		44-40267	no
Baby	15AF			yes	Bad Penny III	34			no
Baby	90	320	41-24094	yes	Bad Penny IV	34			no
Baby	98	344	41-24026	yes	Badger Beauty	376	515	44-41062	yes
Baby	90	400	42-72798	no	Baffling Brat	467	789	42-52512	no
Baby				yes	Bag O' Bolts	448	715	42-7746	no
Baby (C-109)			44-48999	yes	Bag-O-Bolts	448	715	42-7764	no
Baby (The)	456	746	42-51855	yes	Bag-O-Bones	448			no
Baby Boots	456	746	42-51688	yes	Baggy Maggy	93	409	42-100416	yes
Baby Bug	493		42-94865	no	Bagin' Lulu	446			no
Baby Bug	490	850	42-94865	yes	Bail Out Belle	380	529	42-72951	yes
Baby Bug II				yes	Bakadori	392	578	42-7502	yes
Baby Doll	448			no	Baldy & His Brood	44	506	41-24201	yes
Baby Doll	493		42-50554	yes	Ball of Fire	30			yes
Baby Doll (The)	489	844	42-52698	yes	Ball of Fire	44			no
Baby Jane	456	745	42-78239	no	Ball of Fire	448			no
Baby Ruth			41-24292	no	Ball of Fire	HALP		41-11624	no
Baby Sandy II	11	98	42-73013	no	Ball of Fire	93	328	41-23667	yes
Baby Shoe (The)	486	833		no	Ball of Fire	93	328	42-72869	no
Baby Shoe II (The)	486	833		no	Ball of Fire	93	329	41-23670	no
Baby Shoe III (The)			44-6202	no	Ball of Fire III	93			no
Baby Shoes	492		42-50555	no	Ball of Fire Jr.	93	328	41-23874	no
Baby Shoes	448	712	41-28611	no	Ball of Fire, Junior	93	328	42-40128	yes
Baby Shoes	458	753	42-50555	yes	Ballot Baker	491	853	42-110186	no
Baby's Shoes			41-28611	no	Balls 'n All(C-87)				yes
Bachelor Bomber	451	725	42-52158	yes	Balls O' Fire	307		42-40202	yes
Bachelor's Baby	34		42-99991	yes	Balls O' Fire	455	740	44-41115	yes
Bachelor's Bedlam	AZON		44-40287	no	Balls of Fire	445	700	42-109796	yes
Bachelor's Bedlam	450	723		yes	Balls of Fire	449	718	42-109796	yes
Bachelor's Bedlam	458	753	44-40287	yes	Balls of Fire				yes
Bachelor's Brothel	380	531	44-50927	yes	Balls of Fire No. 2	93	328	41-23667	yes
Bachelor's Delight	445		42-78481	no	Ballsafire	445	700	42-7643	no
Bachelor's Delight	448			no	Bama Baby	454	739	42-52205	no
Bachelor's Lady	34	391	41-29562	no	Bama Bound- Lovely Libby	RCM	36	42-50622	no
Bachelor's Party	34	391	41-29562	no					
Bachelor's Roost	464	776	41-29453	yes					

Name	Grp.	Sq.	Serial	Pic.	Name	Grp.	Sq.	Serial	Pic.
Bama Bound-Lovely Libby		801	42-50622	no	Battle Dragon	446	705	42-50431	yes
Bambi	98	345	41-11813	yes	Battle Package	453	732	42-52201	no
Bambi	34	4	41-29567	yes	Battle Weary	380	528	42-41243	yes
Banana Barge (The)	44	506	42-110045	yes	Battlin' Baby	44	68	42-94892	no
Banana Boat	450	720	42-7742	no	Battlin' Baby	448	713	42-99971	yes
Banger			41-29567	no	Battlin' Baby	467	791	42-99971	no
Banger	446	705	41-29140	yes	Battlin' Bitch	RCAF		42-64224	yes
Bangi	446			no	Battlin' Bitch	308	375	41-24237	yes
Bangin' Lulu	446	707	44-48829	yes	Battlin' Bitch	7	9	41-24237	yes
Banshee	448			no	Battling Betsy	489			no
Banshee	44	66	42-63965	no	Battling Bitch	30	392	42-72985	yes
Banshee (The)	44	66	42-7536	yes	Battling Boops	492	858	44-40159	no
Banshee II	44			no	Battling Hornet	30	392	42-73281	yes
Banshee II	448			no	Be Comin' Back	464	778	44-41043	no
Banshee III	44	66		no	Beach-Belle	446	705	44-50513	no
Banshee IV	44	66	42-99980	no	Bear Baby	456	747	42-64470	no
Bar Fly	448		42-95055	no	Bear Down	93	328	42-72863	no
Bar Fly	446	706		no	Bear Down	93	328	42-72869	no
Bar Fly	446	707		yes	Beast (The)	445		42-50743	no
Bar Fly (The)	307	372	42-40096	yes	Beast (The)	446	704	42-7679	no
Bar Made	7			yes	Beast (The)	454	736	42-99758	no
Bar Que				no	Beast (The)	458	755	42-50743	yes
Barbara Ann	460			yes	Beast of Bourbon	482	36	42-50385	yes
Barbara Jane	456	745	42-52304	yes	Beast of Bourbon	RCM	36	42-50385	yes
Barbara Jane II	456	744	44-40592	no	Beast of Bourbon		801	42-50385	yes
Barbara Jean (F-7)	43	65	44-40980	yes	Beaufort Belle	11		44-49528	yes
Barber Pole (The)				no	Beaufort Belle		WEA		yes
Barfly	44	67	42-99986	yes	Beautiful Beast	380	528	42-73167	yes
Barfly	44	67	42-99996	yes	Beautiful Betsy	380	528	42-40387	yes
Barney's Buzz Wagon	446	705	42-50316	yes	Beautiful Takeoff	459	756	44-49732	yes
Barrelhouse Bess	453			no	Beautiful Takeoff	489	844	42-50451	yes
Barrelhouse Bessie	376	515	42-40317	yes	Beautiful Takeoff	491	854	42-50451	no
Barrelhouse Bessie	11	98	42-73027	yes	Beaver's Baby	93	409	42-50597	yes
Barumska	455	742	42-51990	no	Bebe	380	531	42-41248	yes
Bashful	98	343	41-11776	yes	Becky	453		42-51216	no
Bashful Bessie	487			no	Becky	453	735	42-94850	no
Bashful Marion			41-28820	no	Becky	458	752	42-95216	no
Basil				yes	Becomin' Back	380	528	44-50390	yes
Bastard	446	704	42-7628	yes	Becomin' Back	491	855	44-10575	no
Bastard	453	734	42-50720	no	Becoming Back	453	735	44-10575	yes
Basterpiece	RCAF		3704	yes	Bee Line Betty	308	374	44-41292	yes
Bat (The)	ZI			yes	Beelzebub's Babe	487		42-52745	yes
Bat (The)	451	725	41-28740	no	Before (and After)				yes
Bat Out of Hell	11			no	Begin the Beguine	453	732	41-28619	no
Bat Out of Hell	30	392	42-73024	yes	Bela	376	513	41-23918	no
Bat Out of Hell	44	68	41-23806	no	Bela	44	67	41-23918	no
Bat Outa Hell	448			no	Belchin' Bertha	98	344	42-40742	yes
Bathless	30	392	42-109838	yes	Belchin' Bessie	34	7	41-29559	yes
Bathless	11	431	42-109838	yes	Bell Hotel				no
Bathtub Bessie	93	330	41-23678	yes	Belle				no
Batter Bam	491			no	Belle	466	785	42-51099	yes
Battin' Lady				no	Belle				yes
Battle Axe	98	345	42-40793	yes	Belle (The)	494			no
Battle Axe	44	66	42-40793	yes	Belle of Boston	458	754	41-29299	yes
Battle Axe	446	706	42-51073	yes	Belle of Boston	458	754	42-52404	yes
Battle Crate	461	764	41-29289	yes	Belle of Texas	11	42	42-73156	yes
					Belle of the Brawl				yes

Name	Grp.	Sq.	Serial	Pic.	Name	Grp.	Sq.	Serial	Pic.
Belle of the Brawl	389		42-94904	no	Betty	458	755		yes
Belle of the Brawl	34	391	42-94904	no	Betty	459	756		yes
Belle of the Brawl	376	512	42-94904	no	Betty Ann	449	719	41-29215	no
Belle of the Brawl	456	746		no	Betty Anne	459	758	42-51262	no
Belle of the Brawl	11	98	44-40280	yes	Betty Coed	451	725	44-41109	yes
Belle of the East	467	789	42-110187	no	Betty Coed	454	739	41-28656	no
Belle of the East	491	854	42-110187	yes	Betty G.	308	375	41-24279	yes
Belle Ringer	464			no	Betty J				yes
Belle Ringer	460	762	42-52347	yes	Betty J.	11	42	44-41551	yes
Belle Ringer	465	781	42-52503	no	Betty Jane	34		42-94768	no
Belle Ringer	491	852	42-52347	no	Betty Jane	460			no
Belle Ringer	491	855	42-51296	yes	Betty Jane	493		42-94768	no
Belle Starr	308	425	42-40879	yes	Betty Jane	801		42-94768	no
Belle Wringer	90	400	44-50694	yes	Betty Jane	SOP		42-94768	no
Belle Wringer				yes	Betty Jane	389	565	44-40092	yes
Belligerent Bess	2AD			no	Betty Jane	453	733	xx-x3387	yes
Bells of St. Jo	484	826	44-49828	no	Betty Jean	449	719	41-28625	yes
Belzebub	465		41-29444	no	Betty Jean	453	733	xx-x3387	no
Belzebub	464	777	41-29444	no	Betty Jo	451	725	42-51682	no
Ben Buzzard	43			no	Betty Lee	389			no
Benghazi Express	376	514	41-11631	yes	Betty(Bette) Anne	44	67	41-23783	no
Benutz Joy	492			no	Betty-Jim (The)	489	847	42-94947	yes
Benutz Joy	SOP			no	Betty-Jim (The)	491	954	42-94947	no
Berlin Bitch	392	579	42-95103	no	Beverly Ann	459	759		no
Berlin Bound	466	784	42-50717	no	Beverly Joy	SOP			no
Berlin Box Car	448			no	Beverly Joy	492	857	42-50492	yes
Berlin Express				no	Bewitching Witch	376	512	41-24024	no
Berlin Express	Navy			yes	Bewitching Witch	44	67	41-24024	yes
Berlin First	482		42-32002	no	Bi-U Baby	44	66	42-95619	no
Berlin Sleeper	448			no	Bi-U Baby	491	855	42-95619	yes
Bertha/Lady Jane	93	329	42-40804	no	Bif Bam	466	785	42-95283	yes
Bess				yes	Biff Bam	458	752	41-28718	no
Bessie				no	Big 'Un	491	855	42-50680	yes
Bessie May Mucho				no	Big Alice from Dallas	485	829	42-52730	no
Bestwedu	449	718		no	Big Ass Bird				no
Bestwedu	455	741	42-52257	yes	Big Ass Bird				yes
Bestwedu	459	756		yes	Big Ass Bird	392	578	42-7490	no
Bet's Bet	459	759	42-52257	yes	Big Ass Bird	43	65	42-73478	yes
Beth				no	Big Ass Bird	448	713	42-64441	no
Betsie	487		42-52736	no	Big Ass Bird (The)	380	528	42-73113	yes
Betsy	15AF		42-50610	yes	Big Ass Bird II (The)	380	531	42-72801	yes
Betsy	90	321	42-72956	yes	Big Ass Bird III (The)	380	531	44-40396	yes
Betsy	491	854	42-50610	yes	Big Ast Bird	487	836	41-29520	no
Betsy II	389			no	Big Axe	453	732	41-29250	yes
Betsy Jane	448		42-95169	no	Big Az Bird (The)	7			no
Betsy Jay	448			no	Big Bad Wolf	448	715	41-29479	no
Betta Duck				no	Big Bad Wolf	487	836	41-29479	no
Betta Duck			41-23783	no	Big Banner	44	66	42-7638	no
Betta Duck	493		44-40454	no	Big Big				yes
Betta Duck	34	7	44-49454	no	Big Bill	449		42-64400	yes
Betta Duck	466	785	44-40454	yes	Big Bimbo	90	321		no
Bette Ann	44	67	41-23783	no	Big Bimbo	90	321		no
Better Late than Never	98	345	42-51364	no	Big Black Bitch	307		41-24269	yes
Better Late than Never	485	828	42-78446	no	Big Black Bitch	90	400	41-24269	no
Betty	AD4			no	Big Boober Girl	451	727	41-29199	yes
Betty	445	703	42-7562	no	Big Brown Jug (The)	389		42-110148	no
Betty	451	727		yes	Big Brown Jug (The)	492	856	42-110148	no

Name	Grp.	Sq.	Serial	Pic.	Name	Grp.	Sq.	Serial	Pic.
Big Brute	466	784	42-29419	yes	Big Sugar	491	855	42-110170	no
Big Burn	456			no	Big Time Operator	448			no
Big Chief	90	321	42-72774	yes	Big Time Operator	98	344	41-24040	no
Big Chief Cockeye	43	403	42-40351	yes	Big Time Operator	380	529	42-73193	no
Big Chief Cockeye	380	529	42-40351	yes	Big Time Operator	380	530	42-41214	yes
Big Chief Lil'					Big Time Operator	44	66	42-50480	no
Beaver	458		42-51514	yes	Big Time Operator	458	753	41-29288	yes
Big Dealer	93	330	41-23665	yes	Big Time Operator	460	763	42-94923	no
Big Dealer	493	862	42-52759	yes	Big Time Operator	494	864	44-40757	yes
Big Dear				no	Big Time Operators	392	577	42-94897	yes
Big Dick	484	825	42-94740	yes	Big Wheel	446	707	44-10529	yes
Big Dick, Hard to Hit	448			no	Big Wheeler Dealer	464	778	42-78374	no
Big Dick, Hard to Hit	458	754	41-28682	yes	Big-Az-Bird (The)	308			yes
Big Dog	392	578	42-7483	no	Bigast Bird (The)	389	567	42-51233	yes
Big Dog & Nine					Bigast Boid	389			no
Old Men	454	739	41-28815	no	Bigger Boober Girl	451	727	41-28957	no
Big Drip	484	824	42-52708	no	Biggest Boid			42-51233	no
Big Drip	487	836	41-29524	yes	Bill Flap and				
Big Drip (The)	446	705	41-29524	yes	Gear Specialist	491			no
Big Drip, Jr. (The)	487		42-52636	no	Billie B.	307	370	42-40076	yes
Big Eagle	93	330	41-23678	no	Billie Babe	445	703	42-7523	no
Big Emma	90	321	41-23764	no	Billie K.	461	765	44-49038	yes
Big Fat Butterfly			42-99939	no	Billie Mae	453			no
Big Fat Butterfly	44	66	42-64166	yes	Billy Jo	307		42-110080	no
Big Fat Mama	446		44-40067	no	Billy Mae	453			no
Big Fat Mama	392	578	44-40067	yes	Billy the Kid	2AD			no
Big Fat Mama	464	779	44-41213	yes	Bim Bam Bola	448	714	42-94735	no
Big Fat Mama	466	786	44-40067	no	Bing's Big Box	44	68	42-7501	no
Big Fat Mama	492	856	44-40067	no	Bingo	461	764	44-49897	yes
Big Fat Momma	451	726	42-52429	no	Bird (The)	458	752	42-100425	yes
Big Gas Bird	455	743	42-78081	yes	Bird Dog				no
Big Gas Bird				yes	Bird Dog	98	343	42-40341	yes
Big Headed Kid	44	506	44-50748	no	Bird Dog	466	784	42-95084	yes
Big Idjit	451	724	42-52099	yes	Bird Dog	491	854	42-110187	no
Big Job	93	330	42-40627	no	Bird of Paradise	30	27	44-40677	yes
Big Joe	445	703	41-29123	no	Bird of Paradise	30	392	42-72984	no
Big Marge	376	512	41-28920	no	Bird's Eye View	30	38	44-42158	yes
Big Mogul	451	726	42-52078	yes	Bird's Eye View	11	431		yes
Big Nig	376	515	42-73428	no	Birdie Schmidt ARC	392	576	42-50387	yes
Big Noise				no	Birmingham Blitz				
Big Noise	93	330	42-40969	yes	Buggy	448			no
Big Noise from Kentucky	449	718	42-52149	yes	Birmingham				
Big Noise II	93	330	42-94969	no	Express	93	329	42-63968	no
Big Noise III				yes	Biscay Belle	479			yes
Big Operator				yes	Bit XX Big Joe	445	703	41-29123	no
Big Operator	98	344	42-41023	yes	Bitch Kitty	30	392	42-72965	no
Big Operator (The)	98	344	41-24040	yes	Bitch's Sister (The)	308	375	42-73319	yes
Big Operator's					Bitchurquitchin'	307	372	42-40134	yes
Scoreboard				yes	Bitchurquitchin' II	307	372	44-40599	yes
Big Red	308			yes	Bizzy Bitch	485	830	42-51166	yes
Big Sleep (The)	5			yes	Black Cat	466	784	42-95592	yes
Big Sleep (The)	307	370	42-73270	yes	Black Cat	494	864	44-40704	yes
Big Sleep (The)	308	373		yes	Black Fox (The)	464	779	41-29398	no
Big Stinky	461	765	41-28717	no	Black Fox (The)	464	779	42-78618	no
Big Stoop	485	830	41-28842	no	Black Hal	464	779	42-51083	no
Big Stud				yes	Black Item	464	779	42-51663	no
Big Stuff	448			no	Black Jack				no

Name	Grp.	Sq.	Serial	Pic.	Name	Grp.	Sq.	Serial	Pic.
Black Jack	445			no	Blind Date	449	716	41-29243	no
Black Jack	466			no	Blind Date				yes
Black Jack	44	68	41-23816	yes	Blitz Buggy	465		44-40632	no
Black Jack II	484	824	44-40941	yes	Blitz Queen	307	424	42-40858	yes
Black Jed 654	453	735	42-52244	yes	Blockbuster	466	787	42-110164	no
Black Jig	464	779	42-78671	no	Blockbuster	491	853	42-110164	yes
Black M			42-100093	yes	Blockbuster Bernard	455	742	41-29570	no
Black Magic	376		42-40662	yes	Blond Bomber	7		41-11895	no
Black Magic	44			yes	Blonde Baby	90			no
Black Magic	492			no	Blonde Blitz	6	397	AL628	yes
Black Magic	98	415	42-40662	yes	Blonde Bomb Baby				no
Black Magic	380	528	42-40393	yes	Blonde Bomber	467		42-50471	yes
Black Magic	392	576	42-7527	yes	Blonde Bomber	98	343	41-11760	yes
Black Magic	43	64	42-41224	no	Blonde Bomber	98	343	41-11895	yes
Black Magic	43	65	42-41116	yes	Blonde Bomber	376	515	42-100253	yes
Black Magic	446	706	42-110093	yes	Blonde Bomber	464	777	42-78333	no
Black Magic	459	757		no	Blonde Bomber (The)	90	320	42-40942	yes
Black Magic	489	846	42-52737	yes	Blonde Bomber (The)	464	776	42-78431	no
Black Magic				yes	Blonde Bomber II	98	343	41-23659	yes
Black Mariah	376	513	41-11593	no	Blonde Bombshell (The)	455	742	42-52230	yes
Black Mike	464	779	44-41053	no	Blonde Bombshell II	455	740	42-78620	no
Black Nan	464	779	44-49710	yes	Blondes Away	453			no
Black Oboe	464	779	42-51129	no	Blondes Away	389	567	42-40793	yes
Black Roger	464	779	44-49028	no	Blondes Away	43	64	42-110006	no
Black Sheep	VPB	120	Bu59745	yes	Blondes Away				yes
Black Sheep	44	67	42-41021	no	Blondie Saunders (The)	11			yes
Black Sheep	494	867	44-40760	yes	Blondie's Folly	458	755	41-29331	yes
Black Sheep (The)	376	512	42-72776	no	Blood and Guts	453	733	44-50671	no
Black Swan	485			yes	Blow Job	487	839	41-28837	yes
Black Velvet	380	529	42-41239	no	Blowing Bubbles	98	344	42-72779	no
Black Widow				yes	Blubber Butt		2PCS	42-64254	yes
Black Widow	487			no	Blue 1	465	783	41-28853	yes
Black Widow	380	528	42-40967	yes	Blue Bell	VD	5		yes
Black Widow	392	576	42-7527	no	Blue Circle	491	854	44-40242	no
Black Widow	446	707	42-7542	no	Blue Circle	491	855	44-40108	Pic.
Black Widow	448	713	42-100109	yes	Blue Diamond	VPB	106	Bu59396	yes
Black Widow	464	779	42-95336	yes	Blue Dragon	6PR	24CM	44-41680	yes
Black Widow II	392		42-94912	no	Blue Goose	HALP		41-11597	no
Black Zebra	464	779	42-50867	no	Blue Goose	44	67	41-11653	no
Black Zombie	406		41-29602	no	Blue Jay	5	31	44-40607	yes
Blackie's Bastards	489	846	42-52288	no	Blue M for Mike	460	760	44-41252	no
Blackjack	446	707		no	Blue N	465	783	44-41106	no
Blake's Snakes	448			no	Blue Streak	376	514	41-11613	yes
Blanid's Baby	392	576	42-7560	yes	Blue Streak (The)	376	514	42-51635	yes
Blasted Event				yes	Blue-J	5	31	44-40607	yes
Blasted Event	445			no	Blues in the Night	448	713		no
Blasted Event	453			no	Blunderbus				yes
Blasted Event	455		42-95334	yes	Blunderbus	Navy			yes
Blasted Event	SOP		41-23682	yes	Blunderbus	389	565	42-7593	yes
Blasted Event	93	329	41-23682	yes	Blunderbus	446	704	42-7593	no
Blasted Event	93	409	42-7682	no	Blunderin' Ben	494	864	44-40746	yes
Blasted Event	487	837	42-52487	no	Blushing Virgin	459			no
Blastin' Bastard	93	330	41-23707	no	Blythe's Old Maid	ZI		42-41185	yes
Bleeding Heart	467	791	42-51227	no	Bo / Bif Bam	458	752	41-28718	yes
Blessed Event	307		42-40533	yes	Bo 41	458		42-7718	yes
Blind Bat (The)	479		42-40750	yes	Bo II	458			no
Blind Date				yes	Boardwalk Flyer	459			no

Name	Grp.	Sq.	Serial	Pic.	Name	Grp.	Sq.	Serial	Pic.
Bob Alfred				no	Bonnie	466	784	41-29459	yes
Bob Alfred II				no	Bonnie	456			no
Bob's Hope	43	64	44-40395	yes	Bonnie B.			44-40378	no
Bobbie				no	Bonnie B.	493		42-51195	no
Bobbie Lou	307		44-49617	yes	Bonnie Belle	308	425	42-40103	yes
Bobbie Lou Too	307		44-51617	no	Bonnie D. or Dee	445	700	42-95128	no
Bobbit				yes	Bonnie Vee	445	700	42-95128	no
Bobby Anne of Texas	90	319	44-40228	yes	Bonnie's Boys	449	719	42-50307	no
Bodacious	93			no	Bonnie's Pride				no
Bodacious Critter	451	727	42-64450	yes	Bonnie-Annie-Laurie	464	778	42-51760	yes
Bodacious Critter II	451	727	42-78157	yes	Boobie Trap	ZI			yes
Bodacious Idjit	11	98	44-41948	yes	Boobie Trap	461	767	41-29332	yes
Boilermaker	98	415	41-11918	yes	Booby Trap				no
Boilermaker	376	513	41-11910	yes	Booby Trap	90	321	44-40193	yes
Boilermaker II	98	415	41-23782	yes	Booby Trap	490	850	42-94802	yes
Boise Babe	453	735	42-50715	yes	Boogie Joy	448			no
Boise Belle	461	766	42-52398	no	Boogow	28	404	41-23941	yes
Boise Bronc	90	320	44-40728	no	Boom Boom	449	718		no
Boise Bronc	30	392	44-40728	yes	Boomerang				yes
Boisterous Bitch	7	9	41-24302	yes	Boomerang				no
Bold 75	448			no	Boomerang	308		41-23944	no
Bold Sea Rover (The)	34	18	42-94745	no	Boomerang	376		42-52726	yes
Bold Sea Rover (The)	493	861	42-94745	no	Boomerang	445			yes
Bold Venture III	467	788	42-50675	no	Boomerang	460			yes
Bold Venture III	492	859	42-50675	no	Boomerang	493		44-40957	no
Bolicat	490	851	41-29473	no	Boomerang	376	514	41-29425	yes
Bolicat	493	861	41-29473	no	Boomerang	389	566	42-40115	yes
Bolivar	30	27	42-72994	yes	Boomerang	448	712	42-52132	no
Bolivar, Jr.	11	98	44-42151	yes	Boomerang	448	714	42-52115	no
Bomb Babe				no	Boomerang	451	725	41-29219	yes
Bomb Babe	494	866	44-40709	yes	Boomerang	492	857	44-40171	no
Bomb Baby	489	847	42-94829	yes	Boomerang			42-52215	no
Bomb Boogie	376	515	42-40229	yes	Boomerang II	93	330	42-63969	no
Bomb Boogie	392	577	42-50792	no	Boomerang II	93	409	42-40974	no
Bomb Boogie	448	713	42-52120	no	Boomerang the Sad				
Bomb Boogie	467	789	42-50792	no	Sack	445	703		yes
Bomb Em Baby				no	Boomerang, Back Again	7	493	41-23887	yes
Bomb Jockier	459			no	Boop	492	858	44-40159	no
Bomb Lullaby	11		42-72988	yes	Boot in the Ass	451	724	42-51369	yes
Bomb Lullaby	30	392	42-72988	yes	Bootling Boop	492	858	44-40159	yes
Bomb Totin' Mama	458	754	41-29295	yes	Boots	98	343	42-40313	yes
Bomb Wacky Wabbit				yes	Boots	482	36	41-29599	no
Bomb Wacky Wabbit	22			no	Boots	34	391		no
Bomb-Ah-Dear	458	755	41-29342	yes	Boots	490	850	41-29599	yes
Bombat			xx-xx134	yes	Boots and His Buddies	451	724	42-78414	no
Bomber's Moon	489	844	42-94903	yes	Boozer	485	830	42-52702	no
Bomble Bee	493	860	44-40414	yes	Boozin' Susan	464	779	42-52502	yes
Bombs Away	458	753	42-95096	yes	Born to Lose	449	719	41-29258	yes
Bombs for Nippon	90	400	41-23942	yes	Born to Lose	451	724	41-29258	yes
Bombs to Nippon	5		42-73147	yes	Borrowed Time	376	513	42-64474	no
Bombs To Nippon	307	371	42-73147	yes	Borrowed Time	454	739	42-64474	no
Bomerang	93	328	41-23722	yes	Borsuk's Bitch	453	735	42-64496	yes
Bomerang	376	514	41-29425	yes	Boston				no
Bomerang Jr.				no	Boston Deb	6AF			yes
Bona Venture	484	825	44-49580	no	Bottle Baby	492	858	44-40169	yes
Bonnie				no	Bottom's Up	451	727	42-51674	no
Bonnie	330			yes	Bottoms Up			44-40487	yes

Name	Grp.	Sq.	Serial	Pic.	Name	Grp.	Sq.	Serial	Pic.
Bottoms Up			44-40489	yes	Bubble Trouble	451	726	42-78497	yes
Bottoms Up	98			yes	Bubble Trouble	461	764	42-78437	no
Bottoms Up	90	319	42-100232	yes	Bubbles	376	514	42-72846	yes
Bottoms Up	98	415	42-72908	no	Bubbling Lady	445	702	42-7597	no
Bottoms Up	450	721	42-64448	yes	Buccaneer Bunny	VPB	121	Bu59478	yes
Bottoms Up	460	760	42-51926	yes	Buck Benny Rides Again	90	400	44-40340	yes
Bottoms Up				yes	Buck Eye Belle	446			yes
Bottoms Up (F-7)				yes	Buck Fifty Job	93			yes
Boudoir Commandos	376	515		no	Buck Shot	489	846	42-94761	no
Boulder Buf	448			no	Buckaroo (The)	446	706	42-95203	no
Boulder Buff	492	857	44-40195	yes	Bucket O' Bolts				yes
Bouncin' Betty			Bu59741	no	Bucket of Bolts	448			no
Bourbon Boxcar	6PR	20CM	42-73048	yes	Bucket of Bolts	449	718	41-28600	yes
Bowen's Banshee			44-40773	no	Bucket of Bolts II	455	740	42-50400	no
Box Car Babe	487		42-52646	no	Buckeye Belle	450	720	42-7748	no
Boy's Howdy			41-29138	no	Bucksheesh Benny	389	566	41-24112	yes
Boys from Hell	466			no	Bucksheesh Benny	44	68	42-40094	no
Bozo	VB	103	Bu32039	no	Bucksheesh Benny				
Br'er Rabbit	801		42-63798	yes	Rides Again	44	68	41-24112	no
Brady's Gang	449	716	42-7769	yes	Buckshot	389			yes
Brainchild of Warchant	466	784	42-94915	no	Buckshot	446	705	42-7625	yes
Brass Monkey	449	717	41-28846	no	Buckshot Annie	489	846	42-94819	yes
Breadline in '49	380	528	44-42201	yes	Buelah	450	723	41-29228	no
Breezie Weesie	451	727	41-28806	yes	Buffalo	453			no
Breezie Wheezie	450	723	42-78613	no	Buffalo Bill				no
Breezy	5		42-100270	yes	Buffalo Gal	448			no
Breezy Lady	458	755	42-110141	yes	Buffalo Gal	454	738	42-52297	no
Breezy Lady	492	859	42-110141	no	Bug Drip	487			no
Brewery Wagon	376	512	41-24294	yes	Bugs	465	780	42-78259	no
Brief	494	867	44-42058	yes	Bugs Bomby	392		42-72998	no
Briefed for Action	308	374	44-41443	yes	Bugs Bomby	30	392	42-72998	yes
Bright Eyes	454	739	41-28790	no	Bugs Bomby, Jr.	11	42	44-41466	yes
Briney Marlin	453	733	42-52139	no	Bugs Buggy	494	864	44-40707	yes
Briney Marlin	458	755	42-95183	yes	Bugs Bunny				no
Bring 'em Back Alive	448			no	Bugs Bunny	448			no
Broad and High	492		42-50439	no	Bugs Bunny	489			no
Broad and High	467	788	42-50439	no	Bugs Bunny	98	344	42-41029	no
Broadway Bill	448			no	Bugs Bunny	445	700	42-95210	no
Broganelle Fireball				no	Bugs Bunny	458	754	42-50640	no
Broken Dollar	459	759		no	Bugs Bunny	459	757		no
Bronco Nagurski	392	579	41-29552	no	Bugs Bunny	467	791	42-52530	yes
Bronx Express (The)	491	854	44-40248	yes	Bugs Bunny Jr.	494	865	44-40654	no
Brooklyn Rambler	HALP		41-11596	yes	Bull Bat	392	578	42-7472	yes
Brooklyn-No Name Jive	448	714	41-29230	no	Bull II (The)	494	865	44-40688	yes
Brown Bagger's Retreat			Bu65385	yes	Bull Moose	376	514	42-72778	yes
Brown Knowser	446	704	42-99942	no	Bull O' the Woods	44	66	42-7548	yes
Brown Knowser	446	705	42-7659	yes	Bull of the Woods	6	397	AL583	yes
Brown Nose	486		42-94821	no	Bull of the Woods	Navy			yes
Brown Nose	464	778	42-52485	yes	Bull Snooker (The)	494	864	42-40405	yes
Brown Nose	490	849	42-94821	no	Bull Snooker (The)	11	98	42-40405	yes
Brown Nose 2	464	778	42-52485	no	Bulldog	VD	3	Bu31986	no
Brownie	448	714	42-50727	no	Bullet Serenade	445	703	42-64439	no
Bruise Cruiser	454	736	42-52324	no	Bulltoria				no
Brunnhilda	11	42	41-23838	yes	Bums Away	43	403	42-40198	no
Brute (The)(Lft. side)	466	784	41-29419	yes	Bums Away	43	403	42-40812	yes
BTO	448	712	44-50678	no	Bums Away	43	403	42-40822	no
Bubble Trouble	451	725	42-51360	no	Bums Away	380	528	42-110123	no

Name	Grp.	Sq.	Serial	Pic.	Name	Grp.	Sq.	Serial	Pic.
Bums Away	446	704	42-7494	no	Cactus	44	506	41-24191	no
Bums Away		868	42-40812	yes	Cactus Kid	7	9	44-44175	yes
Bundles for Japan	307		41-23965	yes	Cajun Kate	460		42-52401	yes
Bunnie	2AD			no	Cal'donia	490	850	41-28882	no
Bunnie	445		42-51349	no	Calaban	44	67	41-24232	yes
Bunnie	34	4	41-29567	no	Calamity Jane	11	26		yes
Bunny	445			no	Calamity Jane	98	344	42-41220	yes
Bunny	389	565	42-95077	no	Calamity Jane	308	374	44-42019	yes
Bunny Hop	43		42-41091	no	Calamity Jane	451	725	42-52440	yes
Bunny/Asbestos Alice	445	700	42-7619	no	Calamity Jane	7	9		yes
Burgundy Bombers				no	Calamity Jane II	98	344	44-41221	no
Burma	307	424	44-40601	yes	California Rocket	459	757	42-51714	yes
Burma Babe from					California's Golden Bare	486	832	42-52691	no
Birmingham				no	Calis Clipper	93			no
Burma Bound	451	725	41-28861	no	Call House Madam				yes
Burma Bound	451	725	41-28897	yes	Call Me Later	446			yes
Burma Queen	308	425	42-73255	no	Call Me Later	392	579	42-95035	yes
Burma Roadster				yes	Call Me Savage	493		42-94937	no
Burma Virgin				yes	Call Me Savage	490	849	42-94937	yes
Burton's Iron Man	389			no	Callipygia	446	704	42-94920	yes
Bust-er	389	565	44-40052	yes	Callipygia	489	847	42-94920	yes
Butch	453			no	Canadian Cutie	RAF	159		yes
Butch	5		44-41842	yes	Cancelled Leave (T.S.)	456		42-78673	yes
Butch	98	415	42-73138	no	Cancer	458		42-52650	no
Butch	376	515	42-40321	yes	Cancer	486	834	42-52650	yes
Butch	485	831	42-50486	no	Cancer	486	834	42-52665	no
Butch-My-Love	464	778	42-78340	yes	Cancer	486	834	xx-xx500	no
Butcher Boy (The)	90	320	41-24108	yes	Cannon Fodder	451	726	42-78102	yes
Butcher Shop	448			no	Cape Cod Special	44	506	42-51181	no
Butcher's Daughter (The)	90	319	44-40190	yes	Capricorn	493			no
Butchie Darlin'	449	716	44-41049	yes	Capricorn	93		42-52744	yes
Buttercup	454	737	42-52193	no	Capricorn	98			no
Buzz Buggy	446	706	42-7577	no	Capricorn	486	834	42-52744	no
Buzz Job	22	408	42-100290	no	Capricorn	486	834	xx-xx605	yes
Buzz Job	454	738	42-52252	yes	Capt. Eddie				
Buzz Job	455	741	42-78435	yes	Rickenbacker				yes
Buzz Job	485	830	42-52724	yes	Capt. Tom's Cabin				yes
Buzz Job	485	830	42-95203	no	Captain & His Kids (The)	389		41-24213	yes
Buzz Job #2	484	825	42-78268	no	Captain & His Kids (The)	30	819	44-40518	yes
Buzz Job Two	454	738	42-94967	no	Captain & His				
Buzz Tail	487		42-52669	no	Kids Ride Again	44	68	41-23800	no
Buzz Tail II	487		42-52653	yes	Captain & His				
Buzz Tail II	492	859	42-50447	yes	Kids Ride Again	44	68	41-24213	yes
Buzz Trail	487		42-52669	no	Captain & the Kids	489			no
Buzz-z Buggy	308	375	42-73327	yes	Captain & the Kids (The)	11	431	42-73013	no
Buzzer (The)	449	719	41-29307	yes	Captain & the Kid (The)	11	431	42-73018	no
Buzzin Bear	44	67	41-24229	yes	Captain and the				
Buzzin' Bessie	487		42-52736	no	Kids, 2nd Edition	44			no
Buzzzz Job				yes	Captain Gene (The)			42-7085	yes
By Fong Club	449	718		no	Captain John Silver	34	7	42-94818	no
By the Numbers	491	854	44-40121	yes	Careeme Back				no
C.E.Shack	308	425	41-24292	yes	Career Girl	380	528	42-41234	no
C.O.D.-Knot to Tojo	90	321	41-23836	yes	Careless	380	531	42-40500	no
Cabin in the Sky	491			no	Carioca Bev	466			no
Cabin in the Sky	98	343		yes	Carioca Bev	93	330	42-51191	yes
Cabin in the Sky	308	425	42-40849	no	Carioca Joe	RCAF			yes
Cabin in the Sky	453	735	42-64478	yes	Carl "Hen" Chick	93	329	42-63981	no

Name	Grp.	Sq.	Serial	Pic.	Name	Grp.	Sq.	Serial	Pic.
Carol Ann				yes	Cherokee Strip	43	65	44-40198	yes
Carol Ann	392	578	42-7473	yes	Cherokee Strip	451	724	44-49585	no
Carol Ann II	392	579	41-29448	no	Cherrie	90	320		yes
Carol Marie	448	712	42-110040	yes	Cherrie	454	737	42-52075	yes
Carol Marie	448	712	42-51079	no	Cherry	98			no
Carol-N-Chick				no	Cherry	446	705	42-51184	no
Carol-N-Lick	448	712	42-7739	no	Cherry	459	758	42-78106	yes
Carolina Lick				no	Cherry	464	778	42-64441	no
Carolina Moon	490	851	42-94944	no	Cherry II	459	758	42-78106	no
Carolyn Chick	93	329	42-63981	no	Cherub (The)	467		42-94943	no
Carolyn Chick	448	712	41-29981	no	Cherub (The)	490	851	42-94943	no
Carolyn Chick	448	712	42-63981	no	Cheryl Kay	456	747	44-10573	yes
Carolyn Sue	446	707	42-95190	no	Chesty	34	391	41-28598	yes
Carousin' Cock	491	855	44-40202	yes	Chicago Ann	11	26	42-109880	no
Carpenter's					Chicago Red	467		41-29370	no
Masterpiece	376	514	42-78425	yes	Chicago Red	466	787	41-29370	no
Carrier Pigeon					Chicago Shirl	458	755	42-110184	no
(The)	389	564	42-51451	yes	Chick	464	777	42-95340	no
Carrot Top	380	528	42-73114	yes	Chick's Chick	VP	106		yes
Carry Me Back	448			no	Chicken Ship	454	738	44-49406	no
Carter's Kids				no	Chief	801		41-28781	no
Cat's Ass (The)	458	752	42-94946	yes	Chief	SOP		41-28781	no
Catherine	11	26	42-109947	yes	Chief	98	345	41-11774	yes
Catherine	11	98	44-50960	yes	Chief (The)	466	784	44-49850	no
Caught in the Draft	487		42-52776	no	Chief and Sack Artists	44	67	42-100073	no
Cave Girl	451	726	42-7687	no	Chief Jo-Jon	465	781	41-29414	yes
Ceaseless Cindy	90	321	44-42262	no	Chief Manatee	93		41-24309	yes
Cecilia	456	746	44-41092	no	Chief Manhattan				no
Cee Cee	453	735	42-52186	no	Chief Oshkosh	493		41-29510	no
Cee Cee II	453	735	42-64490	yes	Chief Oshkosh	486	833	41-29510	no
Celhalopdos	93	330	41-23675	yes	Chief Wahoo	376	512	41-24279	yes
Censored				yes	Chief Wapello	44	506	42-52618	yes
Censored	455		42-52271	yes	Chief Wapello	44	66	42-52618	yes
Censored	11	431	42-100229	yes	Chief Wapello	487	839	42-52618	yes
Censored	376	514	41-11686	no	Chief's Delight	454	736	44-49370	yes
Censored	489	846	42-94905	yes	Chief's Flight	454	739	42-52314	no
Century Limited (The)	484	824	42-52641	yes	Chiefton (The)	392	577	42-51169	no
Century Queen	453	735	42-95166	no	China Clipper	308	425	44-41448	yes
Chain Lightning	5		42-40636	no	China Doll			41-24066	no
Chambermaid (The)	30	38	42-100227	yes	China Doll	308	425	42-40066	yes
Change-O-Luck	448			no	China Gal	308	425		no
Change-O-Luck	90	320	41-11868	yes	China Gal	7	493		yes
Channel Hopper	44	68	42-95226	yes	Chippie Doll	461	764	42-52458	yes
Channel Shy	453			no	Choo Choo Baby	448			no
Character	485	831	42-52727	no	Choo Choo Baby	453	734	42-52298	no
Chariot				no	Chosef	90	319	41-23767	no
Charlot the Harlot	307	370	41-11823	yes	Chris' Crate	466	785		no
Charlotte the Harlot	480		42-40339	yes	Chris' Crate II	460		42-110160	no
Chattanooga	376	513	42-72854	yes	Chris' Crate II	98		42-110160	yes
Chattanooga Choo Choo				yes	Chris' Crate II	466	784	42-110160	yes
Chattanooga Choo Choo	389	565	42-40782	yes	Chris' Crate II	491	853	42-110160	no
Chattanooga Choo Choo	455	740	41-28994	yes	Chubby Champ				no
Cheec Hako	491	852	44-50884	yes	Chubby Champ	93	329	42-7655	no
Cherokee	454	737	42-52323	no	Chubby Champ	448		42-7655	no
Cherokee	461	766	42-52389	yes	Chuck's Chicken Coop	308	375	42-73441	yes
Cherokee Maiden	459	756	42-52427	yes	Chuck-A-Lug	454	737	42-99801	no
Cherokee Strip	6PR	20CM	44-40198	yes	Chuck-O-Luck	454	737	42-52236	yes

19

Name	Grp.	Sq.	Serial	Pic.	Name	Grp.	Sq.	Serial	Pic.
Chug-A-Lug	98	344	42-41029	no	Coconut Queen	11	98	42-72992	yes
Chug-A-Lug	98	345	41-11766	yes	Cokey Flo				no
Chug-A-Lug	98	345	41-23766	no	Cokey Flo	34	18	42-94745	no
Chug-A-Lug	308	425	41-24251	yes	Cokey Flo	34	7	44-40486	yes
Chug-A-Lug Jr.	308	425	42-73310	yes	Cokey Flo	491	854	44-40486	no
Chum II	389			no	Cold Turkey	487		42-52425	no
Chum U	389			no	Collapsible Susie	34	18	42-94758	yes
Chum V	376	515	41-11630	yes	Collapsible Susie	34	18	42-94879	no
Chum VII	376	515	42-40392	yes	Collapsible Susie	484	824	42-94758	no
Chute the Works	11	431	44-40302	yes	Collapsible Susie	493	861	42-94745	no
Cielito Lindo	376		42-40081	yes	Collapsible Suzy	449	718		no
Cielito Lindo	98	345	42-41033	yes	Colorado Rose				no
Cindy				yes	Colossal Fossil	43	403	42-40863	yes
Cindy	98	345	41-11806	yes	Com-Bat	464	778	42-78091	yes
Cindy	466	784	44-49529	no	Comair Wolfpack II	Navy			yes
Cinnsy's Margie	449	717	42-7723	yes	Comanche (The)	448	714	42-64447	yes
Circus Wagon	11	26	44-42066	yes	Combatty	464	776	42-52520	no
Circus Wagon	30	392	44-42066	no	Come Along Boys	448	715	42-100322	no
Cisco Kid	5		42-73455	no	Come and Get It	43	65	44-40403	no
Cisco Kid	5	31	42-40174	yes	Come and Get It	90			no
Citadel (The)	451	725	42-52168	no	Come Closer	30	38	42-72973	yes
City of					Come N' Get It	VPB	121		yes
Plainfield, NJ	449	719	42-51763	no	Come N' Get It	43	64	42-40941	yes
City of Waco	449	719		no	Come-N'-Get-Me-				
Clam Winkle	2AD			no	You-Bastards	465	781	41-29414	no
Clarence	RAF	356		yes	Comfy N' Cozy	448			no
Clarine from Abilene	380	528	44-50998	no	Coming Home Soon				yes
Classy Chassis	492		42-51291	no	Commando	RAF		AL504	yes
Classy Chassis	SOP		42-51291	no	Commando	448	713	41-28602	no
Classy Chassis	449	717	42-52157	yes	Complete Miss	30	27	44-40810	yes
Classy Chassis	490	849		no	Con Job	451	727	42-78145	no
Classy Chassis II	490	849	42-50291	no	Connell's Special	90	320	41-23765	yes
Classy Chassy				yes	Connell's Special				
Classy Chassy				no	The 2nd	90	400	42-73129	yes
Classy Chassy	448			no	Connie	93	409	42-7682	yes
Classy Chassy	486			no	Connie	446	707	41-29124	yes
Classy Chassy	492		42-95198	no	Connie	466	785	42-7682	no
Classy Chassy	446	704	42-95198	yes	Conquest Cavalier	445	703	41-29126	yes
Clay Pigeon	445	702	42-7604	no	Conquest Cavalier	446	704	41-29126	no
Clique and Shudder (F-7)		4PCS	44-42710	yes	Consolidated Mess	453			no
Cloo-Lus	RCAF			yes	Consolidated Mess	458			no
Cloud Hopper	392			no	Consolidated Mess	489	.	42-100429	yes
Cloud Hopper II	392			no	Consolidated Mess	98	415	44-40630	yes
Cloud Hopper III	392			no	Consolidated Mess	44	506	42-100429	yes
Cloud Hopper IV	392	579	44-49886	yes	Consolidated Mess	44	506	42-7568	no
Cloudy Joe	11	431	42-73499	yes	Consolidated Mess	445	701	42-7568	no
Cloudy Joe	30	819	42-73499	no	Consolidated Mess	448	715	42-64444	no
Club 400	454	736	41-28808	yes	Consolidated Mess	449	719	42-52159	yes
Clumsy Baby	5	31	42-73461	no	Consolidated Mess	451	727	42-64445	no
Cock o' the North				yes	Consolidated Mess	466	785	44-10545	yes
Cock O' the Walk	11	431	44-42347	yes	Consolidated Mess	486	833		no
Cock of the Sky	34	7	41-29569	no	Consolidated Mess	11	98	42-73218	yes
Cock of the Sky	493	861	41-29569	no	Consolidated Mess II	453			no
Cockpit Trouble	445			no	Consolidated Miss				
Cocktail Hour	43	64	44-40428	yes	Carriage	459	756		yes
Cocky Bobby	308	425	44-41427	no	Constant Menace	376	514	41-24310	yes
Cocky Crew	451	724	42-78274	yes	Constant Menace	376	514	41-29563	yes

Name	Grp.	Sq.	Serial	Pic.	Name	Grp.	Sq.	Serial	Pic.
Contrary Mary				yes	Crow's Nest	453			yes
Contrary Mary	494	864	44-40739	yes	Crow's Nest	93			no
Cookie	801		42-40549	no	Crow's Nest	466	786	42-95010	yes
Cookie	SOP		42-40549	no	Crud Wagon	448	712	42-52098	no
Cookie	90	321	41-23839	yes	Cruisin' Susan	380	531	42-73201	yes
Cookie	458	752	42-95165	yes	Crusader	7			no
Cookie	458	755	42-50499	no	Cryin' Lion (The)	459			yes
Cookie's Wailing Wall	34	391	42-52696	no	Cubby	487		42-52766	no
Cooter	453	732		no	Cubby Champ	448			no
Copenhagen Kid			44-40289	no	Cuddles	460	763	42-52337	yes
Coral Princess			42-72977	yes	Culham's Yardbirds				no
Coral Princess	376		41-11931	no	Cupid	11	98	41-24190	no
Coral Princess	449			no	Curly	453			no
Coral Princess	98	344	41-11931	no	Curly Bird	11		44-40683	yes
Coral Princess	98	344	42-41011	no	Curly Bird	30	819	44-40683	yes
Coral Princess	98	344	42-41023	no	Curly Top	456	746	42-64492	no
Coral Princess	98	345	42-100266	no	Custer's Folly	465	781	41-29356	no
Coral Princess	392	576	42-7529	yes	Cute Lil Lass	7	9		yes
Coral Princess	5	868	42-40833	no	Cyclone	489			yes
Coral Princess	43		42-40833	no	Cyclone	6PR	24CM	42-64103	yes
Coral Queen (The)	90	400	41-11870	yes	Czechem	90	321	42-40352	no
Coral Rivers	376			no	D for Dog	44			no
Corky	44	68	42-51101	yes	D'Artagnan	98	415	41-24231	yes
Corky	44	68	42-63971	no	D'nif	491	852	44-40100	yes
Corky Bergundy Bomber	446	706	42-52234	yes	D'nif Annie	487		42-52640	no
Corky Bergundy Bomber	453	733	42-52234	yes	D-Bar Fly	44	67	42-99986	yes
Cornfed	376	513	42-72776	yes	D-Cup	93	330	42-40938	no
Cornhusker	98	415	42-40322	yes	D-Day Patches	389	565	42-50474	yes
Corrine	489	815	42-94793	yes	D-Day Patches	389	565	42-50643	yes
Corsica Kid	459	759	42-78269	no	Daddie's Ray				no
Count (The)	445	700	42-50639	no	Daddy of 'em All	90	321	44-40431	no
Countess Inn	459	758		no	Daddy of 'em All	380	529	44-49860	yes
Courageous	2AD			no	Daddy's Boy				no
Courtin'				no	Daddy's Girl	22	33	44-41852	yes
Cover Girl	449			yes	Daisy Mae				yes
Cover Girl	VPB	121		yes	Daisy Mae	445		42-51349	no
Cover Girl	487	839	44-10576	yes	Daisy Mae	454			no
Cover Girl	489	845	42-94945	yes	Daisy Mae	491			no
Cowbird	494	867	44-40790	yes	Daisy Mae	5			no
Cowtown Blonde	455	742	42-52282	no	Daisy Mae	SOP		xx-xx581	no
Cowtown's Revenge	90	321	41-23750	yes	Daisy Mae	5	23	44-41620	yes
Crack Shot	44	67	42-40126	no	Daisy Mae	307	372	41-23983	yes
Crack Up	464	778		no	Daisy Mae	308	373	41-24218	yes
Crash Kids	494	865	44-40756	yes	Daisy Mae	98	415	41-11815	yes
Crater Maker	451	727	41-28614	yes	Daisy Mae	98	415	42-41031	yes
Crater Maker				yes	Daisy Mae	11	42	41-23983	yes
Craven Raven	451	727	42-52103	no	Daisy Mae	376	513	42-41031	no
Crazy Mary	448	715	41-28601	no	Daisy Mae	448	715	42-94972	yes
Crescent of the					Daisy Mae	449	718	42-7726	no
Half Moon	465	781	41-29415	no	Daisy Mae	450	723	42-78404	no
Crew Chief	392	576	42-7540	yes	Daisy Mae	451	726	42-50952	no
Crippled Bitch (The)	446		41-29371	no	Daisy Mae	458	754	42-100362	no
Crippled Bitch (The)	467		41-29371	no	Daisy Mae	492	856	xx-xx581	no
Crippled Bitch (The)	466	786	41-29371	no	Daisy Mae	492	858	44-40135	no
Crosair	90	319	41-23752	no	Daisy Mae Skraggs	446	704	42-109830	yes
Crosby's Curse	90	321	41-23835	yes	Dakota Queen	455		42-50892	no
Crow's Nest	34		42-94766	no	Dakota Queen	455		42-78166	no

Name	Grp.	Sq.	Serial	Pic.	Name	Grp.	Sq.	Serial	Pic.
Dallas Lady	2641	885	42-78243	no	Desperate Virgin	466	785	41-28747	no
Dally's Dilly	380	528	42-73112	yes	Destination Tokio				yes
Damfino	98	343		yes	Destiny's Deb	450	720	42-78170	no
Damifino	466	784	42-50465	yes	Destiny's Digit				yes
Damned Yankee	484	825	42-52438	no	Destiny's Tot	451	724	42-51590	no
Damsel Easy				yes	Destiny's Tot	490	849	42-97875	no
Damyankee	451	724	42-78414	yes	Detail			xx-xx098	yes
Dangerous Critter	11	26	44-40382	yes	Deuces Wild	98	415	42-78222	no
Dangerous Dance	493	860	44-40361	yes	Deuces Wild	450	721	41-29222	no
Danny Boy			42-50441	no	Deuces Wild	456	746	42-52222	yes
Daring Dame			44-40222	yes	Devil's Delight	43		42-40832	yes
Dark Eyes	801	406	42-50652	no	Devil's Delight	459			no
Dark Rhapsody	466	785	41-29466	no	Devil's Delight		868		yes
Darling Darlene	484	826	42-52633	yes	Devil's Duchess	451	725	42-52094	yes
Darling VI	449	719	44-10633	no	Devil's Henchmen	449	716	42-52089	yes
Dashin' Daisy	30	27	42-72986	no	Devil's Hostess	467	790	42-51531	yes
Dauntless Dottie	380	530	42-40495	yes	Devil's Messenger (The)	93			no
Davy Jones' Helper	480	1	41-24002	yes	Devil's Mistress (The)	459	758	42-51367	no
Dazy May	Navy			yes	Devil's Own				no
Dazzlin' Duchess					Devil's Stepchild	490	851	41-28868	no
& the Ten Dukes	455	743	42-64500	yes	Diamond Lil	CAF	rest.	LB-30	yes
De Boid	479		42-40499	no	Diana Lynn	456	745		yes
De Boid	93	330	42-7499	no	Dic's Delight				yes
De Icer	93	330	42-109830	no	Dick's Dixie				yes
De-Icer	376			no	Diddlin' Dollie	451	724	42-52077	no
De-Imp				no	Diddlin' Dollie II	376	512	41-28786	no
Deacon's Flivver	451	727		yes	Diddlin' Dollie II	451	724	41-28786	no
Dead End Kids				no	Dina Might	307	424	xx-xx547	no
Dead End Kids	448	712	42-94992	yes	Dina-Mite				no
Dead Eye	30	392	42-72997	no	Dina-Mite				yes
Dead Eye II	30	392	42-73425	yes	Dinah Might	460			yes
Dead-Eye Dick	308			no	Dinah Might	30	27	42-73154	no
Deanna's Dreamboat	380	530	44-42244	yes	Dinah Might	450	723	42-52164	no
Dear Duchess				yes	Dinah Might	454	737	42-64359	yes
Dear Mom	458		41-29277	yes	Dinah Mite				yes
Death Dealer	392		42-40611	yes	Dinah Mite	455		42-64481	no
Death Dealer	93	409	42-40611	yes	Dinah Mite	93	328	42-95014	yes
Death of Me Yet	464	777	42-78241	no	Ding Dong Daddy				
Dee Luck	490			no	from Dixie	486	834	42-52765	yes
Defiance				no	Ding Hao				yes
Delayed Action	392	578	42-100117	no	Ding Hou				yes
Delayed Action	454	736	42-52242	no	Ding How Dottie	308	374	44-40788	yes
Delayed Action	459	757	42-52187	no	Dinky	90	320	42-40325	yes
Delectable Deb	389			no	Dinky Duck	458		41-29142	no
Delectable Doris	389	566	42-50551	yes	Dinky Duck	446	706	41-29142	yes
Delectable Lady	389			no	Dippy Dave and His 8				
Delirious Delores	491	853	44-40200	yes	Dippy Diddlers	308	373	41-24143	yes
Deliverer	380	531	42-40522	yes	Dirtie Gertie	90	319	41-23731	yes
Delores Jean	466	787	42-50368	yes	Dirty Deed (The)	446	707	42-50545	yes
Demaio's Delinquents	484	824	42-51988	no	Dirty Gertie				yes
Demon's Delight	448			no	Dirty Gertie	376	514	42-52557	yes
Denver Zephyr	448	714	42-50357	no	Dirty Gertie	392	578	42-50571	no
Der Flittermouse	456		41-29606	no	Dirty Gertie	451	727	42-50298	yes
Der Flittermouse	376	514	41-29606	no	Dirty Gertie	466	786	41-29366	no
Desert Fury	376	512	42-78206	no	Dirty Nell	30	392	42-72995	yes
Desert Lilly	376	512	41-24258	yes	Dirty Nell II	30	392	42-73290	yes
Desperate Desmond	446	706	42-7498	yes	Dirty Shame				no

Name	Grp.	Sq.	Serial	Pic.	Name	Grp.	Sq.	Serial	Pic.
Dirty Tale	491			yes	Dorly	98	343	42-64393	no
Dirty Woman (The)	11	26		no	Dorothy	389	564	42-63960	yes
Dis-Gusted	380	528	42-40486	no	Dorothy	445	733	42-51707	yes
Display of Arms	90	320	44-41274	yes	Dorothy Anne (The)	90	400	42-41077	no
Dissapated Duck	446	707	42-94994	no	Dorothy Anne (The)	43	64	42-41093	yes
Ditney Hill	460	760	42-78678	yes	Dorothy K	454	738	41-29310	no
Dixie	466	785	44-10499	yes	Dorty Treek	491	852	44-10485	yes
Dixie Belle	458			no	Dot's Queen of Queens	98	345	42-50417	yes
Dixie Belle	449	719	41-29193	yes	Dot's Queen of Queens	98	345	42-72854	no
Dixie Belle II	458	754	42-95163	yes	Dot's Queen of Queens	376	513	42-72051	no
Dixie Dew Cup				no	Dot's Queen of Queens	376	514	42-72854	no
Dixie Dumper	392	576	42-99938	no	Dottie Ann	30	38	42-100376	yes
Dixie Flyer	445	701	42-52247	no	Dottie the New Hamp-				
Dizzy E. Easy	453	734	42-50317	yes	shire Troubadour	485	829	44-41144	no
Dizzy R. Roger	453	734	44-50577	yes	Dottie's Double				yes
Do Bunny	448	713	42-95185	yes	Dottie's Double	380	530	42-72964	yes
Do-Jin-Don	446	706	disputed	yes	Dotty Do	485	831	42-51872	no
Doc	98	343	41-11921	yes	Double Shot	90	321	42-40359	no
Doc's Delight	VPB	111	Bu38746	yes	Double Shot Nell				yes
Docile Dragon	22			no	Double Shot Sam	376	514	44-50393	no
Dodo	6PR	24CM	44-42687	yes	Double Trouble				yes
Dog Fight				no	Double Trouble				yes
Dogpatch Clipper	466	785	41-28949	yes	Double Trouble	43		42-40671	yes
Dogpatch Express	93	328	41-24192	no	Double Trouble	90	320	42-40358	yes
Dogpatch Express	30	392	42-73001	no	Double Trouble	93	328	41-23672	yes
Dogpatch Express	11	42	41-24214	yes	Double Trouble	7	493	44-40989	yes
Dogpatch Express	459	756	44-10626	yes	Double Trouble	380	530	44-50602	yes
Dogpatch Express	459	756	44-49750	yes	Double Trouble	392	578	42-100100	yes
Dogpatch Raider			41-24215	no	Double Trouble	449	717	42-50742	yes
Dogpatch Raider	93	328	41-24192	yes	Double Trouble	451	725	41-29244	no
Dogpatch Raider II	93			no	Double Trouble	455	740	41-29282	yes
Doidie Ann	30	38	42-100376	no	Double Trouble	467	791	41-29385	yes
Doity Boid	93	330	41-24104	no	Double Trouble	485	829	42-78149	no
Doity Goity / Peggy	11	42	41-24110	yes	Double Trouble	494	865	44-40563	yes
Doll Baby	448			no	Down and Go	448			no
Dollar Ride	464	777	42-78257	no	Down De Hatch	44	506	42-95016	yes
Dolly	450	720	42-50277	no	Down De Hatch	389	564		no
Dolly's Sister	453	734	41-29005	yes	Down Wind	458	786	42-52566	no
Dolores	28	404	44-50598	yes	Downwind Leg	458	755	41-29331	yes
Don't Cry Baby	389	565	42-110084	yes	Draga	456			no
Don't Fence Me In	448	714	42-50525	yes	Draggin' Lady	453			no
Don't Fence Me In	489	847	42-50525	no	Draggin' Lady	HALP		41-11592	no
Donald Duck	34		42-94890	no	Draggin' Waggin	449	716	42-99770	yes
Donna D Wanna				yes	Dragon and His				
Donna K.				yes	Tail (The)	43	64	44-40973	yes
Donna Mia	458		42-40939	yes	Dragon Fly				no
Doodle Bug	93	409	41-23724	yes	Dragon Lady				yes
Doodle Bug	392	576		no	Dragon Lady				yes
Doodle Bug	449	718	41-23742	yes	Dragon Lady	5	23	44-49753	yes
Doodlebug				no	Dragon Lady	93	409	41-23748	no
Doodlebug	308	373	42-24223	yes	Dragon Lady	11	42	44-40670	yes
Doodlebug	376	512	41-23724	yes	Dragon Lady	308	425	44-41446	yes
Doodlebug	380	531	42-73117	yes	Dragon Lady	389	565	42-7593	yes
Dopey	98	343	42-40268	yes	Dragon Lady	392	577	42-94906	yes
Dopey	98	343	42-78600	yes	Dragon Lady	446	706	42-50306	yes
Dopey	98	343	42-94762	yes	Dragon Lady	449	717	42-52134	no
Dopy Goldberg	376	515	42-40319	yes	Dragon Lady	454	737	42-94978	yes

Name	Grp.	Sq.	Serial	Pic.
Dragon Lady	455	740	42-52223	no
Dragon Lady	455	742	42-51290	no
Dragon Lady #2	449	719	41-28647	yes
Dragon Wagon	43	63		no
Dragonass	450	722	42-51848	no
Dragonass	465	781	42-51858	no
Drawers	389	565	42-100017	yes
Drawers	389	566	42-50760	yes
Dream Gal	380	529	44-40919	yes
Dream Girl				no
Dream Girl	6	29	44-40824	yes
Dream Street Rose	376	515	41-11935	yes
Dreamboat	487		42-52657	no
Dreamboat	458	753	41-28706	yes
Dreyer's Devils	307		44-40954	no
Drip	90	321	42-41105	no
Drip (The)	392	579	42-7477	no
Drip (The)	392	579	42-7481	no
Drip (The)	451	726	44-49659	yes
Drive Me Home	7		44-50866	yes
Dronkie	SAAF	34		yes
Droop Snoot	5	31	42-41246	no
Droopy Drawers				yes
Drop 'em N' Run	448	714		no
Drunk Skunk				no
Drunkard Dram				no
Drunkard's Dream	380	531	42-110115	yes
Dry Bones	98	344	42-40329	no
Dry Run	446	706	41-29137	yes
Dry Run	449	717	42-78017	yes
Dry Run	461	767	42-52395	yes
Dual Sack	448	714	42-95089	yes
Dual Sack	491	855	42-110168	no
Dual Sack	11	98	42-100168	yes
Duboney	448	713	42-95185	no
Duchess	90		42-100262	no
Duchess	28	404	41-11924	no
Duchess	450	723	42-78311	no
Duchess	490	849	42-94821	no
Duchess				yes
Duchess (The)	448			no
Duchess (The)	22	33	44-49865	yes
Duchess (The)	22	33	44-50865	yes
Duchess (The)	93	330	41-24120	no
Duchess (The)	93	330	41-24147	yes
Duchess (The)	98	345	42-73439	no
Duchess (The)	34	391	42-94861	no
Duchess (The)	376	514	42-72874	yes
Duchess (The)	43	65	44-40567	yes
Duchess (The)	494	867	44-40567	yes
Duchess (The) II	494	867	44-40754	no
Duchess II	450	723	44-50481	no
Duchess of Paducah	90		42-109991	yes
Duchess of Paducah	380	530	42-109991	yes
Duck (The)	484	827	42-94737	no
Duckin' Ducklin' II	30	38	42-72971	no
Dude (The)	90	320	42-40326	yes
Duffy's Tavern	466	784	42-51699	yes
Dugan	453		44-51276	no
Dugan	392	578	44-50493	no
Dugan Wagon	493			no
Dugan Wagon	34	7	41-29557	no
Dugan Wagon (The)	34	18	44-40482	yes
Dugan Wagon II	493		42-94757	no
Dugan Wagon II (The)	34	18	44-40482	yes
Dugar	467	788	42-50641	no
Duke (The)	93	328	41-23729	no
Dumbo	30	26	42-72832	yes
Dumbo	307	370	42-41085	yes
Dumbo	449	716	42-7741	no
Dumbo	449	718	41-29217	no
Dumbo	453	735	41-28943	no
Dumbo Delivers	RCAF			yes
Dumbo the Avenger	11	26	42-72832	yes
Dumbo the Avenger	307		41-23906	yes
Dumbo the Pistol Packin' Pachyderm	453	735	41-28943	no
Duration +	464		42-78093	yes
Duration Baby				no
Dust Storm	98	343	42-51168	no
Dusty Deamons	445	701	42-64440	no
Dwatted Wabbit				yes
Dwatted Wabbit	484		42-52658	no
Dwatted Wabbit	485		42-50827	no
Dwatted Wabbit	461	766	41-29337	no
Dwatted Wabbit	461	766	42-50827	no
Dye's Dynamiters	467	789	42-50515	no
Dynahmite Dodo	34	4	41-29522	no
Dysentery Special(C-87)	ATC		42-107267	yes
E for Easy	490		44-40424	no
E Pluribus Aluminum	466	784	42-52590	yes
E Pluribus Aluminum	467	789	42-52590	no
E-Z Duzit	44	66	42-99980	yes
Eager Beaver	44		42-40731	yes
Eager Beaver	446		41-23737	no
Eager Beaver	448			no
Eager Beaver	466			no
Eager Beaver	480		41-24196	no
Eager Beaver	HALP		41-11600	no
Eager Beaver	93	328	41-23737	yes
Eager Beaver	307	371	41-24012	yes
Eager Beaver				yes
Eager Beaver (The)	90	320	41-23849	yes
Eager Beaver II	487			no
Eager Beavers	98	343	41-11897	yes
Eager Cleaver (The)	389	564	44-40864	yes
Eager Eagle	389	564	42-40753	no
Eager Edgar	487		42-52592	no
Eager Edgar II	487		42-52592	no
Eager Eve	44	68	42-40731	no
Eager One	448		42-50326	no
Eager One	448	712	44-10517	yes
Eagle	482		44-42344	no

Name	Grp.	Sq.	Serial	Pic.	Name	Grp.	Sq.	Serial	Pic.
Eagle (The)	494	865	44-40751	no	El Pagliaccio	484	824	42-51925	yes
Eagles Wrath	448			no	El Sluggo				no
Early Bird (The)	494	865	44-40748	yes	El Toro	93	328	42-63982	no
Early Delivery	459	757	42-52319	no	El Toro, Bull of				
Earthquake	376	515	41-24033	yes	the Woods	446	707	41-29136	yes
Earthquake McGoon	RCAF			yes	Eli Swof, Jr.	467	790	42-51171	no
Earthquake McGoon	44	506		yes	Elie	491			no
Earthquake McGoon	44	506	41-24235	yes	Ellen	445	703	42-7602	no
Earthquake McGoon	466	787	42-50448	yes	Ellen Ann	456	746		yes
Earthquake McGoon	India	R385		yes	Elmer	458	753	42-100070	no
Eastern Beast	466	785	41-28743	yes	Elmer	458	755	42-110141	no
Eastern Queen				no	Elmer	492	859	42-110141	no
Easy Breeze	43		42-110118	no	Elmer's Blitz	459	756		yes
Easy Does It	451	724	41-29253	yes	Eloise	11			yes
Easy Maid			Bu38923	yes	Eloise	392	578	41-29571	yes
Easy Maid	464			no	Els-Notcho	VPB	108	Bu59460	yes
Easy Maid	Navy		44-40096	yes	Elsie	376	513	41-23796	yes
Easy Maid	VB	102	Bu32323	no	Elusive Elcy				no
Easy Maid	449	718	44-41119	yes	Elusive Elcy II				no
Easy Maid	455	742		no	Elusive Elcy III				no
Easy Maid	465	781	42-78352	yes	Elusive Elsie				no
Easy Maid (PB4Y-1)	Navy		44-41328	no	Elusive Elsie 2nd				no
Easy Margie	98	343	42-41007	no	Embarrassed	380	531	44-40189	yes
Easy Movement				yes	Emily	98	415	44-40633	no
Easy Queen	466		44-40456	no	Emmy Lou	44	67	41-23988	no
Easy Queen	493		44-40456	no	Emmy Lou II	44	67	42-72878	no
Easy Queen	449	716	42-95269	yes	En-Diving	480		42-40333	no
Easy Takeoff	454	738	42-78377	yes	Envy of 'em All			42-49180	no
Easy Way (The)	491	853		yes	Envy of 'em All	492		42-50279	no
Edie	490	849	42-94958	no	Envy of 'em All	392	579	42-50279	no
Edith	459	759	44-48789	no	Envy of 'em All	458	754	42-50279	no
Edna Elizabeth	98		41-11620	no	Envy of 'em All II	458	754	42-95108	yes
Edna Elizabeth	HALP		41-11620	yes	Eophus	93	330	42-95254	yes
Edna Elizabeth	376	512	41-11620	no	Eophus	466	784	42-95108	no
Eephus			42-95108	no	Eophus	466	784	42-95254	no
Eephus	93	330	42-95254	yes	Ernie's Beavers	466	786	44-40173	no
Eephus	466	784	42-95254	no	Ernie's Beavers	492	857	44-40173	no
Eh, What's Up Doc	380	529	42-73488	no	Erotic Edna	7	9		yes
Eight (8) Ball	90	321	41-23714	yes	Escalator	308	374	41-24296	no
Eight (8) Ball	376	514	42-40206	yes	Escalator III	308	374	42-73438	yes
Eight Ball				no	Eskimo Nell	451		42-78428	no
Eight Ball				yes	Esky	308	373	42-73286	yes
Eight Ball	494		44-40744	yes	Esky Special				yes
Eight Ball	93			no	Esmeralda	376	513	41-11848	no
Eight Ball	449	718		no	Esmeralda II	380	529	42-40507	no
Eightball	44	67	44-40282	no	Esquire	380	531	42-73481	yes
Eightball	459	759	42-95265	no	Estelle of Fort Smith				no
Eighty (80) Days	308	425	42-100267	yes	ETO	489			no
Eighty (80) Days Major	380	530	42-40508	yes	ETO Playhouse	458	752	42-50314	yes
Eileen	445	702	42-50324	no	Eton Pussy	308		42-40758	no
El Capitan	392	578	41-28772	yes	Euroclydon	93	328	42-40612	no
El Diablo				no	European Clipper	493	863	44-40049	yes
El Flako	453	735	42-64469	yes	Evasive Action	30	819	42-109809	yes
El Korab	448			no	Evasive Ann				no
El Lobo	93	344	41-23692	yes	Eveless Eden	448	713	42-51123	yes
El Lobo	392	579	42-7510	yes	Evelyn				no
El Pagliaccio	461	764	42-51925	yes	Evelyn E.	455	740	44-49366	no

Name	Grp.	Sq.	Serial	Pic.	Name	Grp.	Sq.	Serial	Pic.
Everybody's Baby	484			no	Fearless Fosdick	461	765	42-52438	yes
Everybody's Baby	449	718	42-7756	yes	Fearless Fosdick	467	791	42-50698	no
Everybody's Sweetheart	98	345	42-73434	no	Fearless Freddie	446		41-23737	yes
Everything's Jake	467		42-95234	no	Fearless Freddie	466			no
Everything's Jake	492		42-95234	no	Fearless Freddie	93	328	41-23737	no
Evil Weevil	461	764	41-29335	yes	Fearless Freddie II	446	707	42-7654	no
Evil Weevil Too	461	764	42-51816	no	Fearless Joe	376			no
Exasperatin' Gazaborator	459	756	42-78221	yes	Feather Injun	446		42-94886	no
Exterminator	93	329	41-23717	yes	Feather Merchant				no
Exterminator	392	579	41-29135	yes	Feather Merchant	448		42-73477	no
Exterminator	392	579	42-7470	yes	Feather Merchant	493			yes
Exterminator	448	715	42-7717	no	Feather Merchant	801			no
Exterminator II	392	577	42-7556	no	Feather Merchant	SOP			no
Extra Joker	490			no	Feather Merchant	44	66	41-28788	yes
Extra Joker	451	725	41-29588	no	Feather Merchants (The)	484	824	42-94733	no
Extra Joker	451	725	42-95379	yes	Feathermerchants Folly	22	2	42-100293	yes
Eyes of Texas	389			yes	Ferdie	11	42	42-100350	yes
F for Freddie			41-23770	no	Ferp Finesco	451	725	41-28933	yes
F for Freddie	44	67	42-72865	no	Fertile Myrtle				yes
Fabulous Fanny	7	492		yes	Fertile Myrtle	453			no
Fairy Belle			42-73505	no	Fertile Myrtle	98	415	41-24023	yes
Fairy Belle	392		42-72998	no	Fertile Myrtle	376	513	42-40236	no
Fairy Belle II	392	577	42-52415	no	Fertile Myrtle	451	724	42-78471	yes
Falcon (The)	90	321	41-23828	yes	Fertile Myrtle	461	764	42-78123	yes
Falcon (The)	466	785	42-95248	yes	Fertile Myrtle	484	824	42-52371	no
False Alarm				no	Fertile Turtle	465	781		no
Fan Dancer (The)	466	787	41-29423	no	Fertile Turtle (The)	464	777		yes
Fargo Express	484	825	42-78289	no	Feudin Wagon	467		44-40155	no
Fargo Express (The)	98	415	42-78382	yes	Feudin Wagon (The)	466			no
Fart Sack Phyllis	454		42-78638	no	Feudin' Rebel	448			no
Fascinatin' Witch	44	66	41-23811	no	Feudin' Wagon				no
Fascinating Lady	448	713	42-72981	yes	Feudin' Wagon	34		42-94873	no
Fast Company	34	7	41-28877	yes	Feudin' Wagon	482			no
Fast Freight / Samoa	SCA		AL626	yes	Feudin' Wagon	44	506	44-40155	no
Fast Number	464	779	42-52469	yes	Feudin' Wagon	492	859	44-40155	no
Fat Stuff	43	403	42-41171	yes	Feudin' Wagon (The)	44	506	42-110082	yes
Fat Stuff	43	403	42-41171	yes	Feudin; Rebel				no
Fat Stuff II	458	712	42-7591	yes	Fickle Finger	449	716	42-52550	yes
Fatass	456	747	42-52287	no	Fickle Finger	451	727	42-51564	yes
Favorite Gal	448			no	Fickle Finger of Fate	467	790	42-50354	no
Fay Day	466	787	41-28938	no	Fifinella				yes
Fay Day	489	844	42-94874	yes	Fifinella	493		42-110102	yes
Faye	451	725	41-29588	yes	Fifinella	6AF			yes
Fearless Fosdick				no	Fifinella	44	66	42-95329	yes
Fearless Fosdick				yes	Fifinella	44	67	42-63763	yes
Fearless Fosdick	446			no	Fifty (.50) Cal. Gal	90	321	41-23759	no
Fearless Fosdick	453			no	Fightin' Gremlin	491			no
Fearless Fosdick	466		42-50698	no	Fightin' Pappy	448			no
Fearless Fosdick	491			no	Fightin' Rebel	493		41-28849	no
Fearless Fosdick	Navy			yes	Fightin' Rebel	34	391	41-28849	no
Fearless Fosdick	392	578	44-50568	yes	Fightin' Sam	389	567	42-40807	yes
Fearless Fosdick	44	67	42-95049	no	Fightin' Sam II	389	566	42-52579	no
Fearless Fosdick	445	702	41-29604	yes	Fighting Mudcat			42-52392	no
Fearless Fosdick	448	714	42-50698	yes	Fighting Mudcat	459	756	42-42342	yes
Fearless Fosdick	449	716	42-51375	no	Fighting Sam	389	566		no
Fearless Fosdick	459	756	41-29438	yes	Filthy Annie	392	579	42-7471	no
					Filthy McNaughty	458	755	42-50608	no

Name	Grp.	Sq.	Serial	Pic.	Name	Grp.	Sq.	Serial	Pic.
Final Approach	454	736	42-78432	yes	Flak Shak III	489		42-51501	no
Final Approach	458	752	42-52457	yes	Flak Strainer	484	824	42-99851	yes
Final Approach II	454	736	42-78489	no	Flak Target	448			no
Final Objective	11	431	44-41945	yes	Flak-Shy				yes
Final Objective	494	864	44-41945	yes	Flakman (The)	464	779	42-95332	yes
Finito Benito	98	344	42-72891	no	Flame McGoon	376	513	42-72767	yes
Finito Combatt				yes	Flame of the Squadron				yes
Fink's Jinks	448	713	42-7681	no	Flamin' Mame	465	781	42-51631	no
Finnigan's Female				no	Flamin' Mamie				yes
Firebird	491	852	42-110167	yes	Flamin' Mamie	389			no
Firefly				no	Flamin' Mamie	491			no
Firepower	380	528	42-109986	yes	Flamin' Mamie	43	403	42-41062	yes
First Nighter	380	529	42-73340	yes	Flamin' Mamie	464	776	44-41337	yes
First Sergeant	93	329	42-40127	no	Flamin' Mamie	453			yes
First Sergeant	458	754	42-40127	yes	Flaming Amie	5	31	44-42392	yes
Firtil Myrtle	376			yes	Flamingo	308	374	41-24181	no
Firtil Myrtle	43	63	42-100037	yes	Flamingo II	308	373	42-72835	no
Five by Five	308	425	42-40062	no	Flap and Gear Specialist				yes
Five Grand	455	742	44-10560	yes	Flash	28	404	42-41157	yes
Five Thousandth					Flexible Flyer	448			no
Ford-Built	11		42-51623	yes	Flight Chief	SCA		AL617	no
Flabbergasted					Floogie	308	374	42-40614	no
Fanny	451	726	41-29242	yes	Floogie Boo	493		44-40441	no
Flak Alley	44	68	42-24225	yes	Floogie Boo	34	391	44-40441	no
Flak Alley II	44	68	41-29544	no	Floogie Boo	308	425	44-41441	no
Flak Alley Sally	455	742	41-28815	yes	Floogie Boo Bird	98	415	41-11810	yes
Flak Bait	446	706	42-7581	no	Floogie!				yes
Flak Ducker (The)	448			no	Floogie, Jr.				yes
Flak Ducker (The)	392	576	42-7598	yes	Florida Cracker	ATC		42-107255	yes
Flak Finder	461	767	42-52399	yes	Florine Jo-Jo	HALP		41-11613	no
Flak Fled Flapper	90			no	Flossie	493	862	42-50762	no
Flak Fled Flapper	380	528	44-40434	yes	Flossie Flirt	44	66	42-40777	no
Flak Hack	453		42-110100	yes	Flossye	445	701		yes
Flak Happy	44			no	Flower	98			yes
Flak Happy	448			no	Flutter Duck	448			no
Flak Happy	30	27	42-72996	yes	Flutterbye	487	838	42-52577	no
Flak Happy	453	735	42-110100	no	Fluxuation Kate	487			no
Flak Happy	454	736	42-78324	no	Flyer's Fancy	445		42-94840	no
Flak Happy	454	739	42-50910	no	Flyer's Fancy	490	849	42-94840	no
Flak Happy	456	747	42-78328	no	Flyin' Duchess (The)	464			no
Flak Happy Pappy	487		42-52666	no	Flyin' Fool	460		42-52408	no
Flak Happy Too	30	27	42-73279	no	Flyin' Patches	464	778	42-52522	no
Flak Happy, Too	30	27	42-73279	no	Flyin' Pay	494	865	44-40732	yes
Flak Jack	448			no	Flying (Outhouse)				yes
Flak Magnet	93	409		no	Flying 8 Ball	11	26	41-11923	yes
Flak Magnet	389	567	42-99992	no	Flying 8 Ball, Jr.	11	26	42-109840	yes
Flak Magnet	44	68	42-50349	no	Flying Anvil (The)	6PR	24CM	42-64158	no
Flak Magnet	44	68	42-50596	yes	Flying Ass (The)	491			no
Flak Magnet	458	753	41-29373	yes	Flying Ass (The)	451	727		yes
Flak Magnet	467	788	41-29373	no	Flying Box Car	465	781		no
Flak Magnet II				no	Flying Boxcar	494	867	44-40749	yes
Flak Magnet II	458	753	41-28962	yes	Flying Boxcar				yes
Flak Magnet II	467	790	41-28962	no	Flying Boxcar (The)	493		41-29587	no
Flak Sack	98	344	41-23692	yes	Flying Boxcar (The)	490	848	41-29587	yes
Flak Shack	485	831	41-29534	no	Flying Bull	491	852	42-110138	no
Flak Shack II	485	831	44-49899	no	Flying Carpet	30			yes
Flak Shack III	485	831	42-78501	no	Flying Cloud	308	374	42-100235	yes

Name	Grp.	Sq.	Serial	Pic.	Name	Grp.	Sq.	Serial	Pic.
Flying Cloud (The)				no	Flying Wolf	43	403	42-50447	yes
Flying Cock	93	409	41-23724	yes	Flying Wolf	451	727	42-78411	yes
Flying Cock II	93	328	42-63972	no	Flying Wolf (The)	43	403	42-40905	no
Flying Coffin	ZI			yes	Flying Wolves	93	330	42-72872	yes
Flying Commode (The)	486	832		no	Flying Wolves (The)				no
Flying Crusader /My Diversion	392	578	42-7478	yes	Flying Zebra	464	779	42-50867	no
Flying Devil (The)	34	4	41-29548	no	Foe Flusher	98	344	41-28825	no
Flying Devil (The)	493	862	41-29548	no	Foil Proof	93			no
Flying Dragon	448			no	Foil Proof	453	735	42-94805	yes
Flying Duchess (The)				yes	Foil Proof Mary	380	531	42-73126	yes
Flying Duchess (The)	464			no	Fools Paradise	30	38	42-73282	yes
Flying Dutch	392		xx-xx131	no	Ford's Follies	458	754	42-52515	no
Flying Dutchman (The)				yes	Ford's Folly	389		42-94842	no
Flying Dutchman (The)	466			no	Ford's Folly	392		42-94842	no
Flying Dutchman (The)	VPB	108		no	Ford's Folly	458			no
Flying Dutchman (The)	484	826	42-52775	yes	Ford's Folly	376	515	42-78412	no
Flying Eightball	44	67	42-7624	no	Ford's Folly	392	578	42-50466	yes
Flying Fanny	43	403	42-72780	yes	Ford's Folly	450	723	42-78412	no
Flying Fay	494	865	44-40732	yes	Ford's Folly	453	732	42-50296	yes
Flying Fifer	494	865	44-40742	yes	Ford's Folly	455	741	42-52224	no
Flying Finger (The)	461	765	42-50953	no	Ford's Folly	455	741	42-52249	no
Flying Fool				no	Ford's Folly	459	757	42-51911	no
Flying Fool	460		42-78408	no	Ford's Folly	489	844	42-94842	no
Flying Fool (The)	93	409	42-94991	no	Ford's Mistake	451	725	41-29590	no
Flying Ginny			42-51296	no	Ford's Other Folly	455	741	42-52249	no
Flying Ginny	44	67	41-28944	no	Forever Amber	308	374	42-73188	yes
Flying Ginny	490	849	42-94894	no	Forever Amber	448	714		no
Flying Ginny (J?)	98	344	42-41006	no	Forky	44			no
Flying Goose				no	Forky II	44	66	42-40182	yes
Flying Home				no	Form I-A	90	321	44-40229	yes
Flying Home	454	736	41-28914	no	Form I-A	30	392	44-40229	yes
Flying Home	467	789	42-95073	no	Fort Worth Maid	445	702	42-50321	no
Flying Jackass (The)	491	853	44-40239	yes	Forty Two (42) - Kay	451	727	44-41056	yes
Flying Jenny	11	431	42-109943	yes	Foul Ball	448		42-50290	no
Flying Log	44	506	42-50328	no	Foul Ball	490		42-50290	no
Flying Moose (The)	93	409	44-10578	no	Four (4) F	448			no
Flying Patch	392	578	41-29131	no	Four (4) F	493		44-40418	yes
Flying Patch	392	578	41-29511	no	Four (4) F	451	727	44-40418	yes
Flying Patches				no	Four (4)-Q-2	44	67	41-23779	yes
Flying Pay	494	865	44-40732	yes	Four (4)-Q-2	445	700	41-29149	no
Flying Phartsac (The)	464	779	41-28999	no	Four (IV) F	493		44-40380	no
Flying Pin-Up Girl	486		42-52714	no	Four Beers	492	856	44-40227	no
Flying Potty	464			no	Four Eyes	98	343	42-40655	no
Flying Redhead				no	Four Eyes	98		42-40665	no
Flying Rumor	492	859	42-50447	yes	Four Fan Fanny (Fancy)	5	31	44-41669	yes
Flying Sac (The)	448	712	42-110098	yes	Four Five Time	34	391	41-28820	no
Flying Seadog (The)	Navy		Bu32161	yes	Four Flusher	448			no
Flying Sheriffs	491	854	44-40240	yes	Four Fruits	376	514	42-64468	no
Flying Squaw				no	Four or Five Times	489		41-28820	no
Flying Stud	90	320	42-41118	yes	Four Roses	307	370	42-40219	no
Flying Submarine				yes	Four to the Bar	376	513		yes
Flying Tail	Navy			yes	Four-F (4-F) Charlie	43	403	42-72946	no
Flying Wac/China Doll	308	425	42-40066	no	Four-Five Time				no
Flying Witch (The)	466	787	42-95194	no	Four-Five Time	491	855	44-40232	no
Flying Wolf	93	330	42-72872	yes	Four-Five-Time	491	854	41-28820	no
					Fox (The)	489			no
					Foxy Lady				no

Name	Grp.	Sq.	Serial	Pic.	Name	Grp.	Sq.	Serial	Pic.
Foxy Lady	AD4			no	G I Gal	44	67	42-40371	yes
Foxy Phoebe	493		41-29527	no	G.I. Ginnie	376	514	42-40657	yes
Foxy Phoebe	487	839	41-29527	yes	G.I. Jill	458	754	42-51170	no
Fran	466	784	44-49582	yes	G.I. Joe				no
Frances Fury				no	G.I. Joe	492	857	42-110151	no
Frankie C.				no	G.I. Wife	493		44-40477	no
Frankie Ferocious	376	515	42-72773	yes	Gabe's Angels	2AD			no
Frannie Belle	489			no	Gadget	450	723	41-28620	no
Freckle Face			42-7608	no	Gag 'N Vomit	490	850	41-29544	no
Free and Easy	454	736	42-78503	yes	Gag N' Vomit	493		41-29544	no
Free Delivery	464	776	42-52484	no	Gal 'O Mine II	460	763	42-78270	yes
Free For All	380	531	44-42412	yes	Gallant Lady	445	700	42-7550	yes
French Dressing				yes	Gallavantin' Gal	44	506	42-7509	no
French Dressing	466			no	Gallavantin' Gal	392	577	42-7509	no
French Dressing	491	853	44-50299	yes	Gallopin' Gertie	389	566	42-100332	yes
Frenchy-N-More	448			no	Gallopin' Ghost	389		41-23783	no
Frendlin (The)	308	425	42-73265	yes	Gallopin' Ghost	467		41-29439	no
Frenisi	307	370	42-40323	yes	Gallopin' Ghost	44	67	41-23783	no
Friday the 13th	93	328	41-23713	no	Gallopin' Ghost	456	744	41-28934	no
Friday's Cat			41-29513	yes	Gallopin' Ghost	466	787	41-29439	yes
Friday's Cat	93	328	41-23713	no	Gallopin' Katie	389	564	42-50367	yes
Fridget Bridget	445	703	42-51342	no	Galloping Ghost	453			no
Frightful Old Pig (The)	454		42-64364	no	Galloping Ghost	VB	102	Bu31977	no
Frigid Frances	28		41-23858	no	Galloping Ghost of the				
Frisco Frannie	380	530	42-73451	yes	English Coast				no
Frisco Frisky	448	715	42-51247	yes	Galloping Gus	30	819	42-72999	no
Frisco Kid Alias					Galvanized Goose	11	26	42-73015	yes
The Whip	459	756	42-95265	yes	Gambler's Luck				yes
Frisco Trudy	448	714	42-95006	yes	Gambling Lady	93	329	44-40113	yes
Frisky	43	64	42-40667	no	Gambling Lady	492	857	44-40113	no
Fritzi	458	752	41-29329	yes	Gang Bang	454			no
Frivolous Freddie	489			no	Gang Bang	451	727	42-51750	yes
Frivolous Sal	480	1	41-23984	yes	Gangrene Gerty	ZI		42-100052	yes
Frivolous Sal	34	18	42-94893	yes	Gargantua	455	742		no
Frivolous Sal	34	4	42-94815	no	Gas House	451	724	41-29195	no
Frowning Flossie				no	Gas House	451	724	42-52474	no
Frozen, Hot To Go	7	9	42-72803	no	Gas House Gus	487	839	41-29483	yes
Fubar				no	Gas House Jr.	451	724	42-78236	no
Fuddles	5			no	Gas House Mouse	492			no
Fuedin' Rebel	448			no	Gas House Mouse	SOP			no
Fuel Cell Fanny	464		42-52453	yes	Gas House Mouse	458	752	42-95050	yes
Full Boost	454	736	42-52311	yes	Gas House Mouse	487	839	41-29476	no
Full House	389		42-99966	no	Gashouse Gus	392	578	41-29476	no
Full House	448			no	Gashouse Mouse	392	578	41-29476	no
Full House	44	68	42-99966	yes	Gashouse Mouse	458	752	41-29329	no
Full House	451	724	44-10621	no	Gasoline Alley	RCAF			yes
Full House	455	741	42-94949	no	Gator	458	755	42-7516	yes
Fun House	464	776	42-78248	no	Gawgia Peach	485	831	42-52709	no
Fun House (The)	392			no	Gemini	34			no
Fun, Wasn't It?				yes	Gemini	486		42-52639	no
Funny Face	446	704	42-95121	no	Gemini	486		xx-xx762	no
Fur Wagon	451	727	42-50240	yes	Gemini	44	506	41-29496	no
Furious Sal	43			no	Gemini	451	727	41-29496	yes
Furtle Murtle	380			yes	Gemini	486	834	41-29496	yes
Fuzzy Wuzzy	307		41-23730	yes	Gemini II	34			no
Fyrtle Myrtle	376	513	44-40236	yes	Gemini II	486	834	xx-xx762	no
Fyrtle Myrtle	380	531	42-40485	yes	Gen	459	759	42-51772	no

Name	Grp.	Sq.	Serial	Pic.	Name	Grp.	Sq.	Serial	Pic.
Gene's Hare Power	461	765	44-48993	yes	Girl Crazy	454	736	42-78668	yes
General Ike	466			no	Glad To See Ya	466	787	42-95361	yes
Generator Jenny	490		44-40320	no	Gladys	90	400	44-40804	yes
Generator Jenny	493		44-40320	no	Glammer Gal	455	742	41-29296	no
Generator Jenny	34	18	44-40320	no	Glamour Girl	34	391	41-29572	no
Generator Jenny	466	785	44-40320	no	Glamouras'	90		44-40616	yes
Generator Joe	484	827	42-52700	yes	Glamouras'		4 PCS	44-40616	yes
Generator Kid	459	758		no	Glass House				no
Genii	454	737	42-52203	no	Glenna Bee II	11	26	42-73010	yes
Gentle Annie	376	514	42-40661	yes	Glidin' Home	494		44-41238	no
Gentleman Jim	43	403		yes	Glo Girl			44-41138	no
Gentleman Jim	454	737	42-52263	no	Glo Girl	5	72	44-41698	yes
George	456		42-51955	no	Glo Hop	90	321	42-40863	yes
Georgia				no	Globe Trotter	93	409	41-23748	no
Georgia Belle	392	578	42-7543	no	Globe Trotter II	93	330	42-7634	yes
Georgia Cracker	376	512	42-40318	yes	Glorious Lady				no
Georgia Peach				yes	Glory Bee	44	67	42-52616	yes
Georgia Peach	308		42-73445	yes	Glow Worm	93	330	41-23665	no
Georgia Peach	448			no	Go Better	467	789	41-28744	no
Georgia Peach	93	330	42-40985	yes	Go Better	467	789	42-50479	no
Georgia Peach	445	700	42-64434	no	Go-Go Girls	93			no
Georgia Piece				no	Go-Ta-Hay-It	460	760	42-51285	no
Georgie	307	424	44-42428	yes	God Bless Our Ship	93	329	42-7586	no
Geraldine	43	403	42-41065	yes	God Bless Our Ship	445	701	42-7586	no
Gerenime				no	Godfather's Inc.			42-97266	no
Gerocko	93		41-29386	no	Goin' Home-Tennessee				yes
Gerocko	467	791	41-29386	yes	Goin' My Way	446	707	44-10526	yes
Gerocko	467	791	42-50484	no	Goin' My Way	446	707	44-10528	yes
Geronimo	44			yes	Goin' Up, Doc?	487			no
Geronimo	93	409	41-23744	yes	Going My Way	491			no
Gertie the Gremlin	446	707	42-7649	yes	Going My Way	11	431	44-40674	yes
Gertie the Gremlin II	446			no	Going My Way	30	819	44-40674	no
Get Away Gertie	446			no	Going My Way	490	850		no
Ghost (The)	454	738	44-40483	yes	Gol Walloper				no
Ghost of the Omar	449	716	42-52140	yes	Golden Gaboon	453	733	41-28645	yes
Ghost, Too	466	784	42-95609	yes	Golden Gator (The)	380	529	42-40518	yes
GI Gal	44	67	42-40371	yes	Golden Girl	446			yes
GI Jane Pallas Athene	392	578	42-100187	yes	Golden Girl	446			no
GI Wife	487	836	41-29483	yes	Golden Goose (The)	380	528	42-40521	yes
GI Wife	493		44-40477	no	Golden Lady	90	321	42-40914	yes
Gidi Gidi Boom Boom	449	717	41-28846	no	Golden Sandstorm (The)	389	565	42-40795	yes
Gin	376	514	42-78262	yes	Gone With the Wind	90	400	41-24286	yes
Gin Mill Jill	486	835	42-52758	no	Good Conduct	392	577	42-110096	yes
Gin Rae	376	512	42-109831	yes	Good Heavens	455			no
Gin Rae	456	746	41-28643	yes	Good Heavens	454	736	44-41059	no
Ginee	464			yes	Good Heavens	454	739	41-29592	yes
Ginger	446	706	41-29177	yes	Good Nuff	445	700	42-7534	no
Ginnie	467		44-48816	no	Good Ship	450	722	42-78448	yes
Ginnie	453	733	41-28615	no	Good Time Charley	376	515	41-24030	yes
Ginnie	459	736		yes	Goofy	RCAF			yes
Ginny	454	738	44-41009	no	Goofy	459	756	42-52400	yes
Ginny	458	754	41-28669	no	Goon (The)	308	374	41-24183	yes
Ginny	458	754	41-28682	no	Goon (The)	43			no
Ginny	11	98	44-40491	yes	Goose's Garbage				
Ginny Gal	389	565	42-95077	yes	Wagon				yes
Ginny Lynn	30	27	42-72968	yes	Goosy Lucy	451	726	42-78250	yes
Gipsy Queen	44	68	42-109805	yes	Gopher Gus	7		AL-573	yes

Name	Grp.	Sq.	Serial	Pic.	Name	Grp.	Sq.	Serial	Pic.
Gorgeous Gal	389			no	Grim Reaper (The)	458		42-100404	no
Gorgeous Gal	392			no	Ground Happy				no
Government Gal	389	565	42-7582	no	Ground Hog	11AF	404	41-23892	no
Gracie (Fields)				yes	Groundhog	6AF			yes
Gran Slam				no	Grove Hill				
Gran Slam	466	784	42-51094	yes	Blunderbus	307	372	42-72824	yes
Granpappy (XB-24)			39-680	yes	GRRR	90	320		yes
Gravel Gertie	376	513	42-73083	yes	Gruesome 16	307	372	44-41290	yes
Gravel Gertie	451	727	42-73083	yes	Gruesome Goose	466	787	41-28747	yes
Gravel Gertie	454	737	42-78278	no	Grumpy	98	343	41-11825	yes
Gravel Gertie				yes	Guardian Angel				yes
Gravy Train (The)	376		40-2376	yes	Guardian Angel	454			no
Gravy Train (The)	RCM	36	42-51546	no	Guardian Angel	464		42-78115	no
Gray Goose	455	743	41-29583	no	Guardian Angel	449	719	42-7715	no
Grease Ball	491	854	44-40172	yes	Guardian Angel	450	722	41-29376	no
Great Iron Bird	449	717		no	Guardian Angel	465	781	41-29376	yes
Great Speckled Bird	459	757	42-50299	yes	Guardian Angel	484	824	42-52687	no
Great Speckled					Guardian Angel II	465	781	41-28959	no
Bird (The)	484	825	44-48988	yes	Guess What's Left	446	705	42-52598	no
Green Apple	98	415		no	Guess Who's Here	446	705	42-52598	no
Green Banana	11			no	Guess Who's Here	466	787	42-52598	yes
Green Dragon	453			no	Guiding Light (The)				yes
Green Dragon	453		41-23683	no	Gulliver	ATC	PW	41-11608	yes
Green Dragon	389	567	41-23683	yes	Gulliver II	ATC			yes
Green Dragon	466	784	42-51094	no	Gum Drop	464		42-52449	no
Green Dragon (The)	93	329	41-23683	no	Gump the Sniffer				
Green Eye Ikey	98	344	42-50225	no	Chief	98	345	44-50654	no
Green Eyes				no	Gun Moll	90	319	41-23755	yes
Green Gremlin	445	701	42-7515	no	Gun Moll 2nd	90	319	42-40970	yes
Green Hornet	307	372	41-24097	yes	Gun Site	11	26	42-72995	no
Green Hornet	445	702	41-29542	no	Gun Site	11	42	42-73005	yes
Green Hornet (The)	493		44-40286	yes	Gung Ho	448	712	44-10505	no
Green Hornet (The)	392	579	42-52504	yes	Gung Ho	448	713	42-50463	no
Green Hornet (The)	445	701	42-94940	yes	Gunga Din	485	835	41-29505	no
Green Hornet (The)	464	778	42-52504	no	Gunga Din	486	835	41-29505	no
Green Hornet (The)	491	852	44-40286	yes	Gunner's Sight	30	819	44-42526	yes
Greenwich	44	506	41-29153	yes	Gus			42-40255	yes
Gregory the Great	392	577	42-7493	no	Gus' Ball of Fire	458	753	42-52392	yes
Gremlin	307			no	Gus' Bus	380	530	42-40504	yes
Gremlin	11	42		yes	Gus' Bus II	380	530	42-41125	yes
Gremlin (The)				no	Gus' Jokers	11	26	44-41848	no
Gremlin (The)	376	514	41-24110	yes	Gus' Jokers	5	31	44-41848	yes
Gremlin Gus	450	723	42-52161	no	Gussie				yes
Gremlin's Delight			41-23858	yes	Gwen	458	755	42-110184	yes
Gremlin's Delite	449	719	42-64389	yes	Gwen	492	857	42-110184	yes
Gremlin's Gripe	455	743	42-52271	no	Gypsy	380	528	42-41133	yes
Gremlin's Gripe II	455	741	42-52281	yes	Gypsy from Pokipsie				yes
Gremlin's Haven	308			yes	Gypsy Jane (The)	RCM	36	44-50502	no
Gremlin's Haven		868	42-40653	no	Gypsy Queen	448		42-95197	no
Gremlin's Roost	448			no	Gypsy Queen	449		42-95197	no
Gremlin's Roost	445	703	42-7512	no	Gypsy Queen	453		42-109896	no
Gremlin's Roost	486	832	xx-xx601	no	Gypsy Queen	93	409	42-95024	no
Gremlin's Roost	490	848	41-29601	no	Gypsy Queen	392	578	42-109896	no
Gremlin's Roost (The)	93	330	42-50505	no	Gypsy Queen	453	735	42-50327	no
Gremlin's Roost (The)	392	579	44-49577	yes	Gypsy Queen	458	754	42-95196	no
Greyhound Express	93	409	42-40610	no	H for Helen	448			no
Grim Reaper	459	759		no	Hadley's Harem	98	344	41-24311	yes

Name	Grp.	Sq.	Serial	Pic.	Name	Grp.	Sq.	Serial	Pic.
Hag Mag the Hangar Queen	44	66	42-40731	no	Hard To Get	451	725	42-7738	yes
					Hard To Get	454	736	42-78450	yes
Hag Mag the Mothball Queen	44	66	42-40731	no	Hard To Hit				yes
Hail Columbia	98	343	41-11825	yes	Hard Way (The)	459	758	44-40877	yes
Hair Power	454	736		no	Hard Way Ten	376	515	44-40330	yes
Hairless Joe	44		44-40437	no	Hare Force			42-97948	yes
Hairless Joe	456		42-51284	no	Hare Power	454	738	42-51959	no
Hairless Joe	7		42-41252	no	Hare Power	454	739	41-29325	no
Hairless Joe	376	513	42-40081	yes	Hare Power	461	765	41-29325	no
Hairless Joe	454	738	42-52228	yes	Hare Power	491	854	44-40117	yes
Hairless Joe	459	758	42-52228	no	Hare's To Ya	93	329	41-23710	no
Hairless Joe	493	860	44-40437	yes	Harmful Lil' Armful	448	715	42-7754	no
Hairless Joe	11	98	42-41136	no	Harper's Ferry	449	718	41-28621	yes
Half & Half				no	Harriet's Secret	5		42-41155	no
Half & Half			44-49577	yes	Harry S. Truman (The)	90	321	44-40229	yes
Half-Moon Trio (The)	392	576	41-28991	no	Harry S. Truman (The)				yes
Hamtramch Mama				yes	Harry the Horse	376	515	42-73090	yes
Hangar Annie	484	825	42-50394	yes	Hart's Ease				no
Hangar Queen	460	763	42-51084	yes	Hassan the Assassin	449	719	41-29237	no
Hangar Queen				yes	Hassan the Assassin	459	757	41-29237	no
Hangover				yes	Hattie Belle	453	735	44-40292	yes
Hangover Haven II	6PR	20CM	42-64053	yes	Hawaiian Air Depot	307		41-23911	yes
Hap Hazard	392		42-7580	yes	Hawaiian Woman	494	867	44-40754	no
Hap Hazard	446		42-7580	yes	Hawk (The)	454	736	42-52266	no
Hap Hazard	445	703	42-7580	yes	Hawk (The)	454	736	44-49341	no
Hap-N-Hank	11	431	44-50145	yes	Hay Maker	90	319	44-40729	yes
Happy				no	Hay Maker	494	867	44-40729	yes
Happy	98	343	42-40256	yes	Hazee	392	576	44-50527	yes
Happy Go	446			no	Hazee	453	733	44-50527	yes
Happy Go Lucky	446	705	42-7625	yes	Hazel! Which Hazel?	11			yes
Happy Go-Lucky			42-52772	yes	He Dood It	28	404	41-23888	yes
Happy Hangover	448			no	Head Wind Herky	445	702		no
Happy Warrior	448		42-94860	no	Heading for Home	449	719	42-50406	yes
Happy Warrior	489		42-50587	yes	Heat of the Night	451	727	42-52049	no
Happy Warrior	467	791	42-50621	no	Heat's On (The)	485	828	42-78474	no
Happy Warrior	489	846	42-94860	no	Heater (The)	43			no
Hard Guy	461	765	41-28681	no	Heather Angel	307	372	42-72783	yes
Hard Hearted Hannah	464	778	41-28755	yes	Heaven Can Wait				no
Hard Luck				no	Heaven Can Wait				yes
Hard Luck				no	Heaven Can Wait	484			no
Hard Luck	466	787	44-40253	yes	Heaven Can Wait	90	400	42-41216	yes
Hard T' Find	458		42-50373	yes	Heaven Can Wait	389	565	42-40370	yes
Hard T' Find	466	786	42-50373	yes	Heaven Can Wait	389	565	42-40744	no
Hard T' Find	487	839	42-50373	yes	Heaven Can Wait	392	576	42-7507	no
Hard T' Get			42-52299	yes	Heaven Can Wait	392	576	44-50505	no
Hard T' Get	486		41-29486	no	Heaven Can Wait	44	68	42-7507	yes
Hard T' Get	487			no	Heaven Can Wait	448	715	42-7758	no
Hard T' Get	486	835	42-52753	yes	Heaven Can Wait	455	740	42-52210	no
Hard Times	448	714	42-7755	no	Heaven Can Wait	459	758		no
Hard To Get				yes	Heaven Can Wait	461	765	42-51971	no
Hard To Get	467		42-94988	no	Heaven Can Wait	461	766	41-28679	yes
Hard To Get	486			no	Heaven Can Wait	30	819	42-72831	no
Hard To Get	392	578	42-7518	no	Heaven Can Wait	489	845	41-28832	yes
Hard To Get	446	705	42-94988	no	Heaven Can Wait II	489	845	42-94786	no
Hard To Get	450	720	42-78156	no	Heaven Can Wait II	494	866	44-42061	yes
Hard To Get	451	724	42-78523	no	Heaven Can Wait, Don Ameche	11	98	42-73496	yes

Name	Grp.	Sq.	Serial	Pic.	Name	Grp.	Sq.	Serial	Pic.
Heaven's Above	464			yes	Hell's a-Poppin'	449	718	42-52166	yes
Heaven's Above	450	720	41-28757	yes	Hell's Angels	454			no
Heaven's Above				yes	Hell's Angels	93	329	42-40781	no
Heaven's Devils	98	343	42-73077	no	Hell's Angels	90	400	41-11903	yes
Heavenly Body	445		42-94939	no	Hell's Angels	380	529	42-40502	yes
Heavenly Body	453		41-29210	yes	Hell's Angels	458	754	41-29596	no
Heavenly Body	34	18	41-28878	yes	Hell's Angels	485	831	41-29494	no
Heavenly Body	90	400	41-11867	yes	Hell's Bell's	454	739	42-52310	yes
Heavenly Body	308	425	42-73116	yes	Hell's Belle	448			no
Heavenly Body	380	528	42-73116	yes	Hell's Belle	466			no
Heavenly Body	392	577	41-28875	yes	Hell's Belle	487			no
Heavenly Body	43	63	42-73484	yes	Hell's Belle	98	345	42-41183	yes
Heavenly Body	449	716	42-7708	yes	Hell's Belle	34	391	42-94893	no
Heavenly Body	455	741	42-94938	no	Hell's Belle	34	4	42-94815	yes
Heavenly Body	456	746	41-28768	yes	Hell's Belle	90	400	41-24290	yes
Heavenly Body	459	757	44-42417	no	Hell's Belle	380	530	42-41222	yes
Heavenly Body	490	849	42-94939	no	Hell's Belle	446	704	42-99937	yes
Heavenly Body	491	852	42-110135	no	Hell's Belle	459	756	42-52358	yes
Heavenly Daze	93	330	42-63970	no	Hell's Belle	459	756	44-40926	yes
Heavenly Daze	93			yes	Hell's Belle	465	781	42-52505	no
Heavenly Hideaway	AZON		44-40277	no	Hell's Belle	494	864	44-40715	yes
Heavenly Hideaway	93	409	41-23734	no	Hell's Belle				yes
Heavenly Hideaway	458	753	44-40277	yes	Hell's Belle Peggy	487			no
Heavenly Lamb Chop	5	31	44-40585	yes	Hell's Belles				yes
Heavy Date	11	26	42-100228	yes	Hell's Bells	98	343	42-94998	no
Heavy Date	389	566	42-7766	yes	Hell's Bells	464	776	42-51953	yes
Heavy Date	389	567	42-40747	yes	Hell's Bells II	464	778	44-41227	no
Heine Headache	491	855	44-40203	no	Hell's Bells(e)	11			yes
Heine Hunter	466		42-95266	no	Hell's Express	93	409	42-63762	no
Heine Hunter	446	704	42-95266	no	Hell's Hangover	484	827	44-49936	no
Heinie Hunter	93	328	41-23990	no	Hell's Hep Cats	451	724	42-51314	no
Helen	460	760		yes	Hell's Kitchen	44	66	41-24236	yes
Helen B. Happy	44	66	42-40764	yes	Hell's Kitchen	448	713	41-24236	no
Helen Hywater	44	68	42-63971	yes	Hell's Kitten	44	68	41-24236	yes
Helen's Revenge	43	64	42-40913	yes	Hell's Kitten	448	713	41-24236	yes
Helenbak	445		42-94921	no	Hell's Natural	448	713	41-24236	no
Helfer College	389		41-29131	no	Hell's Warrior	445	701	42-7563	no
Helfer College II	389	567	41-29451	no	Hell's Wench	93	328	42-40994	no
Hell and Back			44-48288	no	Hell-O-Trouble	307			yes
Hell and Back	493		42-95170	yes	Hell-O-Trouble	307		41-23864	no
Hell and Back	493		44-42951	no	Hellcat	93			no
Hell and Back	801		42-95170	no	Hellcat	11	431	42-109944	yes
Hell and Back	SOP		42-95170	no	Hellcat Belle	11	98	42-73153	yes
Hell Cat	93			no	Hellcat Honey	5		42-109944	yes
Hell Cat	445	703	42-7585	no	Heller B. Happy	44			no
Hell Cat (The)	392	576	42-7524	no	Heller B. Happy				no
Hell for Hitler	453			no	Hellno				no
Hell from Heaven	307		42-72829	yes	Hello Natural	448	712	41-29191	yes
Hell from Heaven	30	819	42-109941	yes	Hello Natural II	448	712	42-50606	no
Hell from Heaven	30	819	44-40528	yes	Hello Natural II	448	712	42-52606	yes
Hell from Heaven	485	830	42-52722	no	Hello-ver Burma	7	436	44-42460	yes
Hell N' Hiwater II	307		44-41422	yes	Hells Belle	34	391	42-94893	no
Hell Wagon				yes	Hellsadroppin'				no
Hell Wagon	453		42-7492	no	Hellsapoppin'	376		41-11601	no
Hell Wagon (The)	392	576	42-7492	yes	Hellsapoppin'	93	329	41-23723	yes
Hell's A Droppin'	93	329	41-23723	yes	Hellzadroppin'	448		41-23809	no
Hell's A Droppin' II	93	329	41-23809	yes	Hellzadroppin'	392	579	42-7488	no

Name	Grp.	Sq.	Serial	Pic.	Name	Grp.	Sq.	Serial	Pic.
Hellzapoppin'	90	319	41-23719	yes	Home James	455	743	41-28952	no
Henry	493		44-40279	no	Home James	30	819	44-40527	yes
Henry	44	66	44-40279	yes	Home Stretch	7			yes
Henry's Ford	454	738	42-52313	no	Home Town	448			no
Henry's Pride	446	704	42-7574	yes	Homesick Angel				yes
Her Baroness			42-40252	yes	Homesick Angel	11		42-73153	yes
Her Man	453			no	Homesick Angel	454	736	42-52125	no
Herd of Hainan	43			no	Homesick Angel	466	784	41-29395	no
Here I Come Again	458			no	Homesick Angel	490	850		no
Here I Go Again	458	752	42-95179	yes	Homesick Lass	489	845	42-94906	yes
Here's To You	93	329	41-24230	yes	Homesick Moe	459			no
Herk's Jerks	492	858	44-40125	yes	Homesick Susie				no
Hey Mac	449	716	42-99803	yes	Homesick Susie	98	343	42-40312	yes
Hey Man	449			no	Homeward Angel	466	784	41-29395	no
Hey Ride	446	704	44-49523	no	Homeward Angel	485	829	44-41157	no
Hey, Doc	98	344	42-109813	yes	Homeward Angel	456			no
Hey, Moe	451	725	42-51090	yes	Homeward Bound	467	790	41-29378	yes
Hi Ho Silver	461		42-51778	no	Homing Pigeon			44-40247	no
Hi Ho Silver	461	766	41-29336	no	Homing Pigeon (The)	491			no
Hi Pockets	450	721	42-95385	no	Homma Homma Kid	380	528	42-40497	no
Hi-Priority Stuff		2 PCS	44-40967	yes	Homma Homma Kid II	380	529	42-41238	no
High Hopes	487		42-52581	no	Honey	307	371	42-40869	yes
High Hopes	487		42-52592	no	Honey Bucket	489			no
High Life	449	719	41-28972	yes	Honey Child	451	725	41-29220	no
Hillbilly	98	415	42-40379	no	Honey Chile	376	515	42-40664	yes
Hilo Hattie	11	431	41-23844	yes	Honey Chile	449	717	42-78372	yes
Hip Parade	90		42-73002	yes	Honey Chile	460	760	42-52538	no
Hit Parade	448			no	Honey Gal	466	787	42-95246	yes
Hit Parade	11	26	42-73002	no	Honey Lee	93	330	41-23712	no
Hit Parade	43	64	44-40430	yes	Honey Lulu				yes
Hit Parade (The)	34		42-94883	no	Honeybucket	448			no
Hit Parade (The)	489		42-94883	no	Honeysuckle Rose	98	344	42-72890	yes
Hit Parade (The)	44	506	42-94883	no	Honky Tonk Gal	93	409	42-40265	yes
Hit Parader	449			no	Honorable Patches	487			no
Hit Parader	90	319	42-41087	yes	Hoo Jive	453	734	42-52174	yes
Hit Parader II	22	33	42-41087	yes	Hookem Cow	466			no
Hitler's Egg Men	485	831	42-52601	no	Hookem Cow	458	755	42-95120	yes
Hitler's Headache	44	67	41-23774	no	Hoopee	479		42-63779	no
Hitler's Hearse	445			no	Hoosier Pete	464	779	44-49713	no
Hitler's Hearse	389	567	42-40544	no	Hoot Owl Express	307	372	42-40235	yes
Hitler's Nightmare	93		41-23774	no	Hop Scotch	451	727	41-29209	yes
Hitler's Nightmare	44	67	41-23774	no	Hoppy	449	718		no
Hitler's V-4s	448			no	Hornet's Nest				no
Hmm, What A Lick	389	566	42-100185	no	Horrible Bastard	465		42-51583	no
Ho Hum	90	400	42-109983	yes	Horrible Monster	494	864	44-40690	yes
Hobo Queen	451	725	42-64353	no	Horse Fly	44	67	42-40267	yes
Holiday Inn				no	Hot & Bothered	459	758	42-52295	yes
Holiday Mess	44	506	42-40989	no	Hot and Available				yes
Holiday Mess II	44	66	42-7533	no	Hot As Hell	308	425	42-40075	yes
Holiday Raiders	458	753		no	Hot As Hell	308		42-73308	no
Hollywood & Vine	453	734	41-28610	no	Hot Box	458	753	42-100431	no
Holy Joe	34	391	42-50613	yes	Hot Box	466	785	41-29374	yes
Holy Joe	449	717	41-29225	yes	Hot Dish				no
Holy Joe the 2nd	449	717	42-50282	no	Hot Freight	93	330	41-23666	yes
Home Alive in '45				yes	Hot Garters	90	321	42-41188	no
Home Breaker	446	706	42-52612	yes	Hot Lips	93	329	42-40986	no
Home for Christmas	464	778	42-52437	yes	Hot Mathilda	465	781	44-41122	yes

Name	Grp.	Sq.	Serial	Pic.	Name	Grp.	Sq.	Serial	Pic.
Hot Nuts	308	374	41-24266	no	I Yam Wot I Yam				yes
Hot Pants	485	831	42-51872	no	I'll Be Around				yes
Hot Rock				no	I'll Be Around	494			no
Hot Rock	445	703	42-51532	no	I'll Be Around	43	63	42-100042	yes
Hot Rock	446	705	42-51532	no	I'll Be Around	492	859	44-40132	no
Hot Rock	449	718	41-29218	yes	I'll Be Around	90			no
Hot Rock	454	737	42-52225	yes	I'll Be Around?	491		44-40132	no
Hot Rock	491	855	44-40162	no	I'll Be Back	44	506	42-52305	no
Hot Rocks	98	345	42-40197	no	I'll Be Back	44	506	42-52332	no
Hot Rocks	380	531	42-73489	yes	I'll Be Back	392	579	41-28788	no
Hot Rocks	484	827	42-52683	yes	I'll Be Back	458	754	41-29305	yes
Hot Shot Charlie	446	704	42-95126	yes	I'll Be Back	458	754	42-52305	no
Hot Shotsie	454	739	42-78214	yes	I'll Be Seeing You	380	529	44-40923	yes
Hot Sketch	459	756	42-52356	no	I'll Be Seeing You	491	854	44-40210	no
Hot Stuff	453			no	I'll Get By	93			no
Hot Stuff	93	330	41-23728	yes	I'll Get By	Navy			yes
Hot Stuff	98	415	42-41028	yes	I'll Get By	98	343	44-49041	no
Hot Stuff	389	565	42-51087	yes	I'll Get By	450	723	42-64339	no
Hot To Go	449	719	41-29003	yes	I'll Get By	494	864	44-40743	yes
Hot to Go	7	9	42-73303	yes	I'se a Royal				
Hot To Go				yes	Hawaiian	11	26	42-41198	yes
Hot to Go, Frozen	7	9	42-72803	no	I've Had It!	389	567	42-95071	no
Hotcha Babe	484	824	42-51694	no	Ice Cold Katie	448	713	41-28595	yes
Hotcha Baby				no	Ice Cold Katie	451	726	42-7751	no
Hotcha Baby	454	736	42-50285	yes	Ice Cold Katie	456	746	42-64477	no
Hottest ??? in Town	461	766	41-29313	no	Ice Cold Katie II	451	726	41-29541	no
Hottest ??? in Town (The)	485	831	42-78139	yes	Iceberg Inez	28	404	42-40910	no
House of Bourbon	307	424	41-23943	yes	Idiot's Dee Light	98	345	41-23780	yes
House of Rumor	491	854	44-40271	yes	Idiot's Dee Light	376	514	41-23780	yes
How Am I Doin'?	98	415	42-64370	no	Idiot's Delight	392	578	42-50623	no
How'm I Doin'?	90	319	42-41223	yes	Idiot's Delight	490	848	42-94839	yes
Howling Banshee	AZON		44-40273	no	Idiot's Delight	491	853	42-51530	no
Howling Banshee	458	753	44-40207	no	Idle Curiosity	6PR	20CM	44-40423	yes
Howling Banshee	458	753	44-40273	yes	Idle Curiosity	90			no
Hubba Hubba	98			yes	Iggy	461		42-51xxx	no
Hubba Hubba	450	721	42-50776	yes	Iggy	11AF	404	41-1104	no
Hubba Hubba II	450	721	42-78506	no	Ike & Monty	491	852	42-94855	no
Huckle De Buck	493		44-40235	no	Ike and Monty	489	845	42-94855	no
Hula Wahine	446	704	42-7578	yes	Imagine	484	826	44-49738	yes
Hula Wahine II	446	704	42-52467	yes	Imp (The)	456	745	41-29297	no
Hull's Angels	466	787	42-50581	yes	Impatient Lady				no
Hump Time	308	374	44-42117	yes	Impatient Lady	308	374	44-41441	yes
Humpshot	453	732		no	Impatient Virgin	44	67	41-29231	yes
Humpty Dumpty	449	716		no	Impatient Virgin	450	720	42-7697	no
Hussy Lin	448			no	Impatient Virgin	451	724	41-29251	no
Hustlin' Hussy	453	734		no	Impatient Virgin (The)	389		41-29231	no
Hustlin' Hussy	484	827	42-52677	no	Impatient Virgin (The)	448	714	41-29231	no
Hydra	448			no	In God We Trust	486	833	42-52475	no
Hypochondriac	458			no	In The Mood	451	725	42-51222	no
I - Ink	93	328	42-99845	no	In The Mood	486	838	42-52664	no
I Hope So!	446	704	44-50523	yes	Incendiary Blonde	448		42-95158	no
I Tell You, Boys,					Incendiary Sue	30	392	42-72991	yes
It's Heaven	11	26	44-40953	yes	Indian Maid / Redwing	VPB	106	Bu59586	yes
I Walk Alone	RCM	36	42-51546	no	Indian Thummer	307		44-49442	yes
I Walk Alone	392	579	42-51150	no	Inhoomin Critter (The)	449	718	42-78341	yes
I Walk Alone Also			42-51546	no	Innocence A-Broad	494	865	44-40733	yes
I Wanted Wings	486	833	42-52740	yes	Innocence Abroad				yes

Name	Grp.	Sq.	Serial	Pic.	Name	Grp.	Sq.	Serial	Pic.
Innocent Infant III	308	375	44-49649	yes	Jail Bait	491	853	42-110161	yes
Inspector's Squak	453			no	Jake	453		xx-xx219	no
Instable	449	717	42-78195	no	Jake's Nabor	461	765	42-51346	no
Into the Blue	454	738	42-78079	yes	Jamaica?	466	785	41-28746	yes
Invader (The)	93			no	Jamey				yes
Invictus	461	765	41-28725	no	Jane	446			no
Irish Angel II	461	765	42-52486	yes	Jane	460	760	42-78413	no
Irish Lass (The)	449			yes	Jane and Sharon Ann	487			no
Irish Lassie	98	344	42-51147	yes	Jane Lee (The)	451	727	42-94877	yes
Irish Lassie	98	344	42-95352	no	Jane's White Rabbit	34		42-52750	no
Irish Lassie	455	741	44-40517	yes	Jane's Wittle Wabbit	492		42-52757	no
Irish Lassie	459	757		yes	Jane's Wittle Wabbit	493	861	42-52751	no
Irishman's Shanty	492	857	44-40166	yes	Janeen Ann	98	415	42-51986	no
Irma Kay	456	746		yes	Janet	389			yes
Iron Ass	93	329	42-40769	yes	Janet Lee	451	725	41-28766	no
Iron Ass	389	566	42-40769	no	Janie	307	424	44-40535	yes
Iron Bird	5	31	44-41850	yes	Jap Trap	HALP		41-11629	no
Iron Corset	44			no	Jap-A-Nazi Jinx	454	738		no
Iron Duke	458	754	44-10491	no	Jasper's Jokers	90	321	44-49480	no
Ironbird	448			no	Jawja Boy	392	578	42-52548	no
Is This Trip Necessary	466			no	Jay Bird (The)				no
Is This Trip Necessary?				yes	Jay's Pool Hall	392	578	42-50446	no
Is This Trip Necessary?	389		42-50532	yes	Jay's Poolhall	392	578	42-51121	no
Is This Trip Necessary?	491	853	42-50532	yes	Jayhawker	458	752	41-28667	yes
Is This Trip Necessary?	98			yes	Jazz Ax Blues (The)		2PC		no
Island Dream				yes	Je Revien	453	735		no
Island Queen				yes	Je Reviens	380	529	42-72808	yes
Island Queen	5	31	42-100022	yes	Jean	456	744	42-99799	no
Island Queen	22	408	42-100230	no	Jean B				no
It Ain't So Funny	43	64	44-49853	yes	Jeanie	451	724	44-41335	yes
It Had To Be You	459			no	Jeannie C.	307	424	42-40211	yes
It Had To Be You	454	738	41-28608	no	Jeannie with the				
It's A Dog's Life	458	753	44-40281	yes	Light Brown Hair	493			no
It's For You	6AF			yes	Jeeter Bug (The)	11	42	44-40661	yes
It's T.S. Boys	389	567	42-72856	no	Jeeter Bug (The)	30	819	44-40661	yes
Itty Bitty Commando	93			yes	Jennie	466	784	42-95617	no
Ity Fad	448			no	Jennie Ann	456	747		no
IV F Sack Time Sally			44-40380	yes	Jenny	44	66	41-23778	yes
J-Bar	44			no	Jeremiah	307	424	41-23877	yes
J-Bird	456	747	42-52345	no	Jerilyne Sue	467	789	42-52499	yes
J. C. Poolhall	392	578	42-50446	no	Jerilynne Sue	44			no
J.F.Whiggles					Jerk's Berserks	493		44-40443	no
Delivery Service				yes	Jerk's Berserks	34	4	44-40443	no
Jabberwock	453	732	41-28641	no	Jerk's Natural	34		44-40473	no
Jack & Charlie's "21"	464			yes	Jerk's Natural	93	328	41-23711	yes
Jack Frost	93	329	41-23982	no	Jerrie Ann (The)	485	828	42-78116	no
Jack Frost	93	329	41-24259	no	Jersey Bounce	93	330	42-40609	yes
Jack Pine Joe	465	780	42-52466	yes	Jersey Jackass	98	343	41-11776	yes
Jack Pot	90	321	42-40280	no	Jersey Jerk	44	66	44-10548	no
Jack the Ripper	467			no	Jersey Jerks	98	343		yes
Jack the Ripper II	467	791	42-52424	yes	Jersey the Gremlin				no
Jackass Billy	11	98	42-40406	yes	Jesse James	451	724	42-94808	no
Jackass Mule (Male)	389	565	42-72866	no	Jest for Laughs				no
Jackie Boy	459	756	42-52717	no	Jester				no
Jackie's Boy	376	514	42-72844	no	Jeva	486	833	42-50651	no
Jacob's Ladder	456	744	44-10628	no	Jewel	489			no
Jail Bait	44	66	42-110161	yes	Jewel Sa	446			no

Name	Grp.	Sq.	Serial	Pic.	Name	Grp.	Sq.	Serial	Pic.
Jezabelle	491	852	44-40213	yes	Jolly Annette	44			no
Jezebel	11	26	41-24267	yes	Jolly Duck	392	578	42-95241	no
Jezebelle	380	529	42-72953	yes	Jolly Roger	493		44-40475	yes
Jig's Up (The)	RCM	36	42-51232	no	Jolly Roger	98	343	44-50449	yes
Jig's Up (The)		801	42-51232	yes	Jolly Roger	451	727	42-52081	yes
Jigg's Up!	491			yes	Jolly Roger	451	727	44-40425	yes
Jiggs	446	704	42-52733	yes	Jolly Roger	458	752	44-40475	yes
Jiggs	93		xx-xx362	no	Jolly Roger	458	755	42-50864	no
Jigs Up (The)				no	Jolly Roger (The)	90			yes
Jilted Joker				no	Jolly Roger Express	90			no
Jini	Austr.			no	Jolly Roger Special	90			no
Jinny	491			no	Jolly Rogers	5	31		no
Jinx	98	344	42-40742	no	Joltin' Janie	90	321	42-40233	yes
Jinx (The)				yes	Joltin' Janie	43		41-24233	no
Jinx (The)	449			yes	Joltin' Janie II	90	321	42-40065	yes
Jinx (The)	308	374	41-24184	yes	Joltin' Janie II	43	403	42-40233	yes
Jinx (The)	392	577	42-7496	no	Jonny Reb	448			no
Jinx (The)	44	68	42-7551	no	Jonny Reb	449	716	42-7768	no
Jinx (The)	490	848	42-94837	yes	Joplin Jalopy	44	506	42-50535	yes
Jita	11	431	41-24100	no	Jose				yes
Jive Bomber	392	579	42-109814	yes	Jose Carioca			42-100078	yes
Jive Bomber -					Jose Carioca	93	409	42-40617	yes
Hilarious Hell				no	Jose Carioca	44	66	42-50643	yes
Jizzy Outch	461	767	41-28724	no	Jose's "El Diablo"	5AF			yes
Jo	489	847	42-94783	yes	Journal Square Express	93			no
Jo Jo's Special Delivery	389	567	41-23683	yes	Joy	22		41-23973	no
Jo-Jo's Special Delivery	93	329	41-23683	yes	Joy Ride	93	409	42-7621	no
Jodey	454	736	42-52261	yes	Joy Rider	Navy			yes
Jodey	454	736	42-78503	no	Ju Ju	2AD			no
Joe				yes	Juanita	449	719	42-52126	yes
Joe E. Brown	90			yes	Juanita	459	756		yes
Joe E. Brown	489	847	42-94783	no	Juarez				no
Joe-gia Wolf	465	781	42-52321	yes	Juarez Whistle	380	530	42-40496	yes
Joey Uptown	376	515	42-40232	yes	Judith Ann				no
Johnny Come Lately	491	855	42-110154	yes	Judith Ann	98	345	42-73418	yes
Johnny Doughboy	308	425	42-72842	no	Judith Ann	459	756	44-49771	yes
Johnny Reb	489	844	42-94826	no	Judith Lynn	93	329	42-40983	yes
Johnson's Jalopy	489	844	42-94788	no	Judy	487	836	41-29478	no
Joint Venture	450	722	42-78194	no	Judy Ann	456	744	41-29501	no
Joisey Bounce	93	328	41-24228	yes	Judy Lee	5			no
Joker				yes	Judy Lee	450	723	42-7752	yes
Joker	389		42-95253	no	Judy Sue				no
Joker	93	330	42-7504	no	Judy Sue	458			no
Joker	98	415	42-40205	yes	Judy Sue	466	787	42-50791	yes
Joker	389	564	42-95555	no	Judy's Buggy	458		42-52293	no
Joker	446	705	41-29151	no	Judy's Buggy	44	67	42-52293	no
Joker	454	737	41-28993	no	Jug Haid	479			no
Joker	465	782	42-78287	no	Jug Head	453	732	42-51102	no
Joker (The)				yes	Jugglin' Josie	380	530	42-41237	yes
Joker (The)	493		44-40472	yes	Juicy Lady	30	819		no
Joker (The)	93	330	44-40472	yes	Juicy Lucy	30	27	42-40074	yes
Joker (The)	307	372	41-23962	no	Juicy Lucy	11	431	42-40074	yes
Joker (The)	308	372		yes	Jukie L. Lynn				no
Joker (The)	98	415	42-40205	yes	Julie	98			no
Joker (The)	466	787	42-51317	yes	Jumping Jive	448			no
Joker's Wild (The)			42-40772	yes	June Bride	43			no
Jokers (The)				no	Jungle Jig	7	492		yes

37

Name	Grp.	Sq.	Serial	Pic.	Name	Grp.	Sq.	Serial	Pic.
Jungle Princess	392	576	42-7537	no	Kelly	446	704	42-7564	no
Jungle Pussy	308	374	42-40503	yes	Ken's Men	43		44-40980	yes
Jungle Queen			AL640	no	Ken-O-Kay	453	732	42-52302	yes
Jungle Queen	43	65	42-40863	yes	Ken-O-Kay II	453	732	42-52301	no
Jungle Queen II	380	529	42-40510	yes	Ken-O-Kay III	453	732	42-94990	no
Junior	448			no	Kentucky Babe II	389			no
Junior	458	754	42-95116	no	Kentucky Babe III	389		42-7553	no
Junior	460	763	42-99763	no	Kentucky Baby	392	578	42-99979	no
Junior	486	833		no	Kentucky Belle	493		44-40268	no
Junior II	460	763	44-41014	no	Kentucky Belle	446	706	44-40268	yes
Junior Miss	479	6		yes	Kentucky Colonel	446	706	44-40268	no
Just Around the Corner	458			no	Kentucky				
Just F/O 20%	487			no	Kloudhopper	803		44-40380	yes
Just for You	466	784		yes	Kentucky Virgin	43	403	42-41053	yes
Just Jeanne	RCM	36	42-51307	no	KentuckyKloud				
Just One More Time	493		44-40464	no	Hopper III	7	9		yes
Just One Time	446	704	41-29411	no	Kickapoo	98	344	41-11768	yes
Justa 24	307		44-40542	yes	Kickapoo Kid	30	27	42-72983	yes
K - King	460	762	41-28883	no	Kill-Joy	446	706	41-29141	yes
K for King			41-23811	no	Kilocycle Kitty	AACS			yes
K Lucy II	11	26	42-109861	yes	King Bird	491			no
K-Bar	44	506	42-50733	yes	King High	44		42-7648	no
K-Lucy	30	392	44-40302	no	King Kong	445	702	42-50340	no
K. O. Katy	376	515	42-100253	no	King Kong	445	702	42-50383	no
K. O. Katy II	376	515	42-72847	no	King of Clubs	43	63	42-40949	no
K. O. Kid (The)	380	529	44-40342	yes	King of the Pack	455	741	42-52280	no
K.K. & His Abort Kids	93	328	44-40157	no	King Pin	44	66	42-50761	no
Kajun Kate	15AF			yes	King's "X"	308	375	44-40584	yes
Kamikaze Miss (The)	Navy			yes	King's ETO Express	93			no
Kandy Kourier	308	425	42-73318	yes	Kingpin	44	66	42-50761	no
Kangaroo Kate	Austr.			yes	Kisco Kid	34		42-94930	no
Kansas City Kitty	90		44-41480	yes	Kiska Katie	30	21	41-23896	yes
Kansas City Kitty	5	31	44-41480	yes	Kiss Me Baby	AZON		44-40264	yes
Kansas City Kitty	22	33	44-41255	yes	Kiss Me Baby	458	753	44-40264	yes
Kansas Cyclone	11	26	42-73025	yes	Kissed Off Kids	461	766	42-52408	no
Karachi Kourier	308	425	42-73318	no	Kit's Tadger	307	371	44-40604	yes
Karioka Joe	RCAF			yes	Kitrinka	493			no
Kate Smith	98	345		yes	Kitten	450	723	41-28821	no
Kathleen	450	723	42-51603	no	Kitty Quick	376	514	41-11630	yes
Kathleen	392			yes	Kiwi Bird	464	779	42-50920	no
Kathryn Ann	98	343	42-78600	yes	Klunker	451	726	41-28955	no
Kathy	380	531	42-40517	no	Knight of the Eighth	389	566	42-99982	no
Katie Did	454	738	44-41163	no	Knit Clipper	11	26	42-40177	no
Katrinka	493	863	42-51197	yes	Knock It Off	451	724	42-7765	no
Katy	467	789	42-52535	no	Knockers Up	451	727	42-52054	no
Katy Bug	93	328	41-23745	yes	Knockout	454	736	42-78288	no
Katy Did	308	375	41-24284	yes	Knockout	455	741	41-29290	no
Katy-Did				no	Knockout	455	741	42-52260	no
Kay Bar				yes	Knockout	484	827	42-94738	yes
Kay-18	6PR	20CM	44-40656	yes	Knucklehead	392	578	41-29509	no
Kay-Lyn	11		44-40362	no	KO! Kidde		55W	44-49527	yes
Kay-Lyn	30	38	44-40362	yes	Koko	11	26	42-73014	no
Kay-O	22	408	42-109990	no	Kongo Kutie	ATC		41-11709	yes
Kay-Rashun	30	27	42-73236	yes	Kontagious Katie	30	819	42-73493	yes
Kayo	90	321	42-63990	yes	Krachy Kourier				yes
Kayo	451	727	42-78576	yes	Kraut Killer	93	328	42-40801	no
Kelly	445	703	42-7559	no	Kuuipo's	484		44-40xx3	no

Name	Grp.	Sq.	Serial	Pic.	Name	Grp.	Sq.	Serial	Pic.
Kuuipo's	494	864	44-40559	yes	Lady Jane	466	785	44-50484	no
L'il Peach				no	Lady Jane (The)	93	329	42-40804	no
L. A. City Limits	389	567	42-63977	yes	Lady Jane II		868	44-41464	yes
L. A. City Limits	389	567	42-72833	no	Lady Jeanne	380	529	42-40511	yes
La Borracha	459	756	42-52319	no	Lady Jeanne II	380	529	42-40571	yes
La Chiquitae	491			no	Lady Katherine	454	736	41-28873	no
La Mamie	448			no	Lady Katherine	454	736	42-51398	no
Lace	453	732	42-95076	yes	Lady Katherine	459	756		no
Lacey	453			no	Lady Kaye	11			yes
Lackanookie	308	374	42-40630	no	Lady Kaye	494	867	44-40647	yes
Laden Maid	466	786	42-52560	yes	Lady Kessler	490	850	42-94856	yes
Laden Maid	466	786	44-10521	no	Lady Lee	450	723		yes
Laden Maid Again	466	786	44-10521	no	Lady Leone	389			no
Laden Maiden	307	424	42-72819	yes	Lady Leone	494	864	44-40736	yes
Laden Maiden	466	786	44-48781	yes	Lady Liberty	389	564	42-72871	yes
Laden Maiden				no	Lady Lightnin'	449	719	42-52760	no
Laden Raider	446		42-52549	yes	Lady Lightnin'	486	832	42-52760	no
Ladies Delight	454	736	42-78204	no	Lady Lightning	466	784	42-52597	yes
Lady	466	787	42-95255	no	Lady Lora	448	714	42-50799	no
Lady	11	98	42-73004	yes	Lady Luck				yes
Lady (The)	485	828	42-52725	no	Lady Luck			42-40778	no
Lady Barbara (The	446	706	42-99978	no	Lady Luck	389		41-23778	no
Lady Be Good	376	514	41-24301	yes	Lady Luck	7			no
Lady Beverly	90	319	41-23760	no	Lady Luck	VPB	1	Bu38892	no
Lady Corinne	456	747	44-40485	yes	Lady Luck	5	31	44-49845	yes
Lady Diana	392	579	42-50593	no	Lady Luck	90	321	41-11901	yes
Lady Diana II	392	579	42-51459	no	Lady Luck	22	33	44-50795	no
Lady Doris	RCM	36	42-95507	yes	Lady Luck	98	345	42-64391	no
Lady Dot	44	68	42-100112	no	Lady Luck	308	374	44-41430	yes
Lady Duzz	464			yes	Lady Luck	380	528	42-110116	yes
Lady Duzz	494			no	Lady Luck	380	528	44-41430	no
Lady Edith	461	765	41-29284	no	Lady Luck	43	63	42-41058	no
Lady Esther	464	776		yes	Lady Luck	44	66	41-23778	yes
Lady Eva	90	321	41-23762	yes	Lady Luck	446	704	41-29128	yes
Lady Eva II	90	320	41-23772	no	Lady Luck	448	715	41-28578	yes
Lady Eve	392	577	42-95164	yes	Lady Luck	450	723	42-51777	yes
Lady Fifinella	44	67	42-63763	no	Lady Luck	458	754	42-110070	yes
Lady from Bristol	448	714	42-52100	no	Lady Luck	458	755	42-110141	no
Lady from Hades				no	Lady Luck	484	826	42-52774	yes
Lady from Hades	11	26	44-41613	yes	Lady Luck II	7			no
Lady from Hades	30	392	44-41613	yes	Lady Luck II	VPB	108	Bu59446	yes
Lady from Hell	486	835	42-52573	yes	Lady Luck II	491	852	42-40722	no
Lady from Leyte	43	65	44-40807	yes	Lady Luck II	494	865	44-42131	yes
Lady Geraldine	44	68	44-10504	no	Lady Luck II		868	xx-xx780	no
Lady Godiva	448			no	Lady Luck III	VPB	116	Bu59459	yes
Lady Grace	SOP			yes	Lady Margaret	448	714	42-95134	no
Lady Grace	492	858	42-95011	yes	Lady Margaret (The)		868	42-40639	no
Lady Gwen	93	330	44-50553	no	Lady Marian	446	703	42-50592	yes
Lady Halitosis	448			no	Lady Marie	445	702	41-29117	no
Lady in the Dark	449		42-50665	no	Lady Marion	487	837	41-29466	no
Lady in the Dark		36	42-50665	no	Lady Mary		885	44-49336	no
Lady in the Dark	449	716	42-95286	yes	Lady Millie	90	319	41-23753	no
Lady in the Dark	454	739	42-50570	no	Lady of Leisure	Navy			yes
Lady Irene	389	564	42-40697	no	Lady of Loretto	454	739	42-52262	no
Lady Irene		885	42-40697	no	Lady of the Lake	93		41-24130	no
Lady Jane		36	42-51188	no	Lady Patricia (The)	456	745	42-51672	no
Lady Jane	458	753	42-95133	no	Lady Peace	466	784	42-95557	no

Name	Grp.	Sq.	Serial	Pic.	Name	Grp.	Sq.	Serial	Pic.
Lady Peach	466	784	42-95557	no	Lazy Lady	307	371	42-41092	yes
Lady Penny				no	Lazy Lady	461	764	42-51762	no
Lady Pete			42-109969	yes	Lazy Lady	487	838	42-52444	no
Lady Shamrock	445	701	42-7614	yes	Lazy Lou	RCM		42-7609	no
Lady Tabie	11		42-109979	yes	Lazy Lou	801	36	42-7609	no
Lady Too (The)	466	784	42-95511	no	Lazy Lou	446	704	42-95198	no
Lady Will (The)				yes	Lazy Lou	446	706	42-7609	yes
Lady X	RCAF			yes	Le Petite Fleur	451	727	42-51874	no
Lady X	India	45		yes	Leacherous Lou	491		41-29528	no
Lakanooki	307	371	42-40857	yes	Leacherous Lou	487	838	41-29528	no
Lakanooki	308	374	41-24188	yes	Lead Poison	445	703	42-7532	no
Lakanookie			42-50789	yes	Leading Lady	448			no
Lakanookie	451	725	42-7734	yes	Leading Lady	453			no
Lakanookie II	451	725	42-52614	no	Leading Lady	467		xx-xx201	no
Lakanookie II	484	824	42-52614	no	Leading Lady	93		44-40488	no
Lakanooky	464			yes	Leading Lady	93	330	44-50487	yes
Laki-Nuki	448	712	42-7733	no	Leading Lady	451	727	42-95509	yes
Lambsy Divey				no	Leading Lady	461	765	41-28685	yes
Lambsy Divey	491	853	44-40170	yes	Leading Lady	467	790	42-95094	no
Lamplighter (The)					Leading Lady	484	824	42-52647	no
(XC-109)	451	725	42-7721	no	Leading Lady (The)		406	41-28871	no
Lamplighter II (The)	451	725	42-52156	no	Leakin' Deacon	455	743	41-29271	yes
Lamsy Divey				no	Leakin' Deakom				yes
Land's End				no	Leaking Lucy			41-23736	yes
Lane Tech of Chicago				no	Leaky Tub	450	723	41-29226	no
Larrupin' Libby	448			no	Leave Me Be	490	851	42-94844	no
Larrupin' Libby (The)	451	724	44-49460	no	Lee Mee Bee	490	850		no
Larrupin' Linda	492	857	44-40118	yes	Lee Mee Bee II	490	850		no
Larry	453	735	41-29259	no	Lee Mee Bee III	490	850		no
Larry	455	742		no	Leevus Bee	490	851	42-50490	yes
Lascivious Lil				yes	Left Out				yes
Lassie Come Home	AZON		44-40283	no	Leila Bell	459	759	42-52317	yes
Lassie Come Home	392	578	42-51235	no	Lelia Belle	380	531	42-40527	yes
Lassie Come Home	446	707	42-51356	yes	Lemon	30	27	42-72993	yes
Lassie Come Home	456	746	42-52215	yes	Lemon (The)	Navy	VD1		yes
Lassie Come Home	456	746	42-64480	no	Lemon (The)	22	2	42-100333	no
Lassie Come Home	458	753	44-40283	yes	Lemon (The)	466	785	42-52524	yes
Lassie I'm Home	7	436		yes	Lemon (The)/Drip	90	321	42-41105	no
Last Card Louie	458	755	42-52441	yes	Lemon Drop	44	68	41-23699	yes
Last Frontier	392	579	41-29135	no	Len Dee Luck	490	848	42-94922	yes
Last Frontier	392	579	42-52605	no	Leo	493		42-52768	yes
Last Horizon	43			yes	Leo	34	391	41-29605	yes
Last Roundup (The)			xx-xx927	no	Leo	486	834	41-29605	yes
Late Again 4F	486	834		no	Leo	486	834	42-52768	yes
Late Date	392	577	42-100346	yes	Les Miserables	11	431	42-73026	yes
Late Date II (The)	392	577	42-109824	no	Les Miserables	494	866	44-40666	yes
Late Date II (The)	392	577	42-109826	no	Let 'er Rip	93	329	41-23717	no
Late Frate	455	740	42-99748	no	Let 'er Rip	93	330	41-24121	no
Latest Rumor (The)				no	Let 'er Rip	466	785	44-50548	yes
Latrine Rumor (The)	93	409	42-95199	no	Let's Go	376	513	41-24032	yes
Latrine Rumor (The)	389	564	42-99975	yes	Lethal Lady	389	567		no
Latrine Rumor (The)	491	854	44-40271	no	Lethal Linda	489	845	42-94776	yes
Laude End				no	Lethal Louise	459	759	41-28646	no
Laura Jo	492	858	44-40086	no	Lettie Jo	6	397	AL632	yes
Laura Sue	454	736	42-99802	no	Li'l Cookie			42-7461	no
Laurippin' Laura	458	755	42-50502	no	Li'l De Icer	98	415	41-11836	yes
Lazy Eight	485	828	42-52674	no	Li'l Edie	490	850		no

Name	Grp.	Sq.	Serial	Pic.	Name	Grp.	Sq.	Serial	Pic.
Li'l Max	446	707	42-100347	no	Lil' Butch II	451	727	42-50389	no
Li'l Pudge/Rum Dum		36	42-51230	no	Lil' Cookie			42-94842	no
Libby Raider	30	38	42-100396	yes	Lil' Cookie	489		42-7552	yes
Libby Raider	451	724	41-28642	no	Lil' Cookie	44	67	42-7552	yes
Libby Raider	453	734	41-28642	no	Lil' D-Icer	380	530	42-72795	yes
Libby Raider	464	779		no	Lil' D-Icer	380	530	42-72799	no
Liberal Lady	450	720	42-52148	no	Lil' Daisy Cutter	43	63	42-40666	yes
Liberandos Boomerang	376	514	41-29425	yes	Lil' De Icer	376	512	41-11836	yes
Liberator			42-52117	yes	Lil' De-Icer				yes
Liberator (The)	489			no	Lil' De-Icer				yes
Liberator Express				yes	Lil' Eight Ball	453	734	42-52180	no
Liberty Bell	22			no	Lil' Gramper	491	852	42-40722	no
Liberty Belle	448		42-94996	no	Lil' Gypsy	392	579	41-29127	yes
Liberty Belle	RCM		42-30039	no	Lil' Gypsy	446	704	41-29127	yes
Liberty Belle	90	321	41-23920	yes	'Lil Hoot	493		44-40140	yes
Liberty Belle	93	328	42-95095	no	'Lil Hoot	493		44-40440	no
Liberty Belle	380	529	44-50894	yes	Lil' Jo Toddy	5	31	42-110137	yes
Liberty Belle	392	576	42-50647	yes	Lil' Jo Toddy	449	717	42-99856	yes
Liberty Belle	392	578	42-7626	no	Lil' Joe	98	343	41-11886	yes
Liberty Belle	44	66	42-95095	no	Lil' Jughaid	98	415	42-40758	yes
Liberty Belle	44	67	42-99970	yes	Lil' Jughaid	98	415	42-63758	yes
Liberty Belle	445	703	42-7508	no	Lil' Max	446	705	42-100347	yes
Liberty Belle	466	784	42-51134	yes	Lil' Nilmerg	380	529	44-40861	yes
Liberty Belle	30	819	44-40708	yes	Lil' Pudge	482		44-42344	yes
Liberty Belle			xx-xx656	yes	Lil' Pudge	RCM	36	42-51230	no
Liberty Belle (The)	458	754	42-95199	no	Lil' Snooks	446	707	42-94936	yes
Liberty Belle II	22	33	44-41234	yes	Lil' Texas Filley	ZI		44-40848	yes
Liberty Lad	93	409	41-23742	yes	Lilas Marie	90	400	41-24269	yes
Liberty Lass	93	409	41-23732	yes	Lilas Marie The 2nd	90	400	44-42260	yes
Liberty Lass	44	67		yes	Lili Marlene	308		42-73442	no
Liberty Lib	458	752	41-29303	yes	Lili Marlene	308		42-73494	no
Liberty Limited	93	328	41-23874	yes	Lili Marlene	44	506	42-95309	no
Liberty Run				yes	Lili Marlene	44	66	42-7638	yes
Liberty Run	453	733	42-110078	yes	Lili Marlene II	308	374	42-100244	yes
Liberty's Belle	455	741	42-50425	no	Lilli Marlene	44	506		no
Libra	486	834	42-52508	yes	Lilli Marlene	44	68	42-95260	yes
Libra	486	834	xx-xx693	no	Lillian Ann	445	700	42-7558	no
Lid's ON - Lid's OFF	489			no	Lillian Ann II	445	700	42-7571	yes
Life	485	830	42-52728	yes	Lillie Belle	453	735	42-52191	no
Lil Audrey	389	565	42-100280	no	Lilly's Sister	448	715	44-50787	yes
Lil De-Icer				yes	Lily Ann	93	409		no
Lil De-Icer	11AF	404		no	Lily Marlene	458	752	42-95117	yes
Lil Mike	453	734	41-29257	no	Lily Marlene				yes
Lil Nemo	453	732	42-50471	no	Lily of the Desert	376	512	42-72816	yes
Lil Peach	467	788	41-29373	yes	Limpin' Ol Sadie	448			no
Lil Peach	467	791	41-29375	yes	Limpin' Ole Sadie	44	68	42-95021	yes
Lil Snooks	466			no	Lincoln Heights	455	742	42-52238	no
Lil' Abner	98	344	41-11779	yes	Linda Ann	459	758	44-49789	no
Lil' Abner	376	513	41-11779	yes	Linda Ann & Her Wee R			44-40492	no
Lil' Abner	44	67	42-63761	yes	Linda Kay	456	746		no
Lil' Audrey					Linda Lou	453	735	42-50764	no
Grows Up	11	431	42-73016	yes	Linda Mae	448	712	42-51075	no
Lil' Blon Dee	98	415	42-73424	yes	Lindie	93		42-95043	no
Lil' Blon Dee II	98	345	44-49260	no	Lingering Lil				yes
Lil' Butch	376		42-64363	no	Liquidator	494	866	44-42052	yes
Lil' Butch	308	425	41-24193	yes	Little Agnes	453	735	42-52178	no
Lil' Butch	449	718	42-64363	no	Little Angus	453			no

Name	Grp.	Sq.	Serial	Pic.	Name	Grp.	Sq.	Serial	Pic.
Little Audrey			41-29522	no	Little Iodine	489	847	41-28941	yes
Little Audrey	44			yes	Little Iron Pants	490	849	42-94781	yes
Little Audrey	448			no	Little Isadore	376	515	42-40203	no
Little Audrey	482			no	Little Jo	376			yes
Little Audrey	489		44-10615	yes	Little Jo	448	713	41-28958	yes
Little Audrey	389	565	42-100280	no	Little Jody	90			no
Little Audrey	445	701	42-50579	yes	Little Joe	458			no
Little Beaver	449			yes	Little Joe	98	345	41-11886	yes
Little Beaver	90	320	42-40984	yes	Little Joe	30	392	42-72984	yes
Little Beaver	43	403	42-40984	yes	Little Joe	98	415	41-24195	yes
Little Beaver	44	67	41-23807	yes	Little Joe	11	42	44-40678	yes
Little Beaver	450	721		no	Little Joe	392	576	42-7560	no
Little Beaver	491	855	44-40194	yes	Little Joe	392	577	42-51238	no
Little Behind	466			yes	Little Joe	453	732	42-52185	yes
Little Bill	445	702	42-7566	no	Little Joe	484	824	42-50934	yes
Little Bold				no	Little Joe	491	854	44-40084	yes
Little Brother				yes	Little Joe				yes
Little Bryan	453	733	41-28649	no	Little Joe (F-7)	6PR	20CM	42-64054	yes
Little Butch	22	2	42-109997	yes	Little Joe Buffalo				no
Little Butch	28	404	41-23884	yes	Little Jos	448			no
Little Butch	308	425	41-24193	yes	Little King	446	706	42-50790	yes
Little Butch	451	727	42-7465	no	Little Lackassaky	490	850	42-94812	no
Little Butch	451	727	42-7759	yes	Little Lackassaky	493	862	42-94812	no
Little Butch	451	727	42-7765	no	Little Lady	93	409	41-23754	yes
Little Butch	459	759		no	Little Lady	93	409	42-40754	yes
Little Chief Big Dog	98	345	42-40106	yes	Little Lady Joyce	450	723	42-52519	no
Little Chum	93	328	42-51280	no	Little Lambsy Divey	458	752	42-100407	yes
Little Chum	467	790	42-51180	no	Little Lass	7	436		no
Little Chum	467	790	42-51280	no	Little Lee	93	330	42-50505	no
Little Clamwinkle			44-8424	no	Little Lulu			44-40147	no
Little Corporal	389			yes	Little Lulu	25		44-40233	yes
Little Darling				no	Little Lulu	465		42-52479	no
Little Davey			44-40459	no	Little Lulu	493		44-40233	no
Little De-Icer	376		41-28806	yes	Little Lulu	380	529	42-109999	yes
Little De-Icer	451	725	41-28806	yes	Little Lulu	392	577	42-95223	no
Little Dumbo	11	26	41-23841	yes	Little Lulu	464	776	42-52479	yes
Little Dumbo	307	370	41-23841	yes	Little Lulu	466	787	41-29391	yes
Little Egypt	308	374	44-49569	yes	Little Lulu	492	856	42-110143	yes
Little Emma	485	829	42-78136	no	Little Mac	484	825	42-50642	yes
Little Eva	466			no	Little Max	446	707	42-100347	yes
Little Eva	HALP		41-11609	no	Little Mick	307			yes
Little Eva	490	849	41-28869	no	Little Mike	93	409	44-50781	yes
Little Eve	380	528	42-40493	no	Little Milo	445	701	42-7586	no
Little Fellow				no	Little Miss Muff-It	464		42-78131	yes
Little Flower	308	375	41-24288	yes	Little Mitch	98	343	41-28810	yes
Little Flower		406		no	Little Moe the				
Little Gel	448			no	Peacemaker	456	746	42-64486	yes
Little General (The)	30	392	42-73030	yes	Little Nancy	453	732	42-52472	yes
Little Girl	28	404	41-23886	yes	Little Orphan Annie	445			no
Little Gizmo	464	776	42-78133	yes	Little Orphan Annie II	445	703	42-7571	no
Little Gizmo II	464	776	42-78376	no	Little Pete	467			no
Little Gramper (The)	389	566	42-40722	yes	Little Queen II	SAAF			yes
Little Gramper (The)	491		42-40722	yes	Little Queen Mary	5	394	44-40474	yes
Little Gramper, Jr.	389	566	44-40085	yes	Little Rebel	466	786	41-29593	no
Little Hiawatha	11	431	41-24187	yes	Little Rebel	490	851		no
Little Iodine	448		41-28941	yes	Little Red	494	866	44-40693	yes
Little Iodine	448	714	44-10516	no	Little Richard	376	513	42-40660	yes

Name	Grp.	Sq.	Serial	Pic.	Name	Grp.	Sq.	Serial	Pic.
Little Rocket	464	778	42-50962	yes	Lost Angel	22	408	42-109992	yes
Little Rollo	446	707	42-95289	yes	Lotta Laffs	454	738	44-41341	yes
Little Shepherd	458		41-29359	no	Lotta Stern	490	850	42-94876	no
Little Sheppard	448	712	41-28711	yes	Lotta Stern	490	850	xx-xx851	no
Little Stinker	450	723	42-52090	no	Lotta Tayle	VPB	121		yes
Little Stinker (The)	308	375	42-40413	yes	Louie	458			no
Little Warrior	490	850	42-94812	yes	Louise Mary	307	372	44-41354	yes
Little Warrior	493	862	42-94812	yes	Louisiana Belle	44	66	42-50806	yes
Little Willie	464	776	42-51178	yes	Louisiana Belle	44	68	42-50806	no
Live Wire	90	320	44-41235	yes	Louisiana Lady	450	723	42-78175	no
Lively Lady	464	777	44-41070	no	Louisiana Lil	VPB	121	Bu59475	yes
Lizzy	445	701	42-7555	no	Louisiana Lullaby	90	319	42-63986	yes
Lizzy Belle	493			no	Lovable Lorena				yes
Lizzy Belle	490	848	42-94884	yes	Love 'em All	490	851	41-28946	no
Lo-An-Roy	451	727	44-50443	yes	Lovell's Air Force				no
Lobo the Wolf	90	320	42-40830	no	Lovely Annette	43	64	44-40808	no
Local Yokel	448			no	Lovely Heads	449	718		no
Loco Moco	44	66	44-50597	no	Lovely Lady	466	786	42-52569	no
Lone Ranger	44	68	44-40098	yes	Lovely Lady	466	786	xx-xx567	no
Lone Star Avenger	90	321	42-72934	yes	Lovely Lady's Avenger	466	786	44-40093	yes
Lonely Heart	467	791	42-95224	yes	Lovely Louise				yes
Lonely Lair	98	415	44-41185	no	Lovely Louise	90	319	44-41332	yes
Lonesome Lady	494	866	44-40680	yes	Lover's Lane	453	735	42-64473	no
Lonesome Lois	445	701	42-95020	yes	Lovey's Dovies	465	781	42-51628	yes
Lonesome Lou	448	714	42-50677	no	Lucifer	RAF	335		yes
Lonesome Polecat				no	Lucille	34		42-52759	no
Lonesome Polecat	449			no	Luck and Stuff	446	706	41-28664	no
Lonesome Polecat	93	330	42-63978	yes	Luck and Stuff	446	706	42-100360	yes
Lonesome Polecat	308	425	42-40850	yes	Luck O' the Irish	448			yes
Lonesome Polecat	376	515	42-64467	no	Luck's Stuff				no
Lonesome Polecat	389	564	42-95205	yes	Lucky	445			no
Lonesome Polecat	392	577	42-52097	no	Lucky	380	529	42-40514	yes
Lonesome Polecat	451	726	42-52114	no	Lucky (Lucky				
Lonesome Polecat	453	734	41-29249	yes	Gordon)	93	409	41-24215	yes
Lonesome Polecat	454	738	42-64467	no	Lucky _____				yes
Lonesome Polecat	456	747	42-78098	yes	Lucky 1	492	856	44-40134	yes
Lonesome Polecat (The)	489	846	42-94857	yes	Lucky 13	459	757	42-52413	no
Lonesome Polecat, Jr.				yes	Lucky 15	448			no
Lonesome?	449	719	42-7732	yes	Lucky 7 (The)				yes
Lonesome? II	449	719	42-51652	yes	Lucky Babe	455	743	41-28658	no
Long Distance			xx-x0640	yes	Lucky Buck	491	852	42-110158	yes
Long Island Belle		2REC	42-64327	no	Lucky Dog	11		44-40679	yes
Long John Silver	450	721	41-28756	no	Lucky Dog	30	38	44-40679	yes
Long John Silver	450	723	42-78196	no	Lucky Don	380	529	42-73485	yes
Long John Silver	465	781	41-28915	no	Lucky Ducky	451	726	42-78208	no
Loni (League of					Lucky Gordon	445		41-24215	yes
Nations, Inc.)	34	18	41-28865	no	Lucky Gordon	93	409	41-24215	yes
Lonnie	11	431	42-73007	yes	Lucky Lady	93	330	41-23962	no
Look Who's Here				no	Lucky Lady	7	492		no
Lookin' Good	491	852	42-50918	no	Lucky Lady	459	757	42-51344	no
Loose Goose	376	512	42-73089	yes	Lucky Lady	461	764	42-50970	no
Lorelei	458	755	41-29300	yes	Lucky Lady Betty	389	565	44-51153	no
Loretta	30	27	44-40809	no	Lucky Lady Betty II	389	565	44-51153	yes
Loretta Ann (The)	490	850	41-29602	no	Lucky Lass	93	329	41-24245	yes
Lorraine	98			no	Lucky Lass	492	857	44-40157	yes
Lorraine	376	513	41-11591	yes	Lucky Lass II			42-95023	no
Los Lobos	449	719	42-7761	yes	Lucky Leone	389		42-110077	no

43

Name	Grp.	Sq.	Serial	Pic.	Name	Grp.	Sq.	Serial	Pic.
Lucky leven,					Mac's Mighty Midgets	487		42-52625	no
Always a Winner	467	791	44-48820	yes	Mac's Sack	392	576	42-7471	yes
Lucky Lois	455	743	42-78470	yes	Mac's Sack II	392	579	42-7561	no
Lucky Lucille	43	65	42-41224	yes	Mac's Sack III	392	579	42-7599	yes
Lucky Lucille	43	65		no	Macahyba Maiden	VP	107		yes
Lucky Lucy	43	65		no	Mad Frenchman (The)	VPB	121	Bu59566	yes
Lucky Penny			42-40169	no	Mad Madeleine	491			no
Lucky Penny	446			no	Mad Mis Fit				no
Lucky Penny	453	734	42-52169	yes	Mad Monk (The)	466	786	41-29402	yes
Lucky Penny	453	734	42-7734	no	Mad Russian	43	65	44-41846	yes
Lucky Penny II	453	734	42-52169	yes	Madam Queen	380	529	42-109999	yes
Lucky Puss	VPB	111	Bu38896	yes	Madam Shoo-Shoo	34		42-94762	no
Lucky Seven (The)	461	764	41-29362	yes	Madame (The)	466	787	42-52610	no
Lucky Strike				yes	Madame II (The)	466	787	41-29392	yes
Lucky Strike			44-40146	no	Madame Libby,				
Lucky Strike	44	506	41-29172	no	the Sea Ducer	43		42-40838	yes
Lucky Strike	380	530	44-41876	yes	Madame Libby,				
Lucky Strike	44	68	42-110095	no	the Sea Ducer	5	838	42-40838	yes
Lucky Strike	458	755	41-28709	yes	Madame Libby,				
Lucky Strike	464	777	42-52487	yes	the Sea Ducer	307		42-40838	yes
Lucky Strike	492	856	42-110148	yes	Madame Pele	11		42-109851	yes
Lucky Ten	451	727	42-51409	no	Madame Pele	30	819	42-109851	yes
Lucky Thirteen	448			no	Madame				
Lucky Thirty				no	Shoo Shoo	450	722	42-99805	yes
Lucky Tiger	389	565	42-63958	no	Madcap Margie	465	781	41-28756	no
Lucky-Leven	Navy			yes	Mademoiselle Zig-Zig	467	790	44-40070	yes
Lucy Quipment				no	Madson's Madhouse				no
Lucy Quipment	44	68		no	Mag Drop	2641	859	42-95731	no
Lucy Quipment	490	851	41-29545	yes	Mag Drop	801	859	42-95131	no
Lucy's Lucky	98	345	42-40320	yes	Mag the Hag	43	64	42-41084	yes
Lumberin' Liz	487		42-52578	no	Maggie	454			no
Lurchin' Urchin	449	717	41-29233	no	Maggie	44	67	41-23832	no
Lurchin' Urchin II	449	717	42-52092	no	Maggie - The War				
Lus Shus Lay Dee				yes	Horse				no
Luscious Duchess (The)	98	345	42-52009	no	Maggie's Drawers	98	344	42-41008	yes
Luscious Lace	7	9		no	Maggie-Nut (The)				yes
Luscious Lady	487			no	Magic Carpet				no
Lusty Lib	489			no	Magic Carpet	RAF	231	41-11741	yes
Luvablas'	11	431	44-42264	yes	Magic Carpet (The)	389	567	42-95122	yes
Luvablass	380	529	44-41263	yes	Mah Aikin Back	491	853	44-40226	yes
Lynda Lee	489		41-28976	no	Mah Ideal	392	578	42-7588	no
Lyndy	44		42-7518	no	Maid in the U.S.A.	454		42-64372	no
Lyndy	392	577	42-110058	yes	Maid in U.S.A.			44-40776	yes
Lyndy	392	578	42-7518	no	Maid in USA	90	321	44-40341	yes
Lyndy II	445		42-110058	yes	Maid of Fury	34	7	42-94849	no
Lyndy II	392	577	42-110058	yes	Maid of Fury	453	733	41-28613	no
Lynn Bari	44	506	42-40068	no	Maid of Fury II	453	732	42-50337	no
Lynn Bari II	44	506	42-40172	no	Maid of Honor	30	392	44-41476	no
M for Mike				no	Maid of Orleans	448	715	42-7739	no
Ma's Folly	93			no	Maid of Tin	448	715	42-7709	no
Ma's Little Angel	491			no	Maiden America	491			no
Ma's Worry	93	328	41-29437	no	Maiden America	450	723	42-78356	yes
Mabel			42-64182	yes	Maiden America				yes
Mabel	98	345	41-28928	no	Maiden Montana	5		44-41549	yes
Mabel	RCAF		42-64182	yes	Maiden the USA	90		xx-xx341	no
Mabel's Labels	43	64	44-50853	yes	Maiden USA	464	776	42-78392	yes
Mac's Flop House	451	724	42-64465	no	Mailbox	461	764	44-41039	no

Name	Grp.	Sq.	Serial	Pic.	Name	Grp.	Sq.	Serial	Pic.
Mairsy Doats	392	579	42-94891	no	Marez-EE-Doates	458			yes
Mairzy Doats	392	579	42-109789	yes	Margaret Ann	44	68	41-24009	yes
Mairzy Doats	445	703	42-109789	yes	Margaret Ann II	44	67	42-40071	yes
Mairzy Doats	451	724	42-78188	yes	Margaret L.	448			no
Mairzy Doats	490	848	42-94891	yes	Marge	450	722	42-52122	no
Major Hoople	446	707	42-100288	no	Margie	43		41-24018	yes
Major-ette	307			yes	Margie	98		42-41007	yes
Makin' Believe				no	Margie	90	320		no
Makin' Believe	466			yes	Margie	RCM	36	42-95221	no
Mal Function				no	Margie Ann				no
Male				no	Margie Ann II	44	67	42-40071	yes
Male Box	451	725	44-49868	yes	Margie Ann III				no
Male Call				yes	Margie the Magnificent	465	783	44-48990	no
Male Call				yes	Margie/Ready N' Able	801	36	42-95221	no
Male Call	445			no	Marguerite	44	506	41-23936	no
Male Call	34	4	42-94869	no	Marie	43	64	42-40922	yes
Male Call	380	531	42-72799	yes	Marie	458	753	42-110163	no
Male Call	453	734	42-52154	yes	Marilyn	456	745		no
Male Call				yes	Marion	93	409	42-73503	no
Malfunction	392	577	42-7489	no	Marion	392	577	42-94898	no
Malfunction Junction	SOP		42-94825	no	Marion	489	845	42-94898	no
MalfunctionJunction	489	847	42-94825	no	Marizy Doats				no
Malfunction Sired By					Marjorie H.	461	765	42-51610	no
Ford	461	767	41-28670	yes	Mark's Farts	VB	104	44-40313	yes
Malfunction					Marlene				yes
Sired by Ford	484	826	42-52668	yes	Martha	389			no
Malicious	376	512	41-11603	yes	Martha R.	458			no
Malignant Lady	489			no	Martha R.	389	565	42-110068	yes
Mallet Head	43	63	42-41050	no	Mary				yes
Mama Foo Foo	90	320	44-42094	yes	Mary - Big Wheels				yes
Mama Foo Foo	90	320	44-42094	no	Mary Dinah	460	762	42-51602	no
Mama Foo Foo	308	374	44-42094	yes	Mary Ellen	376	515	42-50960	no
Mama's Angels	446			yes	Mary Harriet	453		42-110049	no
Mama's Kids					Mary Harriett	44	68	42-110049	no
Bombs Away				no	Mary Harriett	491	854	42-110149	no
Mama's Lil' Angel	466	785	44-10558	yes	Mary Jane	450	723	41-29338	no
Mama's Lil' Angel	491	852	44-10558	yes	Mary L.	392	576	42-95464	no
Mamma's Kids				yes	Mary Lee	458			no
Mammy Yokum				yes	Mary Lou	5			no
Mammy Yokum	307	424	42-40221	yes	Mary Lou	6PR	20CM	44-42239	yes
Mammy Yokum	376	513	42-72782	yes	Mary Louise	307	372	44-41345	yes
Mammy Yokum	466	784	42-52596	no	Mary Louise	392	576	42-95031	no
Mammy Yokum II	307			yes	Mary M.	380	530	44-40370	yes
Man From Down					Mary Michele	448			no
Under	458			no	Mary O	464	776	42-51423	no
Man-O-War				no	Mary, the Flying				
Man-O-War	307	371	41-23966	yes	Redhead	389	565	42-100319	no
Man-O-War	456	746	41-28831	yes	Mascot	307	371	42-73450	yes
Mandy J.	490			no	Mask-A-Raider	5		44-40547	yes
Mandy J. II	490	850		no	Massa's Dragon	308			no
Mandy J. III	490	850		no	Massachusetts	454			no
Manhattan Maiden	308	374	44-42142	yes	Massachusetts Girl	492		42-50614	no
Manila Calling	43	65		yes	Massachusetts Girl	467	788	42-50614	no
Manistee	489	847	41-28870	yes	Massilon Tiger	467	789	44-10488	yes
Marcia	459	758	42-52322	yes	Matchless Jeep	489	846	42-94817	yes
Marcia Ann	44	67	41-23818	no	Maternity Ward				yes
Marco Polo	RAF	231	AL 578	yes	Maternity Ward	376		42-40663	yes

Name	Grp.	Sq.	Serial	Pic.	Name	Grp.	Sq.	Serial	Pic.
Maternity Ward	98	345	42-40663	yes	Miakinback	490			no
Maui Maid	449	719	41-28623	yes	Miasis Dragon	449	717	42-52172	yes
Maulin' Mallard	93	330	42-109867	yes	Michigan	43	64	44-40429	yes
Maw Stricknine	449	716	42-52104	yes	Mickey	465		42-52526	no
Max Sack				no	Mickey	464	779	42-52526	yes
Maxie's Nightmare	491	854	44-40459	yes	Mickey Finn	93	329	42-7629	no
Maxie's Nightmare	493		44-40459	yes	Mickey Finn	454	738	42-64485	yes
Maximum Effort	484		44-50450	no	Mickey Mouse	493		42-94851	no
Maximum Effort	446	706	42-95188	yes	Mickey Mouse	NLS		42-94851	no
Maxwell House	308	373	41-24164	yes	Mickey Mouse	801	406	42-94851	no
Maxwell House	460	761	41-28702	yes	Mickey Mouse	34	7	42-94851	no
Maxwell House	490	849	42-94885	no	Mickey Mouse	459	756		yes
Maxwell House II	308	373	42-100240	no	Midge	446	704	42-7531	yes
Maxwell House II	308	373	42-73425	no	Midnight Mistress	487		42-52461	no
Maxwell House III	308	373	42-100280	yes	Midnight Mistress		406		no
May Bell	460		44-48769	yes	Midnight Mistress	451	727	41-28897	no
Mayflower (The)	43	64	42-40853	yes	Midnight Mistress	492	857	42-50483	yes
Mazie	459	757	42-51601	yes	Midnight Mistress II	801	36	42-50750	no
Mazie	459	758	42-51601	yes	Midnite Mistress	487		42-94756	no
McNamara's Band	458	752	42-52353	no	Might of the Eighth	389	566	42-99982	no
McSwine's Flying Comet				yes	Mighty Eightball (The)	308	425	41-24224	yes
Me Worry?	34	391	42-94796	no	Mighty Mouse	446	704	44-50775	yes
Me Worry?	484	824	41-28935	no	Mighty Mouse	449	719	41-28594	no
Me Worry? II	34	7	42-94942	no	Mighty Seven /				
Mean Kid	493		44-40468	no	Tojo's Doom Gal				yes
Mean Kid	34	18	44-40468	yes	Mighty Warrior	446			no
Mean Widdle Kid	487	838	42-52763	no	Mike, Spirit of LSU	486	832	42-52731	no
Meat Around					Mike, Spirit of LSU	486	832	42-52764	no
the Corner	459	754	41-28738	yes	Milady	380	531	42-73134	yes
Meddlesome Maggie				yes	Militant Mistress	492	858	44-40115	no
Melodee Blondee	98	343	42-72424	no	Military Secret	93			no
Melodie	98	345	42-73429	yes	Military Secret	464	778	42-52446	yes
Melody Lane	453			no	Milk Run	446			no
Melon Patch Special	98	415	42-41027	no	Milk Run	464			no
Memphis to St. Joe	98	344	41-23801	yes	Milk Run	466			no
Men from Mars				no	Milk Run Mamie				no
Menace (The)	448	712	41-29232	no	Milk Wagon Express				yes
Menacing Messalina	455	742	42-64482	no	Milkrun Betty	491			yes
Merchant	493	862	42-94789	yes	Miller High Life				yes
Merchant (of Menace)	492			yes	Miller's Reluctant Raiders	VPB	109		no
Merchant of Menace	491	855	44-40089	no	Millie's Daughter	11	98	42-109876	yes
Merchant of Venice	466	785	41-28664	yes	Million $ Baby				yes
Merle	459	759	42-51627	no	Million $ Baby	43	403	44-40335	yes
Merle Lee	446	706	42-7584	yes	Million $ Baby	392	576	42-7487	yes
Merle Lee II	446	706	42-99983	no	Million $ Baby II	43	403	44-50768	yes
Merry Barbara	451	726	42-78484	no	Million Dollar Baby			42-97268	no
Merry Boozer	11	26	42-109945	yes	Minerva	389		41-23689	yes
Merry Max (The)	446		42-7713	no	Minerva	93	329	41-23689	yes
Merry Max (The)	448	715	42-7713	yes	Minerva	392	579	41-23689	yes
Messie Bessie	467	790	42-50354	no	Minerva	44	66	41-23689	yes
Methusela	34	4	41-29555	no	Minnehaha	494	864	44-41578	yes
Mexicali Rose	460	760	44-40514	no	Minnesota Marge	376	512	42-78242	yes
Mi A'kin Back	28	404		no	Minnesota Mauler	451	724	42-50906	yes
Mi Akin Ass	446			no	Minnie	446	706	41-28628	yes
Mi Akin Ass	44	67	42-94846	yes	Minnie	458	755	41-28628	yes
Mi Akin Ass	450	722	44-40927	no	Minnie Ha-Cha	455	740	42-64497	no
Mi-Akin-Ass	446	704	42-7613	no	Minniehaha	494	864	44-41578	yes

Name	Grp.	Sq.	Serial	Pic.
Mirage (The)	43			no
Mis Bea Havin'	487		42-52761	no
Mis-Chief	34		42-94775	no
Mis-Chief	34	4	42-94880	yes
Mis-Chief	449	717	42-64388	yes
Misanthrope	448	715	42-94953	no
Misanthrope	490	851	42-94953	no
Misbehavin'				yes
Mischief	93		42-94880	no
Mischief Maker	490	850		no
Misery Agent	34	4	41-28838	no
Misfit	489			yes
Mismyshaktime	464	779	41-29361	no
Mispah	458	754	42-100366	no
Mispah	489	845	42-94788	no
Miss "U"	455		42-52278	no
Miss Alda Flak	491			no
Miss America			44-10554	yes
Miss America	389	566	42-50558	yes
Miss America	392	577	42-7503	no
Miss America	451	727	42-52084	yes
Miss America 1944	454	739	42-52312	yes
Miss Ann		55W	44-49555	yes
Miss Annabelle Lee	6	397	xx-xx957	yes
Miss Annie	459	758		no
Miss B-Haven	RCM	36	42-50844	yes
Miss B-Haven		801	42-50844	yes
Miss Bad Penny	449	719		no
Miss Barbara	389		42-109903	no
Miss Bea Haven	98	415	42-52058	no
Miss Bea Haven	449	717	42-64394	no
Miss Bee Haven	11	98	42-73082	yes
Miss Behave	456	746	42-52232	no
Miss Behavin'	448			no
Miss Behavin'	VPB	118	Bu59392	yes
Miss Behavin'	6	397		yes
Miss Behavin'	449	717	42-52086	no
Miss Behavin'	459	757	42-52007	yes
Miss Beryl	308	374	44-40832	yes
Miss Bubbles	43		42-40836	no
Miss Bubbles		868	42-40836	no
Miss Carriage	448			no
Miss Carriage	458			no
Miss Carriage	308	374	42-40624	yes
Miss Carriage	90	400	41-24207	yes
Miss Carriage	459	756	42-78427	yes
Miss Carriage	43			no
Miss Charlotte	2641	885		yes
Miss Conduct	308	375	44-41118	no
Miss Conduct	456	746	42-51548	yes
Miss D Meaner	43	64	42-41224	no
Miss D. Meaner	90		42-41227	no
Miss De Flak	449	717	42-78125	yes
Miss Dede Belle				yes
Miss Deed	90	321	42-41070	yes
Miss Delores	44	67	41-24229	no
Miss Delores	44	67	41-24278	no
Miss Diane	44	67	41-23784	no
Miss Dorothy				yes
Miss Dorothy	454	739	42-78169	yes
Miss Edna	454	738	42-51542	no
Miss Elise	380	531	44-42381	no
Miss Emmy Lou	44			no
Miss Emmy Lou II	44	67	42-72878	no
Miss Fire	484	826	42-52675	yes
Miss Fire!!	451	724	42-51984	no
Miss Fit	30	392	44-40557	yes
Miss Fit	455	742	42-78292	no
Miss Fitz	485	829	41-29503	no
Miss Fortune	450	720	42-7728	no
Miss Fortune	460	760	41-29291	yes
Miss Fortune	467	790	42-52559	yes
Miss Francia	491	854	42-51267	no
MIss Fury	450	721	42-7746	no
Miss Gay				no
Miss Ginnie	454	736	42-78244	no
Miss Giving				yes
Miss Giving	380	528	42-40489	yes
Miss Gus	489			yes
Miss Hap (The)	380	529	42-100221	yes
Miss Happ	448	713	41-29523	no
Miss Happ	487	836	41-29523	no
Miss Hilda	7	9	44-40859	yes
Miss Hotcha	490	849	42-94862	no
Miss I Hope	454	736	42-78213	no
Miss I Hope	455	740	42-51624	no
Miss Ileen	5	23	44-42418	yes
Miss Irene	492	859	44-40211	no
Miss Irish			42-97998	no
Miss Jolly Roger	90	321	44-41190	yes
Miss Jones	307	371	41-24016	yes
Miss Judy	449	718	42-51639	no
Miss Judy	467	788	42-50641	no
Miss Judy	467	789	42-52507	no
Miss Julie	98	344	41-23763	yes
Miss Kay	461	764	42-78103	yes
Miss Kiwanis	90	319	44-40314	yes
Miss Lace	308		44-42133	yes
Miss Lace	389			yes
Miss Lace	461	764	44-49511	yes
Miss Laid	11			yes
Miss Laid	456	746	42-51678	yes
Miss Led				yes
Miss Lee	449	716	42-7737	no
Miss Liberty				yes
Miss Liberty	389	564	42-72871	yes
Miss Liberty	43	63	42-40479	yes
Miss Lincoln Heights	455	742	42-52238	no
Miss Maggie	454	738	42-52207	no
Miss Mandy				yes
Miss Manookie				yes
Miss Mar-Jan	30	819		no
Miss Marcia	459	758	42-52322	yes
Miss Marcia Ann	44	67	41-23818	no

Name	Grp.	Sq.	Serial	Pic.	Name	Grp.	Sq.	Serial	Pic.
Miss Marie	454	738	42-50416	no	Miss Zeke	456			no
Miss Marion	44	66	44-10503	no	Miss-B-Haven	448			yes
Miss Marjorie	455	743	44-41055	no	Miss-B-Haven	RCM		42-94811	no
Miss Mary	380	528	42-40492	no	Miss-B-Haven	482	36	42-50844	no
Miss Maryland II	307		42-73145	yes	Miss-B-Haven	801	36	42-94811	no
Miss Maryland II	5	72	42-73145	no	Miss-B-Haven	467	788	42-94811	no
Miss McCook	43	403	42-41070	yes	Miss-B-Havin'				
Miss McKrachin				yes	Minnie	464	776	42-52540	yes
Miss Me	490	848	42-94847	no	Miss-I-Hope	449	718	42-78624	yes
Miss Milovin'	VPB	116	Bu59617	yes	Miss-Ma-Nookie				no
Miss Minerva II	456		41-29294	no	Miss-N-Moan	449	717		yes
Miss Minerva II	376	512	41-29294	no	Miss-U	454	738	42-64493	no
Miss Minnesota	30	38		yes	Misschief	34	4	42-94880	yes
Miss Minnie	392	578	42-95041	no	Misschief Maker	93		42-94880	no
Miss Minnie II	392	578	42-78477	yes	Missile Packin'				
Miss Minookie	490	851	42-94798	no	Mama	VPB	121		yes
Miss Minooky				no	Mission Belle	90	400	42-40389	yes
Miss Minooky	30	38	42-72972	no	Mission Belle	465	780	42-51421	no
Miss Minooky	466	786	42-50438	yes	Mission Belle	487	839	41-29514	no
Miss Minuki	454	736	42-52027	no	Mission Complete				yes
Miss Myloven	485	830	42-50921	no	Mission Complete	308			yes
Miss N' Moan	449	717	42-64394	yes	Mission Maid				yes
Miss N-U	98	344	42-52258	yes	Missouri Belle	44	66	41-28690	no
Miss Nadine	11	42	42-109934	yes	Missouri Mauler	389	567	42-63980	yes
Miss O. Lanious	376	514	41-24220	yes	Missouri Miss	380	530	44-41811	yes
Miss Oklahoma	376	514	42-72849	yes	Missouri Mule	490	848	42-51281	no
Miss Ourlovin'	456	746	42-99853	yes	Missouri Mule (The)	494	864	44-40717	yes
Miss Pam	489			no	Missouri Sue	93	409	41-24122	no
Miss Pandemonium	Navy			yes	Missouri Sue	44	66	41-28690	no
Miss Pat	458	754	42-95106	no	Mist'er Chance	466	785	41-28691	yes
Miss Please	98	344	42-51994	yes	Mistah Chick	392		42-100146	no
Miss Polly	454	738	41-29246	no	Mistah Chick	389	567	42-100146	yes
Miss Possum				yes	Mister Five by Five	380	531	42-40505	yes
Miss Possum / My Texas				yes	Mister Period	461	764	41-28726	yes
Miss Red Dauber	11	42	44-41381	yes	Mister Period!	98	344	42-73136	no
Miss Red Dauber	11	42	42-40961	yes	Mister. (period)				yes
Miss Sea Ducer	VPB	121	Bu59582	yes	Mites Pet				no
Miss Sherry	11	42	44-40710	yes	Mitsu Butcher	90	320	42-40326	no
Miss Snow Job	484	827	42-94751	no	Mitsu Butcher	90	320	42-72810	yes
Miss Stardust			41-29522	no	Mitzi-Bishi	Navy	VB106		yes
Miss Stardust	93			no	Mixed Nuts	460			no
Miss Stardust		406	42-37522	no	Miz-Pah	34		42-94845	no
Miss Take	93	329	42-50372	yes	Miz-Pah	801		42-94845	no
Miss Take XIII	93	329	44-49298	no	Miz-Pah	SOP		42-94845	no
Miss Tech Supply	11	42	44-40377	yes	Miz-pah	485	830	42-52713	no
Miss Temptation				yes	Mizpah				yes
Miss Tennessee	7	9		yes	Mizpah	458	754	42-100366	yes
Miss Tit	485	829	42-78141	no	Mizpah	489	845	42-94778	no
Miss Traveler	11	98	44-40530	yes	Mizry Merchant	490	850	41-29561	no
Miss Traveller	43		44-40530	no	Mizry Merchant	493	863	41-29561	no
Miss Used	AZON		44-40277	no	Moby Dick	90	320	41-24047	yes
Miss Used	458	753	44-40277	yes	Moby Dick	455	741	41-29266	no
Miss Vicky	464	778		yes	Moby Dick	465	783	42-52589	no
Miss Virginia	44	68	42-40094	no	Moby Dick	490	851	42-94789	no
Miss You	Navy			yes	Model T	392	578	42-52517	no
Miss Yourlovin'	376			yes	Modest Maid	RCM	36	42-51308	yes
Miss Yourlovin'	456	746	42-99853	yes	Modest Maiden	22	19	44-41537	yes

Name	Grp.	Sq.	Serial	Pic.	Name	Grp.	Sq.	Serial	Pic.
Modest Maiden	308	375	42-40865	no	Multa Bona	455	742	42-51332	yes
Modest Maiden	43	403	42-109994	yes	Multi Bono	450	722	42-7714	no
Modest Maiden	491	853	42-95264	yes	Munda Belle	5		42-73144	no
Modest Miss	VPB	111		yes	Munda Belle	307	370	42-40144	yes
Modest Miss	VPB	116	Bu38733	yes	Murphy's Mighty Mob	466	787	42-52609	no
Modest O'Miss				yes	Murphy's Mighty Mob	487	836	42-52609	no
Modest O'Miss	Navy			yes	Murphy's Mother-in-Law	ATC		44-49017	yes
Moe's Meteor	484	825	44-50557	yes	Murphy's Motley Mob	466	787	42-52609	no
Mohawk	308	373	42-40786	no	Muscle Bound				no
Mohawk Chief	454	736	42-78451	no	Muscle Bound II				no
Mohawk Chief	454	738	42-51415	no	Mutzie B			42-98014	no
Mojalajab	492	859	44-40132	no	Mutzie B			42-98019	no
Momentary Dysentary	307		42-40254	yes	My A'kin' Back	28	404		no
Mon Cheri	Navy			yes	My Achin' Back	448			yes
Mona	458	754		yes	My Achin' Back	449	718	42-52434	yes
Mona the Lame Duck	HALP		41-11615	no	My Achin' Rod	11			no
Mongrel	98	415	41-11932	yes	My Aching Back	376	513	42-52181	yes
Monotonous Maggie	448		42-95151	yes	My Aiken Back	492		44-40226	no
Monotonous Maggie	392	577	42-95151	yes	My Akin' Ass	450	722	44-40927	no
Monsoon Maiden	308	425	42-100276	yes	My Arkansas Sweetheart	460			yes
Monster			44-40474	no	My Assam Dragon	6PR	24CM	42-64055	no
Monster	467	788	44-40166	no	My Assam Dragon	44	66	42-52332	no
Monster (The)	467		42-50720	yes	My Assam Wagon	6PR	24CM	42-64170	no
Monster (The)	464	778	41-29394	yes	My Babs	453	733	42-95276	yes
Monty	486	835	41-29461	yes	My Baby	487		42-52771	no
Monty's Return	486	835	41-29461	yes	My Baby	448	713	42-95305	no
Moo Juice	454	737	42-52209	no	My Beloved Norma				no
Moonbeam McSwine	454	736	42-50315	no	My Bill				yes
Moonbeam McSwine	455	743	44-49625	yes	My Boy Jerry				yes
Moonlight Maid	11		44-42331	yes	My Briney Marlin	485	831	42-78134	no
Moonlight Maid	380	529	44-42331	yes	My Brother and I	485	828	42-52703	no
Moonlight Marge	493		44-40325	no	My Buddy				no
Moonlight Marge	466	787	44-40325	no	My Buddy	446	714	42-95083	yes
Moonshine Express	489			no	My Bunnie	458	752	41-29567	yes
Moonshine Express	492		42-95215	no	My Bunnie II	93		42-51270	yes
Moonshine Express	466	784	44-48807	yes	My Bunnie II	458	752	42-51270	yes
Moose (The)	491	853	44-40205	yes	My Devotion	11	431	42-100361	yes
Morbid Moe, the Moron	380	530	42-41071	yes	My Devotion	380	528	44-42248	yes
Moron (The)	459			no	My Devotion	446	704	42-7587	no
Mors Ab Alto	7	493		yes	My Devotion	446	704	44-50734	yes
Mother Goose	93			yes	My Diversion	392	578	42-7480	yes
Mother of Ten	448	713	44-10556	yes	My Dying Ass			44-40088	no
Mother's Boy	489			no	My Everlovin' Gal	44	506	41-28829	yes
Mountin Time	487		42-52619	yes	My Everloving Gal	44	67		no
Mouse (The)				no	My Gal	451	725	42-78227	no
Mr. 5 x 5	44	506	41-24234	yes	My Gal Eileen	487		42-52767	no
Mr. Five x Five	380	531	42-40505	no	My Gal Sal	44	506	42-50626	yes
Mr. Invader	491	852	42-110038	yes	My Heart Belongs to Daddy			44-41696	yes
Mr. Kip	VPB	121	Bu38733	yes	My Heart Belongs To Daddy	307		44-42698	yes
Mr. Period	98	415	42-73136	no	My Homely Chum	487	837	41-29469	no
Mrs. Lucky				yes	My Ideal	5	31	44-41868	yes
Mrs. Lucky	454	738	44-10571	yes	My Ideal	30	392	42-72985	no
Muck's Mauler	VB	103	Bu32035	no	My Irish Colleen	5	31	44-41462	yes
Muckalone	VPB	111	Bu38895	no	My Mama Done Told Me	490	849	42-94955	no
Mudfish	308	375	41-24308	no	My Nell	454		44-50791	no
Mudfish II	308	375	42-40620	no					
Mugley Other	451	725	42-50730	no					

Name	Grp.	Sq.	Serial	Pic.	Name	Grp.	Sq.	Serial	Pic.
My Peach	44	506	42-100415	no	Near Miss	494	867	44-40795	yes
My Prayer	392	576	42-51194	no	Near Sighted Robin	34	7	41-28851	yes
My Prayer	459	756	42-78388	no	Nella			42-94940	no
My SAD Ass	44	66	44-10531	no	Nellie	458			yes
My Sugar	2AD			no	Nelly Fly				yes
My Sugar II	2AD			no	Nemsis	98	345	42-73423	no
My Tuffy				no	Nemsis		86CMS	42-73032	yes
My Wild Irish Rose	467	790	41-29270	no	Net Results	380	528	44-41875	yes
Myakinback	493		42-94918	no	Neva Lorraine	446	704	42-50308	no
Myakinback	490	850	42-94918	no	Never A Dull Moment	98	415		no
Myasis Draggin'	489			no	Never Mrs.	34	7	42-95167	no
Myasis Dragon	28	404	44-49483	yes	Never Mrs.	453	734	42-95167	yes
Myrtle the Fertile Turtle	44	67	42-99967	yes	Never Mrs. Too	453	734	44-50477	no
Myrtle the Fertile Turtle	44	67	44-50578	no	Niagara Special	392	578	42-51121	no
N - Nan	460	762	44-41233	no	Nice N' Naughty	44	66	42-7476	yes
Nan Fox	30	392	42-72965	no	Nickel Plate Crate	451	727	41-28876	no
Nana	307	424	44-51455	no	Night and Day	11	431	44-41695	yes
Nana	389	566	42-94973	yes	Night Knight	492	858	44-40119	no
Nana	43	63	44-40938	yes	Night Mission	479		42-40891	yes
Nana	5	838	44-40938	yes	Night Mission	11	26	44-40532	yes
Nancy	493		44-40436	yes	Night Mission	308	374	42-78680	yes
Nancy	380	529	44-42351	yes	Night Mission	6	397	42-40891	yes
Nancy	460	761	41-28997	yes	Night Mission	30	819	44-40532	yes
Nancy	464	779	41-28998	no	Night Mission	11		42-40891	yes
Nancy			44-41498	yes	Night Night (The)	NLS			no
Nancy Anne (The)	456		41-29311	no	Night Raider	44		41-11650	yes
Nancy Girl				no	Night Raider	93	330	41-23665	yes
Nancy Jane	449	716	41-28833	no	Night Raider	93	409	41-23734	yes
Nancy Jane	449	716	41-29512	no	Night-Life-Nellie	392	579	42-52654	no
Nancy Jane II	449	719	41-28866	no	Nightmare				yes
Nancy Lee	93			yes	Nightmare	459			no
Nancy Lee	451	725	42-99754	no	Nightmare	489			no
Nani Wahine	389			no	Nightmare	98	343	41-11896	yes
Nasty 'Lil	6PR	24CM	42-64055	no	Nightmare	451	725	42-52079	yes
Natchely	454	736	42-52255	no	Nightmare Express	308		42-63778	yes
Natchez to Mobile	98	344	41-11797	yes	Nine Yanks & a Jerk	445	703	41-29118	yes
Natchez-Belle	44	68	42-40373	no	Nip Nipper	308	373	42-40391	yes
Nature's Nymphe	446	705		yes	Nipper (The)	90	319	41-11866	yes
Nature's Nymphe	466	785		yes	Nippo Nippin' Kitten	VPB	109		no
Naughty 40	456	745	42-99807	yes	Nipponese Clipper	30	38	42-72966	yes
Naughty Angel	459	757	42-52341	yes	Nipponese Nipper		36,435	AL570	no
Naughty Blue Eyes	90	319	42-73797	yes	Nipponese Sunset	307	371	41-23797	yes
Naughty But Nice	451	725		no	Niquotina	11			yes
Naughty Mariette	487		42-52739	no	Niquotina	307	371	41-24107	yes
Naughty Nan	93	328	42-99949	yes	Nita			41-29146	no
Naughty Nan	446	705	42-51581	no	Nita	450	723	42-51841	no
Naughty Nan	460	761	41-28997	yes	Nite Mare	465	781		no
Naughty Nan			42-51581	no	Nitemare	308			no
Naughty Nan II	446	705	42-52594	yes	Nitemare	480	2	42-40328	yes
Naughty Nanette	11	42	41-24155	no	Nitemare	451	727	42-52079	yes
Naughty Nanette	11	42	42-40961	yes	No Dice	11		44-41318	yes
Naughty Nell	44	68	41-29538	no	No Duds	5		42-73256	yes
Naughty Norma	389		42-9783x	no	No Excuse	464	778	42-51840	no
Naughty Norma	93	329	41-23934	yes	No Feathered Injun	392	579	42-94886	no
Naval Body	VPB	121	Bu59406	yes	No Feathered Injun	466	787	42-94886	yes
Navel Maneuvers	90	319	44-49864	yes	No Love, No Nothin'	493		44-40471	no
Near Miss	466		44-40795	no	No Love, No Nothin'	465	782	42-52533	yes

Name	Grp.	Sq.	Serial	Pic.	Name	Grp.	Sq.	Serial	Pic.
No Love, No Nothing	448	713	42-95138	no	Octane Ozzie				no
No Love, No Nothing	460	762		no	Odessa				yes
No Name				no	Off Limits				yes
No Name Baby				no	Off Limits	480		41-24263	no
No Name Jive	448	714	41-29230	no	Off Limits	487			no
No Nook Ee Now	489	846	42-94909	yes	Off Limits	34	18	42-94782	yes
No Nookie Now	489	846	42-94854	yes	Off Limits	464	776	42-73432	yes
No Nothing	448	714	41-28945	no	Off Limits Again	466	786	42-94974	yes
No Strain	Navy			yes	Off Limits II	34			no
Noah Borshuns	30			no	Off We Go		2PCS	42-64185	yes
Noble Effort	490	850	42-94981	no	Oh Joy	451	725	42-52168	no
Nobody	449	717	42-99856	no	Oh Kay	376		41-11934	yes
Nobody Else's Butt	VPB	116	Bu59520	yes	Oh, Mona	458	755	44-49544	yes
Nobody's Baby				no	Oh, Mona	466	787	42-52343	no
Nobody's Baby	90	319	42-40346	no	Oh, My Sufferin' Head	448			no
Nobody's Baby	465	783	42-52403	yes	Oh, My Sufferin' Head	44	506	42-100423	yes
Nobody's Baby	466	787	42-52518	yes	Ohio Silver	453	732	42-95206	yes
Nobody's Baby II	466	785	42-95283	no	Oklahoma				no
Nobody's Darling	380	528	44-50913	no	Oklahoma Gal	446	704	42-50567	yes
Nocturnal Mission			44-41263	yes	Oklahoman (The)	389	566	42-40738	yes
Nocturnal Mission	380	529	44-42250	yes	Ol' 45	484	825	42-52635	no
Nocturnal Nemesis				yes	Ol' Blunderbus	VPB	121	Bu59564	yes
Nokish	453			no	Ol' Buddy	448		42-94774	yes
Nokkish	458	752	41-29302	yes	Ol' Buddy	489			yes
Nona Rhea	446	706	42-7612	yes	Ol' Soak	448	712	41-29358	no
Norma	90	400	42-72948	yes	Ol' Soak	466	785	41-29358	yes
Norma	459	756		no	Ol' Tom Cat	466	785	42-52555	no
Norma Nan	446			no	Ol' Witch				yes
Norman S. Mackie (The)	494	864	44-42055	yes	Old 26				no
Normandy Queen	467	790	44-50250	no	Old 75	448			no
Normandy Queen	467	791	42-95237	no	Old 933	446	706	42-51933	yes
North American Express	98	345	42-78527	yes	Old 99 Proof	ZI		44-49001	yes
Northern Lass	44	68	42-100110	yes	Old Acquaintance	308	375	44-40826	yes
Northern Star	98	343	41-11921	yes	Old Bag of Bolts			40-2376	no
Northern Star	376	512	41-11921	no	Old Baldy				yes
Nosie Josie	6PR	24CM	42-64258	yes	Old Baldy	93			no
Nosie Rosie	6PR	24CM	42-64102	yes	Old Baldy	98	345	42-40102	yes
Not Hard To Take				yes	Old Baldy	308	375	42-40848	no
Not In Stock	90	400	42-41077	yes	Old Baldy	445	701	42-94853	no
Not In Stock	43	64	42-41093	yes	Old Baldy	445	701	42-94863	no
Nothing Sacred	380	529	42-40509	yes	Old Baldy	490	849	42-94853	no
Nov Schmoz Ka Pop	446	704	41-29411	yes	Old Bessie	6AF	29	41-23681	yes
Nov Schmoz Ka Pop	461	764	41-28734	no	Old Big Sugah				no
Nudist Kay	485	829	42-78147	no	Old Bird	461	764	41-29334	no
Nudist Kay III	485	830	42-51992	no	Old Black Magic	5		44-42303	no
Nuff Said	389	565	42-109794	yes	Old Black Magic	5	31	44-50333	yes
Nut-Cracker Sweet	7	492		yes	Old Blister Butt	489		42-40776	yes
O for Oboe	389			no	Old Buck	389			no
O'Reilly's Datter	456	745	42-78598	yes	Old Buster Butt	389			no
O'Riley's Daughter	459	757	42-50432	yes	Old Butch	453	735	41-29250	no
O'Riley's Daughter				yes	Old Consistent			40-2375	no
O-Bar				no	Old Crow	44	506	41-24283	yes
O-Bit-U-Airy Mary	93	409	42-50485	no	Old Crow	44	506	42-7509	no
O-Bitch-U-Air-Mary	93	409	42-50485	no	Old Crow II	445	701	42-7509	no
O-O-Nothing	448	713	42-50468	yes	Old Crow III	30	392	44-41985	yes
Oakland County, Mich.				yes	Old Daddy	392	577	42-7497	no
Ocie Boo	98			no	Old Doc's Yacht	458	754	42-95018	yes

Name	Grp.	Sq.	Serial	Pic.
Old Dutch Cleanser	459	757	42-52500	yes
Old Dutch Cleanser	465	780		yes
Old Faithful	389			no
Old Faithful	SCA		AL633	no
Old Faithful	446	706	42-7605	yes
Old Faithful II	389			no
Old Flak Alley				no
Old Fud	490	850	42-94928	no
Old George				no
Old George	494	866	44-40747	yes
Old Glory	448			no
Old Glory	389	565	42-100372	yes
Old Glory	389	565	42-63956	no
Old Glory	392	579	41-28742	no
Old Goat (The)				no
Old Gran-Dad	464	777		yes
Old Grandad's Dream	464	777	42-78092	yes
Old Grey Gull	487		42-52748	no
Old Grey Wolf	392	576	42-51934	no
Old Grey Wolf	459	756	42-51934	yes
Old Hickory	380	530	42-40827	yes
Old Hickory	446	707	42-110043	no
Old Irish	93			no
Old Iron Ass	464	777	42-52462	no
Old Iron Corset	44	67	42-95318	yes
Old Iron Pants	467	789	42-110168	no
Old Iron Pants	491	855	42-110168	yes
Old Iron Sides	90	320	42-110053	yes
Old Ironsides	380	530	42-110117	no
Old Ironsides	449	717	42-52170	yes
Old King Solomon	376	513	41-11617	yes
Old Man Boston Marclar	392	577	42-100005	no
Old Mutual (The)				yes
Old Ned's Bells	98	345	42-72849	no
Old Ned's Bells	376	514	42-72849	no
Old Patches	93	409	xx-xx334	no
Old Patches (F-7)		4PR		yes
Old Pop	448			no
Old Reliable	308		44-41437	yes
Old Reliable	448			no
Old Sack	493		44-40425	no
Old Sack	449	719	44-40321	yes
Old Spare Ribs	376	513	41-11646	yes
Old Stand By	392	576	42-50430	no
Old Swayback	448	714	42-7722	no
Old Taylor	451	726	42-52111	yes
Old Thunder Mug (The)	446			no
Old Tom Cat	448	714	42-50699	no
Old Tom Cat	466	785	42-50699	no
Old Tub	451	726	42-52151	yes
Old Tub II	451	726	41-29229	no
Old Veteran (The)	389	564	42-95240	yes
Old Yard Dog (The)			42-98006	no
Olde Hellgate (Ye)	458	753	41-28705	yes
Olde Hellgate (Ye)	461	765	41-28705	no
Olde Mother Hubbard				yes
Olde Rugged Curse (Ye)	449	718	42-7762	yes
Ole 410	22		42-73410	no
Ole 76	448			no
Ole 837	308	374	42-72837	no
Ole Andy of Kansas	487			no
Ole Baldy	486			no
Ole Baldy	493		42-94863	no
Ole Baldy	490	851	42-94863	yes
Ole Baldy/Old Baldy	445	701	42-94863	no
Ole Buckshot			42-50139	yes
Ole Buckshot	491		42-50739	no
Ole Buddy	491	855	42-51120	no
Ole Cock	44	506	42-110024	no
Ole Faithful	376	512	41-11595	no
Ole Faithful	449	717	42-64388	yes
Ole Fur Wagon (Ye)	376			yes
Ole Fur Wagon (Ye)	451	727	44-50240	yes
Ole Goat (The)	466	784	41-28910	yes
Ole Herringbone				yes
Ole Irish	493		42-94863	no
Ole Irish	389	564	42-40746	yes
Ole Irish	490	851	42-94863	no
Ole King Cole	93	328	42-7519	yes
Ole King Cole	445	700	42-50565	no
Ole Miss	44	67	42-7650	no
Ole Professor (The)	380	528		yes
Ole Repulsive	460	763	42-52363	yes
Ole Rock	376		41-11618	yes
Ole Rock	HALP		41-11618	yes
Ole Sack	493		44-40421	no
Ole Sarge	376	512		yes
Ole Satan	458	755	42-52432	yes
Ole Tomato	22	33	42-100291	yes
Ole War Horse	392	579	42-7479	no
Ole Worry	459	756	42-52007	yes
Ole-Rock	376			yes
Ollies Trolley	449			no
Oma Akin Bak	492	857	42-51555	no
Omiakinbak	455	741	42-64481	no
On the Ball	90	319	42-40345	no
On the Ball	93	328	42-40990	yes
On-De-Fence	380	530	42-109995	yes
One (The) / Say Uncle	380	528	42-40534	no
One Ball Riley	90	319	42-40681	no
One Eyed Jack (The)	461	764	42-52390	yes
One More Time			44-50702	no
One Night Stand	449	717	41-29584	yes
One Time	90		41-11869	no
One Weakness	44	68	42-50551	no
One-Eyed Jack (The)	461	764	42-52393	yes
Open Bottom	VPB	104		no
Open Post	458	753	42-50449	yes
Open Season	34	4	42-52707	no
Ophelia Bumps	454	736	41-28660	no
Ophelia Bumps	454	736	42-51413	no

Name	Grp.	Sq.	Serial	Pic.	Name	Grp.	Sq.	Serial	Pic.
Ophelia Bumps	454	736	42-78213	no	Out of the Night II	43	63	44-41809	yes
Ore Shack	449			no	Outa This World	22		42-110001	yes
Organized Confusion	455	741	42-78397	yes	Outa This World	30	819	44-40681	yes
Orient Express	308		44-40781	no	Outa This World				yes
Osage Express	467	790	42-52497	no	Outa This World II	22			no
Our Babe	449	719	44-49752	no	Outcast	485	830	42-78089	no
Our Baby			41-29289	no	Over Exposed				yes
Our Baby	11		42-109954	no	Over Exposed		2PC	42-73020	yes
Our Baby	90			yes	Over Loaded		55W	44-49520	yes
Our Baby	98			yes	Over Loaded	494	864		yes
Our Baby	VPB	106		yes	Overloaded(loan)	11			yes
Our Baby	30	27	42-72969	no	Ozark Upstart	451	726	41-29229	no
Our Baby	30	38	42-109954	yes	P - Peter	460	762	42-51845	no
Our Baby	5	394	42-73270	yes	P'Noach	467	791	44-50668	no
Our Baby	392	578	42-7570	no	P-Peter	392		42-95031	no
Our Baby	449	719	41-29428	yes	Pablo	22		42-100317	no
Our Baby	453	735	41-29259	no	Pacific Avenger	30	38	42-72975	yes
Our Baby	454	736	42-52173	yes	Pacific Passion	11			yes
Our Baby	459	756	42-51265	yes	Pacific Passion	494			yes
Our Baby	461	767	42-52388	yes	Pacific Passion	30	392	44-41500	yes
Our Baby	465	781	42-50723	yes	Pacific Passion		4PC	44-40147	yes
Our Baby	466	784	41-29413	no	Pacific Scamp	90		42-72838	yes
Our Baby	494	867	44-40689	yes	Pacific Tramp	11		42-40067	no
Our Baby, Too	449	719	44-49752	yes	Pacific Tramp III	11		42-109936	yes
Our Burma	458	755	42-50740	yes	Pacific Tramp III	7AHQ		42-109936	yes
Our Burma	458	755	42-50864	no	Pacific Vamp	494	867	41-24168	no
Our Devotion	459	758		no	Pacific Vamp	11	98	41-24168	yes
Our Gal			42-100508	no	Packet for Hitler	467			no
Our Gal	492		42-100308	no	Packy's Packrat	Navy			yes
Our Gal	22	33		no	Paddlefoot	487			no
Our Gal	392	579	42-100308	yes	Paddlefoot	458	755	41-28719	yes
Our Gal	445	702	42-100308	yes	Paddlin' Madelin				yes
Our Gal	451	727	44-41152	yes	Paddy's Wagon	491	855	44-40114	no
Our Gal	90			no	Painted Lady	484	824	44-49988	no
Our Gal II	22	33		no	Pal Joey	5		44-40590	no
Our Gal III	22	33	42-100313	yes	Pal Joey	7		44-40590	no
Our Girl	30	819		no	Palace Meat Market	467	791	42-52394	yes
Our Hobby	461			no	Palace of Dallas	389		42-109791	no
Our Hobby II	460			yes	Pale Ale	466	784	42-50336	yes
Our Hobby II	484	826	44-50364	yes	Pallas Athene...	392	576	44-50505	no
Our Honey				no	Pancho	491			yes
Our Honey	448	713	42-50302	yes	Pancho				yes
Our Honey	466	786	42-52480	yes	Pandora's Box	486	832	xx-xx714	no
Our Joy	448	713	42-51291	no	Paoli Local	450	723	44-41058	no
Our Kay	485	830	44-41157	no	Paper Doll				no
Our Kissin' Cousin			40-2369	no	Paper Doll	5		42-72812	yes
Our Lady and					Paper Doll	98	415	42-51981	no
Her Knights	454	738	42-99773	no	Paper Doll	98	415	42-99860	no
Our Last Hope				no	Paper Doll	376	512	41-29279	no
Our Little Guy	454	738		no	Paper Doll	380	529	42-73187	yes
Our Love	455	742	42-78240	no	Paper Doll	44	68	42-100110	yes
Our Mom	454			no	Paper Doll	34	7	42-94799	no
Our Private Stock	308	373	42-73247	yes	Paper Doll	445	702	42-7579	no
Our Sweetheart	459	756		yes	Paper Doll	449	719	42-7691	yes
Out House Mouse	392	579	42-52083	no	Paper Doll	453	734	42-52237	no
Out of Season,					Paper Doll	459	756	42-52316	yes
Don't Shoot	466	785	42-52574	no	Paper Doll	464	779	41-29351	yes

Name	Grp.	Sq.	Serial	Pic.
Paper Doll	465	781	42-52521	yes
Paper Doll	466	786	42-94799	yes
Paper Doll	482	812	42-3492	no
Paper Doll	489	846	42-52688	no
Paper Doll	489	846	42-94932	yes
Paper Doll	456			no
Paper Doll (The)	486		42-52688	yes
Paper Doll II	445	702	42-7590	no
Pappy	446		41-24137	no
Pappy	98	415	44-40324	yes
Pappy Yokum	376	514	41-11933	yes
Pappy Yokum	458	755	42-110059	no
Pappy's Passion	90	319	42-100222	yes
Pappy's Passion II	380	531	42-73121	yes
Pappy's Persuaders	491	852	44-40144	yes
Pappy's Pill	490	850	42-94792	no
Pappy's Pride	460	760		yes
Pappy's Pride	464	776		no
Pappy's Puss	464	776	41-29410	no
Pappy's Yokum	467		42-50624	no
Pappy's Yokum	376	514	41-11933	yes
Pappy's Yokum	450	721	41-11933	yes
Pappy's Yokum	458	755	42-110159	no
Pappy's Yokum	491	853	41-110159	yes
Pardon Me	450	723	44-50845	no
Park N' Strip Patty	494		42-109948	no
Parkin' Strip Patty	30	38	42-109948	yes
Parson's Chariot	466	784	42-110162	no
Parson's Chariot	466	784	44-40699	yes
Parson's Chariot	491	853	42-110162	yes
Partial Payment	453	732	42-50333	no
Party Girl	467	788	42-94811	no
Passion Pit	44	506	42-95150	yes
Passionate Pirate	450	720	44-41041	no
Passionate Witch	487			no
Passionate Witch	11	26	42-41124	yes
Passionate Witch	380	530	42-41124	yes
Passionate Witch	450	722	42-7731	no
Passionate Witch (The)	5			no
Pastime	VPB	121	Bu59504	yes
Patched Up Piece	6PR	20CM	42-64047	yes
Patches	15AF			yes
Patches	464		42-52449	no
Patches	5		42-41115	yes
Patches	11	26		yes
Patches	90	319	41-23673	yes
Patches	34	391	42-94889	no
Patches	93	409	42-100334	no
Patches	11	431	42-73018	yes
Patches	380	531	42-73471	yes
Patches	445	700	42-110022	no
Patches	445	700	42-95015	yes
Patches	449	719	42-52155	yes
Patches	454	737	42-51978	no
Patches	459	756	42-51978	no
Patches	465	781	42-52449	no
Patches	30	819	44-40518	no
Patches	Navy			yes
Patches (Constant Menace)	376	514	41-24310	yes
Patches (D-Day)	389	565	42-50474	yes
Patches II	449	719	41-29428	no
Patches, the Tin-Tappers Delight	451	726	42-78465	yes
Patchie	448			no
Patchie	458	752	42-95219	yes
Patdue	458			no
Pathfinder	494	866	44-40684	no
Patient Kitten	484			no
Patient Kitten	22	33	44-41031	yes
Patricia Ann	448			no
Patricia Ann	460	761	42-51536	yes
Patricia Ann				yes
Patrick Dempsey	448			no
Patriotic Patty	11			no
Patriotic Patty	446	707	42-50734	yes
Patriotic Patty	30	819	42-73494	yes
Patsy	453	735		no
Patsy	453	735	xx-xx282	no
Patsy Ann	44	68	42-50339	yes
Patsy Ann II	44	68	42-100170	no
Patsy Jack	451	727	42-64445	yes
Patty Girl	445	703	42-50811	no
Patty's Pig	380	531	44-40398	yes
Patuxent River Wart Hog	Navy		Bu32096	no
Paulette	7	492	42-100239	yes
Paulette	461	764	42-51324	no
Pay Day			41-28938	yes
Pay Day	Navy			yes
Pay Day	453	732		no
Pay Day	466	787	41-28938	no
Pay Off	93	329	41-23982	no
Payday	491	855	41-28938	no
Pay Load patty				no
Peace Feeler	VPB	116	Bu59755	yes
Peace Maker	455	743	41-28982	no
Peace Maker	459	757		yes
Peace Offering	43	403		no
Peace Offering	380	529	44-50811	yes
Peace Offering	44	68	42-7672	no
Peace Offering	482	814	42-7672	no
Peace Persuader	RCAF		44-10286	yes
Peace Terms	451	726	41-29541	yes
Peace Terms (The)	22			yes
Peace-Maker (The)	451	724	42-52101	no
Peacemaker	448			no
Peacemaker (The)	455	743	41-28982	no
Peacemaker (The)	459	757		yes
Peaches	90	320		no
Peck's Bad Boys	RCM	36	44-50576	no
Peck's Bad Boys	466	785	42-51353	yes
Peck's Bad Boys II	466	785	42-51353	yes
Pecker Red				yes

Name	Grp.	Sq.	Serial	Pic.
Peekin' Thru	450	723	42-51159	no
Peel Off	455	741	42-64476	yes
Peelin' Off	450	723	41-28919	no
Peelin' Off	450	723	44-40949	no
Peep Sight	44	506	42-7535	yes
Peep Sight	392	579	42-7535	yes
Peerless Clipper	449	717	41-29216	yes
Peerless Clipper II	449	716	42-64354	no
Peg	93	329	41-23658	no
Peg O My Heart	487	838	41-29468	no
Peg O' My Heart	389			no
Peg O' My Heart	450	720	42-7735	no
Peg O' San Antone	446	706	42-50852	yes
Peg the Pig	389			no
Pegasus	491	854	44-40164	no
Pegasus the Flying Horse	466	784	42-51141	yes
Peggy				no
Peggy			42-40502	no
Peggy	389			no
Peggy	376	512	42-78400	no
Peggy	11	98	41-24110	yes
Peggy Ann	466	787	42-50666	no
Peggy Ann	466	787	42-51185	no
Peggy Ann	484	827	44-50476	yes
Peggy Jo			42-94744	no
Peggy Rose				yes
Pelican (The)	308	373	41-24124	yes
Pelican (The)	308	373	41-24183	no
Pelican (The)	466	785	42-52574	yes
Pelly-Can	90	319	41-23688	yes
Pelly-Can	7	9	41-23688	no
Pelton's Pissed Off	445	701		yes
Penelope	98	415	42-40195	no
Pennies From Heaven	98	343	41-11894	no
Pennsy Belle	490	850	42-2882	no
Pennsy City Kitty	307		44-41480	yes
Pennsy City Kitty	5		44-41480	yes
Penny	450	720	42-78405	no
Penny C.	455		42-64498	no
Penny C.	454	738	42-64488	no
Pennys From Heaven	98	343	41-11918	yes
Pennys From Heaven	98	343	41-11894	yes
Penthouse for Ten	466	785	42-95268	yes
Peppy	449	717	41-28590	no
Pepsodent Kid				no
Pepsodent Maid				yes
Per Diem II (The)	376	514	41-11935	yes
Percolatin' Pete	34	4	42-52755	no
Perfect Lady (The)	467	789	42-110168	no
Perils of Pauline				no
Perils of Pauline	467	790	42-95162	yes
Perry & the Pirates	465	780	41-28761	no
Persuader (The)	307	372	42-73277	no
Pete				yes
Pete	490			yes
Pete	448	714	42-95006	yes

Name	Grp.	Sq.	Serial	Pic.
Pete the Carrier	90	400	42-40920	yes
Pete the Pelican	490	848	42-94821	no
Pete the POM Inspector	467		41-29393	no
Pete the POM Inspector	44	506	42-40370	no
Pete the POM Inspector II	467		42-40370	yes
Peter Heater (The)	90	320	42-40917	yes
Petty Gal	43	63	44-42128	yes
Phantom Revegada Le Simulacre Renegat	491	852	42-110185	no
Phiddis II	30	27	42-73283	yes
Philly Filly (The)	392	577	41-28841	no
Philly Filly (The)	490	848	41-28841	no
Phoney Express	489	844	42-94833	yes
Phoney Express II	456	744	42-78403	yes
Photo Fanny (F-7)		2PCS	42-73157	yes
Photo Queen (F-7)	6PR	20CM	42-73049	yes
Photo Sailor	VPB	121	Bu59406	yes
Phyllis	44	67	42-109896	no
Phyllis	44	67	42-110031	no
Phyllis T. of Worcester	90	319	42-109988	yes
Piccadilly Commando				no
Piccadilly Commando	448			no
Piccadilly Commando	466	787	42-50305	yes
Piccadilly Commando	467	788	44-10600	no
Piccadilly Commando	489	847	42-51128	yes
Piccadilly Filley	93	329	41-24111	yes
Piccadilly Filly	34	4	44-40458	no
Piccadilly Lady	448			no
Piccadilly Lily	491			no
Piccadilly Lily	466	784	44-49553	yes
Piccadilly Lucy	34		41-29518	no
Piccadilly Lucy	493		41-29518	no
Piccadilly Pam	RNavy			yes
Piccadilly Pat	448			no
Piccadilly Pete	448	712	42-52118	yes
Piccadilly Tilly	34	4	42-94911	yes
Piccadilly Tilly	485	828	44-40458	no
Piccadilly Tilly	493	861	44-40458	yes
Piccidilly Lilly	448	715	42-50341	yes
Pick Up	485	830	42-94750	no
Pickled Peach				yes
Pidgeon Coop				yes
Piece Maker	461	765	42-51599	yes
Piece Maker	461	765	42-52368	no
Piece Maker	466	784	42-51599	yes
Piece Maker (The)	456	746	42-64486	yes
Piece Time	308	373	44-49491	yes
Pied Piper (The)	454	739	42-52245	yes
Pied Piper (The)	458	752	42-51206	yes
Pig Dealer			42-94851	no
Pilikie Oke Iaponi	11			no
Pilot Error	494	865	44-40738	no
Pima Paisano			44-44175	yes
Pin Down Girl	455	741	42-52241	no
Pin Up Girl	446	705	42-94941	no
Pin Up Girl	489	844	42-94941	yes

Name	Grp.	Sq.	Serial	Pic.	Name	Grp.	Sq.	Serial	Pic.
Pindown Girl	455	741	42-52260	yes	Pittsburgh Babe				yes
Pink Avenger	98			yes	Pizz and Moan	44	68	42-99987	yes
Pink Elephant	98	344	41-11814	yes	Plane Sane	448			no
Pink Lady	98	415	41-11764	yes	Plastered Bastard				no
Pink Lady	376	513	41-24000	yes	Plastered Bastard (The)	461			no
Pink Lady	392	578	42-99945	no	Plate's Date	389		42-94830	no
Pink Panties	454	737	42-64466	no	Plate's Date	801		42-94830	no
Pink Tub	392	579		no	Plate's Date	SOP		42-94830	no
Pinky the Pimp	98	343	41-11895	no	Plate's Date	489	847	42-94830	yes
Pinocchio			42-40355	yes	Play Boy				yes
Pious Plunderer	494	867	44-40668	yes	Play Boy	494	867	44-40791	yes
Pirate Lady	307		42-72822	yes	Playboy	466	784	41-29399	yes
Pirate Princess	VPB	121	Bu59492	yes	Playboy's Friend	494	867	44-40791	yes
Pirate Princess		86CM	42-64174	no	Playhouse	458			no
Pis-s-st	93	330	42-95242	no	Playmate	RCM		52-51685	no
Pisces	454	739	42-52179	no	Playmate	SOP			no
Pisces	486	834	41-29517	yes	Playmate		36	42-51685	no
Pisces	486	834	xx-xx490	no	Playmate	11	431	44-40791	no
Pistol Packin' Bomma	446	707	42-7654	yes	Playmate	389	567	42-63980	yes
Pistol Packin' Mama				yes	Playmate	492	856		no
Pistol Packin' Mama				yes	Playmate	801		42-63980	yes
Pistol Packin' Mama	448			no	Playmate (R. Side)				no
Pistol Packin' Mama	453			no	Playboy (L. Side)	494	867	44-40791	yes
Pistol Packin' Mama	98			yes	Pleasant Bent	460	762	44-49693	no
Pistol Packin' Mama	Navy			yes	Pleasant Peasants	376	513	44-40845	yes
Pistol Packin' Mama	RCAF			yes	Pleasant Surprise	392	578	42-50804	no
Pistol Packin' Mama	VB	101	Bu31973	yes	Pleasant Surprise	392	579	42-51268	yes
Pistol Packin' Mama	VB	102		yes	Pleasure Bent	22		42-73440	yes
Pistol Packin' Mama	VB	102		yes	Pleasure Bent	376	515	42-78386	yes
Pistol Packin' Mama	VPB	108		no	Pleasure Bent	380	530	42-73440	yes
Pistol Packin' Mama	11	26	42-40689	yes	Pleasure Bent	392	578	42-50358	no
Pistol Packin' Mama	90	319	42-41209	no	Pleasure Bent	465	781	41-29357	yes
Pistol Packin' Mama	90	321	42-40954	yes	Pleasure Cruise				no
Pistol Packin' Mama	90	321	42-41209	no	Pleasure Cruise II				no
Pistol Packin' Mama	307	370	41-23987	yes	Pleasure Cruise III				no
Pistol Packin' Mama	30	38	42-72989	yes	Plenty on the Ball	490			no
Pistol Packin' Mama	389	566	42-40783	yes	Plenty on the Ball	491			no
Pistol Packin' Mama	445	702	42-7513	yes	Plow Jockey	467	789	42-50309	no
Pistol Packin' Mama	446	707	42-7654	yes	Plucky Lucky	489	844	42-94820	yes
Pistol Packin' Mama	449	716	42-52146	yes	Plum Lake	456	745	42-52334	yes
Pistol Packin' Mama	450	720	42-52124	yes	Plunderbus	494	864	44-40712	yes
Pistol Packin' Mama	451	724	41-29175	yes	Pluto	98	345	41-23715	yes
Pistol Packin' Mama	464	776	42-52563	yes	Pluto	459	756		no
Pistol Packin' Mama				yes	Pluto Crate	466	784	42-50670	no
Pistol Packin'Mama II	VPB	121		yes	Pluto's Dog Days	90	400	42-72947	yes
Pistol Packin' Mama II	90	321	42-41209	no	Plutocrat	458		42-52455	yes
Pistol Packin' Mama II	446	707	42-51278	no	Plutocrat	93		42-52455	no
Pistol Packin' Mama III	Navy			no	Pocahontas	98	415	41-23768	yes
Pistol Packin' Mamma	449	718	41-28597	yes	Pocatello Chief	392	576	42-99976	no
Pistol Packin' Parson	454	737	42-78150	no	Poco Hero	392			no
Pistol Packin' Parson	455	741	42-52216	no	Poco Loco	392	577	42-7658	yes
Pistol Packing Bomma II	446	707	42-51278	yes	Poco Moco	308		44-49451	yes
Pith and Moan	465	783	42-52473	yes	Poco Moco	445			no
Pithonu	455		42-52271	no	Poison Ivy	376	514	41-23660	yes
Pitti-Sing	43	63	42-41051	no	Poker Hat	389			no
Pittsburgh Babe	454	739	42-78264	yes	Pokey	308		42-100040	no
Pittsburgh Babe	455	742	42-78453	yes	Polaris II	466	784	42-50488	no

Name	Grp.	Sq.	Serial	Pic.	Name	Grp.	Sq.	Serial	Pic.
Polaris the Heavenly Body				yes	Pretty Prairie Special				yes
Polaris, the Heavenly Body	466	787	41-29384	yes	Pride of Fondy	90	321	44-40338	no
Politicians (The)	451	726	42-78478	no	Pride of the Cornhuskers	43			yes
Pollyana	389	566	42-109817	no	Pride of the Yanks	90	400	41-11904	yes
Pom Pom Express			44-50459	yes	Princ-Ass(ess)	44	506	42-63962	yes
Pom Pom Express	380	531	44-50396	yes	Prince	44	506	42-63962	yes
Ponderous Pachyderm	491	853	42-94753	yes	Prince Charming	98	343	42-40082	yes
Pontiac Squaw (The)	484	826	42-52774	yes	Prince Charming II	98	343	42-109802	yes
Poo Tinky	448			no	Prince Valiant	380	531	42-40526	yes
Poochie	380	528	42-40369	no	Princess (The)	446	706	42-7620	yes
Poochie	380	528	42-40491	no	Princess Carol		3	44-41331	yes
Poon Tang	5			no	Princess Charlotte	44	66	41-23769	yes
Poontang	30	38	42-72999	yes	Princess Helen	449	716	42-78479	yes
Poop (The)	30	38	41-23746	no	Princess Konocti	389	565	42-100190	yes
Poop Deck Pappy	448			no	Princess Marie	485	830	42-52694	no
Poop Deck Pappy	392	577	42-7521	yes	Princess O'Rourke	446	705	42-7572	no
Poop Deck Pappy	44	67	41-29161	yes	Princess Pat	448			no
Poop Deck Pappy	44	67	42-7521	no	Princess Pat	450	723	44-50245	no
Pop	448			yes	Princess Pat	458	752	42-95316	yes
Pork	44			no	Princess Pat	464	779	42-78350	no
Porky	453	733	42-95111	no	Princess Pat	465	781	42-51894	no
Porky	456	746		yes	Princess Pat				yes
Porky	465	783	44-41137	no	Princess Sheila	6		AL639	yes
Porky II	44		42-40182	no	Problem Child				yes
Portland Annie	453	735	42-52175	no	Problem Child	448			no
Portland Rose	464	778	42-78431	yes	Problem Child	34	18	41-28884	no
Pot Luck	389	567	42-95071	yes	Problem Child	308	375	42-41164	no
Pot Luck	484	825	42-51851	no	Problem Child	376	514	42-78347	yes
Pouting Squaw (The)	484	825	42-94753	yes	Problem Child	450	723	42-7724	no
Powder Ann	98	344	42-73421	no	Problem Child	487	838	41-28813	no
Powder Room	454	737	42-78297	yes	Problem Child				yes
Powerful Katrinka	34	4	41-29555	no	Prodigal Son (The)	448	712	41-28593	no
Powers Girl (The)				yes	Professor D	376	514	41-24034	yes
Powers Girl (The)	90	400	42-72807	yes	Prop Wash	380	530	42-73475	yes
Precious Jewell	389		42-110103	no	Proud Mary	44	506	42-7630	no
Predominant Yankee	466	787	42-50516	no	Prowler (The)	491	854	42-110171	yes
Preg-Peg	456	747	41-29283	no	Psycology	308	425	42-40070	no
Pregnant Angel	93	330		no	Pub Hound	466	786	42-95211	yes
Pregnant Cow	44	67	41-11673	no	Puddle Jumper	11		44-40829	yes
Pregnant Duck	454	739	44-49264	no	Puddle Jumper	30	819	44-40829	yes
Pregnant Peg	392			yes	Puddle Jumper II	11		44-41946	yes
Pregnant Peg	44	506	42-50328	yes	Puddle Jumper II	30	819	44-41946	yes
Pregnant Peg	392	577	42-7491	no	Pudgy				no
Pregnant Peg II	392	577	42-52649	yes	Pudgy	90	320	41-23830	yes
Pregnant Peggy	489	847	42-94913	yes	Pudgy	93	330	42-40613	yes
Pregnant Polecat	90	400	42-72789	yes	Pug	380	529	42-40518	yes
Pregnant Swan	308	425	42-40069	no	Pug	453	732	42-52147	no
Pretty Baby	392			no	Pug				yes
Pretty Baby	460			no	Pug II	380	530	42-40526	yes
Pretty Baby	90	319	42-109987	yes	Pug Nose	90		41-23823	yes
Pretty Kitty				yes	Pug Nose Annie	454			no
Pretty Little Lass	466	785	42-95202	no	Puggy II	449	719	42-7747	no
Pretty Mickey				yes	Pugnacious Peggy	449	716	42-52269	yes
Pretty Mickey	454	736	42-50423	no	Pugnacious Princess Pat	389	566	44-10579	yes
Pretty Petty				yes	Punjab	30	38	42-72974	yes
					Punjab	90	400	41-11902	no
					Punkie				yes

57

Name	Grp.	Sq.	Serial	Pic.	Name	Grp.	Sq.	Serial	Pic.
Pupil Packin' Mama	376			yes	Queenie	93	409	41-24298	no
Puritanical Bitch	44	68	42-50427	no	Queenie	446	707	42-50773	yes
Puritanical Witch	44	68	42-50427	no	Queenie	453	735	41-28631	no
Purple Shaft				no	Queenie	466	785	44-10518	no
Purple Shaft				yes	Queenie	490	851		no
Purple Shaft	466			no	Queenie(Miss Delores)	44	67	41-24278	no
Purple Shaft	453	734	42-52296	yes	Queer Deer	380	528	42-40935	yes
Purple Shaft	454	736	42-78256	yes	Question Mark (The)				no
Purple Shaft	454	738	41-28811	no	Quit Shovin'	493		42-94916	no
Purple Shaft (The)	451	724	42-51880	yes	Quit Shovin'	490	851	42-94916	no
Purple Shaft Special	448			no	Quitcherbitchin	448			no
Pursuit of Happiness				yes	Quivering Box	446	705	42-100315	yes
Pursuit of Happiness	492		42-95272	no	R-Baby	454	736		no
Pursuit of Happiness	392	576	42-95272	no	Rabbit Habit				no
Pursuit of Happiness	392	579	42-94886	no	Rabbit Habit	466			no
Purty Baby	493		44-40299	yes	Rabbit Habit	451	725	42-51764	yes
Purty Baby	376	515	44-40299	no	Rabduckit	448			yes
Push Over	392	578	42-7518	no	Rackem' Back	487	837	41-29525	no
Puss 'N Boots	454	739	42-51905	no	Racken Jumper	456			no
Puss 'n Boots	491	853	44-50340	yes	Racy Tomato	449	718	42-78266	yes
Puss in Boots	449	718	44-49403	yes	Rag Doll			42-95099	no
Puss in Boots	484	826	41-28835	yes	Rag-A-Das	449	717	42-51920	yes
Puss N Boots	392	577	42-95079	no	Rage in Heaven			44-40186	no
Puss N' Boots	380	528	42-72942	yes	Rage in Heaven	450	721		no
Puss N' Boots	389	567	42-95079	no	Rage in Heaven	491	852	44-40165	yes
Q for Queenie	44			no	Ragged But Right	491		44-10622	no
Q for Queenie	445	701	42-51015	no	Ragged But Right	454	736	41-28914	no
QQQQ	448			no	Ragged But Right	454	737	42-52265	no
Quanta Costa	465	782	42-78391	no	Ragged But Right	459		42-78490	yes
Que Pasa?				yes	Raggedy Ann	44	67	42-7603	no
Queen Ann	22	33	42-110119	yes	Raggedy Ann II	44	67	42-72873	no
Queen Anne	44	506	41-23936	no	Raid of Terror	448			no
Queen Anne	450	722	42-95458	no	Raiden Maiden	490	849	42-94763	no
Queen Bee	376	513	41-11591	yes	Railway Express	44	67	41-23794	no
Queen Bee	449	719		no	Rainbow Goddess	453	735	42-64469	no
Queen Hi	380	529	44-40432	yes	Rainbow Virgin				yes
Queen Mae	6PR	20CM	44-40337	yes	Ram It - Damn It	44	68	42-7635	no
Queen Mae	90	319	44-40337	yes	Ramblin Rocket				no
Queen Marguerite	44	506	41-23936	no	Ramblin Wreck II				no
Queen Marlene	44	66	42-72813	yes	Ramblin' Reck	486	835		no
Queen of Angels	5	31	42-72834	yes	Ramblin' Rose	22	33	42-100201	no
Queen of Angels	446	704	42-50735	no	Ramblin' Wreck				yes
Queen of Hearts				yes	Ramblin' Wreck	445	700	42-64438	no
Queen of Hearts	90	320	44-40185	yes	Ramblin' Wreck	466	787	41-28932	yes
Queen of Hearts	98	345		no	Ramblin' Wreck (The)	380	529	44-50776	yes
Queen of Hearts	449	716	42-64367	yes	Ramey's Wreck	380	530	42-73451	yes
Queen of Hearts	449	717	42-64367	yes	Ramp Champ		3PRS	44-41996	yes
Queen of Hearts	450	723	44-50675	no	Ramp Rat	ZI			yes
Queen of Hearts	454	738	42-78074	yes	Ramp Rat	450	721	42-78454	yes
Queen of Hearts	494	866	44-40685	yes	Ramp Rider	11	431		yes
Queen of Peace (The)	392	577	42-7637	yes	Ramp Rooster	SOP			no
Queen of the Clouds	43	403	44-40979	yes	Ramp Rooster	482	36	42-50671	yes
Queen of the Clouds II	43			no	Ramp Rooster	RCM	36	42-50671	no
Queen of the Strip	380	529	44-42214	yes	Ramp Rooster	308	425	41-24222	yes
Queenie	448			no	Ramp Rooster	455	742	41-28640	no
Queenie	98	345	42-78420	no	Ramp Rooster	484	824	42-52576	yes
Queenie	34	4	41-29564	no	Ramp Rooster				yes

58

Name	Grp.	Sq.	Serial	Pic.
Ramp Rooster				yes
Ramp Tramp	5		42-40651	no
Ramp Tramp	449	716	42-7700	yes
Ran Dee Dan	456	747	42-64470	yes
Randy Dandy	493		44-40477	no
Rangoon Raider	7		44-40817	no
Rangoon Rambler	467			yes
Rangoon Rambler	7	436		yes
Rangoon Rambler II	7	436	41-23702	yes
Rangoon Rambler II	467	790	42-52554	no
Rangy Lil	380	528	44-41867	yes
Rap 'em Pappy	392	576	42-95070	no
Rap 'em Pappy	392	579	42-95229	yes
Rape Shape	485	829	42-78137	no
Rapid Robin	11	431	41-24170	yes
Rapid Robin II	11	431	42-73287	yes
Rat Poison	493		41-29560	no
Rat Poison	493		44-40477	no
Rat Poison	34	18	41-29560	no
Rat Poison	93	330	42-50989	yes
Rat Poison	392	579	41-29560	yes
Rat Race	464	776	42-78128	no
Rationed Passion	448			no
Rattler (The)	307	424	41-23925	yes
Rattlesnake Hank	460	763	42-52367	yes
Raunch Rebel (The)	389		42-95063	no
Raunchy	30	27	42-72980	no
Raunchy	98	345	41-11819	yes
Razzle Dazzle				yes
Ready	464	776	42-52402	yes
Ready & Willing	93	330	41-24109	yes
Ready & Willing	98	415	41-11765	yes
Ready & Willing	44	67	41-24109	no
Ready and Waiting				no
Ready and Waiting	466	787	41-28971	yes
Ready and Willing	RCAF			yes
Ready and Willing	466	784	41-24109	no
Ready Bette	30			yes
Ready Betty	487		41-29524	yes
Ready Betty	451	727	42-78254	yes
Ready for Let				no
Ready N' Able	RCM		42-95221	yes
Ready Teddy	93	330	41-23721	yes
Ready Teddy	380	529	42-73488	yes
Ready Teddy	451	726	42-52087	yes
Ready Teddy II	11	98	42-73008	yes
Ready, Willing & Able	90	319	42-41078	yes
Ready, Willing & Able	376	512	42-72768	yes
Ready, Willing & Able	467	790	42-29427	no
Ready, Willing and Able			42-95427	no
Ready-N-Able	RCM	36	42-95221	no
Rebel	98	344	41-23763	no
Rebel (The)				yes
Rebel (The)	448			no
Rebel (The)	44	68	41-23813	yes
Rebel Gal	392	578	42-94838	no
Rebel Gal	489	845	42-94838	yes
Rebel Raigh	454	736	44-50876	yes
Rebel Yell	466	784	41-29422	no
Rebel Yell	466	786	41-29416	no
Record Breakers (The)	43	64	42-110122	yes
Red Ace				no
Red Arrow (The)				yes
Red Arrow (The)	5			yes
Red Ass	93	409	41-23740	yes
Red Ass	446	706	42-95203	yes
Red Ass (The)	380	530	42-40524	yes
Red Ball Express	93		42-40992	no
Red Butt	446	706	42-95203	yes
Red Dog	448			no
Red F	465	780	42-52994	no
Red Head	461	767	44-49501	no
Red Headed Woman	5	31	44-41645	yes
Red Hot Mama	448			no
Red Hot Riden Hood (I)	22	33	42-100212	yes
Red Hot Riden Hood III	22	2		yes
Red Hot Riden-Hood II	22	2	44-40202	yes
Red Hot Ridin' Hood	455	743	42-52204	yes
Red Hot Riding Hood	308			yes
Red Hot Riding Hood	464			no
Red Hot Riding Hood	449	717	42-52086	no
Red Hot Riding Hood	456	747	42-94886	yes
Red Hot Riding Hood	466	786	42-52442	no
Red Hot Riding Hood	490	849	42-52086	yes
Red J - Jig	464			yes
Red O	465	780	42-51421	no
Red Raider (The)	451	726		no
Red Ryder	376	512	42-95285	yes
Red Ryder	451	726	42-52460	yes
Red Ryder	461	764	42-52460	no
Red Sox	448			no
Red Victor	464	776	41-28969	no
Red Wing	376	513	42-40657	no
Red Wing	376	513	42-72902	yes
Red Y	465	780	44-48861	no
Red's Devils	307	371	42-73271	yes
Red's Raiders	376			no
Red-Dee	98		42-100434	no
Red-Hot Riden-Hood II	484			no
Redaz	90			no
Redding's Rummies				yes
Reddy Maid	491			no
Reddy Maid	456	746	44-50382	yes
Reddy Maid	465	746	44-50387	yes
Reddy Teddy				yes
Reddy Teddy	93	330	41-23721	yes
Reddy Teddy	448	715	42-51551	yes
Reddy Teddy Too	455	742	41-28989	yes
Redwing				yes
Redwing	VPB	121	Bu59505	yes
Reliable Babe	466	786	42-52527	yes
Reluctant Beaver	456	745	42-78329	no
Reluctant Dragon	453		41-xx286	yes

Name	Grp.	Sq.	Serial	Pic.	Name	Grp.	Sq.	Serial	Pic.
Reluctant Dragon	487			no	Roberta & Son / Firepower	380	528	42-109986	yes
Reluctant Dragon	491		42-95610	no	Rockcliffe Ice Wagon	RCAF			yes
Reluctant Dragon	308	373	42-40634	yes	Rodger the Lodger	307	372	44-41535	yes
Reluctant Dragon	308	374	42-73xxx	no	Rodney the Rocks	486	835	xx-xx500	no
Reluctant Dragon	491	853	42-51088	yes	Roger the 2nd	464	779	44-49028	no
Reluctant Lady	487		42-52561	no	Roger the Lodger	455	742	42-64482	no
Reluctant Lady	487		42-52769	no	Roger's Rangers	460	763	41-28698	no
Reluctant Liz	449	717	41-28596	yes	Rogue's Retreat	RCAF			yes
Reluctant Virgin	98	415	42-51176	no	Roll Me Over	485		44-49939	no
Renegade (The)	491	852	42-110186	no	Roll Me Over	484	827	44-49939	no
Repulser			41-28843	no	Roman's Candles	451	726	42-52153	yes
Repulsive Raider	464	777	42-95382	no	Rome of New York	448			no
Repulsive Raider II	464	777	42-78365	no	Ronnie	446	704	41-29144	yes
Reputation Cloudy	465	782	41-28906	yes	Ronny				no
Ret by Ford	392		42-7465	no	Roost (The)				no
Retriever	30	27	42-100398	yes	Roost (The)	446	704	42-7679	no
Return Engagement	93	409	42-100336	no	Rooster	453	735	41-28650	no
					Root of All Evil	98	415	41-11808	no
Return Engagement	93	409	44-10578	yes	Rosalie Mae	455	741	42-78166	no
Returner (The)				yes	Rosalyn	467	788	44-10601	yes
Revenge	454	736	42-52272	no	Rose Bud	98	344	41-11764	no
Rhapsody in Junk	389		41-28733	yes	Rose Marie	493		44-40207	no
Rhapsody in Junk	458	753	41-28733	yes	Rose Marie	30	27	44-40680	no
Rhapsody in Rivets	487		42-52622	no	Rose Marie	467	790	41-28695	yes
Rheinmacher	467	790	42-52556	no	Rose O'Day				yes
Rhoda	451	726	44-49866	yes	Rose O'Day's Daughter	6	397	xx-xx961	yes
Rhoda	461	765	41-28740	no	Rose of Juarez	308	375	42-73305	yes
Rhode Island Red	461	765	41-28737	no	Rose of Juarez	392	579	42-7469	yes
Rhode Island Red II	461	765		yes	Rose's Rivets	448	712	42-95544	no
Rhumba Rita	90			no	Roseanna from Indiana	460			yes
Rice Paddy Hattie				yes	Rosebalm	466	786	42-52511	yes
Rice Paddy Hattie	308	374	44-42029	yes	Rosemarie	307			yes
Rice Pattie Hattie	6PR	24CM	42-73038	yes	Rosie	448			no
Ridge Runner	446	704	41-29411	no	Rosie	454	737		yes
Rigor Mortis	446	705	42-7589	no	Rosie o' the Ramp	380	528	42-100213	yes
Rim Runner				no	Rosie Wrecked 'Em	98	345	41-11803	yes
Ring-Dang-Doo	11			yes	Rosie Wrecked 'Em	376	515	41-11803	no
Riot Call	494	864	44-40755	yes	Rough (K)night	380	530	42-100209	yes
Rip Snorter	6PR	20CM	42-73047	yes	Rough and ...				yes
Rip Snorter (The)	494	866	44-40684	yes	Rough Buddy	11	26	42-41198	no
Rip Tide	453	732	41-28627	no	Rough Buddy	446	707	42-95390	yes
Ripper (The)	489	846	42-50360	yes	Rough Cobb	454	737	42-78458	yes
Ripper the 2nd	376	512	42-72852	yes	Rough Deal Lucille	485	828	42-94791	no
Ripper the First	376	515	41-11614	yes	Rough House Annie	485	831	42-50819	no
Ripper's Clipper	489	846	42-50360	yes	Rough House Kate	34	4	41-29542	no
Rita	30	27	44-40633	yes	Rough House Kate	445	702		no
Rita	11	42	44-40633	yes	Rough Night	380	530	42-100209	yes
Ritz	464	776	44-49073	no	Rough on Rats	376	514	44-40149	yes
Road Back (The)				yes	Rough Raiders	487			no
Road to Tokyo	11	42	44-40521	yes	Rough Rid'er				yes
Road to Tokyo	90		44-40521	no	Rough Rid'er	454	739	42-78182	no
Roamin' Josie	90	319	41-23698	yes	Rough Rider	460	470		yes
Roarin' Rosie	90	319	41-23698	no	Rough Riders	458	755	41-29342	yes
Rob				yes	Round Trip	307		42-40644	yes
Robbie L.	380	529	42-40516	yes	Round Trip	451	726	42-50630	no
Robbie L. II	380	531	42-40979	yes	Round Trip Rose	450	723	41-29213	no

Name	Grp.	Sq.	Serial	Pic.	Name	Grp.	Sq.	Serial	Pic.
Round Trip Ticket	494			yes	Rum Runner	489	845	42-94900	yes
Round Trip Ticket	22	33	42-100193	yes	Rumplestiltskin	453	735	42-52182	yes
Round Trip Ticket	389	565	42-40171	yes	Rumplestiltskin II	446		42-64452	no
Round Trip Ticket II	22	33	44-41538	no	Rumplestiltskin II	491		42-64452	no
Rover Boys	448			no	Rumplestiltskin II	453	735	42-64452	no
Rover Boys (The)	451	726	42-78463	yes	Run on Sugar (A)				yes
Rover Boys' Baby	494	865	44-40752	yes	Rupert the Roo	98	415	44-48782	no
Rovin Redhead	VD	5	Bu65299	yes	Rupert the Roo II	98	415	42-64365	no
Rovin' Lady				yes	Ruptured Duck	467			no
Rowdy	98	344	41-11794	yes	Ruptured Duck	492	856	44-40150	no
Rowdy Ann	98	344	41-11796	yes	Ruptured Duck (The)				no
Rowdy Ann	376	512	41-11796	no	Ruptured Duck (The)	493		42-52770	yes
Rowdy Dowdys	450	720	42-78184	yes	Ruptured Duck (The)	34	4	42-52770	yes
Rowdy II	98	344	41-23656	yes	Ruptured Duck (The)	392	576	42-52770	yes
Rowdy II	376	513	42-40656	no	Ruptured Falcon	34	4	42-52770	no
Roy's Boys	93			no	Ruptured Falcon	380	529	42-100215	yes
Royal Carriage	489	847	42-94925	no	Ruptured Falcon	389	529	42-100215	yes
Royal Flush	392			no	Ruptured Falcon	392	576	42-52770	yes
Royal Flush	448			no	Rusty				no
Royal Flush	AZON		44-40291	no	Rusty Dusty	455	742	42-99771	yes
Royal Flush	11	431	44-41318	yes	Ruth Ann	307		44-40945	yes
Royal Flush	458	753	44-40291	yes	Ruth E-K Allah Hassid	489	845	41-29577	yes
Royal Flush II	90	320	42-73131	yes	Ruth E.K. Allah				
Royal Flush II	380	531	42-73131	yes	Hassid (The)	448	714	41-29577	yes
Royal Prod	451	727	41-29241	yes	Ruth Marie	453	734	42-51301	yes
Royal Screw	446	706	42-99983	no	Ruth Marie	467	790	41-28695	no
Royal Screw!				yes	Ruth Please	98	343	42-51161	yes
Rubber Check	459			yes	Ruth-less	448			no
Rubber Check	93	409	42-95294	no	Ruthie the Raider	464	778	42-52537	yes
Rubber Check	44	506	42-110023	no	Ruthless	44	506	41-24282	yes
Rubber Check	446	705	42-95294	yes	Ruthless Ruthie	493		44-40317	no
Rubber Check (The)	455	743	41-29271	no	Ruthless Ruthie	491	854	44-40317	yes
Rubber Check,	446	706	42-99983	yes	S for Sugar	453	735		no
Ruby's Ricksha	90		42-73121	yes	S-S-Sylvia				yes
Rude Nude	307	371	41-24151	yes	S. O. L.	458	753	44-40066	yes
Ruff 'N Ready	465	783	42-52464	no	S. O. L.	492	858	44-40066	yes
Ruff Knights	11		44-40550	yes	Sa Wrong Gal	484	826	42-52671	yes
Ruff Knights	30	38	44-40550	yes	Sabrina	44	506	42-7647	no
Ruff Stuff	459			yes	Sabrina 2	44	506	42-52611	no
Rugged Beloved	VPB	111	44-41308	yes	Sabrina III	44	506	42-95209	no
Rugged Buggy	44	68	41-23819	yes	Sac Rat				no
Rugged But Right	448	715	42-94953	yes	Sacajawea	465	781	42-52558	no
Rugged But Right	490	851	42-94953	no	Sack (The)	489	846	42-94857	no
Rugged Cross	489			no	Sack (The)	489	847	41-29603	no
Rum and Coke	43	65	44-49827	yes	Sack Artists	44	67	42-100073	yes
Rum Boogie	448			no	Sack Bound	43	63	42-73471	yes
Rum Collins	453	733	44-49972	no	Sack Happy	489			no
Rum Dum	RCM	36	42-51230	no	Sack Happy	392	579		no
Rum Dum	465	780		no	Sack Happy	453	734		no
Rum Dum	489	845	42-50280	yes	Sack Happy	466	786	42-52570	yes
Rum Hound	484	825	42-52690	no	Sack Rat				no
Rum Runner	486		42-52496	no	Sack Rat	392			no
Rum Runner	493		42-52496	yes	Sack Rat	491	852	44-40206	no
Rum Runner	308	374	41-24243	no	Sack Shack	98			yes
Rum Runner	34	392	42-52496	no	Sack Time	376			yes
Rum Runner	448	713	42-28583	yes	Sack Time	451		44-40275	yes
Rum Runner	484	824	42-52660	no	Sack Time	467		42-110173	no

Name	Grp.	Sq.	Serial	Pic.	Name	Grp.	Sq.	Serial	Pic.
Sack Time	380	531	42-41219	yes	Salty Dog	449	719	41-28864	yes
Sack Time	490	849	42-94841	no	Salty Dog (Rt. Side)	466	784	41-29419	yes
Sack Time	491	855	42-110173	yes	Salty Sal	30	392	42-100219	yes
Sack Time	492	857	42-110184	no	Salutation Rose	34	391	42-94770	no
Sack Time Sal	494	866	44-40741	no	Salvaged Sally	389	564	42-94964	yes
Sack Time Sal II	11	431		yes	Salvo	90			no
Sack Time Sal II	494	866	44-40796	yes	Salvo Sal	454	738	42-64471	no
Sack Time Sally	389	565	42-40749	yes	Salvo Sally			42-52757	no
Sack Time Sally	493	863	42-110094	yes	Salvo Sally II	484	826	42-52697	yes
Sack Wagon (The)	43	63	42-100034	yes	Sam Sent Me	459			no
Sack Warmer	389	566	41-28824	yes	Same Ole Crap	445		44-40466	yes
Sacktime	467	789	42-94931	no	Same Ole Crap	493		44-40466	yes
Sad Sack				yes	Sammy's Niece	487	838	42-52629	no
Sad Sack	448		42-94988	no	Samoa	11		AL 626	yes
Sad Sack	7AF			yes	San Antonio Rose	454	737	42-95009	yes
Sad Sack	7AF		FP-685	yes	San Antonio Rose	455	742	42-52230	no
Sad Sack	7AHQ		FP-685	yes	San Quentin Quail	11	98	42-41205	yes
Sad Sack	90	320	42-72785	yes	Sand Bomb Special	44	66	42-95124	no
Sad Sack	90	320	42-73133	no	Sand Witch	389	566	42-40735	no
Sad Sack	98	344	42-40208	yes	Sandman (The)	98	345	42-40402	yes
Sad Sack	376	512	42-41175	no	Sandra Kay	380	530	42-72790	yes
Sad Sack	376	515	42-78321	yes	Sandy	460			yes
Sad Sack	380	531	42-73133	yes	Sandy	11	26	42-73019	yes
Sad Sack	44	66	41-29147	yes	Sandy	22	408	42-100324	yes
Sad Sack	446	707	41-29147	yes	Sans Souci	465	783	41-29424	no
Sad Sack	451	726	44-49456	yes	Santa	98	343		yes
Sad Sack	453	733		no	Sassy Lassie	454	737	41-29265	no
Sad Sack	454	736	44-49703	yes	Sassy Lassy				yes
Sad Sack	489	844	42-94831	no	Sassy Lassy	455	740	41-29282	yes
Sad Sack	459			yes	Satan's Angels	93	328	42-40604	yes
Sad Sack (The)			42-99988	no	Satan's Baby				yes
Sad Sack (The)	389			no	Satan's Baby				yes
Sad Sack (The)	480		41-23992	no	Satan's Chariot	93	329	41-24025	no
Sad Sack (The)	480		42-40376	yes	Satan's Flame	392	579	42-7474	no
Sad Sack II	44	66	41-24153	yes	Satan's Gal II	450	720	42-78231	yes
Sadie	90	400	41-24289	yes	Satan's Hell Cats	44	68	42-40995	yes
Safu	489	846	42-94909	yes	Satan's Kite II	11	26	42-40079	yes
Sage Lady	450	723	41-28607	no	Satan's Lady	487			no
Sagittarius	449	716	41-29400	yes	Satan's Little Sister	446	706	42-50318	yes
Sagittarius	486	834	41-29400	yes	Satan's Little Sister	446	706	42-95180	yes
Sagittarius	486	834	xx-xx744	no	Satan's Mate	389	564	42-110074	no
Sahara Sue	93			no	Satan's Mate	458	753	42-100341	yes
Saints & Sinners	30	38	42-100385	yes	Satan's Playmate	458	753	42-100341	no
Saipanda				yes	Satan's Secretary	380	528	42-63683	no
Sakin' Shack	451	724	41-29256	yes	Satan's Secretary	380	528	42-63989	yes
Sakin' Shack II	451	724	44-50591	yes	Satan's Shuttlebus	459	756	41-28802	yes
Sally	484			no	Satan's Shuttlebus	459	756	42-52351	no
Sally				no	Satan's Siren	455	740	42-52239	no
Sally Ann				yes	Satan's Sister	93			yes
Sally Ann	392	578	42-7484	yes	Satan's Sister	93			yes
Sally D II	484		41-29426	no	Satan's Sister	22	2	42-40680	yes
Sally D II	451	725	41-29426	yes	Satan's Sister	43	403	42-40680	yes
Sally Lee	451	727	41-29239	no	Satan's Sister	446	706	42-7610	yes
Salt Lake Katie	98	415	41-28917	yes	Satan's Sister	451	724	41-29258	no
Salt Lake Katie	98	415	42-109799	no	Satan's Sister	489	844	42-50541	yes
Salty Dog	467		41-29419	no	Satan's Sister	491	854	42-50541	no
Salty Dog	11	431	42-41137	yes	Satan's Sister II	93	330	42-100413	no

Name	Grp.	Sq.	Serial	Pic.	Name	Grp.	Sq.	Serial	Pic.
Satan's Sister III	93			no	Seldom Available	460	760	44-40495	yes
Satan's Sister IV	93			no	Seldom Miss	455		42-51341	no
Satan's Sister V	93			no	Semi Eager				no
Satchel Lass	487	838	41-29482	no	Semper Felix	98	345	41-24246	yes
Saucy Pants	467	790	42-95201	no	Senator (The)	494	864	44-40713	yes
Savage	493			no	Send Me Baby	376	513	42-78476	yes
Savanna Sue	456	745	44-49478	no	Sentimental				
Say Uncle	90		42-40534	yes	Journey-Am				yes
Say Uncle	93			yes	Sequina Girl	448	712	42-64451	no
Say When	492	858	44-40103	yes	Sergeant Stripes				
Scarface	491	855	42-95007	no	Forever	5	31	42-73456	yes
Scheherezade	389	564	42-40772	yes	Set 'em Up	450	723	42-94787	yes
Scherezade	308	375	41-24293	yes	Settin' Pretty	308	374	44-41429	yes
School Daze	467	791	42-51832	yes	Seven Up				no
Schooner (The)				yes	Seventh Heaven	7AHQ		AL633	yes
Scootin' Thunder	5			yes	Sex Appeal	93	409	41-24105	no
Scorpia (The)	465	781	42-52762	yes	Sexshun Eight	5	31		no
Scorpia (The)	486	834	42-52762	yes	Sexy Sal	376	514	41-24102	yes
Scorpion				yes	Sexy Sue II	307	424	41-23943	no
Scorpion	90	319	41-24073	no	Sexy Sue IV	307	372	41-23938	yes
Scorpion (drawing)				yes	Sexy Sue IV	11	98	41-23938	yes
Scorpion (The)	308	373	42-40554	yes	Sexy Sue, Mother of Ten	11	98	42-40078	yes
Scotland Taxi	446	707	42-52583	yes	Sexy Sue,				
Scotty Mack	44	68	44-40276	no	Mother of Ten II	11	98	41-23952	yes
Scourge of the Skies	44	66	42-7618	no	Sexy Sue,				
Scrap Drive	445	701	42-100426	no	Mother of Ten III	11	98	42-73017	no
Scrapiron	307		44-41423	yes	Sexy Sue,				
Scrapper	467	788	41-29397	no	Mother of Ten IV	11	98	41-23928	yes
Scrapper	467	790	42-52394	no	Shack (The)			44-40398	no
Scrappy	44	506	41-24014	yes	Shack (The)	487		44-40298	yes
Scrappy II	44	66	42-40375	yes	Shack (The)	493		44-40298	no
Screamer (The)	380	531	44-40189	no	Shack (The)	RCM	36	41-29143	no
Screamin' Meemie	451	726	42-52082	yes	Shack (The)	446	704	41-29000	no
Screamin' Meemie II	451	726	41-29850	yes	Shack (The)	449	718	42-94977	yes
Screamin' Red Ass	448			no	Shack (The)	458	753	44-40298	yes
Screaming (Out) House				yes	Shack (The)	466	786	41-29000	yes
Screaming Meemie	494		44-42055	no	Shack Bunny	494	867	44-40759	yes
Screaming Mimi	389	565	42-40997	yes	Shack Date	454			no
Screwball	467			no	Shack Date	486			no
Screwball	SOP		42-52711	no	Shack Date	466	786	42-52566	yes
Screwball	492	859	42-52711	yes	Shack Happy	449	717	42-7744	yes
Screwball	2641		42-52711	yes	Shack Happy	453	734	42-95252	no
Scrounch	461	764	41-29338	no	Shack II (The)	453			no
Seafood Mama	90	321	41-24219	yes	Shack II (The)	466			no
Seaman's Super					Shack II (The)	SOP		41-29143	no
Snoope	43			no	Shack II (The)	801	36	41-29143	no
Sears Steers	VB	104	Bu32079	no	Shack II (The)	446	704	41-29143	yes
Second Chance	93	330	41-23707	no	Shack Queen	465	783	41-28736	yes
Second Hand Rose	456	746	44-40487	no	Shack Rabbit	448			no
Secret Weapon (The)	455	740	42-52190	no	Shack Rabbit	44	67	42-7767	no
Secrut Weapin	11	98	42-100224	yes	Shack Rabbit	446	707	42-110043	no
Section 8	491	853	42-50365	yes	Shack Rabbit	453	733	42-64460	no
Section Eight	30	38	42-73982	no	Shack Rabbit II			42-30372	yes
Section Eight	465	783	42-52585	no	Shack Rat	90	320	42-40918	yes
Seed of Satan II	44	67	42-7544	no	Shack Rat	307	370	42-40222	yes
Seed-of-Satan			42-40745	no	Shack Rat	44	506	42-94952	no
Seldom Available	451	725	42-7763	no	Shack Rat	392	577	42-7482	yes

Name	Grp.	Sq.	Serial	Pic.	Name	Grp.	Sq.	Serial	Pic.
Shack Rat Special	7	9		no	Sharon D. (The)	445		42-94759	no
Shack Time	451		44-40275	yes	Sharon D. (The)	489	847	42-94759	yes
Shack Time	458	753	44-40275	yes	Sharp Character	392	577		yes
Shack Time II			42-94841	no	Sharpy				no
Shack Time II	389		42-95250	no	Shasta Shack	449	719	41-28833	no
Shack Time II	392	578	42-95250	no	Shasta Shack	449	719	42-64348	no
Shack Wagon	461	765	42-78616	yes	Shawantsta	43	65		no
Shack? Wolf!	449	717	41-29194	yes	Shawnee Raider	43			no
Shack? Wolf!	451	725	41-29194	yes	Shazam	458			no
Shackin' Stuff		2PCS	42-73033	yes	Shazam	389	564	42-110032	yes
Shacking Stuff	449	716	42-50415	no	She 'Asta	380	530	42-40512	yes
Shackup	454	737	42-51323	no	She Devil	458		44-40123	no
Shadie Sadie	446			no	She Devil	491	852	44-40123	yes
Shadow (The)	307		41-23687	yes	She Hasta	451	724	41-29251	no
Shadow (The)	454	737	42-100198	no	She Wolf				yes
Shadrach	34	7	41-29557	yes	She Wolf	AD4			no
Shady Character III				yes	She's Mine	446	704	42-95105	no
Shady Lady				no	Sheila	392	578	42-7596	no
Shady Lady			44-41916	no	Sherezade	308	425	41-24293	yes
Shady Lady	307		44-41370	yes	Sheza Honey	98	345	42-51328	no
Shady Lady	34			no	Shicago Shirl	458	755	42-110184	no
Shady Lady	467		xx-xx791	no	Shif'lus Skonk	446	706	42-7595	yes
Shady Lady	493		44-40439	no	Shilay-Lee	451	727	41-29239	yes
Shady Lady	5			no	Shining Example (The)	43	64	44-40184	yes
Shady Lady	NLS		42-37726	no	Shirley Ann				yes
Shady Lady	307	370	42-40212	yes	Shirley Jean	449	716	42-95397	yes
Shady Lady	307	372	41-24212	no	Shitiningittin'	5			yes
Shady Lady	380	528	42-40291	no	Shitten-and-a-				
Shady Lady	380	528	42-40369	yes	Gettin'	22	33	44-50799	no
Shady Lady	389	566	44-40439	yes	Shittiningittin II	22	33	44-40799	yes
Shady Lady	448	715	42-50759	yes	Shiverless				yes
Shady Lady	450	720	42-7743	no	Shoe Shoe Baby	445	700	42-64434	no
Shady Lady	451	727	42-78436	yes	Shoo Shoo Baby			42-95183	no
Shady Lady	461	766	41-29268	no	Shoo Shoo Baby	465		41-29458	no
Shady Lady	490	850		no	Shoo Shoo Baby	22	408	42-109984	yes
Shady Sadie	446	705	42-95059	yes	Shoo Shoo Baby	44	506	41-29208	no
Shady Sadie	466	786	42-95059	yes	Shoo Shoo Baby	44	506	41-29431	yes
Shady Sadie				yes	Shoo Shoo Baby	446	707	42-52747	yes
Shaft (The)	489	846	42-52737	yes	Shoo Shoo Baby	455	742	41-29407	no
Shake				no	Shoo Shoo Baby	458	754	44-51095	no
Shake II				no	Shoo Shoo Baby	464	779	41-29458	yes
Shake III				no	Shoo Shoo Baby	466	785	42-52587	yes
Shaknstuff		2PCS	42-73033	yes	Shoo Shoo Baby	467	791	41-29393	yes
Shamrock	449	716	42-52243	yes	Shoo Shoo Baby II	487			no
Shamrock	453	735	42-50510	no	Shoo Shoo Baby II	446	704	42-95197	yes
Shamrock	466	784	42-95109	no	Shoo! Shoo Baby				no
Shamrock (The)	307	371	41-23829	no	Shoo! Shoo! Baby			42-50201	no
Shamrock Sherry	90	319	44-40918	yes	Shoo! Shoo! Baby			42-50204	yes
Shanghai Lil				yes	Shoo! Shoo! Baby	392	578	42-50284	yes
Shanghai Lil	98	415	41-11767	yes	Shoo! Shoo! Baby	489	578	42-50284	no
Shanghai Lil	376	514	41-11787	yes	Shoo! Shoo! Baby	448	712	41-29208	yes
Shanghai Lil	43	63	44-41026	no	Shoo! Shoo! Baby	490	849	42-50284	yes
Shanghi Lil	98	415	41-11767	yes	Shoo-Shoo Baby				no
Shanghi Lil's Sister	376		42-40314	yes	Shoo-Shoo Baby				no
Shark (The)	34	4	42-52707	no	Shoo-Shoo Baby	466	785	41-28752	yes
Shark (The)	392	578	42-7486	no	Shoot Fritz,				
Shark (The)	44	67	42-7549	no	You're Faded	389	567	42-40768	yes

Name	Grp.	Sq.	Serial	Pic.	Name	Grp.	Sq.	Serial	Pic.
Shoot Luke	93	328	41-23729	yes	Silver Streak	445	703	42-95192	yes
Shoot the Works	11	98	44-40554	yes	Silver Witch	492	857	44-40136	yes
Shoot, You're Covered	7	9		yes	Silver Wolf (The)	490	848	42-94882	no
Shoot, You're Faded				yes	Sin Ship	445	702	42-7601	no
Shooting Star	308	374	42-73306	yes	Sinful Cynthia	484	827	42-52661	no
Short Arm				yes	Sing Bing	489			no
Short Bier	493		44-40442	no	Sinner's Dream	449	718	41-28605	no
Short Round	392	577	42-52642	no	Sissy	455	743	44-48760	no
Short Round II	486		42-52753	no	Sissy Lee	455	741	42-51974	yes
Short Round II	392	577	44-50753	yes	Sittin' Bull	446	707	42-7575	no
Short Run	494	867	44-40686	yes	Sittin' Pretty				no
Short Snorter				yes	Sittin' Pretty	494	865	44-40711	yes
Short Snorter	15AF			yes	Sitting Girl	43	403	42-73472	no
Short Snorter	392	579	42-99990	yes	Sitting Pretty				yes
Short Snorter II	392	578	44-10495	no	Sitting Pretty	307			yes
Short Stuff	451		44-49043	yes	Six Bits	467	789	42-52525	no
Short Stuff	465		42-78538	no	Six Bitts	380	529	42-100214	yes
Short, Fat & 4F	464			yes	Six O'Clock Joe	449	717	xx-xx061	yes
Shot Load				yes	Skeeter	448			no
Shufti	98	345	44-40494	no	Skeeter	455	742	41-28640	no
Shy Ann				yes	Skeeter II	448	714	42-52638	no
Shy Ann	466			no	Skeezix	480	2		yes
Shy Ann	7	9		yes	Skerby	389	567	44-40245	no
Shy Daddy				no	Ski-Nose	458		42-52160	no
Shy Shark				no	Ski-Nose	392	579	42-52160	yes
Shy-Chi Baby	380	531	44-40902	yes	Skid's Kids	448			no
Shy-Chi Baby	380	531	44-40920	yes	Skin Wagon	465	781	44-49380	no
Siapanda				yes	Skipper				yes
Sick Call	485	828	41-29491	no	Skipper	98	344	41-23733	yes
Sierra Blanca			44-40152	no	Skipper	449	719	42-78172	yes
Sierra Blanca	492	858	44-40167	no	Skipper Junior				no
Silent Yokum	392	576	44-40297	no	Skipper's Clipper	445	701	42-95000	no
Silent Yokum	453	735	44-40297	yes	Skippy				yes
Silent Yokum	466	787	42-50581	no	Skirt Patrol (The)	464	778	42-78096	yes
Silly Filly	2AD			no	Sknappy	492	856	44-40142	yes
Silver Babe	449	716	44-40331	yes	Skotty	34		42-94813	no
Silver Buck (The)	465	781		no	Sky Chief	453	734	42-95173	no
Silver Chief	392	578	42-95033	no	Sky Demon	30	819	42-40143	yes
Silver Chief	467	790	42-95032	yes	Sky Grazer	456	745	42-52309	no
Silver Chief	492	857	44-40201	yes	Sky Lady				yes
Silver Dollar				yes	Sky Lady	90	400	41-24043	yes
Silver Dollar			xx-xx631	no	Sky Lady	90	400	42-109982	no
Silver Dollar	446	704	42-7611	no	Sky Lark	6	29	42-40771	yes
Silver Dollar	466	784	42-51154	yes	Sky Lark	98	345	41-11883	yes
Silver Dollar	486			no	Sky Master	487		42-52746	no
Silver Eagle	93	409	42-50362	yes	Sky Pirate	490	848	42-94823	no
Silver Eagle	466	786	42-50362	yes	Sky Queen	392	576	42-7500	no
Silver Fleet	454	737	42-52256	no	Sky Queen	44	67	42-7547	no
Silver Fox	487			no	Sky Queen	455	741	42-52216	no
Silver Lady	380	530	44-40371	yes	Sky Queen (The)	448	713	41-28583	no
Silver Queen	489	846	42-95267	yes	Sky Queen (The)	448	713	42-110026	no
Silver Queen	491	852	42-95267	yes	Sky Room	458	754	42-50578	yes
Silver Satan	460			yes	Sky Scorpions (The)	389	565	42-40629	yes
Silver Shark				yes	Sky Shark (The)	389	567	42-109915	yes
Silver Shark	454	736	42-51370	yes	Sky Shy	43		42-40683	no
Silver Shark II	454	739	42-78230	no	Sky Skow	30	27	42-72987	yes
Silver Streak	392	577	42-95040	yes	Sky Skow III	30	27	42-73473	yes

Name	Grp.	Sq.	Serial	Pic.	Name	Grp.	Sq.	Serial	Pic.
Sky Tramp	5	72	42-73143	yes	Slick Chick	448	715	42-50460	yes
Sky Watch				yes	Slick Chick	449	716	42-52110	no
Sky Witch				yes	Slick Chick	466	785	42-94979	yes
Sky Witch	90	400	42-72815	yes	Slick Chick	467	788	41-29380	no
Sky Wolf	5		42-73142	yes	Slick Chick	467	791	41-29388	yes
Sky Wolf	98	345	42-73416	no	Slick Chick	489	846	42-50388	yes
Sky Wolf	445	701	42-7569	yes	Slick Chick II	449	716	42-52165	yes
Sky Wolf	455	740	41-29264	yes	Slick Chick With				
Sky Wolf	489	844	41-29547	no	a Hot Lick	460	761	42-50746	no
Sky Wolf Avenger				yes	Slightly Dangerous	22	33	44-40366	yes
Sky Wolves	489			yes	Slightly Dangerous	380	531	42-73333	yes
Sky Wolves	389	566	42-100281	no	Slightly Dangerous	392	577	42-7556	no
Sky Wolves	460	760	42-78429	yes	Slightly Dangerous	445	701	42-50618	no
Sky's Delight	11	431	44-40673	yes	Slightly Dangerous	446	704	42-50618	no
Sky's the Limit	448			no	Slightly Eager	459	759	42-78177	no
Sky's the Limit (The)			44-28276	yes	Slightly Virgin				yes
Skylark	448		44-40224	no	Slim Chance	455	742	42-51645	no
Skylark	98	345	41-11883	no	Slip Stream				yes
Skylark	451	726	42-51677	yes	Slip Stream	5			yes
Slammin' Spammy				no	Slipstream	454	738	42-64459	yes
Slammin' Spammy	486	833	42-52637	yes	Slo Freight			42-50793	no
Sleeping Dynamite	93		42-50839	yes	Slo Freight	491	852	44-40111	yes
Sleeping Time Gal	464			no	Sloppy But Safe	376		44-41008	yes
Sleepless Knight	487		42-52653	no	Sloppy But Safe	451	727	44-41008	yes
Sleepless Knights	487	837	41-29487	no	Slossie	445	701	44-40294	no
Sleepless Nights			41-29487	no	Slow Time Sally	98	345	44-48784	yes
Sleepless Nights	484	825	42-52653	no	Slugger, Jr.	467	788	41-29397	yes
Sleepout Sam	376			no	Sluggin' Sal	494	865	44-40750	yes
Sleepy	98	344	41-11761	yes	Small Change				yes
Sleepy Time Gal				yes	Small Change	489			no
Sleepy Time Gal				yes	Small Change	466	786	42-50585	no
Sleepy Time Gal				yes	Small Change II	34	391	42-50585	no
Sleepy Time Gal	389			no	Small Change III	34	391		no
Sleepy Time Gal	448			no	Small Fry	451	726	42-52429	no
Sleepy Time Gal	458			no	Smitty	11	26	42-73288	yes
Sleepy Time Gal	487			no	Smitty	34	4	42-94780	no
Sleepy Time Gal	Navy			yes	Smokey	34	18	41-28840	no
Sleepy Time Gal	22	33	44-41311	no	Smokey	459	756	42-52406	yes
Sleepy Time Gal	7	493	44-51030	yes	Smokey Joe	487		42-52620	no
Sleepy Time Gal	380	530	42-110120	yes	Smokey Stover	11	26	42-73011	yes
Sleepy Time Gal	449	718	42-7745	yes	Smooth Sailing				yes
Sleepy Time Gal	453	735	42-50426	yes	Smooth Sue	6PR	24CM	42-64168	yes
Sleepy Time Gal	464	776	42-99813	yes	Smooth Takeoff				yes
Sleepy Time Gal	484	826	42-94734	yes	Smoothie	455		42-99771	yes
Sleepy Time Gal II	449	719	42-95271	no	Snafu				yes
Sleepy Time Gal II	464	776	44-99813	yes	Snafu	93			no
Sleepytime Gal				yes	Snafu	NLS		41-24614	no
Sleepytime Gal				yes	Snafu	98	343	41-24275	yes
Sleepytime Gal			42-98007	yes	Snafu	98	345	41-24275	yes
Sleepytime Gal			44-41503	yes	Snafu	308	373	42-73246	yes
Sleepytime Gal	93	328	42-95095	no	Snafu	380	529	42-40513	yes
Sleepytime Gal	450	720	42-78211	no	Snafu	44	66	40-2354	yes
Sleepytime Gal II	449	719	42-95271	no	SNAFU	44	67	42-40354	no
Slic Chick	485	830	42-95460	no	Snafu	489	846	42-94909	no
Slick Chick				no	Snafu II	380	529	42-41120	yes
Slick Chick	376			no	Snafu Snark	466	785	41-29387	yes
Slick Chick	RCM			no	Snafuperman	490	848	42-94784	no

Name	Grp.	Sq.	Serial	Pic.	Name	Grp.	Sq.	Serial	Pic.
Snag On				yes	Sonia	448			no
Snake Eyes	98	344	44-40102	no	Sonny Boy	450	723	44-50709	no
Snake Eyes	98	345	42-40316	yes	Sooner Queen				no
Snappe	467		xx-xx394	no	Sooper Drooper	380	531	42-40515	yes
Snappin' N' A'Bitin'	90	320	41-23869	yes	Sooper Wabbit	90			no
Snappin' N' A'Bitin'	90	320	41-24045	yes	Sophisticated Lady	449	716	41-29214	yes
Snark			41-29347	yes	Sorry Bird				no
Snark (The)	308	425	42-100242	yes	Southern Belle			44-51082	no
Snatch (The)	450	722	42-78197	no	Southern Belle	460			yes
Sneezy				yes	Southern Belle	98	344	42-51989	no
Sneezy	98	343	41-23795	yes	Southern Belle				yes
Snicklefritz				no	Southern Clipper	467	788	42-50684	yes
Sniffin' Griffin	494	865	44-40705	yes	Southern Clipper	467	788	42-52546	no
Snooky	11	431	42-41257	yes	Southern Clipper II	44	506	42-40778	no
Snooper	467			no	Southern Comfort	448			no
Snooper	467		xx-xx731	no	Southern Comfort	492			no
Snooper	30	27	42-109952	yes	Southern Comfort	44	506	42-40778	yes
Snooper	467	790	42-52571	yes	Southern Comfort	392	576	42-7506	no
Snootie Cutie	801		41-29597	no	Southern Comfort	464	777	41-29441	yes
Snootie Cutie	SOP		41-29597	no	Southern Comfort II	44	506	42-110034	no
Snootie Cutie	490	848	41-29597	yes	Southern Comfort II	44	506	42-7522	yes
Snorky	380	528	42-73164	yes	Southern Comfort III			42-50895	yes
Snottie Dottie	490	851	42-94803	yes	Southern Comfort III	44	506	42-50889	no
Snow Goose	445	700	42-7520	no	Southern Cross	489			no
Snow Job	5	31	42-41230	yes	Southern Cross	467	790	42-52565	no
Snow Job II	5	31	44-40572	yes	Southern Cross Airways No. 4	SCA		FP685	no
Snow Queen	448			no	Southern Gal	465	783	42-52539	yes
Snow White				yes	Southern Lass	44			no
Snow White	15AF			yes	Southern Queen II			42-63959	yes
Snow White	98	343	41-11913	yes	Southern Queen III	389	564		no
Snow White	489	847	42-94834	yes	Southern Queen IV	389	564	42-63959	no
Snow White and the Seven Dwarfs	98	343	42-40364	yes	Southwind	93	409	42-63987	no
Snowball from Hell (The)	308	374	41-24244	yes	Spain			41-23740	no
Snuffie's Pubing Mission	484	825	44-50319	no	Spare Parts				no
Snuffy Smith	11	431	41-24148	yes	Spare Parts	308		42-40635	yes
Snuffy Smith	455	743		yes	Spare Parts	453	732	41-28654	yes
Snuffy's Delight	448			no	Spare Parts	458	753	41-28706	yes
So Round So Firm So Fu				yes	Spare Parts	466	785	41-29350	yes
So Round, So Firm So Fully Stacked	459	759	42-51701	yes	Sparky's Hot Box	491			no
So Round, So Firm, So Fully Packed	491	854	42-95123	yes	Sparky's Hot Box	464	779	44-40928	yes
So Velly Solly			41-23985	no	Special Delivery	98	343		no
So Velly Solly	307	372	41-23929	yes	Special Delivery	451	726	41-28760	no
Sod Buster (The)	451	727	41-29233	yes	Special Delivery	489	845	42-94896	yes
Solid				yes	Special Delivery II	489	844	42-94888	no
Solid Comfort	93	330	42-50501	yes	Special Mission II	451	727	41-28804	no
Solid Comfort	446	705		yes	Spike and Pickles Pub				yes
Solid John	376	514	41-24035	yes	Spirit of '44				yes
Solid Sender	487		42-52431	no	Spirit of '46	392		41-29131	no
Son of a Beach	453	732	42-52185	no	Spirit of '76				yes
Son of Satan	392	576	42-99989	no	Spirit of '76	448			no
Son of Satan II	392	577	42-52704	no	Spirit of '76	487			no
					Spirit of '76	44	68	41-23776	yes
					Spirit of '76	493	860	41-29473	no
					Spirit of '77 (The)	RCM	36	42-7607	no
					Spirit of '77 (The)	446	705	42-7607	yes
					Spirit of 77	446	705	42-7610	no

Name	Grp.	Sq.	Serial	Pic.	Name	Grp.	Sq.	Serial	Pic.
Spirit of Colley H.S.	492		42-50777	no	Star Eyes	11	431	42-109881	no
Spirit of Colley H.S.	448	713	42-50777	no	Star Eyes	11	431	42-40074	yes
Spirit of Illinois	449	716	42-51553	no	Star Eyes	449	719	41-29203	yes
Spirit of Jackson Heights				yes	Star Eyes	453	735	42-51089	yes
Spirit of Lakeland (The)	307	424	41-23945	yes	Star Spangled Hell	492		42-72873	yes
Spirit of London	RAF		44-39237	no	Star Spangled Hell	44	67	42-72873	yes
Spirit of Notre Dame	448			no	Star Spangled Hell	448	712	42-7767	yes
Spirit of Notre Dame	453	734	41-29257	yes	Star Swinger	392	578	42-51205	yes
Spirit of Notre Dame	453	734	42-95102	yes	Star Valley	44	68	42-100181	no
Spirit of Plainfield, NJ	449	719	42-51763	no	Stardust				no
Spirit of Spokane	98	415	41-28799	no	Stardust				yes
Spittin' Kitten	458	754	44-40126	no	Stardust			41-29634	no
Spittin' Kitten	492	858	44-40126	yes	Stardust	467		41-29439	no
Splash	466	785	42-52510	yes	Stardust	376	512		yes
Spook (The)	487	837	41-29553	no	Stardust	450	721	42-64455	no
Spotted Ass Ape	458	754	41-28967	yes	Stardust	453	735	42-52627	yes
Spunky Punky	456	746	42-51637	yes	Stardust	454	737	42-64495	no
Squat 'N' Droppit	458		41-28710	no	Stardust	458	754	42-50516	yes
Squat 'N' Droppit	448	712	41-28710	yes	Stardust	466	784	42-50364	no
Squat N' Drop	455	740	42-95462	no	Stardust	466	784	42-94902	no
Squaw (The)	98	344	41-11761	yes	Stardust	466	787	41-29439	no
Squaw (The)	98	344	41-23795	no	Stardust	466	787	42-50516	no
Squaw Peak	380	529	44-40801	yes	Stardust	485	831	44-50819	no
Squee-Gee	453	735	42-50379	no	Stardust II	455	792	42-50497	yes
Squee-Gee	453	735	42-95086	no	Starduster	307		41-23869	yes
Squee-Gee	489	846	42-95086	no	Starduster	90	321	41-23869	yes
Squeeze	308	374	44-42020	yes	Starduster	307	370	42-40679	no
Squeeze (not 44-42020)	308			yes	Starfu	43			no
Squirrely Shirley	5	31	42-110092	yes	Stars & Stripes	389			no
Squitch	467	788	42-52561	no	State of New York				no
St. Louis Belle	454	738	42-64392	no	Stateside Stuff	380	530	44-50997	yes
St. Louis Blues	6PR	20CM	42-64172	yes	Stateside Stuff	380	530	44-51301	yes
St. Louis Woman				yes	Stella				yes
St. Louis Woman	489			no	Sterile Errol	India			yes
St. Louis Woman	448	714	42-50459	no	Sterile Errol	93	328	42-7641	yes
St. Peter's Ferry	451	727	42-7720	no	Sterile Errol	446	707	42-7641	yes
St. Teresa of Little Flower		406		no	Stevenovich	464	779	44-49710	yes
Stalky	389			no	Stevonovich	464	776	42-51625	no
Stand-by	454	738	42-52248	no	Stew Bum	484	826	42-52602	no
Standby	389	567	42-50774	no	Stinger	389			no
Star Dust			41-29364	no	Stinger	98	415	41-11817	yes
Star Dust	30			no	Stinger?	467	788	42-52542	no
Star Dust	455		41-29267	no	Stingeroo				yes
Star Dust	445	700	42-7576	yes	Stinker	467		42-95201	no
Star Dust	446	705	42-7576	yes	Stinker	489			no
Star Dust	449	718	42-52188	yes	Stinkey	389	565	42-95088	no
Star Dust	453	733	42-51009	no	Stinky				no
Star Dust	454	737	42-78601	no	Stinky				yes
Star Dust	494	867	44-41610	yes	Stinky				yes
Star Dust II	455	743	42-52283	no	Stinky				yes
Star Duster	487		42-52769	no	Stinky	482		42-5793	no
Star Duster	455	740	42-64497	no	Stinky	389	564	42-100085	yes
Star Duster	487	837	42-52651	yes	Stinky	389	565	42-95088	no
Star Duster II	455	742	42-50497	yes	Stinky	453	733	42-110138	no
Star Eyes	22			yes	Stinky	455	742	42-78609	yes
					Stinky	458	755	42-95120	yes
					Stinky	461	764	41-29333	yes

68

Name	Grp.	Sq.	Serial	Pic.	Name	Grp.	Sq.	Serial	Pic.
Stinky	464	779		no	Su Su	489			no
Stinky	489	846	42-94864	yes	Su-Su	389			yes
Stinky	491	852	42-110138	no	Sub Depot Sue	461	767	42-64361	yes
Stinky Avenger	459	759	41-28996	no	Sub-Depot Susy	454	737	44-49392	yes
Stinky Pinky	307		41-24106	yes	Sub-Mission	480		41-24007	no
Stinky Poo	487		42-52452	no	Subconscious	392	579	41-28742	yes
Stinky Poo	451	725	42-52452	no	Subconscious II	480	2	42-40100	yes
Stinky the B.T.O.	449	716	42-64462	yes	Subdued				no
Stinky's Siren	450		42-52085	no	Subtractor				no
Stinky-The Hot Rock	459	759		no	Sugar	VPB	108		yes
Stolen Moment	453			no	Sugar	93	328		no
Stork (The)	98	345	41-11794	yes	Sugar	98	345	42-41240	no
Stork (The)	451	726	42-7687	yes	Sugar	456	745	42-51715	no
Stork Club	389		42-63967	yes	Sugar Baby			42-51091	yes
Stork Club	460	762	42-52333	no	Sugar Baby	98	345	42-41240	no
Stork Club				yes	Sugar Baby	456	746		yes
Storm Cloud	ZI			yes	Sullivan's Travellers	448			no
Stormy	445		42-50574	no	Sully's Saloon	466	786	42-52529	yes
Stormy	466	787	41-29392	no	Sultan II	464	778	42-95348	no
Stormy Weather	11		44-40556	yes	Sultan's Daughter (The)	380	531	42-73489	yes
Stormy Weather	30	38	44-40556	yes	Sultry Sue	34		42-50539	no
Stormy Weather	43	64	44-40184	yes	Sultry Sue	44	67	42-50539	yes
Straight Shot	460	761	42-52385	yes	Sunday Punch				no
Strange Cargo				no	Sunflower Sue	445	703	42-7617	no
Strange Cargo	492			no	Sunrise				no
Strange Cargo	RCM			no	Sunsetter				yes
Strange Cargo	450	720	42-51153	no	Sunsetter (The)	11	431	42-100223	yes
Strange Cargo	461	765	42-51967	yes	Sunsetter (The)	30	819	42-100223	no
Strange Cargo	484	826	42-51967	no	Sunshine	448			no
Strange Cargo II	450	720	42-51623	yes	Sunshine	380	531	42-41225	yes
Strawberry Bitch	376	512	42-72843	yes	Sunshine	389	564	41-28779	no
Strawberry Bitch	450	722	42-7753	no	Sunshine	449	719	42-52106	yes
Strawberry Blonde	376		41-11842	yes	Sunshine	453	735	42-52186	no
Strawberry Blonde	98	345	41-11842	yes	Sunshine Jane			42-94801	no
Strawberry Butch	464	776		yes	Sunshine Jane	466	787	42-52600	yes
Streamliner	5		44-40543	yes	Sunshine Rose	493		44-40323	no
Strictly Business	453			no	Sunshine Rose	34	391	44-40323	no
Strictly from Hunger	464	778	41-29412	yes	Super Baby	11	98	42-109873	yes
Strictly from Hunger	464	778	42-94785	no	Super Chick	494	865	44-40761	yes
Strictly GI	461	766	42-95287	no	Super Chief	445		42-95562	yes
String of Pearls	389	567	42-94982	no	Super Chief	446		42-95562	yes
Strip Polka (The)	90			yes	Super Moose	451	727	42-64442	no
Strip Polka (The)	90	319	42-40970	yes	Super Natural	465	781	42-52470	yes
Stripped for Action	308	425	44-42142	yes	Super Wolf	467	791	42-95080	yes
Stripped for Action	11	431	44-41501	yes	Super Wolf	492	859	44-40050	yes
Strippin' for Action	392			yes	Supercan				yes
Struggle Buggy	489	845	42-94785	yes	Superchick	484			no
Struggle Buggy	489	847	42-94836	no	Superchief (The)	VPB	106		yes
Stubby Gal	489	847	42-94836	yes	Superman	11	26	42-109938	yes
Stubby Gal II	489	846	42-94933	no	Superstitious Aloysius				no
Stubby Gal III	489	847	42-94888	no	Superstitious Aloysius	449	717	42-52136	yes
Stud Duck			44-40538	no	Superstitous Aloysius	376	512	42-73078	yes
Stud Duck (The)	6	397	42-40372	yes	Sure Shot	446			no
Stud Horse	484	825	42-52658	yes	Sure Shot!	44	66	42-63769	no
Stuggot's 1st	43	65		no	Sure Shot!	44	68		no
Stumpy Joe	461	765	44-41162	no	Sure Thing	451	727	42-51680	no
Sturgeon (The)	448	715	42-110066	yes	Surprise Attack	308	374	44-50956	yes

Name	Grp.	Sq.	Serial	Pic.	Name	Grp.	Sq.	Serial	Pic.
Surprise Attack	90			no	Sweet Chariot	450	723	42-78246	no
Susan Diane	451	727	41-29238	no	Sweet Chariot	461	766	41-28689	no
Susie	11		44-40587	yes	Sweet Chariot	492	856	44-40087	yes
Susie	307		44-40587	yes	Sweet Eloise	389		41-29511	yes
Susie's Sister	308	425	42-40407	yes	Sweet Eloise	491			no
Susie's Sister	7	9	41-23893	no	Sweet Eloise	392	578	41-29511	yes
Susu	389			yes	Sweet Eloise	44	66	41-29511	no
Susu	446	707	42-50365	yes	Sweet Gen	464			no
Suzan Jane	449	717	42-52396	yes	Sweet Ginny Lee	484	826	44-10484	yes
Suzy Q	98			no	Sweet Job	490	849	42-94927	yes
Suzy Q.	44	67	41-23774	no	Sweet Job		868	42-94927	yes
Suzy Q.	44	67	41-23817	yes	Sweet Lorraine	458	754	42-110172	yes
Swamp Angel	445		42-51480	no	Sweet Marie	Navy	106		yes
Swamp Angel	389	565	42-100352	no	Sweet Moonbeam				
Swamp Angel	455	741	44-40499	no	McSwine	446	704	42-7592	yes
Swamp Angel	455	742	44-10569	no	Sweet Mother	449	719	41-29309	yes
Swamp Rat	450	721	42-78454	yes	Sweet N Bitter				no
Swan (The)	43	63	42-40475	no	Sweet Pea	389	564	42-94822	no
Swashbuckler	450	723	42-95296	no	Sweet Racket	22	33	42-100188	yes
Sweet Marie	Navy	VB115		yes	Sweet Revenge				yes
Sweet Pea II				no	Sweet Revenge	484	827	42-52648	yes
Sweat Box				yes	Sweet Rose Marie	448			no
Sweat Box			44-50471	yes	Sweet Routine	11	26	44-40527	yes
Sweat Box	487			no	Sweet Routine	30	819	44-40527	yes
Sweat Box	93	330	44-40071	no	Sweet Sioux	34	4	42-94911	no
Sweat Box	44	66	44-40071	yes	Sweet Sioux	448	714	42-7683	yes
Sweat Box	492	857	44-40071	yes	Sweet Sioux Two	448	713	42-95013	no
Sweat Girl	93	330	42-100150	no	Sweet Sixteen	43	63	42-73394	yes
Sweat N' Duck	392	578	42-51249	yes	Sweet Sue				no
Sweat Pea	93			no	Sweet Sue	445		42-95042	no
Sweat'er Gal	492	859	44-40053	yes	Sweet Sue	453		44-10563	no
Sweat'er Out	448			no	Sweet Sue	455		42-51480	no
Sweater Gal	93	330	42-100150	yes	Sweet Sue	455		42-95042	no
Sweater Girl	448			no	Sweet Sue	460			no
Sweater Girl	466			no	Sweet Sue	445	703	42-51480	no
Sweater Girl	489			no	Sweet Sue	449	718		no
Sweatin' It Out	376	515	41-29488	no	Sweet Sue	453	735	42-50301	no
Sweatin' It Out	445	701	42-7541	no	Sweet Sue	454	736	42-78461	no
Sweatin' It Out	455	743	42-52278	no	Sweet Sue	456	745	44-10563	yes
Sweatin' It Out	487	839	41-29488	no	Sweet Thing	5	72	44-42366	yes
Sweating Betty				no	Sweetest Rose of Texas	445	701	42-51105	yes
Sweatty Betty	451	727	42-78254	yes	Sweetheart of				
Sweaty Betty	98	345	42-41026	no	Harlech (The)	34	7	42-94824	no
Swed (The)	453			no	Sweetheart of the				
Swede's John Deere	376	514	41-28624	yes	Rockies	448		44-10544	yes
Swee Pea	461	764	41-28732	yes	Sweetheart of the South	493		44-40469	no
Swee Peaz	389	565	42-95085	no	Swing Shift				no
Swee' Pea II	389			no	Swing Shift	NLS			no
Sweet & Lovely	449	716		no	Swing Shift	30	38	42-109940	yes
Sweet Adeline	389	565	41-23933	yes	Swingtime in the Rockies	486	833		no
Sweet and Lovely	389			no	Swingtime in the Rockies	486	835	42-52681	yes
Sweet and Lovely	449	716		no	Swingtime in the Rockies	486	835	42-52758	no
Sweet and Lowdown	389	567	42-100428	no	Swiss Itch	459		41-29316	yes
Sweet Cecilia	28	404	44-49483	yes	Swivel Chair	490	850	42-94843	no
Sweet Chariot	389		44-40087	no	T S	6PR	20CM	42-64051	yes
Sweet Chariot	93	330	42-50829	no	T'ings Is Tough	451	727	41-28931	yes
Sweet Chariot	392	579	42-100261	yes	T-Bar				no

Name	Grp.	Sq.	Serial	Pic.	Name	Grp.	Sq.	Serial	Pic.
T. N. Toni	34		42-94790	no	Tally Ho	491	854	42-110165	yes
T. S. Boys	389	566	42-73856	yes	Taloa	494	866	44-40716	yes
T. S. Express	460			yes	Tamerlane	459	757	42-52328	no
T. S. Tessie	44	68	42-95001	no	Tangerine				yes
T. S. the Chaplain	451	726	41-28860	no	Tangerine	448			no
Table Stuff	AZON		44-40285	no	Tangerine	98	345	42-64344	no
Table Stuff	458	753	44-40285	yes	Tangerine	376	513	41-11916	yes
Table Stuff	464	779	42-52463	yes	Tangerine	467	790	41-29446	yes
Table Stuff	465	783	41-29360	no	Tanta Lisa	450	722	41-29281	no
Tabu	22			yes	Tanta Lisa	450	722	42-7740	no
Taffy	448			no	Tantalizing Tillie				no
Taffy II	448			no	Tar Baby				yes
Tagalong	98	344	41-24197	yes	Tar Baby	RCM	36	42-51311	no
Tahelenbak	489			no	Tar Heel Baby	392	577	41-29125	yes
Tahelenbak	445	701	42-94921	yes	Tar Heel Baby	446	707	41-29125	yes
Tail Chaser	VPB	121	Bu59491	yes	Tarbaby	448			yes
Tail Dragon	484		42-94732	yes	Tarfu				yes
Tail Dragon	461	767	42-94732	yes	Tarfu	489			no
Tail End Charley	445	702	42-7554	no	Tarfu	Navy			yes
Tail End Charlie	466			yes	Tarfu	11	26	42-109933	yes
Tail End Charlie	30	27	42-109935	yes	Tarfu	93	329	41-23810	no
Tail Heavy	7		42-40xxx	no	Tarfu	448	713	42-99993	yes
Tail Heavy	308	373	41-24125	yes	Tarfu	449	719	42-72165	yes
Tail Heavy	448	715	42-52608	yes	Tarfu II	93			no
Tail Skid Tolly	43			no	Tarfu II	448	714	42-100425	yes
Tail Wind	6AF			yes	Target for Tonight	460		44-48977	yes
Tail Wind	98	344		no	Target for Tonight	43	65	42-41060	yes
Tail Wind	11	431	42-73155	no	Target for Tonite	NLS		41-24615	no
Tail Wind	392	577	42-50792	no	Target for Tonite	464	777	41-28748	yes
Tail Wind	446	707	41-29550	yes	Tarheel baby	446	707	41-29125	yes
Tail Wind		868	44-40467	yes	Taurus	486	834		yes
Tail Wind	22			yes	Taurus	11	98	42-109846	yes
Tailenders	484	824	41-29539	yes	Taylor Maid	308	374	42-73326	yes
Tailwind				yes	Taylor Maid II	308	374	44-41294	no
Tailwind	449			yes	Team GO	93	328	41-29437	no
Tailwind	454			yes	Tear Ass	90	400	44-40720	no
Tailwind	22	33	41-28762	yes	Tear-Ass the Bull	90	321	41-23720	yes
Tailwind	22	33	42-100210	yes	Teaser	489	845	42-95249	no
Tailwind	98	343	42-64346	yes	Teasin' but Pleasin'	459	758	41-28727	yes
Tailwind	11	431	41-24155	yes	Teepee Time Gal	449			no
Tailwind	455	741	42-64456	no	Teepee Time Gal	454	737	42-95380	no
Tailwind	458	755	41-29359	yes	Teepee Time Gal	455	743		yes
Tailwind	467	789	41-29368	yes	Teggie Ann	98		41-23754	no
Tailwind	487	859	41-29481	no	Teggie Ann	93	409	41-23754	yes
Tailwind II	22	33	44-41652	no	Teggie Ann	376	515	42-40664	yes
Tailwind II	467	789	42-50792	no	Teggie Ann II	93	409	41-23999	no
Tailwind II	485	829	42-78416	no	Tell Me More	466	787	41-28754	no
Tain't What You Do...				yes	Temperamental Duchess	392		42-6982	yes
Takeoff	11	42	41-24149	yes	Temperamental Lady	22	408	42-100174	yes
Takeoff Time	98	344	42-51146	yes	Temptacious	11		44-51515	yes
Takeoff Time	450	723	42-7710	no	Temptation	11		44-40617	yes
Takin' Off	15AF			yes	Temptation	308	373	41-24129	yes
Tale of Misfortune	7		44-40991	yes	Temptation	308	373	44-40617	yes
Talisman	43			no	Temptation	446	705	42-50477	no
Tall, Torrid & Texas	459	757	44-50418	yes	Temptation	30	819	44-40617	yes
Tally Ho			42-110173	no	Temptress (The)	449	717	42-52107	yes
Tally Ho	44	66	44-10542	no					

Name	Grp.	Sq.	Serial	Pic.	Name	Grp.	Sq.	Serial	Pic.
Ten Aces with a Queen	445			no	Texas Termite				yes
Ten Fighting Cocks	450	720	42-52119	yes	Texas Termite	494			yes
Ten Gun Dottie	445	700	42-50620	yes	Texas Terror	90	400	41-23825	no
Ten Hi	5	31	42-73470	yes	Texas Twister				no
Ten Hi Hit Parade	389		42-95570	no	Thai Times				yes
Ten High	493		42-50292	no	Thanks A Lot	448			no
Ten High	380	530	44-42405	no	Thar She Blows	448			no
Ten High	380	530	44-50405	no	Thar She Blows	93	329	41-23658	yes
Ten High	389	564	42-40665	yes	Thar She Blows	93	329	42-40127	yes
Ten High	490	849	42-50292	no	Thar She Blows	458	754	42-40127	no
Ten Hits & A Miss	455	741	42-78359	yes	Thar She Blows II	30	392	42-109870	yes
Ten Hits & A Miss	459	758	42-78160	yes	Thar She Blows II	11	42	42-109870	yes
Ten Hits and a Miss	464			yes	Thar She Blows III	11	42	44-40168	yes
Ten Knights in a					Thar She Blows III	492	857	44-40168	yes
Bar Room	90	321	42-72806	yes	That Red Headed Gal	466	784	42-95569	yes
Ten to the Bar	376	513		yes	That's All Brother	467		44-40120	no
Ten-O-K				no	That's All Brother	492	859	44-40120	yes
Ten-O-K II				no	That's Jayhawker	458	752	41-28667	no
Tender Comrade	467	791	41-29369	no	That's Us	464	778	42-52522	yes
Tender Foot	491	853	44-40243	yes	These Guns for Hire	30	819	42-73494	no
Tennessee Belle	308		42-100036	no	Things Is Rough	449	717	42-52091	yes
Tennessee Belle	308		42-109807	yes	Thirty Day Furlough	448	713	42-52123	yes
Tennessee Dottie	445	703	41-28652	yes	Thirty Day Leave	448	713	42-51123	yes
Tennessee Maid	308		42-100036	no	This Above All	5	23	44-41622	yes
Tennessee Rambler	93			no	This Above All	34	391	44-40328	yes
Tennessee					This Above All		4PCS	44-40316	yes
Squirrel Hunter	380	531	42-73201	no	This Above All	466	786	44-40328	yes
Tennessee					This Above All	487		44-40328	yes
Squirrel Hunter	380	531	42-73324	yes	This Above All	493		44-40328	yes
Tenofus	467	789	42-50309	no	This Heart of Mine	30	27		no
Tenovus	445	703	41-29132	no	This Is It Men/				
Tepee Time Gal	449			yes	Bama Bound-				
Tepee Time Gal	455	741	42-94790	yes	Lovely Libba		36	42-50622	no
Tequila Daisy	492	857	44-40168	yes	This Is It!				no
Termite Chaser #1	450	722	42-52141	no	This Is It!	466	785	42-50364	yes
Terri Ann	392	577	42-94898	no	This Is It!	466		44-40328	yes
Terri Ann	489	845	42-94898	yes	This Is It, Men!	RCM	36	42-50622	no
Terrible Terry	454	739	42-95522	no	This Love of Mine	460	760	42-78071	yes
Terrible Terry's Terror	445	700	42-94810	yes	Three (III) Special	467	788	42-94986	no
Terry & the Pirates	466	786	41-29434	no	Three Cornered Kid (A)	464	776		no
Terry & the Pirates	466	786	42-50438	no	Three Dreams				
Terry the Third Cossack	376	512	42-99760	yes	and a Drink				yes
Texan	44	506	41-23787	no	Three Feathers	451	726	42-7636	yes
Texan	44	67	41-23808	no	Three Kisses for Luck	44	67	42-95193	no
Texan II	44	67	41-23818	yes	Throbbing Monster	466	786	42-52570	no
Texarkana Hussy	459			yes	Thumbs Up	448			no
Texas Hellcat	454	738	42-50312	no	Thump Time	308			no
Texas II	44	506	41-24013	no	Thumper	307		42-40073	yes
Texas II	44	506	42-41013	no	Thumper	460			yes
Texas Kate	11		44-40358	yes	Thumper	490			no
Texas Kate	30	392	44-40358	yes	Thumper	5	31	42-41220	no
Texas Lassie II	459	756	42-52373	no	Thumper	308	375	41-24287	yes
Texas Ranger	456			no	Thumper	5	394	42-73220	yes
Texas Refugees	392	576	42-100102	no	Thumper	11	42	42-40073	yes
Texas Rose	445	701	41-28922	no	Thumper	445	703	42-95291	no
Texas Rose	487	839	41-29554	no	Thumper II				yes
Texas Star	485	828	41-29477	no	Thumper II	11			no

Name	Grp.	Sq.	Serial	Pic.	Name	Grp.	Sq.	Serial	Pic.
Thumper II	460			yes	Toddlin' Trollop	451	724	42-78445	yes
Thumper II	490	848	42-94848	no	Toddy	380	531	42-100226	yes
Thunder Bay Babe	449	717	42-7623	yes	Toggle Annie	464		42-52357	yes
Thunder Bird				yes	Toggle Annie	484	826	42-52357	yes
Thunder Mist	454	739	41-28927	no	Tojo				no
Thunder Mist	454	739	44-41165	no	Tokio Express	90	319	41-24074	yes
Thunder Mug	VB	109	Bu32108	no	Tolly	5		42-41189	no
Thunderbird	307			no	Tommy Thumper	467	788	42-94811	no
Thunderbird	93	329	41-23658	no	Tommy Thumper	486	833	41-28838	no
Thunderbird	308	373	41-24166	no	Tommy Thumper II	34	4	41-28838	no
Thunderbird	93	409	41-28626	no	Tommy Thumper II	34	4	42-94811	no
Thunderbird	98	415	41-23789	yes	Tondelayo	34			no
Thunderbird	491	852	44-40238	yes	Tondelayo	460			yes
Thunderbird II	308	375	42-41142	no	Tondelayo	493			no
Thundermug	446			no	Tondelayo	SOP			no
Thundermug	VB	108		yes	Tondelayo	30	27	42-73289	yes
Thundermug	98	328	42-40246	yes	Tondelayo	389	566	42-40706	yes
Thundermug	308	373	42-40621	no	Tondelayo	392	577	42-50343	no
Thundermug	451	726	42-7475	no	Tondelayo	448	713	41-28240	no
Thundermug	454	739	44-41165	yes	Tong Hoy	450	723	41-29345	no
Thundermug	461	765	42-51474	no	Toni-7				yes
Thundermug	467	789	41-28750	yes	Too Tired	445	702	42-7517	no
Thundermug No. 2	456	745	42-64475	yes	Too-Hot-To-Handle	459	756	42-52307	no
Thuper Wabbit				yes	Toonerville Trolley	389			yes
Tidewater Tillie	480		42-40334	yes	Toonerville Trolley	98			yes
Tiger			42-51100	no	Toonerville Trolley	453	733		no
Tiger Bell				no	Toonerville Trolley (The)	464	776		no
Tiger Lady	6	397	AL641	yes	Top O' the Mark	5	23	44-42245	yes
Tiger Lil	480	1	41-24261	yes	Top O' the Mark	458	752	42-95110	yes
Tiger Rag	34	7	42-94908	yes	Top Pull	RCAF			yes
Tiger's Revenge	482	814	42-7646	no	Topper	389			no
Tiger's Revenge	486	832		no	Topper	467	791	42-52303	no
Tiger's Revenge	489	846	42-94816	yes	Topper (The)	307	371	41-23910	yes
Tiger's Revenge	492	858	42-94816	no	Torchy Lena	Navy			yes
Tigers Teeth	449			no	Toretto Taxi	484		44-41110	no
Til Then	494	866	44-40731	yes	Tornado Buster	307		42-40638	yes
Tillie	307	370	41-23915	no	Torney	44	506	42-72833	no
Tim-ber	5			yes	Torney	389	567	42-72833	no
Timb - A - Ah	44	506	42-40606	yes	Tortilla Flat	VPB	197	Bu59398	yes
Time Wounds					Totem Pole	459	756		yes
All Heels				yes	Touch Me Not	449	719	42-78510	yes
Time's A Wastin'	446		42-50569	no	Touch of Texas	389	567	42-40751	yes
Time's A Wastin'	448			no	Touch of Venus	44	67	42-7545	no
Time's A Wastin'	93			no	Tough Boy	28	404	41-23891	yes
Time's A Wastin'	30	27	44-40614	yes	Tough Ship	450	721	41-29244	no
Time's A Wastin'	458	753	42-110163	no	Tough Titti	308		44-40296	yes
Time's A Wastin'	491	855	44-40234	yes	Tough Titti	308	375	44-40898	no
Tinker Belle	44	506	44-40158	yes	Tough Titty	448			no
Tinker Belle	492	857	44-40158	yes	Toughy	380	529	42-40525	yes
Tiny Mac	494	866	44-40672	yes	Toughy	43	64	42-40525	no
Tired Tessie	11	431	42-73155	yes	Tovarich	392			no
TNT	454	736	44-41059	no	Town Hall	HALP		41-11622	yes
To Hell N' Back	448			no	Townsend's Terrible Ten	44	68	42-109822	no
Tobacco Rhoda	376		41-29556	yes	Trade Winds	487			yes
Tobapnwib	392			no	Trader Horn	RAF			yes
Tobasco Keeds				no	Trader Horn	SCA		AL611	yes
Tobias the Terrible	376	515	42-78078	yes	Trail Blazer (The)	11	98	42-72960	yes

Name	Grp.	Sq.	Serial	Pic.	Name	Grp.	Sq.	Serial	Pic.
Travelling Trollop	389	567	42-40784	no	Twang	491			no
Travlin' Bag (The)	458	753	42-50912	yes	Twecherous Wabbit (The)	487		42-52652	yes
Tricky Micky	11	98	44-50960	yes	Twentieth Century Wolf	486	835	42-52483	no
Trips Daily	392	577	42-95012	yes	Twin Nifties	90	400	42-40348	yes
Troop Sleeper	449	716	41-29512	no	Twin Nifties II				yes
Tropic Knight	11			no	Twin Nifties II	90	400	42-40928	yes
Tropic Knight	30	27	42-73151	yes	Twin Tail				yes
Tropic Knight II	11			yes	Twin Tails	448	715	42-100122	no
Tropical Dream	494			no	Twin Tails	450	723	41-28579	no
Tropical Dream	11	98	42-100218	yes	Twin Tails	455	742	42-52259	no
Tropical Trick	90		42-40060	no	Twinkletoes	449	719	42-95314	yes
Tropical Trollop				no	Twitchy Bitch	VPB	118	Bu59430	yes
Tropical Trollop	11		42-100405	yes	Two (2) Down, 1 to Go	93			yes
Tropical Trollop	30	392	42-100405	yes	Two Bob Tillie	90	320		no
Trouble				yes	Two Bob Tillie	43	65	42-41215	yes
Trouble	44	506	41-24013	yes	Two Bob Tillie	43	65	42-73952	no
Trouble Maker	5	394		yes	Two Gun Flossie	445	701	42-64436	no
Trouble Maker	466	787	42-95067	yes	Two Pair				yes
Trouble Maker	484	827	42-52667	yes	Two Time	307		44-40546	yes
Trouble Maker				yes	Two Ton Tessie	449	717	42-52117	yes
Trouble N' Mind	448		44-50519	no	Two-Time	5		44-40546	yes
Trouble N' Mind	389	566	42-41013	no	Typhoon				yes
Trouble N' Mind	448	713	42-95298	no	Tyrranosaurus Rex	90	400	42-40363	yes
Troublesome Twins	493		42-94743	no	U Name It	93			no
Troublesome Twins	490	851	42-94743	no	U Name It Peg	93	329	41-23658	yes
Truculent Turtle	449	717		no	U Name It, We'll Fly It				yes
True Love		55W	44-49502	yes	U Need It	93			no
True Love	466	786	41-29449	yes	U.S. Express	93	329	41-23674	no
Trula Marie				yes	U.S.A.F.I.				yes
TS	465	783	42-52478	no	Ubangi Bag	308	374	41-24194	yes
TS	446			no	Ubangi Bag II	308	374	42-41168	yes
TS-Chaplain (The)	484	824	41-28860	no	Ubangi Bag III	308	374	42-73436	yes
Tu-Yung-Tu	98	415	44-10546	no	Ubangi Webangi	308			yes
Tubarao	491	854	44-40101	yes	Ugly But Tough	98	345	44-48784	yes
Tuff Nut Tessie	454	738	41-29426	no	Ugly Duckling (The)	464	716	42-524xx	yes
Tuff Ship				yes	Umbriago				yes
Tuffy	44	67	42-100279	no	Umbriago	11		44-40327	yes
Tuffy (Hairless Joe)	11	98	42-41136	no	Umbriago	34		42-94824	no
Tug				no	Umbriago	446		42-50280	no
Tulsa Joe				yes	Umbriago	448			yes
Tulsa-American (The)	461	765	42-51430	no	Umbriago	Navy		Bu59390	yes
Tung Hoi	389		44-40230	no	Umbriago	30	392	44-40327	yes
Tung Hoi	491	852	44-40230	yes	Umbriago	392	579	42-51126	yes
Tung Hoi II	44	66	42-95622	yes	Umbriago	34	7	41-28880	no
Tung Hoi II	491	852	42-95622	yes	Umbriago	446	705	42-50330	no
Tung Hoy	450	723	41-29345	yes	Umbriago	449	717	41-28902	yes
Tupelo Lass	93	409	41-24105	yes	Umbriago	449	719	41-28902	yes
Turbo-Culosis	455	743	41-28879	no	Umbriago	465	783	41-29377	yes
Turd Bird	445	703	42-7565	no	Umbriago	467	788	44-40068	no
Turd Bird	454	739	42-52197	no	Umbriago	492	859	44-40068	yes
Turgo Joe	34		44-40303	no	Umbriago II	392	578	42-50337	no
Turgo Joe	493		44-40303	no	Un-Decided	380	530	42-109986	yes
Turnip Termite	392	578	42-7624	no	Un-Invited (The)	34		42-94762	yes
Turnip Termite	44	68	41-29418	no	Unapproachable	Navy	VB106		yes
Turnip Termite	486	832	41-29418	no	Unapproachable	5		44-40548	yes
Turnip Termite II	44	68	42-7624	no	Unapproachable	11	98	44-40551	no
Tuttle Money	90	400	42-40968	no	Uncle Jim		3	44-41315	yes

Name	Grp.	Sq.	Serial	Pic.	Name	Grp.	Sq.	Serial	Pic.
Uncle Sam	43	64	42-72811	yes	V for Victory	44	68	42-100412	no
Uncle's Fury	43		42-40854	no	V Grand	465	783	44-41064	yes
Uncle's Fury		868		no	V Packett	44	68	41-29156	yes
Unconditional Surrender	491	855	42-110146	yes	V-Sure Pop	90	319	42-41073	yes
Undecided	34		42-94748	no	V8			44-51251	yes
Undecided	380	530	42-109986	yes	Va-on	11			no
Undecided	380	531	42-73333	yes	Vadie Raye	448	713	42-73497	yes
Under Exposed	6PR	20CM	42-73052	yes	Vagabond King	389	565	42-40787	yes
Unexpected I	93			no	Valhalla	11	26	41-24168	no
Unexpected II	93			no	Valiant Lady	44		42-41012	no
Unexpected III	93			no	Valiant Lady	467	790	41-29408	no
Unexpected IV	93			no	Valiant Lady II	44		42-7514	no
Unexpected V	93			no	Valiant Virgin-ia	449	716	41-29460	yes
Unexpected VI	93	329		yes	Valiant Virgin-ia	449	716	42-78158	yes
Unfinished Business	459	757	42-52046	yes	Valient Virgin	93	329	42-40765	yes
Unholy Kitten	22	33	44-41031	no	Valkyrie	453	734	42-52176	no
Unholy Virgin	489			yes	Vampin' Vera			41-29301	no
Unholy Virgin	448	712	42-95544	no	Vampin' Vera	453	733	42-52176	yes
Uninvited		36	42-51239	no	Vampin' Vera	458	752	41-29302	no
Uninvited	RCM	36	42-51239	no	Varga Belle	801	859	42-95262	no
Uninvited	491	853	44-40124	no	Varga Girl	445		42-52662	no
Uninvited	11	98	44-40360	yes	Varga Girl	480		41-24196	no
Uninvited (The)	464	776		no	Varga Girl	487		42-52662	no
Uninvited (The)	484	827	42-52683	yes	Varga Virgin	480	2	41-24196	yes
Uninvited (The)	11	98	44-40360	yes	Velma				yes
Union Jack				no	Veni, Vidi, Vici	449	718	42-52150	yes
United...In God					Vera 1	30	27		yes
We Trust	491			no	Vibratin' Virgin	307	372	41-24212	yes
Unlimited (The)	34	4	41-29464	no	Vicious Virgin	448			no
Unlimited (The)	491	853	41-29464	no	Vicious Virgin	484	826	42-52715	no
Unstable Mable	389	564	42-63957	no	Vicious Virgin	484	826	42-94746	yes
Untimely Visitor	5		44-40586	yes	Vicious Vixen	454	738	41-29263	no
Up In Arms	486		42-52621	no	Victor	464	779	42-78434	no
Up In Arms	467	791	42-50621	no	Victoria Vixen	454	737	42-52171	no
Up Late				no	Victory	484	825	42-52715	no
Updraft	5	72	44-40620	yes	Victory Belle	93	328	42-100294	yes
Upshaw the Aught	308	425	41-24265	yes	Victory Gal	464	778		yes
Upstairs Maid	11			no	Victory Ship	389		41-23813	no
Upstairs Maid	15AF			yes	Victory Ship	44	68	41-23813	yes
Upstairs Maid	90		42-73941	no	Viking Maiden	28	404	41-11783	no
Upstairs Maid	461	765	42-52371	yes	Vinegar Joe				yes
Upstairs Maid	30	819	42-109941	yes	Virago (The)	5	72		no
Upsy	98	343		yes	Virgin	90	319		no
Urge Me	VB	109		yes	Virgin Abroad	380	529	44-50941	yes
Urgent Virgin	451	726		yes	Virgin Annie	459		41-28659	no
Urgent Virgin	461	766	42-78446	no	Virgin Annie	454	738	41-28659	no
Urgin' Virgin				yes	Virgin II	90	319	41-23833	yes
Urgin' Virgin			42-40608	yes	Virgin on the Verge				yes
Urgin' Virgin	448			no	Virgin Sturgeon	448			no
Urgin' Virgin	489			no	Virgin Sturgeon	454	736	42-52254	no
Urgin' Virgin	98	345	42-41010	no	Virgin Sturgeon	466	784	42-52516	no
Urgin' Virgin (The)	93	328	42-41004	yes	Virgin Vampire	449			no
US Express (The)				yes	Virgin Vampire	487	839	42-52745	yes
USA Boomerang	308			yes	Virgin Wolf	456	746	42-52227	no
USAFI				yes	Virgin's Vampire				no
Utah Man	93	330	41-24226	yes	Virginia	489			no
V for Victory	392	577	42-50813	no	Virginia Belle	11	42	42-40645	yes

Name	Grp.	Sq.	Serial	Pic.	Name	Grp.	Sq.	Serial	Pic.
Virginia Lee	485			no	War Champ	389	567	42-94951	yes
Virginia Princess (The)	455	742		no	War Champ	466	784	42-94915	no
Virgo	486	834	42-52508	no	War Cloud	98	345	41-23785	yes
Virgo	486	834	42-52532	yes	War Eagle	34	4	41-29566	no
Vitamin P	376			yes	War Eagle	461	764	41-28693	yes
Vivacious Lady	484	826	42-94741	yes	War Goddess	93	409	42-109816	yes
Vivian	389		42-95063	no	War Goddess	446	706	42-100306	yes
Vivie	376	513	41-28965	yes	War Maid	376	512	42-40658	no
Vulgar Virgin	93	328	41-24192	no	War Weary	5	31	44-41667	yes
Vulgar Virgin	93	328	42-40608	no	War Weary	484	827	42-95360	yes
Vulgar Virgin	98	344	41-24198	yes	War Weary Wanda	454	736	42-52229	no
Vulgar Virgin (The)	376		41-24198	yes	Warbird	11		42-100406	yes
Vulnerable Virgin	11	26		yes	Warbird	30	819	42-100406	no
Vulture (The)				yes	Warm Front		55W	44-49524	yes
Vulture (The)				yes	Warrior Maiden	454	738	41-29304	yes
W.R.F.T.F.	11	431	44-40662	yes	Wash's Tub	376	514	41-11636	yes
Wa-Hoo	454	739	44-41074	no	Wasp's Nest (The)	44	67	42-109820	no
Wabash Cannonball	448			no	Watch the Fords Go By	446	704	42-7574	no
Wabash Cannonball	492		42-50313	no	Water Wagon	448			no
Wabash Cannonball	392	578	42-50313	yes	Watta Crok	455			no
Wabbit	467	789	42-52663	yes	Wazzle Dazzle	448	715	42-50767	yes
Wabbit	467	789	42-62663	no	We Dood It	448			no
Wabbit Twacks	448			no	We Go	453	731		no
Wabbit Twacks	VPB	108		no	We Go II	453	731	xx-xx243	no
Wabbit Twacks	458	753	41-29276	yes	We The People				yes
Wabbit Twansit	11	431	42-73006	yes	We'll Get By			44-40118	no
Wac's Delight	11	26	44-40734	yes	We'll Get By	467		42-50697	no
Wacky Donald	445	700	42-7567	no	We'll Get By	392	577	42-50697	yes
Wacky Wabbit				yes	Weary	44	66	42-95189	no
Waco Wench	451	727	42-51680	no	Weary Willie	376		42-99816	yes
Waddlin' Warrior	459	756		yes	Weary Willie	34	4	42-94755	no
Waddy's Wagon				yes	Weary Willie	449	718	42-99816	yes
Wagon	448			no	Weary Willie	451	727	42-99816	yes
Wahoo	98	345	41-11774	no	Weary Willie	484	825	42-94755	no
Wait for Me, Mary	456	744	42-52290	no	Weary Wolf (The)			41-29478	no
Wajid Trouble				yes	Weary Wolf II (The)				yes
Wake Island	11	26	41-23829	yes	Weary Wolfe (The)	487	837	42-52656	yes
Wake Island	307	371	41-23829	yes	Weather Witch		55W	44-49506	yes
Wake Island Sleeper (The)	11	26	41-24254	yes	Weather Witch II		55W	44-49522	yes
Walden Belle				yes	Weaver's Beavers				yes
Wallet A-Abel	445			no	Wedding Belle	446	704	42-95178	yes
Wallowing Wilbert	467	791	41-29421	yes	Wee Willie	28	21		yes
Wana	44	68	42-50509	yes	Wee Willie	93	409	44-50600	no
Wanda Jo	5		42-110135	no	Wee Willie	446	707	42-7583	no
Wanda Lust	446	705		no	Wee Willie	451	725	42-52167	yes
Wandering Wanda	453	735	42-95214	yes	Weesie	451	727	44-41056	yes
Wandering Witch	RAF	355		yes	Weezie	90	320	42-41081	no
Wangering Winds	453	735		no	Weight Ship	389			yes
Wango Wango Bird (The)	6PR	20CM	42-64048	yes	Weiser Witch	446	707	42-95324	yes
					Well Developed	494			no
Want-A-Play?	449	717		yes	Well Developed	11	431	44-40209	yes
Wapello Belle				yes	Well Developed		4PCS	44-40209	yes
War Baby	93	328	42-40128	yes	Wells Cargo	450	723	42-52143	yes
War Bird	30	819	42-100406	yes	Wells Fargo	446	707	42-50365	yes
War Bride	453	734	42-52196	no	Wench (The)	376	515	42-78387	yes
War Bride	489	847	42-94924	yes	Wench (The)	454	737	42-78387	yes
					Wendy	44	506	42-110082	no

Name	Grp.	Sq.	Serial	Pic.	Name	Grp.	Sq.	Serial	Pic.
Werewolf	446	705	42-7572	yes	Who Dare?	98	415	44-40847	no
Wet Dream	451	726	42-51300	yes	Who Dare?	98	415	44-41047	no
Whadahell!	307		42-73144	yes	Who Dat?	307	372	44-41700	yes
Whaler (The)				no	Who Nose	459		41-28699	no
Wham Bam	389		41-23738	no	Who Nose	454	739	41-28699	no
Wham Bam	93	330	41-23738	yes	Who's Next	43	63	42-41049	no
Wham Bam	453	735	41-23738	yes	Whoda Thunkit	98			yes
Wham Bam,					Whodunit 2nd (The)	307			yes
Thank You, Maam	491	854	42-110107	yes	Why Bother	459	759		no
What A Cookie	448			no	Why Daddy?				no
What A Sack	93	409		no	Why Worry?	490	850	41-29568	no
What Da Hell	448	715	44-50846	yes	Wicked Wench (The)	307	372	42-73258	yes
What Da Hell	453	733	41-28591	no	Wicked Wicket	392			no
What Next?	461	765	42-51783	yes	Wicked Wicket II	392			no
What's Cookin'				yes	Wicked Widget	389			no
What's Cookin' Doc?			42-110102	yes	Wicked Widget II	389			no
What's Cookin' Doc?	98	344	41-24040	yes	Wicked Widget III			42-109792	no
What's Cookin' Doc?	389	567	42-99977	no	Wicked Witch	11	42	42-40688	yes
What's Cookin' Doc?	455	742		no	Wicked Witch	44	506	41-24295	no
What's Cookin' Doc?	466	786	42-110157	yes	Wicked Witch	44	506	41-29862	no
What's Cookin' Doc?	491	855	42-110157	yes	Wickie (The)	459	759	42-78207	yes
What's Next Doc?	492	857	44-40167	yes	Widdle Wed Rabbit	376	515	41-24200	no
What's Next?	461	765	42-51783	yes	Wilco	90	319	41-23773	yes
What's Up Doc	492	857	44-40167	no	Wild Ass Ride	11		xx-xx615	yes
What's Up Doc?				yes	Wild Ass Ride	30	38	44-41615	yes
What's Up Doc?	392		44-40137	no	Wild Bill				no
What's Up Doc?	459	757	41-29457	yes	Wild Cherry II	Navy			yes
What's Up Doc?	465	781		no	Wild Hare (The)	493		42-52695	yes
What's Up Doc?	492	858	44-40167	no	Wild Hare (The)	392	579	44-49454	no
What's Up, Doc?	484	825	42-78351	no	Wild Honey	449	717	42-52208	yes
Whatzit?	490	851	42-94912	no	Wild Oats	376	514	42-78190	yes
Whee				yes	Wild Princess	466	786	42-52529	no
Wheel N' Deal	464	778	42-95364	yes	Wild Pussy	466	786	42-52529	yes
Wheels of Justice				no	Wild Wolf (The)	376	513	42-40209	yes
Whirling Dervish	464		41-28741	yes	Will Rogers Special	450	723	42-78593	no
Whiskers	392	579	42-7477	no	Willer Run?	445	702	42-7526	no
Whiskers	392	579	42-7481	no	Willet Run?	392			no
Whiskey Jim	465	780		no	Willie	464		42-78473	no
Whiskey Jingles	453	733	42-51114	yes	Willie Joe	454	738	42-50987	no
Whiskey Kid	450	723	42-52163	no	Willie Maker	308		44-40774	yes
Whiskey Straight	464			yes	Willie the Wolf	454	737	42-51417	no
Whistle Stop	43	403	42-41060	no	Willie Wolves Den	307	371	42-73146	yes
Whistlin' Shithouse	28	404	44-49474	yes	Willie's Folly				yes
Whistling Annie	451	724	44-49747	no	Willie's Sillies	448			no
White Angel(C-109)				yes	Willie's Wild Cat II	VPB	116		yes
White Duck	466	785	42-52574	no	Willie's Worry	93	328	42-100428	yes
White Elephant (The)	466	784	44-49626	yes	Willy	464	777	42-51903	no
White Fang	449	718	41-28606	no	Wilson	34	7	42-52738	no
White H	98	345	42-51910	no	Wimpy's Queen	392	577	42-50901	yes
White J	464	778	42-78682	no	Win With Page				no
White Lit'nin'	446	705	42-95058	yes	Win, Our Little Lady	389	565	42-95088	no
White Mike	460			no	Wind Haven			42-51903	no
White Savage	479		42-40921	yes	Wind Haven	445		42-94853	no
White Savage	482	814	42-40921	yes	Wind Haven	SOP		42-94853	no
White U.	465	782	44-49085	no	Wind Haven	490	849	42-94853	no
White X	465	782		no	Windhaven	448			no
Whitsshits	VB	104	Bu32081	yes	Windy City	451	724	42-7757	no

Name	Grp.	Sq.	Serial	Pic.	Name	Grp.	Sq.	Serial	Pic.
Windy City #2	451	724	42-52378	no	Wolf Wagon 2	456	745	42-99749	yes
Windy City Belle	392	578	42-51240	yes	Wolf Wagon II	451	724	41-28950	no
Windy City II	461	767	42-52378	no	Wolf's Gang	454	737	42-52264	no
Windy City Kitty	90			yes	Wolf's Lair	458	755	44-40470	yes
Windy City Kitty	43	64		yes	Wolfe Pack	307	371	41-24268	yes
Windy Clipper	455	742		no	Wolfe Pack	448	712	42-51221	yes
Windy Clipper	456	746		no	Wolfel Bear	486	833	xx-xx908	no
Windy Winnie	448		44-10599	no	Wolfgang				no
Windy Winnie	448	712	42-50676	no	Wolfgang	458	755	42-52423	yes
Wine, Women & Song	449	718		no	Wolves Lair	458	755	41-29352	yes
Wing and a Prayer	44	68	41-24211	no	Wolves, Inc.	458		41-28981	no
Wing Dinger	44	66	41-24015	no	Wolves, Inc.	467	791	41-28981	yes
Wing Man				no	Won Long Hop	493	861	44-40460	no
Winged Fury				yes	Wonder Gal	43	63	44-40942	yes
Winged Victory	454	739	42-52300	yes	Wondrous Wanda	11		44-40562	yes
Winged Victory	466	784	42-50765	yes	Wondrous Wanda	30	819	44-40562	yes
Winged Victory				yes	Wongo Wongo	376	512	42-40563	yes
Winged Virgin	486	834		no	Woodcutter	RCAF			yes
Wingless Witch	30	392	42-72990	no	Woods Chopper	449	718	42-7750	yes
Winnie	486	834		no	Woody Woodpecker	11		44-41179	yes
Winnie the Pooh	34		42-94771	no	Woody Woodpecker	307	424	44-41179	yes
Winona Belle	485	828	42-50827	no	Workin' for the				
Wise Virgin (The)	449	716	41-28616	yes	Yankee Dollar	491	852	42-51113	yes
Wise Virgin II (The)	449	716	41-29274	yes	Worry Bird	458		44-40470	no
Wishbone	490	850	41-29594	no	Worry Bird	487			no
Wishbone	490	850	42-94797	no	Worry Bird	493		44-40470	no
Wishful Thinking	11			yes	Worry Bird	RCM			no
Wishful Thinking	5			yes	Worry Bird	449	719	42-78173	yes
Wishing Jingles	453			no	Worry Bird	456	745	42-51293	no
Wiskey Jingles	453	735	42-51114	yes	Worry Bird	458	755	42-7516	no
Wistful Vista	446	706	44-40104	yes	Worry Bird (The)				no
Witch (The)				yes	Worry Bird (The)	44			no
Witch (The)	98	343	41-11840	yes	Worry Bird (The)	479		42-40927	yes
Witchcraft	30	38	42-100403	yes	Worry Bird (The)	446	707	42-7616	yes
Witchcraft	467	790	42-52534	yes	Worry Bird (The)	466	787	42-52582	no
Witchcraft II	467	790	42-28631	yes	Worry Bird II	466	787	42-52584	no
Wokkish				yes	Worrybird	VPB	116		yes
Wolf	7			no	Worth Fighting For				yes
Wolf	494	867	44-40737	yes	Wotta Crock	455			no
Wolf (The)	308	374	41-24266	yes	Wrangler (The)	34	18	41-28871	no
Wolf Gang II				no	Wrangler (The)	34	4	42-51209	yes
Wolf Larsen	376	512	42-78375	yes	Wurf'less	458	753	42-52382	yes
Wolf Pack			42-100268	no	Yakamaw	454	737	42-78367	no
Wolf Pack	98	343	42-40207	no	Yakima Kid (The)	460			yes
Wolf Pack	307	370	41-24144	no	Yank	376	512	41-11625	no
Wolf Pack	43	403	42-73476	yes	Yankee Buzz Bomb	458	752	41-29340	yes
Wolf Pack	376	513	42-40315	yes	Yankee Doll	453	734	41-28644	yes
Wolf Pack	448	713	42-52121	yes	Yankee Doll-ah (The)	491			no
Wolf Pack	450	723	42-64454	no	Yankee Dood It	392			no
Wolf Pack (The)	376	513	42-40213	no	Yankee Doodle Dandy	90	319	42-40077	yes
Wolf Pack (The)	376	513	42-40315	yes	Yankee Doodle Dandy	98	344	42-40105	yes
Wolf Patrol				yes	Yankee Doodle Dandy	389	566	42-95588	no
Wolf Patrol				yes	Yankee Doodle Dandy	485	828	42-52718	no
Wolf Patrol (The)	446	705	42-50882	yes	Yankee Fury	450	721	42-52109	yes
Wolf Waggin'	389	565	42-40775	yes	Yankee Gal	22	33	42-100173	yes
Wolf Waggin'	389	565	44-10510	no	Yankee Gal II	22	33	44-40916	yes
Wolf Wagon	451	724	42-64449	yes	Yankee Girl	376	513	42-51658	no

Name	Grp.	Sq.	Serial	Pic.	Name	Grp.	Sq.	Serial	Pic.
Yankee Maid				yes	Zell Bee	308	425	42-63771	yes
Yankee Maid	34		42-94794	yes	Zeus	453	735	42-95353	no
Yankee Maid	449	716	42-94794	yes	Zippo	493			no
Yankee Maid	487	838	41-29537	no	Zombie	389			yes
Yankee Maid	490	849	42-94794	yes	Zombie	98	415	41-11790	yes
Yankee Rebel	446			no	Zombie	43	63	42-40913	yes
Yankee Rebel	459	756	44-48763	yes	Zombie of 69	461		42-51501	yes
Yankee Rebel					Zoomin' Zombie	389	565	42-63961	yes
Harmony	389	564	42-99975	no	Zoot Chute	308	373	42-100184	yes
Yanks from Hell	90	321	41-23716	yes	Zoot Snook the				
Yanks from Hell II	90	400		no	Shark	93			no
Yard Bird	RAF		AL515	no	Zoot Suiter (The)	454	737	42-94978	no
Yardbird	90	400	42-40905	yes	ZZGGAAKK (The)				yes
Ye Olde Rugged Curse	449	718		yes					
Ye Olde Thunder Mug	446	704	42-7539	yes					
Yegg Beaters	448			no					
Yellow 28	450	723	44-41025	no					
Yellow Fever	308	374	44-50803	yes					
Yellow H	465	781		no					
Yellow How	464	777	44-41231	no					
Yellow L	464	777	44-49328	no					
Yellow Mike	464	777	44-10566	no					
Yellow Rose of Texas	445			no					
Yen Tu	98	415	42-40520	yes					
YMCA Flying Service	392	577	42-50758	no					
YMCA Flying									
Service (The)	392	577	41-28700	yes					
YMCA Flying									
Service II (The)	392	577	42-50901	no					
Yo Yo	456	746		no					
Yo-Yo	455	740	44-41199	yes					
Yokum Boy	458	752	42-109812	no					
Yoo Hoo	376	515		yes					
You Bet	458	755	44-10602	yes					
You Can't Take									
It With You	458		42-51097	yes					
You Cawn't Miss It	448		41-23809	yes					
You Cawn't Miss It	93	329	41-23809	no					
You Cawn't Miss It	389	565	44-10510	yes					
You Name It				no					
You Speak	454	737	42-51366	yes					
You're Gonna Get It	11		41-24100	yes					
You're Safe at Home	445		42-94828	no					
You're Safe At Home	448			no					
You're Safe at Home	490	851	42-94828	yes					
Your Gal	392	579	42-52615	yes					
Yours Truly	389	565	42-40716	no					
Yours Truly	389	566	42-100167	yes					
Youthful Rocket	453	732	42-50898	no					
Yuk-Yuk	490	848	42-94899	no					
Yum Yum	376	514	42-94987	yes					
Yum Yum Wild Oats	376	512	41-24252	no					
Yuvadit	453	735	42-64472	yes					
Yvonne, Yippee	RAF	159		yes					
Z	7	22	44-40396	no					
Z	22		44-40396	no					
Z-Bar	44	506	42-95016	yes					

AIRCRAFT NAMES BY UNIT

5TH BOMB GROUP

Name	Grp.	Sq.	Serial	Pic.
About Average	5	23	42-72777	yes
American Beauty (F7A)	5		42-73065	no
Big Sleep (The)	5			yes
Blue Jay	5	31	44-40607	yes
Blue-J	5	31	44-40607	yes
Bombs to Nippon	5		42-73147	yes
Breezy	5		42-100270	yes
Butch	5		44-41842	yes
Chain Lightning	5		42-40636	no
Cisco Kid	5		42-73455	no
Cisco Kid	5	31	42-40174	yes
Clumsy Baby	5	31	42-73461	no
Coral Princess	5	868	42-40833	no
Daisy Mae	5			no
Daisy Mae	5	23	44-41620	yes
Devil's Delight		868		yes
Dragon Lady	5	23	44-49753	yes
Droop Snoot	5	31	42-41246	no
Flaming Amie	5	31	44-42392	yes
Four Fan Fanny (Fancy)	5	31	44-41669	yes
Fuddles	5			no
Glo Girl	5	72	44-41698	yes
Gus' Jokers	5	31	44-41848	yes
Harriet's Secret	5		42-41155	no
Heavenly Lamb Chop	5	31	44-40585	yes
Hellcat Honey	5		42-109944	yes
Iron Bird	5	31	44-41850	yes
Island Queen	5	31	42-100022	yes
Jolly Rogers	5	31		no
Judy Lee	5			no
Kansas City Kitty	5	31	44-41480	yes
Lady Luck	5	31	44-49845	yes
Lil' Jo Toddy	5	31	42-110137	yes
Little Queen Mary	5	394	44-40474	yes
Madame Libby, the Sea Ducer	5	838	42-40838	yes
Maiden Montana	5		44-41549	yes
Mary Lou	5			no
Mask-A-Raider	5		44-40547	yes
Miss Ileen	5	23	44-42418	yes
Miss Maryland II	5	72	42-73145	no
Munda Belle	5		42-73144	no
My Ideal	5	31	44-41868	yes
My Irish Colleen	5	31	44-41462	yes
Nana	5	868	44-40938	yes
No Duds	5		42-73256	yes
Old Black Magic	5		44-42303	no
Old Black Magic	5	31	44-50333	yes
Our Baby	5	394	42-73270	yes
Pal Joey	5		44-40590	no
Paper Doll	5		42-72812	yes

Name	Grp.	Sq.	Serial	Pic.
Passionate Witch (The)	5			no
Patches	5		42-41115	yes
Pennsy City Kitty	5		44-41480	yes
Poon Tang	5			no
Queen of Angels	5	31	42-72834	yes
Ramp Tramp	5		42-40651	no
Red Arrow (The)	5			yes
Red Headed Woman	5	31	44-41645	yes
Scootin' Thunder	5			yes
Sergeant Stripes Forever	5	31	42-73456	yes
Sexshun Eight	5	31		no
Shady Lady	5			no
Shitiningittin'	5			yes
Sky Tramp	5	72	42-73143	yes
Sky Wolf	5		42-73142	yes
Slip Stream	5			yes
Snow Job	5	31	42-41230	yes
Snow Job II	5	31	44-40572	yes
Squirrely Shirley	5	31	42-110092	yes
Streamliner	5		44-40543	yes
Sweet Thing	5	72	44-42366	yes
Ten Hi	5	31	42-73470	yes
This Above All	5	23	44-41622	yes
Thumper	5	31	42-41220	no
Thumper	5	394	42-73220	yes
Tim-ber	5			yes
Tolly	5		42-41189	no
Top O' the Mark	5	23	44-42245	yes
Trouble Maker	5	394		yes
Two-Time	5		44-40546	yes
Unapproachable	5		44-40548	yes
Untimely Visitor	5		44-40586	yes
Updraft	5	72	44-40620	yes
Virago (The)	5	72		no
Wanda Jo	5		42-110135	no
War Weary	5	31	44-41667	yes
Wishful Thinking	5			yes

6TH BOMB GROUP

Name	Grp.	Sq.	Serial	Pic.
Alley Oop	6	3	42-63793	yes
Blonde Blitz	6	397	AL628	yes
Bull of the Woods	6	397	AL583	yes
Dream Girl	6	29	44-40824	yes
Lettie Jo	6	397	AL632	yes
Miss Annabelle Lee	6	397	xx-xx957	yes
Miss Behavin'	6	397		yes
Night Mission	6	397	42-40891	yes
Princess Sheila	6		AL639	yes
Rose O'Day's Daughter	6	397	xx-xx961	yes
Sky Lark	6	29	42-40771	yes
Stud Duck (The)	6	397	42-40372	yes
Tiger Lady	6	397	AL641	yes

Name	Grp.	Sq.	Serial	Pic.

7TH BOMB GROUP

Name	Grp.	Sq.	Serial	Pic.
Apocalypse	7	436	41-23879	no
Bar Made	7			yes
Battlin' Bitch	7	9	41-24237	yes
Big Az Bird (The)	7			no
Blond Bomber	7		41-11895	no
Boisterous Bitch	7	9	41-24302	yes
Boomerang, Back Again	7	493	41-23887	yes
Cactus Kid	7	9	44-44175	yes
Calamity Jane	7	9		yes
China Gal	7	493		yes
Crusader	7			no
Cute Lil Lass	7	9		yes
Double Trouble	7	493	44-40989	yes
Drive Me Home	7		44-50866	yes
Erotic Edna	7	9		yes
Fabulous Fanny	7	492		yes
Frozen, Hot To Go	7	9	42-72803	no
Gopher Gus	7		AL-573	yes
Hairless Joe	7		42-41252	no
Hello-ver Burma	7	436	44-42460	yes
Home Stretch	7			yes
Hot to Go	7	9	42-73303	yes
Hot to Go, Frozen	7	9	42-72803	no
Jungle Jig	7	492		yes
Kentucky Kloud-Hopper III	7	9		yes
Lady Luck	7			no
Lady Luck II	7			no
Lassie I'm Home	7	436		yes
Little Lass	7	436		no
Lucky Lady	7	492		no
Luscious Lace	7	9		no
Miss Hilda	7	9	44-40859	yes
Miss Tennessee	7	9		yes
Mors Ab Alto	7	493		yes
Nut-Cracker Sweet	7	492		yes
Pal Joey	7		44-40590	no
Paulette	7	492	42-100239	yes
Pelly-Can	7	9	41-23688	no
Rangoon Raider	7		44-40817	no
Rangoon Rambler	7	436		yes
Rangoon Rambler II	7	436	41-23702	yes
Shack Rat Special	7	9		no
Shoot, You're Covered	7	9		yes
Shy Ann	7	9		yes
Sleepy Time Gal	7	493	44-51030	yes
Susie's Sister	7	9	41-23893	no
Tail Heavy	7		42-40xxx	no
Tale of Misfortune	7		44-40991	yes
Wolf	7			no
Z	7	22	44-40396	no

11TH BOMB GROUP

Name	Grp.	Sq.	Serial	Pic.
Alice the Goon	11	26	41-23868	yes
Angel Face	11	98	42-40960	no
Angel Face 3rd	11	98		no
Angel Face the 2nd	11		42-73217	no
Angel Face the 2nd	11	98	42-100217	yes
Angel Face the 3rd	11	98	42-109949	yes
Angela	11	42	44-40498	yes
As-cend Charlie	11	98	42-73009	yes
Baby Sandy II	11	98	42-73013	no
Barrelhouse Bessie	11	98	42-73027	yes
Bat Out of Hell	11			no
Bathless	11	431	42-109838	yes
Beaufort Belle	11		44-49528	yes
Belle of Texas	11	42	42-73156	yes
Belle of the Brawl	11	98	44-40280	yes
Betty J.	11	42	44-41551	yes
Bird's Eye View	11	431		yes
Blondie Saunders (The)	11			yes
Bodacious Idjit	11	98	44-41948	yes
Bolivar, Jr.	11	98	44-42151	yes
Bomb Lullaby	11		42-72988	yes
Brunnhilda	11	42	41-23838	yes
Bugs Bomby, Jr.	11	42	44-41466	yes
Bull Snooker (The)	11	98	42-40405	yes
Calamity Jane	11	26		yes
Captain & the Kids (The)	11	431	42-73013	no
Captain & the Kids (The)	11	431	42-73018	no
Catherine	11	26	42-109947	yes
Catherine	11	98	44-50960	yes
Censored	11	431	42-100229	yes
Chicago Ann	11	26	42-109880	no
Chute the Works	11	431	44-40302	yes
Circus Wagon	11	26	44-42066	yes
Cloudy Joe	11	431	42-73499	yes
Cock O' the Walk	11	431	44-42347	yes
Coconut Queen	11	98	42-72992	yes
Consolidated Mess	11	98	42-73218	yes
Cupid	11	98	41-24190	no
Curly Bird	11		44-40683	yes
Daisy Mae	11	42	41-23983	yes
Dangerous Critter	11	26	44-40382	yes
Dirty Woman (The)	11	26		no
Dogpatch Express	11	42	41-24214	yes
Doity Goity, Peggy	11	42	41-24110	yes
Dragon Lady	11	42	44-40670	yes
Dual Sack	11	98	42-100168	yes
Dumbo the Avenger	11	26	42-72832	yes
Eloise	11			yes
Ferdie	11	42	42-100350	yes
Final Objective	11	431	44-41945	yes
Five Thousandth Ford-Built	11		42-51623	yes
Flying 8 Ball	11	26	41-11923	yes
Flying 8 Ball, Jr.	11	26	42-109840	yes

Name	Grp.	Sq.	Serial	Pic.	Name	Grp.	Sq.	Serial	Pic.
Flying Jenny	11	431	42-109943	yes	Miss Traveler	11	98	44-40530	yes
Galvanized Goose	11	26	42-73015	yes	Moonlight Maid	11		44-42331	yes
Ginny	11	98	44-40491	yes	My Achin' Rod	11			no
Glenna Bee II	11	26	42-73010	yes	My Devotion	11	431	42-100361	yes
Going My Way	11	431	44-40674	yes	Naughty Nanette	11	42	41-24155	no
Green Banana	11			no	Naughty Nanette	11	42	42-40961	yes
Gremlin	11	42		yes	Night and Day	11	431	44-41695	yes
Gun Site	11	26	42-72995	no	Night Mission	11	26	44-40532	yes
Gun Site	11	42	42-73005	yes	Night Mission	11		42-40891	yes
Gus' Jokers	11	26	44-41848	no	Niquotina	11			yes
Hairless Joe	11	98	42-41136	no	No Dice	11		44-41318	yes
Hap-N-Hank	11	431	44-50145	yes	Our Baby	11		42-109954	no
Hazel! Which Hazel?	11			yes	Overloaded(loan)	11			yes
Heaven Can Wait,					Pacific Passion	11			yes
Don Ameche	11	98	42-73496	yes	Pacific Tramp	11		42-40067	no
Heavy Date	11	26	42-100228	yes	Pacific Tramp III	11		42-109936	yes
Hell's Bells(e)	11			yes	Pacific Vamp	11	98	41-24168	yes
Hellcat	11	431	42-109944	yes	Passionate Witch	11	26	42-41124	yes
Hellcat Belle	11	98	42-73153	yes	Patches	11	26		yes
Hilo Hattie	11	431	41-23844	yes	Patches	11	431	42-73018	yes
Hit Parade	11	26	42-73002	no	Patriotic Patty	11			no
Homesick Angel	11		42-73153	yes	Peggy	11	98	41-24110	yes
I Tell You, Boys,					Pilikie Oke Iaponi	11			no
It's Heaven	11	26	44-40953	yes	Pistol Packin' Mama	11	26	42-40689	yes
I'se a Royal Hawaiian	11	26	42-41198	yes	Playmate	11	431	44-40791	no
Jackass Billy	11	98	42-40406	yes	Puddle Jumper	11		44-40829	yes
Jeeter Bug (The)	11	42	44-40661	yes	Puddle Jumper II	11		44-41946	yes
Jezebel	11	26	41-24267	yes	Ramp Rider	11	431		yes
Jita	11	431	41-24100	no	Rapid Robin	11	431	41-24170	yes
Juicy Lucy	11	431	42-40074	yes	Rapid Robin II	11	431	42-73287	yes
K Lucy II	11	26	42-109861	yes	Ready Teddy II	11	98	42-73008	yes
Kansas Cyclone	11	26	42-73025	yes	Ring-Dang-Doo	11			yes
Kay-Lyn	11		44-40362	no	Rita	11	42	44-40633	yes
Knit Clipper	11	26	42-40177	no	Road to Tokyo	11	42	44-40521	yes
Koko	11	26	42-73014	no	Rough Buddy	11	26	42-41198	no
Lady	11	98	42-73004	yes	Royal Flush	11	431	44-41318	yes
Lady from Hades	11	26	44-41613	yes	Ruff Knights	11		44-40550	yes
Lady Kaye	11			yes	Sack Time Sal II	11	431		yes
Lady Tabie	11		42-109979	yes	Salty Dog	11	431	42-41137	yes
Les Miserables	11	431	42-73026	yes	Samoa	11		AL 626	yes
Lil' Audrey Grows Up	11	431	42-73016	yes	San Quentin Quail	11	98	42-41205	yes
Little Dumbo	11	26	41-23841	yes	Sandy	11	26	42-73019	yes
Little Hiawatha	11	431	41-24187	yes	Satan's Kite II	11	26	42-40079	yes
Little Joe	11	42	44-40678	yes	Secrut Weapin	11	98	42-100224	yes
Lonnie	11	431	42-73007	yes	Sexy Sue IV	11	98	41-23938	yes
Lucky Dog	11		44-40679	yes	Sexy Sue, Mother of Ten	11	98	42-40078	yes
Luvablas'	11	431	44-42264	yes	Sexy Sue,				
Madame Pele	11		42-109851	yes	Mother of Ten II	11	98	41-23952	yes
Merry Boozer	11	26	42-109945	yes	Sexy Sue,				
Millie's Daughter	11	98	42-109876	yes	Mother of Ten III	11	98	42-73017	no
Miss Bee Haven	11	98	42-73082	yes	Sexy Sue,				
Miss Laid	11			yes	Mother of Ten IV	11	98	41-23928	yes
Miss Nadine	11	42	42-109934	yes	Shoot the Works	11	98	44-40554	yes
Miss Red Dauber	11	42	44-41381	yes	Sky's Delight	11	431	44-40673	yes
Miss Red Dauber	11	42	42-40961	yes	Smitty	11	26	42-73288	yes
Miss Sherry	11	42	44-40710	yes	Smokey Stover	11	26	42-73011	yes
Miss Tech Supply	11	42	44-40377	yes	Snooky	11	431	42-41257	yes

Name	Grp.	Sq.	Serial	Pic.	Name	Grp.	Sq.	Serial	Pic.
Snuffy Smith	11	431	41-24148	yes	Daddy's Girl	22	33	44-41852	yes
Star Eyes	11	431	42-109881	no	Docile Dragon	22			no
Star Eyes	11	431	42-40074	yes	Duchess (The)	22	33	44-49865	yes
Stormy Weather	11		44-40556	yes	Duchess (The)	22	33	44-50865	yes
Stripped for Action	11	431	44-41501	yes	Feathermerchants Folly	22	2	42-100293	yes
Sunsetter (The)	11	431	42-100223	yes	Hit Parader II	22	33	42-41087	yes
Super Baby	11	98	42-109873	yes	Island Queen	22	408	42-100230	no
Superman	11	26	42-109938	yes	Joy	22		41-23973	no
Susie	11		44-40587	yes	Kansas City Kitty	22	33	44-41255	yes
Sweet Routine	11	26	44-40527	yes	Kay-O	22	408	42-109990	no
Tail Wind	11	431	42-73155	no	Lady Luck	22	33	44-50795	no
Tailwind	11	431	41-24155	yes	Lemon (The)	22	2	42-100333	no
Takeoff	11	42	41-24149	yes	Liberty Bell	22			no
Tarfu	11	26	42-109933	yes	Liberty Belle II	22	33	44-41234	yes
Taurus	11	98	42-109846	yes	Little Butch	22	2	42-109997	yes
Temptacious	11		44-51515	yes	Lost Angel	22	408	42-109992	yes
Temptation	11		44-40617	yes	Modest Maiden	22	19	44-41537	yes
Texas Kate	11		44-40358	yes	Ole 410	22		42-73410	no
Thar She Blows II	11	42	42-109870	yes	Ole Tomato	22	33	42-100291	yes
Thar She Blows III	11	42	44-40168	yes	Our Gal	22	33		no
Thumper	11	42	42-40073	yes	Our Gal II	22	33		no
Thumper II	11			no	Our Gal III	22	33	42-100313	yes
Tired Tessie	11	431	42-73155	yes	Outa This World	22		42-110001	yes
Trail Blazer (The)	11	98	42-72960	yes	Outa This World II	22			no
Tricky Micky	11	98	44-50960	yes	Pablo	22		42-100317	no
Tropic Knight	11			no	Patient Kitten	22	33	44-41031	yes
Tropic Knight II	11			yes	Peace Terms (The)	22			yes
Tropical Dream	11	98	42-100218	yes	Pleasure Bent	22		42-73440	yes
Tropical Trollop	11		42-100405	yes	Queen Ann	22	33	42-110119	yes
Tuffy (Hairless Joe)	11	98	42-41136	no	Ramblin' Rose	22	33	42-100201	no
Umbriago	11		44-40327	yes	Red Hot Riden Hood (I)	22	33	42-100212	yes
Unapproachable	11	98	44-40551	no	Red Hot Riden Hood III	22	2		yes
Uninvited	11	98	44-40360	yes	Red Hot Riden-Hood II	22	2	44-40202	yes
Uninvited (The)	11	98	44-40360	yes	Round Trip Ticket	22	33	42-100193	yes
Upstairs Maid	11			no	Round Trip Ticket II	22	33	44-41538	no
Va-on	11			no	Sandy	22	408	42-100324	yes
Valhalla	11	26	41-24168	no	Satan's Sister	22	2	42-40680	yes
Virginia Belle	11	42	42-40645	yes	Shitten-and-a-Gettin'	22	33	44-50799	no
Vulnerable Virgin	11	26		yes	Shittiningittin II	22	33	44-40799	yes
W.R.F.T.F.	11	431	44-40662	yes	Shoo Shoo Baby	22	408	42-109984	yes
Wabbit Twansit	11	431	42-73006	yes	Sleepy Time Gal	22	33	44-41311	no
Wac's Delight	11	26	44-40734	yes	Slightly Dangerous	22	33	44-40366	yes
Wake Island	11	26	41-23829	yes	Star Eyes	22			yes
Wake Island Sleeper (The)	11	26	41-24254	yes	Sweet Racket	22	33	42-100188	yes
Warbird	11		42-100406	yes	Tabu	22			yes
Well Developed	11	431	44-40209	yes	Tail Wind	22			yes
Wicked Witch	11	42	42-40688	yes	Tailwind	22	33	41-28762	yes
Wild Ass Ride	11		xx-xx615	yes	Tailwind	22	33	42-100210	yes
Wishful Thinking	11			yes	Tailwind II	22	33	44-41652	no
Wondrous Wanda	11		44-40562	yes	Tempermental Lady	22	408	42-100174	yes
Woody Woodpecker	11		44-41179	yes	Unholy Kitten	22	33	44-41031	no
You're Gonna Get It	11		41-24100	yes	Yankee Gal	22	33	42-100173	yes
					Yankee Gal II	22	33	44-40916	yes
					Z	22		44-40396	no

22ND BOMB GROUP

Name	Grp.	Sq.	Serial	Pic.
Bomb Wacky Wabbit	22			yes
Buzz Job	22	408	42-100290	no

Name	Grp.	Sq.	Serial	Pic.

25TH BOMB GROUP

Name	Grp.	Sq.	Serial	Pic.
Little Lulu	25		44-40233	yes

28TH BOMB GROUP

Name	Grp.	Sq.	Serial	Pic.
Atchison, Topeka & Santa Fe	28	404	44-49807	yes
Boogow	28	404	41-23941	yes
Dolores	28	404	44-50598	yes
Duchess	28	404	41-11924	no
Flash	28	404	42-41157	yes
Frigid Frances	28		41-23858	no
He Dood It	28	404	41-23888	yes
Iceberg Inez	28	404	42-40910	no
Little Butch	28	404	41-23884	yes
Little Girl	28	404	41-23886	yes
Mi A'kin Back	28	404		no
My A'kin' Back	28	404		no
Myasis Dragon	28	404	44-49483	yes
Sweet Cecilia	28	404	44-49483	yes
Tough Boy	28	404	41-23891	yes
Viking Maiden	28	404	41-11783	no
Wee Willie	28	21		yes
Whistlin' Shithouse	28	404	44-49474	yes

30TH BOMB GROUP

Name	Grp.	Sq.	Serial	Pic.
A-Vailable	30	27	42-72979	yes
A. W. O. L.	30	38	42-72970	no
Angel Face II	30	819		no
Annie	30	392	42-72958	yes
Ball of Fire	30			yes
Bat Out of Hell	30	392	42-73024	yes
Bathless	30	392	42-109838	yes
Battling Bitch	30	392	42-72985	yes
Battling Hornet	30	392	42-73281	yes
Bird of Paradise	30	27	44-40677	yes
Bird of Paradise	30	392	42-72984	no
Bird's Eye View	30	38	44-42158	yes
Bitch Kitty	30	392	42-72965	no
Boise Bronc	30	392	44-40728	yes
Bolivar	30	27	42-72994	yes
Bomb Lullaby	30	392	42-72988	yes
Bugs Bomby	30	392	42-72998	yes
Captain & His Kids (The)	30	819	44-40518	yes
Chambermaid (The)	30	38	42-100227	yes
Circus Wagon	30	392	44-42066	no
Cloudy Joe	30	819	42-73499	no
Come Closer	30	38	42-72973	yes
Complete Miss	30	27	44-40810	yes
Curly Bird	30	819	44-40683	yes
Dashin' Daisy	30	27	42-72986	no
Dead Eye	30	392	42-72997	no
Dead Eye II	30	392	42-73425	yes
Dinah Might	30	27	42-73154	no
Dirty Nell	30	392	42-72995	yes
Dirty Nell II	30	392	42-73290	yes
Dogpatch Express	30	392	42-73001	no
Doidie Ann	30	38	42-100376	no
Dottie Ann	30	38	42-100376	yes
Duckin' Ducklin' II	30	38	42-72971	no
Dumbo	30	26	42-72832	yes
Evasive Action	30	819	42-109809	yes
Flak Happy	30	27	42-72996	yes
Flak Happy Too	30	27	42-73279	no
Flak Happy, Too	30	27	42-73279	no
Flying Carpet	30			yes
Fools Paradise	30	38	42-73282	yes
Form I-A	30	392	44-40229	yes
Galloping Gus	30	819	42-72999	no
Ginny Lynn	30	27	42-72968	yes
Going My Way	30	819	44-40674	no
Gunner's Sight	30	819	44-42526	yes
Heaven Can Wait	30	819	42-72831	no
Hell from Heaven	30	819	42-109941	yes
Hell from Heaven	30	819	44-40528	yes
Home James	30	819	44-40527	yes
Incendiary Sue	30	392	42-72991	yes
Jeeter Bug (The)	30	819	44-40661	yes
Juicy Lady	30	819		no
Juicy Lucy	30	27	42-40074	yes
K-Lucy	30	392	44-40302	no
Kay-Lyn	30	38	44-40362	yes
Kay-Rashun	30	27	42-73236	yes
Kickapoo Kid	30	27	42-72983	yes
Kiska Katie	30	21	41-23896	yes
Kontagious Katie	30	819	42-73493	yes
Lady from Hades	30	392	44-41613	yes
Lemon	30	27	42-72993	yes
Libby Raider	30	38	42-100396	yes
Liberty Belle	30	819	44-40708	yes
Little General (The)	30	392	42-73030	yes
Little Joe	30	392	42-72984	yes
Loretta	30	27	44-40809	no
Lucky Dog	30	38	44-40679	yes
Madame Pele	30	819	42-109851	yes
Maid of Honor	30	392	44-41476	no
Miss Fit	30	392	44-40557	yes
Miss Mar-Jan	30	819		no
Miss Minnesota	30	38		yes
Miss Minooky	30	38	42-72972	no
My Ideal	30	392	42-72985	yes
Nan Fox	30	392	42-72965	no
Night Mission	30	819	44-40532	yes
Nipponese Clipper	30	38	42-72966	yes
Noah Borshuns	30			no
Old Crow III	30	392	44-41985	yes
Our Baby	30	27	42-72969	no
Our Baby	30	38	42-109954	yes
Our Girl	30	819		no
Outa This World	30	819	44-40681	yes
Pacific Avenger	30	38	42-72975	yes

Name	Grp.	Sq.	Serial	Pic.
Pacific Passion	30	392	44-41500	yes
Parkin' Strip Patty	30	38	42-109948	yes
Patches	30	819	44-40518	no
Patriotic Patty	30	819	42-73494	yes
Phiddis II	30	27	42-73283	yes
Pistol Packin' Mama	30	38	42-72989	yes
Poontang	30	38	42-72999	yes
Poop (The)	30	38	41-23746	no
Puddle Jumper	30	819	44-40829	yes
Puddle Jumper II	30	819	44-41946	yes
Punjab	30	38	42-72974	yes
Raunchy	30	27	42-72980	no
Ready Bette	30			yes
Retriever	30	27	42-100398	yes
Rita	30	27	44-40633	yes
Rose Marie	30	27	44-40680	no
Ruff Knights	30	38	44-40550	yes
Saints & Sinners	30	38	42-100385	yes
Salty Sal	30	392	42-100219	yes
Section Eight	30	38	42-73982	no
Sky Demon	30	819	42-40143	yes
Sky Skow	30	27	42-72987	yes
Sky Skow III	30	27	42-73473	yes
Snooper	30	27	42-109952	yes
Star Dust	30			no
Stormy Weather	30	38	44-40556	yes
Sunsetter (The)	30	819	42-100223	no
Sweet Routine	30	819	44-40527	yes
Swing Shift	30	38	42-109940	yes
Tail End Charlie	30	27	42-109935	yes
Temptation	30	819	44-40617	yes
Texas Kate	30	392	44-40358	yes
Thar She Blows II	30	392	42-109870	yes
These Guns for Hire	30	819	42-73494	no
This Heart of Mine	30	27		no
Time's A Wastin'	30	27	44-40614	yes
Tondelayo	30	27	42-73289	yes
Tropic Knight	30	27	42-73151	yes
Tropical Trollop	30	392	42-100405	yes
Umbriago	30	392	44-40327	yes
Upstairs Maid	30	819	42-109941	yes
Vera 1	30	27		yes
War Bird	30	819	42-100406	yes
Warbird	30	819	42-100406	no
Wild Ass Ride	30	38	44-41615	yes
Wingless Witch	30	392	42-72990	no
Witchcraft	30	38	42-100403	yes
Wondrous Wanda	30	819	44-40562	yes

34TH BOMB GROUP

Name	Grp.	Sq.	Serial	Pic.
A-1	34	18	42-94879	no
Ann	34		42-51190	no
Bachelor's Baby	34		42-99991	yes
Bachelor's Lady	34	391	41-29562	no
Bachelor's Party	34	391	41-29562	no
Bad Penny	34		42-94764	no
Bad Penny II	34			no
Bad Penny III	34			no
Bad Penny IV	34			no
Bambi	34	4	41-29567	yes
Belchin' Bessie	34	7	41-29559	yes
Belle of the Brawl	34	391	42-94904	no
Betta Duck	34	7	44-49454	no
Betty Jane	34		42-94768	no
Bold Sea Rover (The)	34	18	42-94745	no
Boots	34	391		no
Bunnie	34	4	41-29567	no
Captain John Silver	34	7	42-94818	no
Chesty	34	391	41-28598	yes
Cock of the Sky	34	7	41-29569	no
Cokey Flo	34	18	42-94745	no
Cokey Flo	34	7	44-40486	yes
Collapsible Susie	34	18	42-94758	yes
Collapsible Susie	34	18	42-94879	no
Cookie's Wailing Wall	34	391	42-52696	no
Crow's Nest	34		42-94766	no
Donald Duck	34		42-94890	no
Duchess (The)	34	391	42-94861	no
Dugan Wagon	34	7	41-29557	no
Dugan Wagon (The)	34	18	44-40482	yes
Dugan Wagon II (The)	34	18	44-40482	yes
Dynahmite Dodo	34	4	41-29522	no
Fast Company	34	7	41-28877	yes
Feudin' Wagon	34		42-94873	no
Fightin' Rebel	34	391	41-28849	no
Floogie Boo	34	391	44-40441	no
Flying Devil (The)	34	4	41-29548	no
Four Five Time	34	391	41-28820	no
Frivolous Sal	34	18	42-94893	yes
Frivolous Sal	34	4	42-94815	no
Gemini	34			no
Gemini II	34			no
Generator Jenny	34	18	44-40320	no
Glamour Girl	34	391	41-29572	no
Heavenly Body	34	18	41-28878	yes
Hell's Belle	34	391	42-94893	no
Hell's Belle	34	4	42-94815	yes
Hells Belle	34	391	42-94893	no
Hit Parade (The)	34		42-94883	no
Holy Joe	34	391	42-50613	yes
Jane's White Rabbit	34		42-52750	no
Jerk's Berserks	34	4	44-40443	no
Jerk's Natural	34		44-40473	no
Kisco Kid	34		42-94930	no
Leo	34	391	41-29605	yes
Loni (League of Nations, Inc.)	34	18	41-28865	no
Lucille	34		42-52759	no
Madam Shoo-Shoo	34		42-94762	no
Maid of Fury	34	7	42-94849	no
Male Call	34	4	42-94869	no
Me Worry?	34	391	42-94796	no
Me Worry? II	34	7	42-94942	no

Name	Grp.	Sq.	Serial	Pic.
Mean Kid	34	18	44-40468	yes
Methusela	34	4	41-29555	no
Mickey Mouse	34	7	42-94851	no
Mis-Chief	34		42-94775	no
Mis-Chief	34	4	42-94880	yes
Misery Agent	34	4	41-28838	no
Misschief	34	4	42-94880	yes
Miz-Pah	34		42-94845	no
Near Sighted Robin	34	7	41-28851	yes
Never Mrs.	34	7	42-95167	no
Off Limits	34	18	42-94782	yes
Off Limits II	34			no
Open Season	34	4	42-52707	no
Paper Doll	34	7	42-94799	no
Patches	34	391	42-94889	no
Percolatin' Pete	34	4	42-52755	no
Piccadilly Filly	34	4	44-40458	no
Piccadilly Lucy	34		41-29518	no
Piccadilly Tilly	34	4	42-94911	yes
Powerful Katrinka	34	4	41-29555	no
Problem Child	34	18	41-28884	no
Queenie	34	4	41-29564	no
Rat Poison	34	18	41-29560	no
Rough House Kate	34	4	41-29542	no
Rum Runner	34	392	42-52496	no
Ruptured Duck (The)	34	4	42-52770	yes
Ruptured Falcon	34	4	42-52770	no
Salutation Rose	34	391	42-94770	no
Shadrach	34	7	41-29557	yes
Shady Lady	34			no
Shark (The)	34	4	42-52707	no
Skotty	34		42-94813	no
Small Change II	34	391	42-50585	no
Small Change III	34	391		no
Smitty	34	4	42-94780	no
Smokey	34	18	41-28840	no
Sultry Sue	34		42-50539	no
Sunshine Rose	34	391	44-40323	no
Sweet Sioux	34	4	42-94911	no
Sweetheart of Harlech (The)	34	7	42-94824	no
T. N. Toni	34		42-94790	no
This Above All	34	391	44-40328	yes
Tiger Rag	34	7	42-94908	yes
Tommy Thumper II	34	4	41-28838	no
Tommy Thumper II	34	4	42-94811	no
Tondelayo	34			no
Turgo Joe	34		44-40303	no
Umbriago	34		42-94824	no
Umbriago	34	7	41-28880	no
Un-Invited (The)	34		42-94762	yes
Undecided	34		42-94748	no
Unlimited (The)	34	4	41-29464	no
War Eagle	34	4	41-29566	no
Weary Willie	34	4	42-94755	no
Wilson	34	7	42-52738	no
Winnie the Pooh	34		42-94771	no
Wrangler (The)	34	18	41-28871	no
Wrangler (The)	34	4	42-51209	yes
Yankee Maid	34		42-94794	yes

43RD BOMB GROUP

Name	Grp.	Sq.	Serial	Pic.
Ace of Spades	43	63	42-40945	no
Art's Cart	43	63	42-40896	yes
At Ease	43	63	42-40955	no
Barbara Jean (F-7)	43	65	44-40980	yes
Ben Buzzard	43			no
Big Ass Bird	43	65	42-73478	yes
Big Chief Cockeye	43	403	42-40351	yes
Black Magic	43	64	42-41224	no
Black Magic	43	65	42-41116	yes
Blondes Away	43	64	42-110006	no
Bob's Hope	43	64	44-40395	yes
Bums Away	43	403	42-40198	no
Bums Away	43	403	42-40812	yes
Bums Away	43	403	42-40822	no
Bunny Hop	43		42-41091	no
Cherokee Strip	43	65	44-40198	yes
Cocktail Hour	43	64	44-40428	yes
Colossal Fossil	43	403	42-40863	yes
Come and Get It	43	65	44-40403	no
Come N' Get It	43	64	42-40941	yes
Coral Princess	43		42-40833	no
Devil's Delight	43		42-40832	yes
Dorothy Anne (The)	43	64	42-41093	yes
Double Trouble	43		42-40671	yes
Dragon and His Tail (The)	43	64	44-40973	yes
Dragon Wagon	43	63		no
Duchess (The)	43	65	44-40567	yes
Easy Breeze	43		42-110118	no
Fat Stuff	43	403	42-41171	yes
Fat Stuff	43	403	42-41171	yes
Firtil Myrtle	43	63	42-100037	yes
Flamin' Mamie	43	403	42-41062	yes
Flying Fanny	43	403	42-72780	yes
Flying Wolf	43	403	42-50447	yes
Flying Wolf (The)	43	403	42-40905	no
Four-F (4-F) Charlie	43	403	42-72946	no
Frisky	43	64	42-40667	yes
Furious Sal	43			no
Gentleman Jim	43	403		yes
Geraldine	43	403	42-41065	yes
Goon (The)	43			no
Heater (The)	43			no
Heavenly Body	43	63	42-73484	yes
Helen's Revenge	43	64	42-40913	yes
Herd of Hainan	43			no
Hit Parade	43	64	44-40430	yes
I'll Be Around	43	63	42-100042	yes
It Ain't So Funny	43	64	44-49853	yes
Joltin' Janie	43		41-24233	no
Joltin' Janie II	43	403	42-40233	yes

Name	Grp.	Sq.	Serial	Pic.
June Bride	43			no
Jungle Queen	43	65	42-40863	yes
Ken's Men	43		44-40980	yes
Kentucky Virgin	43	403	42-41053	yes
King of Clubs	43	63	42-40949	no
Lady from Leyte	43	65	44-40807	yes
Lady Luck	43	63	42-41058	no
Last Horizon	43			yes
Lil' Daisy Cutter	43	63	42-40666	yes
Little Beaver	43	403	42-40984	yes
Lovely Annette	43	64	44-40808	no
Lucky Lucille	43	65	42-41224	yes
Lucky Lucille	43	65		no
Lucky Lucy	43	65		no
Mabel's Labels	43	64	44-50853	yes
Mad Russian	43	65	44-41846	yes
Madame Libby, the Sea Ducer	43		42-40838	yes
Mag the Hag	43	64	42-41084	yes
Mallet Head	43	63	42-41050	no
Manila Calling	43	65		yes
Margie	43		41-24018	yes
Marie	43	64	42-40922	yes
Mayflower (The)	43	64	42-40853	yes
Michigan	43	64	44-40429	yes
Million $ Baby	43	403	44-40335	yes
Million $ Baby II	43	403	44-50768	yes
Mirage (The)	43			no
Miss Bubbles	43		42-40836	no
Miss Carriage	43			no
Miss D Meaner	43	64	42-41224	no
Miss Liberty	43	63	42-40479	yes
Miss McCook	43	403	42-41070	yes
Miss Traveller	43		44-40530	no
Modest Maiden	43	403	42-109994	yes
Nana	43	63	44-40938	yes
Not In Stock	43	64	42-41093	yes
Out of the Night II	43	63	44-41809	yes
Peace Offering	43	403		no
Petty Gal	43	63	44-42128	yes
Pitti-Sing	43	63	42-41051	no
Pride of the Cornhuskers	43			yes
Queen of the Clouds	43	403	44-40979	yes
Queen of the Clouds II	43			no
Record Breakers (The)	43	64	42-110122	yes
Rum and Coke	43	65	44-49827	yes
Sack Bound	43	63	42-73471	yes
Sack Wagon (The)	43	63	42-100034	yes
Satan's Sister	43	403	42-40680	yes
Seaman's Super Snoope	43			no
Shanghai Lil	43	63	44-41026	no
Shawantsta	43	65		no
Shawnee Raider	43			no
Shining Example (The)	43	64	44-40184	yes
Sitting Girl	43	403	42-73472	no
Sky Shy	43		42-40683	no
Starfu	43			no
Stormy Weather	43	64	44-40184	yes
Stuggot's 1st	43	65		no
Swan (The)	43	63	42-40475	no
Sweet Sixteen	43	63	42-73394	yes
Tail Skid Tolly	43			no
Talisman	43			no
Target for Tonight	43	65	42-41060	yes
Toughy	43	64	42-40525	no
Two Bob Tillie	43	65	42-41215	yes
Two Bob Tillie	43	65	42-73952	no
Uncle Sam	43	64	42-72811	yes
Uncle's Fury	43		42-40854	no
Whistle Stop	43	403	42-41060	no
Who's Next	43	63	42-41049	no
Windy City Kitty	43	64		yes
Wolf Pack	43	403	42-73476	yes
Wonder Gal	43	63	44-40942	yes
Zombie	43	63	42-40913	yes

44TH BOMB GROUP

Name	Grp.	Sq.	Serial	Pic.
Amblin' Okie	44	67	41-29174	no
Annie Oakley 'Crack Shot'	44	67	42-40126	yes
Any Gum Chum?	44	68	42-110035	yes
Arrowhead	44	68	42-51108	no
Available Jones	44	67	42-40780	yes
Avenger	44	68	41-23788	yes
Avenger II	44	66	42-40130	no
Bad Penny	44	67	42-7650	no
Baldy & His Brood	44	506	41-24201	yes
Ball of Fire	44			no
Banana Barge (The)	44	506	42-110045	yes
Banshee	44	66	42-63965	no
Banshee (The)	44	66	42-7536	yes
Banshee II	44			no
Banshee III	44	66		no
Banshee IV	44	66	42-99980	no
Barfly	44	67	42-99986	yes
Barfly	44	67	42-99996	yes
Bat Out of Hell	44	68	41-23806	no
Battle Axe	44	66	42-40793	yes
Battlin' Baby	44	68	42-94892	no
Bela	44	67	41-23918	no
Bette Ann	44	67	41-23783	no
Betty(Bette) Anne	44	67	41-23783	no
Bewitching Witch	44	67	41-24024	yes
Bi-U Baby	44	66	42-95619	no
Big Banner	44	66	42-7638	no
Big Fat Butterfly	44	66	42-64166	yes
Big Headed Kid	44	506	44-50748	no
Big Time Operator	44	66	42-50480	no
Bing's Big Box	44	68	42-7501	no
Black Jack	44	68	41-23816	yes
Black Magic	44			yes
Black Sheep	44	67	42-41021	no

Name	Grp.	Sq.	Serial	Pic.	Name	Grp.	Sq.	Serial	Pic.
Blue Goose	44	67	41-11653	no	Gallavantin' Gal	44	506	42-7509	no
Bucksheesh Benny	44	68	42-40094	no	Gallopin' Ghost	44	67	41-23783	no
Bucksheesh Benny					Gemini	44	506	41-29496	no
Rides Again	44	68	41-24112	no	Geronimo	44			yes
Bull O' the Woods	44	66	42-7548	yes	GI Gal	44	67	42-40371	yes
Buzzin Bear	44	67	41-24229	yes	Gipsy Queen	44	68	42-109805	yes
Cactus	44	506	41-24191	no	Glory Bee	44	67	42-52616	yes
Calaban	44	67	41-24232	yes	Greenwich	44	506	41-29153	yes
Cape Cod Special	44	506	42-51181	no	Hag Mag the				
Captain & His Kids					Hangar Queen	44	66	42-40731	no
Ride Again	44	68	41-23800	no	Hag Mag the				
Captain & His Kids					Mothball Queen	44	66	42-40731	no
Ride Again	44	68	41-24213	yes	Hairless Joe	44		44-40437	no
Captain and the					Heaven Can Wait	44	68	42-7507	yes
Kids, 2nd Edition	44			no	Helen B. Happy	44	66	42-40764	yes
Channel Hopper	44	68	42-95226	yes	Helen Hywater	44	68	42-63971	yes
Chief and Sack Artists	44	67	42-100073	no	Hell's Kitchen	44	66	41-24236	yes
Chief Wapello	44	506	42-52618	yes	Hell's Kitten	44	68	41-24236	yes
Chief Wapello	44	66	42-52618	yes	Heller B. Happy	44			no
Consolidated Mess	44	506	42-100429	yes	Henry	44	66	44-40279	yes
Consolidated Mess	44	506	42-7568	no	Hit Parade (The)	44	506	42-94883	no
Corky	44	68	42-51101	yes	Hitler's Headache	44	67	41-23774	no
Corky	44	68	42-63971	no	Hitler's Nightmare	44	67	41-23774	no
Crack Shot	44	67	42-40126	no	Holiday Mess	44	506	42-40989	no
D for Dog	44			no	Holiday Mess II	44	66	42-7533	no
D-Bar Fly	44	67	42-99986	yes	Horse Fly	44	67	42-40267	yes
Down De Hatch	44	506	42-95016	yes	I'll Be Back	44	506	42-52305	no
E-Z Duzit	44	66	42-99980	yes	I'll Be Back	44	506	42-52332	no
Eager Beaver	44		42-40731	yes	Impatient Virgin	44	67	41-29231	yes
Eager Eve	44	68	42-40731	no	Iron Corset	44			no
Earthquake McGoon	44	506		yes	J-Bar	44			no
Earthquake McGoon	44	506	41-24235	yes	Jail Bait	44	66	42-110161	yes
Eightball	44	67	44-40282	no	Jenny	44	66	41-23778	yes
Emmy Lou	44	67	41-23988	no	Jerilynne Sue	44			no
Emmy Lou II	44	67	42-72878	no	Jersey Jerk	44	66	44-10548	no
F for Freddie	44	67	42-72865	no	Jinx (The)	44	68	42-7551	no
Fascinatin' Witch	44	66	41-23811	no	Jolly Annette	44			no
Fearless Fosdick	44	67	42-95049	no	Joplin Jalopy	44	506	42-50535	yes
Feather Merchant	44	66	41-28788	yes	Jose Carioca	44	66	42-50643	yes
Feudin' Wagon	44	506	44-40155	no	Judy's Buggy	44	67	42-52293	no
Feudin' Wagon (The)	44	506	42-110082	yes	K-Bar	44	506	42-50733	yes
Fifinella	44	66	42-95329	yes	King High	44		42-7648	no
Fifinella	44	67	42-63763	yes	King Pin	44	66	42-50761	no
Flak Alley	44	68	42-24225	yes	Kingpin	44	66	42-50761	no
Flak Alley II	44	68	41-29544	no	Lady Dot	44	68	42-100112	no
Flak Happy	44			no	Lady Fifinella	44	67	42-63763	no
Flak Magnet	44	68	42-50349	no	Lady Geraldine	44	68	44-10504	no
Flak Magnet	44	68	42-50596	yes	Lady Luck	44	66	41-23778	yes
Flossie Flirt	44	66	42-40777	no	Lemon Drop	44	68	41-23699	yes
Flying Eightball	44	67	42-7624	no	Liberty Belle	44	66	42-95095	no
Flying Ginny	44	67	41-28944	no	Liberty Belle	44	67	42-99970	yes
Flying Log	44	506	42-50328	no	Liberty Lass	44	67		yes
Forky	44			no	Lil' Abner	44	67	42-63761	yes
Forky II	44	66	42-40182	yes	Lil' Cookie	44	67	42-7552	yes
Four (4)-Q-2	44	67	41-23779	yes	Lili Marlene	44	506	42-95309	no
Full House	44	68	42-99966	yes	Lili Marlene	44	66	42-7638	yes
G I Gal	44	67	42-40371	yes	Lilli Marlene	44	506		no

Name	Grp.	Sq.	Serial	Pic.	Name	Grp.	Sq.	Serial	Pic.
Lilli Marlene	44	68	42-95260	yes	Patsy Ann II	44	68	42-100170	no
Limpin' Ole Sadie	44	68	42-95021	yes	Peace Offering	44	68	42-7672	no
Little Audrey	44			yes	Peep Sight	44	506	42-7535	yes
Little Beaver	44	67	41-23807	yes	Pete the POM Inspector	44	506	42-40370	no
Loco Moco	44	66	44-50597	no	Phyllis	44	67	42-109896	no
Lone Ranger	44	68	44-40098	yes	Phyllis	44	67	42-110031	no
Louisiana Belle	44	66	42-50806	yes	Pizz and Moan	44	68	42-99987	yes
Louisiana Belle	44	68	42-50806	no	Poop Deck Pappy	44	67	41-29161	yes
Lucky Strike	44	506	41-29172	no	Poop Deck Pappy	44	67	42-7521	no
Lucky Strike	44	68	42-110095	no	Pork	44			no
Lucy Quipment	44	68		no	Porky II	44		42-40182	no
Lyndy	44		42-7518	no	Pregnant Cow	44	67	41-11673	no
Lynn Bari	44	506	42-40068	no	Pregnant Peg	44	506	42-50328	yes
Lynn Bari II	44	506	42-40172	no	Princ-Ass(ess)	44	506	42-63962	yes
Maggie	44	67	41-23832	no	Prince	44	506	42-63962	yes
Marcia Ann	44	67	41-23818	no	Princess Charlotte	44	66	41-23769	yes
Margaret Ann	44	68	41-24009	yes	Proud Mary	44	506	42-7630	no
Margaret Ann II	44	67	42-40071	yes	Puritanical Bitch	44	68	42-50427	no
Margie Ann II	44	67	42-40071	yes	Puritanical Witch	44	68	42-50427	no
Marguerite	44	506	41-23936	no	Q for Queenie	44			no
Mary Harriett	44	68	42-110049	no	Queen Anne	44	506	41-23936	no
Mi Akin Ass	44	67	42-94846	yes	Queen Marguerite	44	506	41-23936	no
Minerva	44	66	41-23689	yes	Queen Marlene	44	66	42-72813	yes
Miss Delores	44	67	41-24229	no	Queenie/Miss Delores)	44	67	41-24278	no
Miss Delores	44	67	41-24278	no	Raggedy Ann	44	67	42-7603	no
Miss Diane	44	67	41-23784	no	Raggedy Ann II	44	67	42-72873	no
Miss Emmy Lou	44			no	Railway Express	44	67	41-23794	no
Miss Emmy Lou II	44	67	42-72878	no	Ram It - Damn It	44	68	42-7635	no
Miss Marcia Ann	44	67	41-23818	no	Ready & Willing	44	67	41-24109	no
Miss Marion	44	66	44-10503	no	Rebel (The)	44	68	41-23813	yes
Miss Virginia	44	68	42-40094	no	Rubber Check	44	506	42-110023	no
Missouri Belle	44	66	41-28690	no	Rugged Buggy	44	68	41-23819	yes
Missouri Sue	44	66	41-28690	no	Ruthless	44	506	41-24282	yes
Mr. 5 x 5	44	506	41-24234	yes	Sabrina	44	506	42-7647	no
My Assam Dragon	44	66	42-52332	no	Sabrina 2	44	506	42-52611	no
My Everlovin' Gal	44	506	41-28829	yes	Sabrina III	44	506	42-95209	no
My Everloving Gal	44	67		no	Sack Artists	44	67	42-100073	yes
My Gal Sal	44	506	42-50626	yes	Sad Sack	44	66	41-29147	yes
My Peach	44	506	42-100415	no	Sad Sack II	44	66	41-24153	yes
My SAD Ass	44	66	44-10531	no	Sand Bomb Special	44	66	42-95124	no
Myrtle the Fertile Turtle	44	67	42-99967	yes	Satan's Hell Cats	44	68	42-40995	yes
Myrtle the Fertile Turtle	44	67	44-50578	no	Scotty Mack	44	68	44-40276	no
Natchez-Belle	44	68	42-40373	no	Scourge of the Skies	44	66	42-7618	no
Naughty Nell	44	68	41-29538	no	Scrappy	44	506	41-24014	yes
Nice N' Naughty	44	66	42-7476	yes	Scrappy II	44	66	42-40375	yes
Night Raider	44		41-11650	yes	Seed of Satan II	44	67	42-7544	no
Northern Lass	44	68	42-100110	yes	Shack Rabbit	44	67	42-7767	no
Oh, My Sufferin' Head	44	506	42-100423	yes	Shack Rat	44	506	42-94952	no
Old Crow	44	506	41-24283	yes	Shark (The)	44	67	42-7549	no
Old Crow	44	506	42-7509	no	Shoo Shoo Baby	44	506	41-29208	no
Old Iron Corset	44	67	42-95318	yes	Shoo Shoo Baby	44	506	41-29431	yes
Ole Cock	44	506	42-110024	no	Sky Queen	44	67	42-7547	no
Ole Miss	44	67	42-7650	no	Snafu	44	66	40-2354	yes
One Weakness	44	68	42-50551	no	SNAFU	44	67	42-40354	no
Paper Doll	44	68	42-100110	yes	Southern Clipper II	44	506	42-40778	no
Passion Pit	44	506	42-95150	yes	Southern Comfort	44	506	42-40778	yes
Patsy Ann	44	68	42-50339	yes	Southern Comfort II	44	506	42-110034	no

Name	Grp.	Sq.	Serial	Pic.
Southern Comfort II	44	506	42-7522	yes
Southern Comfort III	44	506	42-50889	no
Southern Lass	44			no
Spirit of '76	44	68	41-23776	yes
Star Spangled Hell	44	67	42-72873	yes
Star Valley	44	68	42-100181	no
Sultry Sue	44	67	42-50539	yes
Sure Shot!	44	66	42-63769	no
Sure Shot!	44	68		no
Suzy Q.	44	67	41-23774	no
Suzy Q.	44	67	41-23817	yes
Sweat Box	44	66	44-40071	yes
Sweet Eloise	44	66	41-29511	no
T. S. Tessie	44	68	42-95001	no
Tally Ho	44	66	44-10542	no
Texan	44	506	41-23787	no
Texan	44	67	41-23808	no
Texan II	44	67	41-23818	yes
Texas II	44	506	41-24013	no
Texas II	44	506	42-41013	no
Three Kisses for Luck	44	67	42-95193	no
Timb - A - Ah	44	506	42-40606	yes
Tinker Belle	44	506	44-40158	yes
Torney	44	506	42-72833	no
Touch of Venus	44	67	42-7545	no
Townsend's Terrible Ten	44	68	42-109822	no
Trouble	44	506	41-24013	yes
Tuffy	44	67	42-100279	no
Tung Hoi II	44	66	42-95622	yes
Turnip Termite	44	68	41-29418	no
Turnip Termite II	44	68	42-7624	no
V for Victory	44	68	42-100412	no
V Packett	44	68	41-29156	yes
Valiant Lady	44		42-41012	no
Valiant Lady II	44		42-7514	no
Victory Ship	44	68	41-23813	yes
Wana	44	68	42-50509	yes
Wasp's Nest (The)	44	67	42-109820	no
Weary	44	66	42-95189	no
Wendy	44	506	42-110082	no
Wicked Witch	44	506	41-24295	no
Wicked Witch	44	506	41-29862	no
Wing and a Prayer	44	68	41-24211	no
Wing Dinger	44	66	41-24015	no
Worry Bird (The)	44			no
Z-Bar	44	506	42-95016	yes

90TH BOMB GROUP

Name	Grp.	Sq.	Serial	Pic.
A+	90		41-23919	no
Aincha Sorry	90		41-23824	yes
Air Pocket	90	319	44-49479	yes
Asterperious Special	90	319	42-73493	yes
Baby	90	320	41-24094	yes
Baby	90	400	42-72798	no
Bad Penny	90	321	44-41314	yes
Belle Wringer	90	400	44-50694	yes
Betsy	90	321	42-72956	yes
Big Bimbo	90	321		no
Big Bimbo	90	321		no
Big Black Bitch	90	400	41-24269	no
Big Chief	90	321	42-72774	yes
Big Emma	90	321	41-23764	no
Blonde Baby	90			no
Blonde Bomber (The)	90	320	42-40942	yes
Bobby Anne of Texas	90	319	44-40228	yes
Boise Bronc	90	320	44-40728	no
Bombs for Nippon	90	400	41-23942	yes
Booby Trap	90	321	44-40193	yes
Bottoms Up	90	319	42-100232	yes
Buck Benny Rides Again	90	400	44-40340	yes
Butcher Boy (The)	90	320	41-24108	yes
Butcher's Daughter (The)	90	319	44-40190	yes
C.O.D.-Knot to Tojo	90	321	41-23836	yes
Ceaseless Cindy	90	321	44-42262	no
Change-O-Luck	90	320	41-11868	yes
Cherrie	90	320		yes
Chosef	90	319	41-23767	no
Come and Get It	90			no
Connell's Special	90	320	41-23765	yes
Connell's Special the 2nd	90	400	42-73129	yes
Cookie	90	321	41-23839	yes
Coral Queen (The)	90	400	41-11870	yes
Cowtown's Revenge	90	321	41-23750	yes
Crosair	90	319	41-23752	no
Crosby's Curse	90	321	41-23835	yes
Czechem	90	321	42-40352	no
Daddy of 'em All	90	321	44-40431	no
Dinky	90	320	42-40325	yes
Dirtie Gertie	90	319	41-23731	yes
Display of Arms	90	320	44-41274	yes
Dorothy Anne (The)	90	400	42-41077	no
Double Shot	90	321	42-40359	no
Double Trouble	90	320	42-40358	yes
Drip	90	321	42-41105	no
Duchess	90		42-100262	no
Duchess of Paducah	90		42-109991	yes
Dude (The)	90	320	42-40326	yes
Eager Beaver (The)	90	320	41-23849	yes
Eight (8) Ball	90	321	41-23714	yes
Falcon (The)	90	321	41-23828	yes
Fifty (.50) Cal. Gal	90	321	41-23759	no
Flak Fled Flapper	90			no
Flying Stud	90	320	42-41118	yes
Form I-A	90	321	44-40229	yes
Gladys	90	400	44-40804	yes
Glamouras'	90		44-40616	yes
Glo Hop	90	321	42-40863	yes
Golden Lady	90	321	42-40914	yes
Gone With the Wind	90	400	41-24286	yes
GRRR	90	320		yes
Gun Moll	90	319	41-23755	yes
Gun Moll 2nd	90	319	42-40970	yes
Harry S. Truman (The)	90	321	44-40229	yes

Name	Grp.	Sq.	Serial	Pic.	Name	Grp.	Sq.	Serial	Pic.
Hay Maker	90	319	44-40729	yes	Norma	90	400	42-72948	yes
Heaven Can Wait	90	400	42-41216	yes	Not In Stock	90	400	42-41077	yes
Heavenly Body	90	400	41-11867	yes	Old Iron Sides	90	320	42-110053	yes
Hell's Angels	90	400	41-11903	yes	On the Ball	90	319	42-40345	no
Hell's Belle	90	400	41-24290	yes	One Ball Riley	90	319	42-40681	no
Hellzapoppin'	90	319	41-23719	yes	One Time	90		41-11869	no
Hip Parade	90		42-73002	yes	Our Baby	90			yes
Hit Parader	90	319	42-41087	yes	Our Gal	90			no
Ho Hum	90	400	42-109983	yes	Pacific Scamp	90		42-72838	yes
Hot Garters	90	321	42-41188	no	Pappy's Passion	90	319	42-100222	yes
How'm I Doin'?	90	319	42-41223	yes	Patches	90	319	41-23673	yes
I'll Be Around	90			no	Peaches	90	320		no
Idle Curiosity	90			no	Pelly-Can	90	319	41-23688	yes
Jack Pot	90	321	42-40280	no	Pete the Carrier	90	400	42-40920	yes
Jasper's Jokers	90	321	44-49480	no	Peter Heater (The)	90	320	42-40917	yes
Joe E. Brown	90			yes	Phyllis T. of Worcester	90	319	42-109988	yes
Jolly Roger (The)	90			yes	Pistol Packin' Mama	90	319	42-41209	no
Jolly Roger Express	90			no	Pistol Packin' Mama	90	321	42-40954	yes
Jolly Roger Special	90			no	Pistol Packin' Mama	90	321	42-41209	no
Joltin' Janie	90	321	42-40233	yes	Pistol Packin' Mama II	90	321	42-41209	no
Joltin' Janie II	90	321	42-40065	yes	Pluto's Dog Days	90	400	42-72947	yes
Kansas City Kitty	90		44-41480	yes	Powers Girl (The)	90	400	42-72807	yes
Kayo	90	321	42-63990	yes	Pregnant Polecat	90	400	42-72789	yes
Lady Beverly	90	319	41-23760	no	Pretty Baby	90	319	42-109987	yes
Lady Eva	90	321	41-23762	yes	Pride of Fondy	90	321	44-40338	no
Lady Eva II	90	320	41-23772	no	Pride of the Yanks	90	400	41-11904	yes
Lady Luck	90	321	41-11901	yes	Pudgy	90	320	41-23830	yes
Lady Millie	90	319	41-23753	no	Pug Nose	90		41-23823	yes
Lemon (The)/Drip	90	321	42-41105	no	Punjab	90	400	41-11902	no
Liberty Belle	90	321	41-23920	yes	Queen Mae	90	319	44-40337	yes
Lilas Marie	90	400	41-24269	yes	Queen of Hearts	90	320	44-40185	yes
Lilas Marie The 2nd	90	400	44-42260	yes	Ready, Willing & Able	90	319	42-41078	yes
Little Beaver	90	320	42-40984	yes	Redaz	90			no
Little Jody	90			no	Rhumba Rita	90			no
Live Wire	90	320	44-41235	yes	Road to Tokyo	90		44-40521	no
Lobo the Wolf	90	320	42-40830	no	Roamin' Josie	90	319	41-23698	yes
Lone Star Avenger	90	321	42-72934	yes	Roarin' Rosie	90	319	41-23698	no
Louisiana Lullaby	90	319	42-63986	yes	Royal Flush II	90	320	42-73131	yes
Lovely Louise	90	319	44-41332	yes	Ruby's Ricksha	90		42-73121	yes
Maid in USA	90	321	44-40341	yes	Sad Sack	90	320	42-72785	yes
Maiden the USA	90		xx-xx341	no	Sad Sack	90	320	42-73133	no
Mama Foo Foo	90	320	44-42094	yes	Sadie	90	400	41-24289	yes
Mama Foo Foo	90	320	44-42094	no	Salvo	90			no
Margie	90	320		no	Say Uncle	90		42-40534	yes
Miss Carriage	90	400	41-24207	yes	Scorpion	90	319	41-24073	no
Miss D. Meaner	90		42-41227	no	Seafood Mama	90	321	41-24219	yes
Miss Deed	90	321	42-41070	yes	Shack Rat	90	320	42-40918	yes
Miss Jolly Roger	90	321	44-41190	yes	Shamrock Sherry	90	319	44-40918	yes
Miss Kiwanis	90	319	44-40314	yes	Sky Lady	90	400	41-24043	yes
Mission Belle	90	400	42-40389	yes	Sky Lady	90	400	42-109982	no
Mitsu Butcher	90	320	42-40326	no	Sky Witch	90	400	42-72815	yes
Mitsu Butcher	90	320	42-72810	yes	Snappin' N' A'Bitin'	90	320	41-23869	yes
Moby Dick	90	320	41-24047	yes	Snappin' N' A'Bitin'	90	320	41-24045	yes
Naughty Blue Eyes	90	319	42-73797	yes	Sooper Wabbit	90			no
Navel Maneuvers	90	319	44-49864	yes	Starduster	90	321	41-23869	yes
Nipper (The)	90	319	41-11866	yes	Strip Polka (The)	90			yes
Nobody's Baby	90	319	42-40346	no	Strip Polka (The)	90	319	42-40970	yes

Name	Grp.	Sq.	Serial	Pic.
Surprise Attack	90			no
Tear Ass	90	400	44-40720	no
Tear-Ass the Bull	90	321	41-23720	yes
Ten Knights in a Bar Room	90	321	42-72806	yes
Texas Terror	90	400	41-23825	no
Tokio Express	90	319	41-24074	yes
Tropical Trick	90		42-40060	no
Tuttle Money	90	400	42-40968	no
Twin Nifties	90	400	42-40348	yes
Twin Nifties II	90	400	42-40928	yes
Two Bob Tillie	90	320		no
Tyrranosaurus Rex	90	400	42-40363	yes
Upstairs Maid	90		42-73941	no
V-Sure Pop	90	319	42-41073	yes
Virgin	90	319		no
Virgin II	90	319	41-23833	yes
Weezie	90	320	42-41081	no
Wilco	90	319	41-23773	yes
Windy City Kitty	90			yes
Yankee Doodle Dandy	90	319	42-40077	yes
Yanks from Hell	90	321	41-23716	yes
Yanks from Hell II	90	400		no
Yardbird	90	400	42-40905	yes

93RD BOMB GROUP

Name	Grp.	Sq.	Serial	Pic.
$64 Question	93	330	42-64437	yes
Able Mabel	93	328	42-110081	yes
Amapola	93	328	42-40269	no
Ambrose	93	330	41-23712	yes
Ambrose #2	93	330	41-23909	no
Ambrose III	93	330		no
Annie's Cousin Mamie	93			no
As You Like It	93	409	41-23748	no
As You See It	93			no
Assender II	93			no
Babby Maggy	93			no
Baggy Maggy	93	409	42-100416	yes
Ball of Fire	93	328	41-23667	yes
Ball of Fire	93	328	42-72869	no
Ball of Fire	93	329	41-23670	no
Ball of Fire III	93			no
Ball of Fire Jr.	93	328	41-23874	no
Ball of Fire, Junior	93	328	42-40128	yes
Balls of Fire No. 2	93	328	41-23667	yes
Bathtub Bessie	93	330	41-23678	yes
Bear Down	93	328	42-72863	no
Bear Down	93	328	42-72869	no
Beaver's Baby	93	409	42-50597	yes
Bertha/Lady Jane	93	329	42-40804	no
Big Dealer	93	330	41-23665	yes
Big Eagle	93	330	41-23678	no
Big Job	93	330	42-40627	no
Big Noise	93	330	42-40969	yes
Big Noise II	93	330	42-94969	no
Birmingham Express	93	329	42-63968	no
Blasted Event	93	329	41-23682	yes
Blasted Event	93	409	42-7682	no
Blastin' Bastard	93	330	41-23707	no
Bodacious	93			no
Bomerang	93	328	41-23722	yes
Boomerang II	93	330	42-63969	no
Boomerang II	93	409	42-40974	no
Buck Fifty Job	93			yes
Calis Clipper	93			no
Capricorn	93		42-52744	yes
Carioca Bev	93	330	42-51191	yes
Carl "Hen" Chick	93	329	42-63981	no
Carolyn Chick	93	329	42-63981	no
Celhalopdos	93	330	41-23675	yes
Chief Manatee	93		41-24309	yes
Chubby Champ	93	329	42-7655	no
Connie	93	409	42-7682	yes
Crow's Nest	93			no
D-Cup	93	330	42-40938	no
De Boid	93	330	42-7499	no
De Icer	93	330	42-109830	no
Death Dealer	93	409	42-40611	yes
Devil's Messenger (The)	93			no
Dinah Mite	93	328	42-95014	yes
Dogpatch Express	93	328	41-24192	no
Dogpatch Raider	93	328	41-24192	yes
Dogpatch Raider II	93			no
Doity Boid	93	330	41-24104	no
Doodle Bug	93	409	41-23724	yes
Double Trouble	93	328	41-23672	yes
Dragon Lady	93	409	41-23748	no
Duchess (The)	93	330	41-24120	no
Duchess (The)	93	330	41-24147	yes
Duke (The)	93	328	41-23729	no
Eager Beaver	93	328	41-23737	yes
Eephus	93	330	42-95254	yes
Eight Ball	93			no
El Lobo	93	344	41-23692	yes
El Toro	93	328	42-63982	no
Eophus	93	330	42-95254	yes
Euroclydon	93	328	42-40612	no
Exterminator	93	329	41-23717	yes
Fearless Freddie	93	328	41-23737	no
First Sergeant	93	329	42-40127	no
Flak Magnet	93	409		no
Flying Cock	93	409	41-23724	yes
Flying Cock II	93	328	42-63972	no
Flying Fool (The)	93	409	42-94991	no
Flying Moose (The)	93	409	44-10578	no
Flying Wolf	93	330	42-72872	yes
Flying Wolves	93	330	42-72872	yes
Foil Proof	93			no
Friday the 13th	93	328	41-23713	no
Friday's Cat	93	328	41-23713	no
Gambling Lady	93	329	44-40113	yes
Georgia Peach	93	330	42-40985	yes
Gerocko	93		41-29386	no

Name	Grp.	Sq.	Serial	Pic.	Name	Grp.	Sq.	Serial	Pic.
Geronimo	93	409	41-23744	yes	Leading Lady	93	330	44-50487	yes
Globe Trotter	93	409	41-23748	no	Let 'er Rip	93	329	41-23717	no
Globe Trotter II	93	330	42-7634	yes	Let 'er Rip	93	330	41-24121	no
Glow Worm	93	330	41-23665	no	Liberty Belle	93	328	42-95095	no
Go-Go Girls	93			no	Liberty Lad	93	409	41-23742	yes
God Bless Our Ship	93	329	42-7586	no	Liberty Lass	93	409	41-23732	yes
Green Dragon (The)	93	329	41-23683	no	Liberty Limited	93	328	41-23874	yes
Gremlin's Roost (The)	93	330	42-50505	no	Lily Ann	93	409		no
Greyhound Express	93	409	42-40610		Lindie	93		42-95043	no
nuypsy Queen	93	409	42-95024	no	Little Chum	93	328	42-51280	no
Hare's To Ya	93	329	41-23710	no	Little Lady	93	409	41-23754	yes
Heavenly Daze	93	330	42-63970	no	Little Lady	93	409	42-40754	yes
Heavenly Daze	93			yes	Little Lee	93	330	42-50505	no
Heavenly Hideaway	93	409	41-23734	no	Little Mike	93	409	44-50781	yes
Heinie Hunter	93	328	41-23990	no	Lonesome Polecat	93	330	42-63978	yes
Hell Cat	93			no	Lucky (Lucky Gordon)	93	409	41-24215	yes
Hell's A Droppin'	93	329	41-23723	yes	Lucky Gordon	93	409	41-24215	yes
Hell's A Droppin' II	93	329	41-23809	yes	Lucky Lady	93	330	41-23962	no
Hell's Angels	93	329	42-40781	no	Lucky Lass	93	329	41-24245	yes
Hell's Express	93	409	42-63762	no	Ma's Folly	93			no
Hell's Wench	93	328	42-40994	no	Ma's Worry	93	328	41-29437	no
Hellcat	93			no	Marion	93	409	42-73503	no
Hellsapoppin'	93	329	41-23723	yes	Maulin' Mallard	93	330	42-109867	yes
Here's To You	93	329	41-24230	yes	Mickey Finn	93	329	42-7629	no
Hitler's Nightmare	93		41-23774	no	Military Secret	93			no
Honey Lee	93	330	41-23712	no	Minerva	93	329	41-23689	yes
Honky Tonk Gal	93	409	42-40265	yes	Mischief	93		42-94880	no
Hot Freight	93	330	41-23666	yes	Miss Stardust	93			no
Hot Lips	93	329	42-40986	no	Miss Take	93	329	42-50372	yes
Hot Stuff	93	330	41-23728	yes	Miss Take XIII	93	329	44-49298	no
I - Ink	93	328	42-99845	no	Misschief Maker	93		42-94880	no
I'll Get By	93			no	Missouri Sue	93	409	41-24122	no
Invader (The)	93			no	Mother Goose	93			yes
Iron Ass	93	329	42-40769	yes	My Bunnie II	93		42-51270	yes
Itty Bitty Commando	93			yes	Nancy Lee	93			yes
Jack Frost	93	329	41-23982	no	Naughty Nan	93	328	42-99949	yes
Jack Frost	93	329	41-24259	no	Naughty Norma	93	329	41-23934	yes
Jerk's Natural	93	328	41-23711	yes	Night Raider	93	330	41-23665	yes
Jersey Bounce	93	330	42-40609	yes	Night Raider	93	409	41-23734	yes
Jiggs	93		xx-xx362	no	O-Bit-U-Airy Mary	93	409	42-50485	no
Jo-Jo's Special Delivery	93	329	41-23683	yes	O-Bitch-U-				
Joisey Bounce	93	328	41-24228	yes	Air-Mary	93	409	42-50485	no
Joker	93	330	42-7504	no	Old Baldy	93			no
Joker (The)	93	330	44-40472	yes	Old Irish	93			no
Jose Carioca	93	409	42-40617	yes	Old Patches	93	409	xx-xx334	no
Journal Square Express	93			no	Ole King Cole	93	328	42-7519	yes
Joy Ride	93	409	42-7621	no	On the Ball	93	328	42-40990	yes
Judith Lynn	93	329	42-40983	yes	Patches	93	409	42-100334	no
K.K. & His Abort Kids	93	328	44-40157	no	Pay Off	93	329	41-23982	no
Katy Bug	93	328	41-23745	yes	Peg	93	329	41-23658	no
King's ETO Express	93			no	Piccadilly Filley	93	329	41-24111	yes
Kraut Killer	93	328	42-40801	no	Pis-s-st	93	330	42-95242	no
Lady Gwen	93	330	44-50553	no	Plutocrat	93		42-52455	no
Lady Jane (The)	93	329	42-40804	no	Pregnant Angel	93	330		no
Lady of the Lake	93		41-24130	no	Pudgy	93	330	42-40613	yes
Latrine Rumor (The)	93	409	42-95199	no	Queenie	93	409	41-24298	no
Leading Lady	93		44-40488	no	Rat Poison	93	330	42-50989	yes

Name	Grp.	Sq.	Serial	Pic.
Ready & Willing	93	330	41-24109	yes
Ready Teddy	93	330	41-23721	yes
Red Ass	93	409	41-23740	yes
Red Ball Express	93		42-40992	no
Reddy Teddy	93	330	41-23721	yes
Return Engagement	93	409	42-100336	no
Return Engagement	93	409	44-10578	yes
Roy's Boys	93			no
Rubber Check	93	409	42-95294	no
Sahara Sue	93			no
Satan's Angels	93	328	42-40604	yes
Satan's Chariot	93	329	41-24025	no
Satan's Sister	93			yes
Satan's Sister	93			yes
Satan's Sister II	93	330	42-100413	no
Satan's Sister III	93			no
Satan's Sister IV	93			no
Satan's Sister V	93			no
Say Uncle	93			yes
Second Chance	93	330	41-23707	no
Sex Appeal	93	409	41-24105	no
Shoot Luke	93	328	41-23729	yes
Silver Eagle	93	409	42-50362	yes
Sleeping Dynamite	93		42-50839	yes
Sleepytime Gal	93	328	42-95095	no
Snafu	93			no
Solid Comfort	93	330	42-50501	yes
Southwind	93	409	42-63987	no
Sterile Errol	93	328	42-7641	yes
Sugar	93	328		no
Sweat Box	93	330	44-40071	no
Sweat Girl	93	330	42-100150	no
Sweat Pea	93			no
Sweater Gal	93	330	42-100150	yes
Sweet Chariot	93	330	42-50829	no
Tarfu	93	329	41-23810	no
Tarfu II	93			no
Team GO	93	328	41-29437	no
Teggie Ann	93	409	41-23754	yes
Teggie Ann II	93	409	41-23999	no
Tennessee Rambler	93			no
Thar She Blows	93	329	41-23658	yes
Thar She Blows	93	329	42-40127	yes
Thunderbird	93	329	41-23658	no
Thunderbird	93	409	41-28626	no
Time's A Wastin'	93			no
Tupelo Lass	93	409	41-24105	yes
Two (2) Down, 1 to Go	93			yes
U Name It	93			no
U Name It Peg	93	329	41-23658	yes
U Need It	93			no
U.S. Express	93	329	41-23674	no
Unexpected I	93			no
Unexpected II	93			no
Unexpected III	93			no
Unexpected IV	93			no
Unexpected V	93			no

Name	Grp.	Sq.	Serial	Pic.
Unexpected VI	93	329		yes
Urgin' Virgin (The)	93	328	42-41004	yes
Utah Man	93	330	41-24226	yes
Valient Virgin	93	329	42-40765	yes
Victory Belle	93	328	42-100294	yes
Vulgar Virgin	93	328	41-24192	no
Vulgar Virgin	93	328	42-40608	no
War Baby	93	328	42-40128	yes
War Goddess	93	409	42-109816	yes
Wee Willie	93	409	44-50600	no
Wham Bam	93	330	41-23738	yes
What A Sack	93	409		no
Willie's Worry	93	328	42-100428	yes
You Cawn't Miss It	93	329	41-23809	no
Zoot Snook the Shark	93			no

98TH BOMB GROUP

Name	Grp.	Sq.	Serial	Pic.
Air Lobe	98	345	42-40312	yes
Alice the Goon	98	344	41-11786	yes
Arkansas Traveler II	98	345	41-23781	yes
Arkansas Traveller	98	345	41-11809	yes
B. T. O.	98	344	41-24040	no
Baby	98	344	41-24026	yes
Bambi	98	345	41-11813	yes
Bashful	98	343	41-11776	yes
Battle Axe	98	345	42-40793	yes
Belchin' Bertha	98	344	42-40742	yes
Better Late than Never	98	345	42-51364	no
Big Operator	98	344	42-41023	yes
Big Operator (The)	98	344	41-24040	yes
Big Time Operator	98	344	41-24040	no
Bird Dog	98	343	42-40341	yes
Black Magic	98	415	42-40662	yes
Blonde Bomber	98	343	41-11760	yes
Blonde Bomber	98	343	41-11895	yes
Blonde Bomber II	98	343	41-23659	yes
Blowing Bubbles	98	344	42-72779	no
Boilermaker	98	415	41-11918	yes
Boilermaker II	98	415	41-23782	yes
Boots	98	343	42-40313	yes
Bottoms Up	98			yes
Bottoms Up	98	415	42-72908	no
Bugs Bunny	98	344	42-41029	no
Butch	98	415	42-73138	no
Cabin in the Sky	98	343		yes
Calamity Jane	98	344	42-41220	yes
Calamity Jane II	98	344	44-41221	no
Capricorn	98			no
Cherry	98			no
Chief	98	345	41-11774	yes
Chris' Crate II	98		42-110160	yes
Chug-A-Lug	98	344	42-41029	no
Chug-A-Lug	98	345	41-11766	yes
Chug-A-Lug	98	345	41-23766	no
Cielito Lindo	98	345	42-41033	yes

Name	Grp.	Sq.	Serial	Pic.	Name	Grp.	Sq.	Serial	Pic.
Cindy	98	345	41-11806	yes	Idiot's Dee Light	98	345	41-23780	yes
Consolidated Mess	98	415	44-40630	yes	Irish Lassie	98	344	42-51147	yes
Coral Princess	98	344	41-11931	no	Irish Lassie	98	344	42-95352	no
Coral Princess	98	344	42-41011	no	Is This Trip Necessary?	98			yes
Coral Princess	98	344	42-41023	no	Janeen Ann	98	415	42-51986	no
Coral Princess	98	345	42-100266	no	Jersey Jackass	98	343	41-11776	yes
Cornhusker	98	415	42-40322	yes	Jersey Jerks	98	343		yes
D'Artagnan	98	415	41-24231	yes	Jinx	98	344	42-40742	no
Daisy Mae	98	415	41-11815	yes	Joker	98	415	42-40205	yes
Daisy Mae	98	415	42-41031	yes	Joker (The)	98	415	42-40205	yes
Damfino	98	343		yes	Jolly Roger	98	343	44-50449	yes
Deuces Wild	98	415	42-78222	no	Judith Ann	98	345	42-73418	yes
Doc	98	343	41-11921	yes	Julie	98			no
Dopey	98	343	42-40268	yes	Kate Smith	98	345		yes
Dopey	98	343	42-78600	yes	Kathryn Ann	98	343	42-78600	yes
Dopey	98	343	42-94762	yes	Kickapoo	98	344	41-11768	yes
Dorly	98	343	42-64393	no	Lady Luck	98	345	42-64391	no
Dot's Queen of Queens	98	345	42-50417	yes	Li'l De Icer	98	415	41-11836	yes
Dot's Queen of Queens	98	345	42-72854	no	Lil' Abner	98	344	41-11779	yes
Dry Bones	98	344	42-40329	no	Lil' Blon Dee	98	415	42-73424	yes
Duchess (The)	98	345	42-73439	no	Lil' Blon Dee II	98	345	44-49260	no
Dust Storm	98	343	42-51168	no	Lil' Joe	98	343	41-11886	yes
Eager Beavers	98	343	41-11897	yes	Lil' Jughaid	98	415	42-40758	yes
Easy Margie	98	343	42-41007	no	Lil' Jughaid	98	415	42-63758	yes
Edna Elizabeth	98		41-11620	no	Little Chief Big Dog	98	345	42-40106	yes
Emily	98	415	44-40633	no	Little Joe	98	345	41-11886	yes
Everybody's Sweetheart	98	345	42-73434	no	Little Joe	98	415	41-24195	yes
Fargo Express (The)	98	415	42-78382	yes	Little Mitch	98	343	41-28810	yes
Fertile Myrtle	98	415	41-24023	yes	Lonely Lair	98	415	44-41185	no
Finito Benito	98	344	42-72891	no	Lorraine	98			no
Flak Sack	98	344	41-23692	yes	Lucy's Lucky	98	345	42-40320	yes
Floogie Boo Bird	98	415	41-11810	yes	Luscious Duchess (The)	98	345	42-52009	no
Flower	98			yes	Mabel	98	345	41-28928	no
Flying Ginny (J?)	98	344	42-41006	no	Maggie's Drawers	98	344	42-41008	yes
Foe Flusher	98	344	41-28825	no	Margie	98		42-41007	no
Four Eyes	98	343	42-40655	no	Maternity Ward	98	345	42-40663	yes
Four Eyes	98		42-40665	no	Melodee Blondee	98	343	42-72424	no
Green Apple	98	415		no	Melodie	98	345	42-73429	yes
Green Eye Ikey	98	344	42-50225	no	Melon Patch Special	98	415	42-41027	no
Grumpy	98	343	41-11825	yes	Memphis to St. Joe	98	344	41-23801	yes
Gump the Sniffer Chief	98	345	44-50654	no	Miss Bea Haven	98	415	42-52058	no
Hadley's Harem	98	344	41-24311	yes	Miss Julie	98	344	41-23763	yes
Hail Columbia	98	343	41-11825	yes	Miss N-U	98	344	42-52258	yes
Happy	98	343	42-40256	yes	Miss Please	98	344	42-51994	yes
Heaven's Devils	98	343	42-73077	no	Mister Period!	98	344	42-73136	no
Hell's Belle	98	345	42-41183	yes	Mongrel	98	415	41-11932	yes
Hell's Bells	98	343	42-94998	no	Mr. Period	98	415	42-73136	no
Hey, Doc	98	344	42-109813	yes	Natchez to Mobile	98	344	41-11797	yes
Hillbilly	98	415	42-40379	no	Nemsis	98	345	42-73423	no
Homesick Susie	98	343	42-40312	yes	Never A Dull Moment	98	415		no
Honeysuckle Rose	98	344	42-72890	yes	Nightmare	98	343	41-11896	yes
Hot Rocks	98	345	42-40197	no	North American Express	98	345	42-78527	yes
Hot Stuff	98	415	42-41028	yes	Northern Star	98	343	41-11921	yes
How Am I Doin'?	98	415	42-64370	no	Ocie Boo	98			no
Hubba Hubba	98			yes	Old Baldy	98	345	42-40102	yes
I'll Get By	98	343	44-49041	no	Old Ned's Bells	98	345	42-72849	no

The lovely FLAK FLED FLAPPER, a B-24J served with the 528th Sq, 380th BG, Fifth AF. She was salvaged on Biak Is. in Sept. 45 after 1,000 plane hours. (Beitling)

FUEL CELL FANNY (astride a Lib fuel tank) was a B-24H with the 464th BG, Fifteenth AF. (Beitling)

Half a world apart, Liberators share a similar fate. Above: After a mission to the Marshall Islands in Dec 1943 THE GREMLIN crash-landed on Makin Island. This B-24D of the 98th Sq, 11th BG bore the name and likeness of SEXY SUE II on the right side of the fuselage. (Lambert) Below: SATAN'S ANGELS, a B-24D of the 328th Sq, 93rd BG, came to a bad end on its belly in England. The 93rd was a pioneering B-24 unit in the Eighth AF. (Beitling)

FEARLESS FOSDICK (one of many Al Capp cartoon characters to appear on warbirds) was a B-24H serving with the 702nd Sq, 445th BG. She came to rest on her belly. (8th AFHS)

A Fifteenth Air Force B-24D, BREWERY WAGON was with the 512th Sq, 376th BG. Original pilot was Robert Storz of Storz Brewery, Omaha. She was lost on the first Ploesti mission, 8 Aug 41, with John Palm as pilot. (Beitling)

A B-24M, OLD BLACK MAGIC, smelted at Kingman, AZ, served with the 31st Sq, 5th Bomb Grp in the Pacific. (Fred Johnsen)

TARGET FOR TONIGHT was a B-24D that served with the 65th Sq, 43rd BG. (Beitling)

AVAILABLE JONES, veteran of the first Ploesti raid, ditched off Greece, crew taken POW, flew with the 67th Sq, 44th BG. (Beitling)

UNAPPROACHABLE was a PB4Y-1 serving with VB-106. Note three Jap aircraft kill flags. (USN via NMNA)

A pair of Fifteenth AF B-24Js. Above: DOGPATCH EXPRESS, 756th Sq, 459th BG, drops her load on a railroad bridge near Padua, Italy. (Lambert) Below: QUEEN OF HEARTS of the 738th Sq, 454th BG was not adorned with nose art but had six German fighter claims to show for just eight missions. (Beitling)

B-24Js of the 90th flew into Pacific battles with these two saucy beauties. The group was known as The Jolly Rogers. (Beitling)

Above: GINEE was a late model B-24 with the 464th Bomb Grp. Note unique nose windows adapted in the field. Artist was **Ray Ingalls**. (Forman) Below: SACK TIME SALLY was a B-24H assigned to the 565th Sq, 389th BG. She was lost over France on 31 Jan 44. (Beitling)

Above: DING DONG DADDY FROM DIXIE was a B-24H of the 834th Sq, 486th BG, pilot, Albert Kite. It carried some of the most bizarre art in the Eighth AF. (Beitling)   Below: This B-24J, BOMB WACKY WABBIT, was with the 33rd Sq, 22nd BG, a pioneer unit in the Pacific. (Beitling)

A B-24J, OLD IRON PANTS flew with the 855th Sq, 491st BG, Eighth AF. (Beitling)

The crew of PIN UP GIRL stands before their Eighth AF B-24H of the 844th Sq, 489th BG. Transferred to 446th BG and lost 4 Apr 45. (M.A. O'Brien via Lambert)

This complex piece of art adorned a PB4Y-1 of VPB-111, the only Navy patrol squadron to serve combat tours in both Atlantic and Pacific. (Fred Johnsen)

BLACK SHEEP was an 867th Sq, 494th Bomb Grp. B-24J with the Seventh AF. Pilot was Lt. Bill Lambert. (Lambert)

Above: A Navy PB4Y-1 of VB-115, SWEET MARIE, is shown here at Biak Is. in 1944. (Norbert Krane via NMNA) Below: OLD TAYLOR, a Fifteenth AF B-24H served with the 726th Sq, 451st BG. It blew up in flight on a Vienna mission, only one crew member surviving. (Beitling)

Libs named **TARFU** flew in both the Pacific (above) and Europe. Above: TARFU was a B-24J of the 26th Sq, 11 BG. She flew 40 missions with the crew of 1st Lt. Henry Slayton and came home with part of a Jap fighter wrapped about #3 engine. (Beitling) Below: TARFU II, was a B-24J of the 448th BG. (8th AFHS)

A pair of Fifteenth AF vets: Above: BOTTOMS UP, a B-24H was with the 721st Sq, 450th BG, flew over 100 missions and is seen here undergoing extensive repairs. (Lambert) Below: This H model Lib of the 830th Sq, 485th BG, had the familiar LIFE magazine logo on its side. (Lambert)

JUNGLE QUEEN, serving with the 65th Sq, 43rd Bomb Group early in the SW Pacific war, was an export version of the Liberator, an LB-30, Serial AL-640. (Beitling)

The 859th Sq, 492nd BG Eighth AF was home to B-24H, SCREW BALL. It was utilized on special operations, leaflets, agent drops, etc. (Beitling)

Above: TAIL WIND, was a B-24H with the 789th Sq, 467th BG. (8th AFHS) Below: A B-24J, PACIFIC TRAMP III, was assigned to HQ Seventh Air Force. Flown on missions by B. Gen. Truman London, CO VII Bomber Command. (Beitling)

Returning home to England was a common theme for all Eighth AF crews. Above: YOU'RE SAFE AT HOME, a B-24H, belonged to the 851st Sq, 490th BG. (8th AFHS) Below: The 735th Sq, 453rd BG claimed BECOMING BACK, a B-24J. She made it back to the U.S. (Beitling)

Above: The PB4Y-1, THUNDER MUG (also dubbed "Olde 8 Ball") was the aircraft of Cdr. Norman Miller, VB-109, shown here on Kwajalein Is. in 1944. With various crews, she sank or damaged 66 ships and claimed 15 enemy planes. (USN via NMNA)

Below: WELL DEVELOPED was well traveled in the Pacific. A B-24J she served briefly with the 494th BG and the 11th BG and then the 2nd Recon Sq under Sid Hendrick as an F7-B. (Beitling)

A pair of long range Pacific photo reconnaissance Libs. Above: PHOTO FANNY adorned this AF B-24J of the 2nd Photo Charting Sq based on Okinawa. (Beitling)
Below: THE LEMON was a PB4Y-1 serving with the Navy's VD-1. She is shown here on Guam in 1945. (USN via NMNA)

Above: A pair of Fifteenth AF casualties. Above: LIL' BLON DEE, a B-24J of the 415th Sq, 98th BG, was a "Mickey", or radar equipped aircraft. After crash landing in Italy, she was repaired. (Beitling) Below: The B-24E, QUEEN OF HEARTS, 717th Sq, 449th BG crashed in Italy and was written off. (Beitling)

The highly polished SEVENTH HEAVEN was the personal aircraft of Seventh AF CG Maj. Gen. Willis Hale. It was an early model Liberator built for export to Britain. (Lambert)

POOP DECK PAPPY, a B-24H, was assigned to the 577th Sq, 392nd BG. She crash landed at Shipdam, England, 16 Nov 44. (8th AFHS)

Old and new Libs of the Fifteenth AF. Above: Wearing her desert paint scheme in 1943 is THUNDER BIRD of the 415th Sq, 98th BG. (Beitling) Below: CALAMITY JANE is seen over Budapest in June 1944. She belonged to the 725th Sq, 451st BG. She was lost over Szony, Hungary, on her 51st mission, 7 Feb 45. (Lambert)

This B-24H, THE NEAR SIGHTED ROBIN, belonged to the 7th Sq, 34th BG. (8th AFHS)

A B-24D converted to a C-87 transport, KONGO KUTIE supported the Ninth AF in Africa. (Beitling)

A pair of Fourteenth AF 308th BG Libs: SNAFU, a word coined in WW II, was the name for this B-24J of the 373rd Sq. The tiger shark mouth was common on this and other China based aircraft. THE BAD PENNY was a B-24D of the 375th Sq. It was lost in combat and the wreckage found on a Japanese airfield at war's end. (Beitling)

LIL' NILMERG (Gremlin spelled backward), a B-24J, seen with the Glenn Horton crew of the 529th Sq, 380th BG, Fifth AF. She had over 1,000 hours of time and 82 missions. (Lambert)

HELL AND BACK, a B-24H served with the 493rd BG. (8th AFHS)

A pair of B-24Js of the 36th Bomb Sq. They were a special unit that flew electronic countermeasure sorties in advance of Eighth AF bombing missions. (Donat Lafond and Richard Sackett via Stephen Hutton)

An irreverent YE OLDE RUGGED CURSE was a B-24E assigned to the 718th Sq, 449th BG in Italy. (Beitling)

RED HEADED WOMAN, a B-24L of the 31st Sq, 5th Bomb Grp, Fifth AF, had flown 90 missions when this photo was taken. (A.B. Goldberg via Fred Johnsen)

This B-24H was assigned to the 786th Sq, 466th BG, Eighth AF. (Beitling)

CHIEF'S DELIGHT was a B-24L of the 736th Sq, 454th BG, Fifteenth AF. (Beitling)

123

MITZI-BISHI served with VB-106 a PB4Y-1 squadron. (USN via NMNA)

Lt. Upfield's crew of Lady Luck II were ship hunters of the independent 868th Bomb Sq, Thirteenth Air Force. The B-24Ms of the 868th were specially equipped with search radar. (Forman)

The B-24D, CHUG-A-LUG, 345th Sq, 98th BG, is shown here returning from her 105th and last mission, including three trips to Ploesti. The veteran Liberator went on bond tours in the U.S. (Lambert) Below: This B-24J was with the 20th Sq, 6th Recon Group. (Beitling)

Patterned after the "Dogpatch" cartoon character was SWEET MOONBEAM MC SWINE, a B-24H of the 704th Sq, 446th BG. (8th AFHS)

ALLEY OOP, yet another cartoon character, was the namesake for this Fifteenth AF, 780th Bomb Sq, 465th BG Lib. (Lambert)

An exceptional artist adorned Seventh AF B-24Js of the 819th Sq, 30th BG with these and other ladies. (Lambert)

The 5,000th Liberator from Consolidated's San Diego plant was signed by employees. A B-24J, it served with the Fifteenth AF, 465th BG. (Lambert)

MUNDA BELLE, named for an oft visited Japanese airfield in the Solomon Is., was a 307th Bomb Grp. B-24D. She carried the last three digits of the serial number on her nose along with the naked lady. (Beitling)

128

Name	Grp.	Sq.	Serial	Pic.	Name	Grp.	Sq.	Serial	Pic.
Our Baby	98			yes	Snow White and the Seven Dwarfs	98	343	42-40364	yes
Paper Doll	98	415	42-51981	no	Southern Belle	98	344	42-51989	no
Paper Doll	98	415	42-99860	no	Special Delivery	98	343		no
Pappy	98	415	44-40324	yes	Spirit of Spokane	98	415	41-28799	no
Penelope	98	415	42-40195	no	Squaw (The)	98	344	41-11761	yes
Pennies From Heaven	98	343	41-11894	no	Squaw (The)	98	344	41-23795	no
Pennys From Heaven	98	343	41-11918	yes	Stinger	98	415	41-11817	yes
Pennys From Heaven	98	343	41-11894	yes	Stork (The)	98	345	41-11794	yes
Pink Avenger	98			yes	Strawberry Blonde	98	345	41-11842	yes
Pink Elephant	98	344	41-11814	yes	Sugar	98	345	42-41240	no
Pink Lady	98	415	41-11764	yes	Sugar Baby	98	345	42-41240	no
Pinky the Pimp	98	343	41-11895	no	Suzy Q	98			no
Pistol Packin' Mama	98			yes	Sweaty Betty	98	345	42-41026	no
Pluto	98	345	41-23715	yes	Tagalong	98	344	41-24197	yes
Pocahontas	98	415	41-23768	yes	Tail Wind	98	344		no
Powder Ann	98	344	42-73421	no	Tailwind	98	343	42-64346	yes
Prince Charming	98	343	42-40082	yes	Takeoff Time	98	344	42-51146	yes
Prince Charming II	98	343	42-109802	yes	Tangerine	98	345	42-64344	no
Queen of Hearts	98	345		no	Teggie Ann	98		41-23754	no
Queenie	98	345	42-78420	no	Thunderbird	98	415	41-23789	yes
Raunchy	98	345	41-11819	yes	Thundermug	98	328	42-40246	yes
Ready & Willing	98	415	41-11765	yes	Toonerville Trolley	98			yes
Rebel	98	344	41-23763	no	Tu-Yung-Tu	98	415	44-10546	no
Red-Dee	98		42-100434	no	Ugly But Tough	98	345	44-48784	yes
Reluctant Virgin	98	415	42-51176	no	Upsy	98	343		yes
Root of All Evil	98	415	41-11808	no	Urgin' Virgin	98	345	42-41010	no
Rose Bud	98	344	41-11764	no	Vulgar Virgin	98	344	41-24198	yes
Rosie Wrecked 'Em	98	345	41-11803	yes	Wahoo	98	345	41-11774	no
Rowdy	98	344	41-11794	yes	War Cloud	98	345	41-23785	yes
Rowdy Ann	98	344	41-11796	yes	What's Cookin' Doc?	98	344	41-24040	yes
Rowdy II	98	344	41-23656	yes	White H	98	345	42-51910	no
Rupert the Roo	98	415	44-48782	no	Who Dare?	98	415	44-40847	no
Rupert the Roo II	98	415	42-64365	no	Who Dare?	98	415	44-41047	no
Ruth Please	98	343	42-51161	yes	Whoda Thunkit	98			yes
Sack Shack	98			yes	Witch (The)	98	343	41-11840	yes
Sad Sack	98	344	42-40208	yes	Wolf Pack	98	343	42-40207	no
Salt Lake Katie	98	415	41-28917	yes	Yankee Doodle Dandy	98	344	42-40105	yes
Salt Lake Katie	98	415	42-109799	no	Yen Tu	98	415	42-40520	yes
Sandman (The)	98	345	42-40402	yes	Zombie	98	415	41-11790	yes
Santa	98	343		yes					
Semper Felix	98	345	41-24246	yes					
Shanghai Lil	98	415	41-11767	yes					
Shanghi Lil	98	415	41-11767	yes					

307TH BOMB GROUP

Name	Grp.	Sq.	Serial	Pic.
Sheza Honey	98	345	42-51328	no
Shufti	98	345	44-40494	no
Skipper	98	344	41-23733	yes
Sky Lark	98	345	41-11883	yes
Sky Wolf	98	345	42-73416	no
Skylark	98	345	41-11883	no
Sleepy	98	344	41-11761	yes
Slow Time Sally	98	345	44-48784	yes
Snafu	98	343	41-24275	yes
Snafu	98	345	41-24275	yes
Snake Eyes	98	344	44-40102	no
Snake Eyes	98	345	42-40316	yes
Sneezy	98	343	41-23795	yes
Snow White	98	343	41-11913	yes

Name	Grp.	Sq.	Serial	Pic.
A+	307		41-23919	no
Annie Fay	307		41-24096	yes
Available	307	370	42-40980	yes
Babes in Arms	307	370	42-73263	yes
Bad Penny (The)	307	370	41-23899	yes
Balls O' Fire	307		42-40202	yes
Bar Fly (The)	307	372	42-40096	yes
Big Black Bitch	307		41-24269	yes
Big Sleep (The)	307	370	42-73270	yes
Billie B.	307	370	42-40076	yes
Billy Jo	307		42-110080	no
Bitchurquitchin'	307	372	42-40134	yes
Bitchurquitchin' II	307	372	44-40599	yes
Blessed Event	307		42-40533	yes

Name	Grp.	Sq.	Serial	Pic.	Name	Grp.	Sq.	Serial	Pic.
Blitz Queen	307	424	42-40858	yes	Nana	307	424	44-51455	no
Bobbie Lou	307		44-49617	yes	Nipponese Sunset	307	371	41-23797	yes
Bobbie Lou Too	307		44-51617	no	Niquotina	307	371	41-24107	yes
Bombs To Nippon	307	371	42-73147	yes	Pennsy City Kitty	307		44-41480	yes
Bundles for Japan	307		41-23965	yes	Persuader (The)	307	372	42-73277	no
Burma	307	424	44-40601	yes	Pirate Lady	307		42-72822	yes
Charlot the Harlot	307	370	41-11823	yes	Pistol Packin' Mama	307	370	41-23987	yes
Daisy Mae	307	372	41-23983	yes	Rattler (The)	307	424	41-23925	yes
Dina Might	307	424	xx-xx547	no	Red's Devils	307	371	42-73271	yes
Dreyer's Devils	307		44-40954	no	Rodger the Lodger	307	372	44-41535	yes
Dumbo	307	370	42-41085	yes	Rosemarie	307			yes
Dumbo the Avenger	307		41-23906	yes	Round Trip	307		42-40644	yes
Eager Beaver	307	371	41-24012	yes	Rude Nude	307	371	41-24151	yes
Four Roses	307	370	42-40219	no	Ruth Ann	307		44-40945	yes
Frenisi	307	370	42-40323	yes	Scrapiron	307		44-41423	yes
Fuzzy Wuzzy	307		41-23730	yes	Sexy Sue II	307	424	41-23943	no
Georgie	307	424	44-42428	yes	Sexy Sue IV	307	372	41-23938	yes
Green Hornet	307	372	41-24097	yes	Shack Rat	307	370	42-40222	yes
Gremlin	307			no	Shadow (The)	307		41-23687	yes
Grove Hill Blunderbus	307	372	42-72824	yes	Shady Lady	307		44-41370	yes
Gruesome 16	307	372	44-41290	yes	Shady Lady	307	370	42-40212	yes
Hawaiian Air Depot	307		41-23911	yes	Shady Lady	307	372	41-24212	no
Heather Angel	307	372	42-72783	yes	Shamrock (The)	307	371	41-23829	no
Hell from Heaven	307		42-72829	yes	Sitting Pretty	307			yes
Hell N' Hiwater II	307		44-41422	yes	So Velly Solly	307	372	41-23929	yes
Hell-O-Trouble	307			yes	Spirit of Lakeland (The)	307	424	41-23945	yes
Hell-O-Trouble	307		41-23864	no	Starduster	307		41-23869	yes
Honey	307	371	42-40869	yes	Starduster	307	370	42-40679	no
Hoot Owl Express	307	372	42-40235	yes	Stinky Pinky	307		41-24106	yes
House of Bourbon	307	424	41-23943	yes	Susie	307		44-40587	yes
Indian Thummer	307		44-49442	yes	Thumper	307		42-40073	yes
Janie	307	424	44-40535	yes	Thunderbird	307			no
Jeannie C.	307	424	42-40211	yes	Tillie	307	370	41-23915	no
Jeremiah	307	424	41-23877	yes	Topper (The)	307	371	41-23910	yes
Joker (The)	307	372	41-23962	no	Tornado Buster	307		42-40638	yes
Justa 24	307		44-40542	yes	Two Time	307		44-40546	yes
Kit's Tadger	307	371	44-40604	yes	Vibratin' Virgin	307	372	41-24212	yes
Laden Maiden	307	424	42-72819	yes	Wake Island	307	371	41-23829	yes
Lakanooki	307	371	42-40857	yes	Whadahell!	307		42-73144	yes
Lazy Lady	307	371	42-41092	yes	Who Dat?	307	372	44-41700	yes
Little Dumbo	307	370	41-23841	yes	Whodunit 2nd (The)	307			yes
Little Mick	307			yes	Wicked Wench (The)	307	372	42-73258	yes
Louise Mary	307	372	44-41354	yes	Willie Wolves Den	307	371	42-73146	yes
Madame Libby, the Sea Ducer	307		42-40838	yes	Wolf Pack	307	370	41-24144	no
Major-ette	307			yes	Wolfe Pack	307	371	41-24268	yes
Mammy Yokum	307	424	42-40221	yes	Woody Woodpecker	307	424	44-41179	yes
Mammy Yokum II	307			yes					
Man-O-War	307	371	41-23966	yes					

308TH BOMB GROUP

Name	Grp.	Sq.	Serial	Pic.
Mary Louise	307	372	44-41345	yes
Mascot	307	371	42-73450	yes
Miss Jones	307	371	41-24016	yes
Acme Beer Barrel	308		42-100249	no
Miss Maryland II	307		42-73145	yes
American Beauty	308	375	44-41251	yes
Momentary Dysentary	307		42-40254	yes
Angry Angel (The)	308	374	42-73436	yes
Munda Belle	307	370	42-40144	yes
Armored Angel	308	374	44-49624	yes
My Heart Belongs				
Assam Wagon	308	374		no
To Daddy	307		44-42698	yes
Available	308	375	42-100269	yes
Axis Nightmare	308	373	41-24138	yes
Bad Penny (The)	308	375	41-24238	yes

Name	Grp.	Sq.	Serial	Pic.	Name	Grp.	Sq.	Serial	Pic.
Battlin' Bitch	308	375	41-24237	yes	Joker (The)	308	372		yes
Bee Line Betty	308	374	44-41292	yes	Jungle Pussy	308	374	42-40503	yes
Belle Starr	308	425	42-40879	yes	Kandy Kourier	308	425	42-73318	yes
Betty G.	308	375	41-24279	yes	Karachi Kourier	308	425	42-73318	no
Big Red	308			yes	Katy Did	308	375	41-24284	yes
Big Sleep (The)	308	373		yes	King's "X"	308	375	44-40584	yes
Big-Az-Bird (The)	308			yes	Lackanookie	308	374	42-40630	no
Bitch's Sister (The)	308	375	42-73319	yes	Lady Luck	308	374	44-41430	yes
Bonnie Belle	308	425	42-40103	yes	Lakanooki	308	374	41-24188	yes
Boomerang	308		41-23944	no	Lil' Butch	308	425	41-24193	yes
Briefed for Action	308	374	44-41443	yes	Lili Marlene	308		42-73442	no
Burma Queen	308	425	42-73255	no	Lili Marlene	308		42-73494	no
Buzz-z Buggy	308	375	42-73327	yes	Lili Marlene II	308	374	42-100244	yes
C.E.Shack	308	425	41-24292	yes	Little Butch	308	425	41-24193	yes
Cabin in the Sky	308	425	42-40849	no	Little Egypt	308	374	44-49569	yes
Calamity Jane	308	374	44-42019	yes	Little Flower	308	375	41-24288	yes
China Clipper	308	425	44-41448	yes	Little Stinker (The)	308	375	42-40413	yes
China Doll	308	425	42-40066	yes	Lonesome Polecat	308	425	42-40850	yes
China Gal	308	425		no	Mama Foo Foo	308	374	44-42094	yes
Chuck's Chicken Coop	308	375	42-73441	yes	Manhattan Maiden	308	374	44-42142	yes
Chug-A-Lug	308	425	41-24251	yes	Massa's Dragon	308			no
Chug-A-Lug Jr.	308	425	42-73310	yes	Maxwell House	308	373	41-24164	yes
Cocky Bobby	308	425	44-41427	no	Maxwell House II	308	373	42-100240	no
Daisy Mae	308	373	41-24218	yes	Maxwell House II	308	373	42-73425	no
Dead-Eye Dick	308			no	Maxwell House III	308	373	42-100280	yes
Ding How Dottie	308	374	44-40788	yes	Mighty Eightball (The)	308	425	41-24224	yes
Dippy Dave and His					Miss Beryl	308	374	44-40832	yes
8 Dippy Diddlers	308	373	41-24143	yes	Miss Carriage	308	374	42-40624	yes
Doodlebug	308	373	42-24223	yes	Miss Conduct	308	375	44-41118	no
Dragon Lady	308	425	44-41446	yes	Miss Lace	308		44-42133	yes
Eighty (80) Days	308	425	42-100267	yes	Mission Complete	308			yes
Escalator	308	374	41-24296	no	Modest Maiden	308	375	42-40865	no
Escalator III	308	374	42-73438	yes	Mohawk	308	373	42-40786	no
Esky	308	373	42-73286	yes	Monsoon Maiden	308	425	42-100276	yes
Eton Pussy	308		42-40758	no	Mudfish	308	375	41-24308	no
Five by Five	308	425	42-40062	no	Mudfish II	308	375	42-40620	no
Flamingo	308	374	41-24181	no	Night Mission	308	374	42-78680	yes
Flamingo II	308	373	42-72835	no	Nightmare Express	308		42-63778	yes
Floogie	308	374	42-40614	no	Nip Nipper	308	373	42-40391	yes
Floogie Boo	308	425	44-41441	no	Nitemare	308			no
Flying Cloud	308	374	42-100235	yes	Old Acquaintance	308	375	44-40826	yes
Flying Wac/					Old Baldy	308	375	42-40848	no
China Doll	308	425	42-40066	no	Old Reliable	308		44-41437	yes
Forever Amber	308	374	42-73188	yes	Ole 837	308	374	42-72837	no
Frendlin (The)	308	425	42-73265	yes	Orient Express	308		44-40781	no
Georgia Peach	308		42-73445	yes	Our Private Stock	308	373	42-73247	yes
Goon (The)	308	374	41-24183	yes	Pelican (The)	308	373	41-24124	yes
Gremlin's Haven	308			yes	Pelican (The)	308	373	41-24183	no
Heavenly Body	308	425	42-73116	yes	Piece Time	308	373	44-49491	yes
Hot As Hell	308	425	42-40075	yes	Poco Moco	308		44-49451	yes
Hot As Hell	308		42-73308	no	Pokey	308		42-100040	no
Hot Nuts	308	374	41-24266	no	Pregnant Swan	308	425	42-40069	no
Hump Time	308	374	44-42117	yes	Problem Child	308	375	42-41164	no
Impatient Lady	308	374	44-41441	yes	Psycology	308	425	42-40070	no
Innocent Infant III	308	375	44-49649	yes	Ramp Rooster	308	425	41-24222	yes
Jinx (The)	308	374	41-24184	yes	Red Hot Riding Hood	308			yes
Johnny Doughboy	308	425	42-72842	no	Reluctant Dragon	308	373	42-40634	yes

Name	Grp.	Sq.	Serial	Pic.
Reluctant Dragon	308	374	42-73xxx	no
Rice Paddy Hattie	308	374	44-42029	yes
Rose of Juarez	308	375	42-73305	yes
Rum Runner	308	374	41-24243	no
Scherezade	308	375	41-24293	yes
Scorpion (The)	308	373	42-40554	yes
Settin' Pretty	308	374	44-41429	yes
Sherezade	308	425	41-24293	yes
Shooting Star	308	374	42-73306	yes
Snafu	308	373	42-73246	yes
Snark (The)	308	425	42-100242	yes
Snowball from Hell (The)	308	374	41-24244	yes
Spare Parts	308		42-40635	yes
Squeeze	308	374	44-42020	yes
Squeeze (not44-42020)	308			yes
Stripped for Action	308	425	44-42142	yes
Surprise Attack	308	374	44-50956	yes
Susie's Sister	308	425	42-40407	yes
Tail Heavy	308	373	41-24125	yes
Taylor Maid	308	374	42-73326	yes
Taylor Maid II	308	374	44-41294	no
Temptation	308	373	41-24129	yes
Temptation	308	373	44-40617	yes
Tennessee Belle	308		42-100036	no
Tennessee Belle	308		42-109807	yes
Tennessee Maid	308		42-100036	no
Thump Time	308			no
Thumper	308	375	41-24287	yes
Thunderbird	308	373	41-24166	no
Thunderbird II	308	375	42-41142	no
Thundermug	308	373	42-40621	no
Tough Titti	308		44-40296	yes
Tough Titti	308	375	44-40898	no
Ubangi Bag	308	374	41-24194	yes
Ubangi Bag II	308	374	42-41168	yes
Ubangi Bag III	308	374	42-73436	yes
Ubangi Webangi	308			yes
Upshaw the Aught	308	425	41-24265	yes
USA Boomerang	308			yes
Willie Maker	308		44-40774	yes
Wolf (The)	308	374	41-24266	yes
Yellow Fever	308	374	44-50803	yes
Zell Bee	308	425	42-63771	yes
Zoot Chute	308	373	42-100184	yes

330TH BOMB GROUP

Name	Grp.	Sq.	Serial	Pic.
Bonnie	330			yes

376TH BOMB GROUP

Name	Grp.	Sq.	Serial	Pic.
Angie the Ox	376	515	41-24031	yes
Aquina	376		40-698	no
Arkansas Traveler	376	515	41-11616	yes

Name	Grp.	Sq.	Serial	Pic.
Arlene the Lincoln Queen	376			yes
Babe the Big Blue Ox	376	515	41-11602	no
Badger Beauty	376	515	44-41062	yes
Barrelhouse Bessie	376	515	42-40317	yes
Bela	376	513	41-23918	no
Belle of the Brawl	376	512	42-94904	no
Benghazi Express	376	514	41-11631	yes
Bewitching Witch	376	512	41-24024	no
Big Marge	376	512	41-28920	no
Big Nig	376	515	42-73428	no
Black Magic	376		42-40662	yes
Black Mariah	376	513	41-11593	no
Black Sheep (The)	376	512	42-72776	no
Blonde Bomber	376	515	42-100253	yes
Blue Streak	376	514	41-11613	yes
Blue Streak (The)	376	514	42-51635	yes
Boilermaker	376	513	41-11910	yes
Bomb Boogie	376	515	42-40229	yes
Bomerang	376	514	41-29425	yes
Boomerang	376		42-52726	yes
Boomerang	376	514	41-29425	yes
Borrowed Time	376	513	42-64474	no
Boudoir Commandos	376	515		no
Brewery Wagon	376	512	41-24294	yes
Bubbles	376	514	42-72846	yes
Bull Moose	376	514	42-72778	yes
Butch	376	515	42-40321	yes
Carpenter's Masterpiece	376	514	42-78425	yes
Censored	376	514	41-11686	no
Chattanooga	376	513	42-72854	yes
Chief Wahoo	376	512	41-24279	yes
Chum V	376	515	41-11630	yes
Chum VII	376	515	42-40392	yes
Cielito Lindo	376		42-40081	yes
Constant Menace	376	514	41-24310	yes
Constant Menace	376	514	41-29563	yes
Coral Princess	376		41-11931	no
Coral Rivers	376			no
Cornfed	376	513	42-72776	yes
Daisy Mae	376	513	42-41031	no
De-Icer	376			no
Der Flittermouse	376	514	41-29606	no
Desert Fury	376	512	42-78206	no
Desert Lilly	376	512	41-24258	yes
Diddlin' Dollie II	376	512	41-28786	no
Dirty Gertie	376	514	42-52557	yes
Doodlebug	376	512	41-23724	yes
Dopy Goldberg	376	515	42-40319	yes
Dot's Queen of Queens	376	513	42-72051	no
Dot's Queen of Queens	376	514	42-72854	no
Double Shot Sam	376	514	44-50393	no
Dream Street Rose	376	515	41-11935	yes
Duchess (The)	376	514	42-72874	yes
Earthquake	376	515	41-24033	yes
Edna Elizabeth	376	512	41-11620	no
Eight (8) Ball	376	514	42-40206	yes

Name	Grp.	Sq.	Serial	Pic.	Name	Grp.	Sq.	Serial	Pic.
Elsie	376	513	41-23796	yes	Old King Solomon	376	513	41-11617	yes
Esmeralda	376	513	41-11848	no	Old Ned's Bells	376	514	42-72849	no
Fearless Joe	376			no	Old Spare Ribs	376	513	41-11646	yes
Fertile Myrtle	376	513	42-40236	no	Ole Faithful	376	512	41-11595	no
Firtil Myrtle	376			yes	Ole Fur Wagon (Ye)	376			yes
Flame McGoon	376	513	42-72767	yes	Ole Rock	376		41-11618	yes
Ford's Folly	376	515	42-78412	no	Ole Sarge	376	512		yes
Four Fruits	376	514	42-64468	no	Ole-Rock	376			yes
Four to the Bar	376	513		yes	Paper Doll	376	512	41-29279	no
Frankie Ferocious	376	515	42-72773	yes	Pappy Yokum	376	514	41-11933	yes
Fyrtle Myrtle	376	513	44-40236	yes	Pappy's Yokum	376	514	41-11933	yes
G.I. Ginnie	376	514	42-40657	yes	Patches (Constant				
Gentle Annie	376	514	42-40661	yes	Menace)	376	514	41-24310	yes
Georgia Cracker	376	512	42-40318	yes	Peggy	376	512	42-78400	no
Gin	376	514	42-78262	yes	Per Diem II (The)	376	514	41-11935	yes
Gin Rae	376	512	42-109831	yes	Pink Lady	376	513	41-24000	yes
Good Time Charley	376	515	41-24030	yes	Pleasant Peasants	376	513	44-40845	yes
Gravel Gertie	376	513	42-73083	yes	Pleasure Bent	376	515	42-78386	yes
Gravy Train (The)	376		40-2376	yes	Poison Ivy	376	514	41-23660	no
Gremlin (The)	376	514	41-24110	yes	Problem Child	376	514	42-78347	yes
Hairless Joe	376	513	42-40081	yes	Professor D	376	514	41-24034	yes
Hard Way Ten	376	515	44-40330	yes	Pupil Packin' Mama	376			yes
Harry the Horse	376	515	42-73090	yes	Purty Baby	376	515	44-40299	no
Hellsapoppin'	376		41-11601	no	Queen Bee	376	513	41-11591	yes
Honey Chile	376	515	42-40664	yes	Ready, Willing & Able	376	512	42-72768	yes
Idiot's Dee Light	376	514	41-23780	yes	Red Ryder	376	512	42-95285	yes
Jackie's Boy	376	514	42-72844	no	Red Wing	376	513	42-40657	no
Joey Uptown	376	515	42-40232	yes	Red Wing	376	513	42-72902	yes
K. O. Katy	376	515	42-100253	no	Red's Raiders	376			no
K. O. Katy II	376	515	42-72847	no	Ripper the 2nd	376	512	42-72852	yes
Kitty Quick	376	514	41-11630	yes	Ripper the First	376	515	41-11614	yes
Lady Be Good	376	514	41-24301	yes	Rosie Wrecked 'Em	376	515	41-11803	no
Let's Go	376	513	41-24032	yes	Rough on Rats	376	514	44-40149	yes
Liberandos Boomerang	376	514	41-29425	yes	Rowdy Ann	376	512	41-11796	no
Lil' Abner	376	513	41-11779	yes	Rowdy II	376	513	42-40656	no
Lil' Butch	376		42-64363	no	Sack Time	376			yes
Lil' De Icer	376	512	41-11836	yes	Sad Sack	376	512	42-41175	no
Lily of the Desert	376	512	42-72816	yes	Sad Sack	376	515	42-78321	yes
Little De-Icer	376		41-28806	yes	Send Me Baby	376	513	42-78476	yes
Little Isadore	376	515	42-40203	no	Sexy Sal	376	514	41-24102	yes
Little Jo	376			yes	Shanghai Lil	376	514	41-11787	yes
Little Richard	376	513	42-40660	yes	Shanghi Lil's Sister	376		42-40314	yes
Lonesome Polecat	376	515	42-64467	no	Sleepout Sam	376			no
Loose Goose	376	512	42-73089	yes	Slick Chick	376			no
Lorraine	376	513	41-11591	yes	Sloppy But Safe	376		44-41008	yes
Malicious	376	512	41-11603	yes	Solid John	376	514	41-24035	yes
Mammy Yokum	376	513	42-72782	yes	Stardust	376	512		yes
Mary Ellen	376	515	42-50960	no	Strawberry Bitch	376	512	42-72843	yes
Maternity Ward	376		42-40663	yes	Strawberry Blonde	376		41-11842	yes
Minnesota Marge	376	512	42-78242	yes	Superstitous Aloysius	376	512	42-73078	yes
Miss Minerva II	376	512	41-29294	no	Sweatin' It Out	376	515	41-29488	no
Miss O. Lanious	376	514	41-24220	yes	Swede's John Deere	376	514	41-28624	yes
Miss Oklahoma	376	514	42-72849	yes	Tangerine	376	513	41-11916	yes
Miss Yourlovin'	376			yes	Teggie Ann	376	515	42-40664	yes
My Aching Back	376	513	42-52181	yes	Ten to the Bar	376	513		yes
Northern Star	376	512	41-11921	no	Terry the Third Cossack	376	512	42-99760	yes
Oh Kay	376		41-11934	yes	Tobacco Rhoda	376		41-29556	yes

Name	Grp.	Sq.	Serial	Pic.
Tobias the Terrible	376	515	42-78078	yes
Vitamin P	376			yes
Vivie	376	513	41-28965	yes
Vulgar Virgin (The)	376		41-24198	yes
War Maid	376	512	42-40658	no
Wash's Tub	376	514	41-11636	yes
Weary Willie	376		42-99816	yes
Wench (The)	376	515	42-78387	yes
Widdle Wed Rabbit	376	515	41-24200	no
Wild Oats	376	514	42-78190	yes
Wild Wolf (The)	376	513	42-40209	yes
Wolf Larsen	376	512	42-78375	yes
Wolf Pack	376	513	42-40315	yes
Wolf Pack (The)	376	513	42-40213	no
Wolf Pack (The)	376	513	42-40315	yes
Wongo Wongo	376	512	42-40563	yes
Yank	376	512	41-11625	no
Yankee Girl	376	513	42-51658	no
Yoo Hoo	376	515		yes
Yum Yum	376	514	42-94987	yes
Yum Yum Wild Oats	376	512	41-24252	no

380TH BOMB GROUP

Name	Grp.	Sq.	Serial	Pic.
108 Missions	380	531	44-40189	yes
A Wing and Ten Prayers	380	528	44-42378	yes
Adelaide Fever	380	531	42-41247	yes
Alley Oop	380	530	41-24248	yes
Angel in de Skies	380	528	42-73464	yes
Atom Smasher	380	530	42-64045	yes
Atomic Blonde	380	531	41-51414	yes
Atomic Blonde	380	531	44-42414	no
Bachelor's Brothel	380	531	44-50927	yes
Bail Out Belle	380	529	42-72951	yes
Battle Weary	380	528	42-41243	yes
Beautiful Beast	380	528	42-73167	yes
Beautiful Betsy	380	528	42-40387	yes
Bebe	380	531	42-41248	yes
Becomin' Back	380	528	44-50390	yes
Big Ass Bird (The)	380	528	42-73113	yes
Big Ass Bird II (The)	380	531	42-72801	yes
Big Ass Bird III (The)	380	531	44-40396	yes
Big Chief Cockeye	380	529	42-40351	yes
Big Time Operator	380	529	42-73193	no
Big Time Operator	380	530	42-41214	yes
Black Magic	380	528	42-40393	yes
Black Velvet	380	529	42-41239	no
Black Widow	380	528	42-40967	yes
Breadline in '49	380	528	44-42201	yes
Bums Away	380	528	42-110123	no
Career Girl	380	528	42-41234	no
Careless	380	531	42-40500	no
Carrot Top	380	528	42-73114	yes
Clarine from Abilene	380	528	44-50998	no
Cruisin' Susan	380	531	42-73201	yes
Daddy of 'em All	380	529	44-49860	yes
Dally's Dilly	380	528	42-73112	yes

Name	Grp.	Sq.	Serial	Pic.
Dauntless Dottie	380	530	42-40495	yes
Deanna's Dreamboat	380	530	44-42244	yes
Deliverer	380	531	42-40522	yes
Dis-Gusted	380	528	42-40486	no
Doodlebug	380	531	42-73117	yes
Dottie's Double	380	530	42-72964	yes
Double Trouble	380	530	44-50602	yes
Dream Gal	380	529	44-40919	yes
Drunkard's Dream	380	531	42-110115	yes
Duchess of Paducah	380	530	42-109991	yes
Eh, What's Up Doc	380	529	42-73488	no
Eighty (80) Days Major	380	530	42-40508	yes
Embarrassed	380	531	44-40189	yes
Esmeralda II	380	529	42-40507	no
Esquire	380	531	42-73481	yes
Firepower	380	528	42-109986	yes
First Nighter	380	529	42-73340	yes
Flak Fled Flapper	380	528	44-40434	yes
Foil Proof Mary	380	531	42-73126	yes
Free For All	380	531	44-42412	yes
Frisco Frannie	380	530	42-73451	yes
Furtle Murtle	380			yes
Fyrtle Myrtle	380	531	42-40485	yes
Golden Gator (The)	380	529	42-40518	yes
Golden Goose (The)	380	528	42-40521	yes
Gus' Bus	380	530	42-40504	yes
Gus' Bus II	380	530	42-41125	yes
Gypsy	380	528	42-41133	yes
Heavenly Body	380	528	42-73116	yes
Hell's Angels	380	529	42-40502	yes
Hell's Belle	380	530	42-41222	yes
Homma Homma Kid	380	528	42-40497	no
Homma Homma Kid II	380	529	42-41238	no
Hot Rocks	380	531	42-73489	yes
I'll Be Seeing You	380	529	44-40923	yes
Je Reviens	380	529	42-72808	yes
Jezebelle	380	529	42-72953	yes
Juarez Whistle	380	530	42-40496	yes
Jugglin' Josie	380	530	42-41237	yes
Jungle Queen II	380	529	42-40510	yes
K. O. Kid (The)	380	529	44-40342	yes
Kathy	380	531	42-40517	no
Lady Jeanne	380	529	42-40511	yes
Lady Jeanne II	380	529	42-40571	yes
Lady Luck	380	528	42-110116	yes
Lady Luck	380	528	44-41430	no
Lelia Belle	380	531	42-40527	yes
Liberty Belle	380	529	44-50894	yes
Lil' D-Icer	380	530	42-72795	yes
Lil' D-Icer	380	530	42-72799	no
Lil' Nilmerg	380	529	44-40861	yes
Little Eve	380	528	42-40493	no
Little Lulu	380	529	42-109999	yes
Lucky	380	529	42-40514	yes
Lucky Don	380	529	42-73485	yes
Lucky Strike	380	530	44-41876	yes
Luvablass	380	529	44-41263	yes

Name	Grp.	Sq.	Serial	Pic.	Name	Grp.	Sq.	Serial	Pic.
Madam Queen	380	529	42-109999	yes	Sad Sack	380	531	42-73133	yes
Male Call	380	531	42-72799	yes	Sandra Kay	380	530	42-72790	yes
Mary M.	380	530	44-40370	yes	Satan's Secretary	380	528	42-63683	no
Milady	380	531	42-73134	yes	Satan's Secretary	380	528	42-63989	yes
Miss Elise	380	531	44-42381	no	Screamer (The)	380	531	44-40189	no
Miss Giving	380	528	42-40489	yes	Shady Lady	380	528	42-40291	no
Miss Hap (The)	380	529	42-100221	yes	Shady Lady	380	528	42-40369	yes
Miss Mary	380	528	42-40492	no	She 'Asta	380	530	42-40512	yes
Missouri Miss	380	530	44-41811	yes	Shy-Chi Baby	380	531	44-40902	yes
Mister Five by Five	380	531	42-40505	yes	Shy-Chi Baby	380	531	44-40920	yes
Moonlight Maid	380	529	44-42331	yes	Silver Lady	380	530	44-40371	yes
Morbid Moe, the Moron	380	530	42-41071	yes	Six Bitts	380	529	42-100214	yes
Mr. Five x Five	380	531	42-40505	no	Sleepy Time Gal	380	530	42-110120	yes
My Devotion	380	528	44-42248	yes	Slightly Dangerous	380	531	42-73333	yes
Nancy	380	529	44-42351	yes	Snafu	380	529	42-40513	yes
Net Results	380	528	44-41875	yes	Snafu II	380	529	42-41120	yes
Nobody's Darling	380	528	44-50913	no	Snorky	380	528	42-73164	yes
Nocturnal Mission	380	529	44-42250	yes	Sooper Drooper	380	531	42-40515	yes
Nothing Sacred	380	529	42-40509	yes	Squaw Peak	380	529	44-40801	yes
Old Hickory	380	530	42-40827	yes	Stateside Stuff	380	530	44-50997	yes
Old Ironsides	380	530	42-110117	no	Stateside Stuff	380	530	44-51301	yes
Ole Professor (The)	380	528		yes	Sultan's Daughter (The)	380	531	42-73489	yes
On-De-Fence	380	530	42-109995	yes	Sunshine	380	531	42-41225	yes
One (The) /Say Uncle	380	528	42-40534	no	Ten High	380	530	44-42405	no
Paper Doll	380	529	42-73187	yes	Ten High	380	530	44-50405	no
Pappy's Passion II	380	531	42-73121	yes	Tennessee				
Passionate Witch	380	530	42-41124	yes	Squirrel Hunter	380	531	42-73201	no
Patches	380	531	42-73471	yes	Tennessee				
Patty's Pig	380	531	44-40398	yes	Squirrel Hunter	380	531	42-73324	yes
Peace Offering	380	529	44-50811	yes	Toddy	380	531	42-100226	yes
Pleasure Bent	380	530	42-73440	yes	Toughy	380	529	42-40525	yes
Pom Pom Express	380	531	44-50396	yes	Un-Decided	380	530	42-109986	yes
Poochie	380	528	42-40369	no	Undecided	380	530	42-109986	yes
Poochie	380	528	42-40491	no	Undecided	380	531	42-73333	yes
Prince Valiant	380	531	42-40526	yes	Virgin Abroad	380	529	44-50941	yes
Prop Wash	380	530	42-73475	yes					
Pug	380	529	42-40518	yes					
Pug II	380	530	42-40526	yes					

389TH BOMB GROUP

Name	Grp.	Sq.	Serial	Pic.
Puss N' Boots	380	528	42-72942	yes
Queen Hi	380	529	44-40432	yes
Queen of the Strip	380	529	44-42214	yes
Queer Deer	380	528	42-40935	yes
Ramblin' Wreck (The)	380	529	44-50776	yes
Ramey's Wreck	380	530	42-73451	yes
Rangy Lil	380	528	44-41867	yes
Ready Teddy	380	529	42-73488	yes
Red Ass (The)	380	530	42-40524	yes
Robbie L.	380	529	42-40516	yes
Robbie L. II	380	531	42-40979	yes
Roberta & Son/				
Firepower	380	528	42-109986	yes
Rosie o' the Ramp	380	528	42-100213	yes
Rough (K)night	380	530	42-100209	yes
Rough Night	380	530	42-100209	yes
Royal Flush II	380	531	42-73131	yes
Ruptured Falcon	380	529	42-100215	yes
Sack Time	380	531	42-41219	yes

Name	Grp.	Sq.	Serial	Pic.
Angel Ann	389			no
Bad Penny (The)	389	564	42-40767	no
Belle of the Brawl	389		42-94904	no
Betsy II	389			no
Betty Jane	389	565	44-40092	yes
Betty Lee	389			no
Big Brown Jug (The)	389		42-110148	no
Bigast Bird (The)	389	567	42-51233	yes
Bigast Boid	389			no
Blondes Away	389	567	42-40793	yes
Blunderbus	389	565	42-7593	yes
Boomerang	389	566	42-40115	yes
Bucksheesh Benny	389	566	41-24112	yes
Buckshot	389			yes
Bunny	389	565	42-95077	no
Burton's Iron Man	389			no
Bust-er	389	565	44-40052	yes
Captain & His Kids (The)	389		41-24213	yes
Carrier Pigeon (The)	389	564	42-51451	yes

Name	Grp.	Sq.	Serial	Pic.	Name	Grp.	Sq.	Serial	Pic.
Chattanooga Choo Choo	389	565	42-40782	yes	Lady Leone	389			no
Chum II	389			no	Lady Liberty	389	564	42-72871	yes
Chum U	389			no	Lady Luck	389		41-23778	no
D-Day Patches	389	565	42-50474	yes	Latrine Rumor (The)	389	564	42-99975	yes
D-Day Patches	389	565	42-50643	yes	Lethal Lady	389	567		no
Delectable Deb	389			no	Lil Audrey	389	565	42-100280	no
Delectable Doris	389	566	42-50551	yes	Little Audrey	389	565	42-100280	no
Delectable Lady	389			no	Little Corporal	389			yes
Don't Cry Baby	389	565	42-110084	yes	Little Gramper (The)	389	566	42-40722	yes
Dorothy	389	564	42-63960	yes	Little Gramper, Jr.	389	566	44-40085	yes
Down De Hatch	389	564		no	Lonesome Polecat	389	564	42-95205	yes
Dragon Lady	389	565	42-7593	yes	Lucky Lady Betty	389	565	44-51153	no
Drawers	389	565	42-100017	yes	Lucky Lady Betty II	389	565	44-51153	yes
Drawers	389	566	42-50760	yes	Lucky Leone	389		42-110077	no
Eager Cleaver (The)	389	564	44-40864	yes	Lucky Tiger	389	565	42-63958	no
Eager Eagle	389	564	42-40753	no	Magic Carpet (The)	389	567	42-95122	yes
Eyes of Texas	389			yes	Martha	389			no
Fightin' Sam	389	567	42-40807	yes	Martha R.	389	565	42-110068	yes
Fightin' Sam II	389	566	42-52579	no	Mary, the Flying				
Fighting Sam	389	566		no	Redhead	389	565	42-100319	no
Flak Magnet	389	567	42-99992	no	Might of the Eighth	389	566	42-99982	no
Flamin' Mamie	389			no	Minerva	389		41-23689	yes
Ford's Folly	389		42-94842	no	Miss America	389	566	42-50558	yes
Full House	389		42-99966	no	Miss Barbara	389		42-109903	no
Gallopin' Gertie	389	566	42-100332	yes	Miss Lace	389			yes
Gallopin' Ghost	389		41-23783	no	Miss Liberty	389	564	42-72871	yes
Gallopin' Katie	389	564	42-50367	yes	Missouri Mauler	389	567	42-63980	yes
Ginny Gal	389	565	42-95077	yes	Mistah Chick	389	567	42-100146	yes
Golden Sandstorm (The)	389	565	42-40795	yes	Nana	389	566	42-94973	yes
Gorgeous Gal	389			no	Nani Wahine	389			no
Government Gal	389	565	42-7582	no	Naughty Norma	389		42-9783x	no
Green Dragon	389	567	41-23683	yes	Nuff Said	389	565	42-109794	yes
Heaven Can Wait	389	565	42-40370	yes	O for Oboe	389			no
Heaven Can Wait	389	565	42-40744	no	Oklahoman (The)	389	566	42-40738	yes
Heavy Date	389	566	42-7766	yes	Old Buck	389			no
Heavy Date	389	567	42-40747	yes	Old Buster Butt	389			no
Helfer College	389		41-29131	no	Old Faithful	389			no
Helfer College II	389	567	41-29451	no	Old Faithful II	389			no
Hitler's Hearse	389	567	42-40544	no	Old Glory	389	565	42-100372	yes
Hmm, What A Lick	389	566	42-100185	no	Old Glory	389	565	42-63956	no
Hot Stuff	389	565	42-51087	yes	Old Veteran (The)	389	564	42-95240	yes
I've Had It!	389	567	42-95071	no	Ole Irish	389	564	42-40746	yes
Impatient Virgin (The)	389		41-29231	no	Palace of Dallas	389		42-109791	no
Iron Ass	389	566	42-40769	no	Patches (D-Day)	389	565	42-50474	yes
Is This Trip Necessary?	389		42-50532	yes	Peg O' My Heart	389			no
It's T.S. Boys	389	567	42-72856	no	Peg the Pig	389			no
Jackass Mule (Male)	389	565	42-72866	no	Peggy	389			no
Janet	389			yes	Pistol Packin' Mama	389	566	42-40783	yes
Jo Jo's Special Delivery	389	567	41-23683	yes	Plate's Date	389		42-94830	no
Joker	389		42-95253	no	Playmate	389	567	42-63980	yes
Joker	389	564	42-95555	no	Poker Hat	389			no
Kentucky Babe II	389			no	Pollyana	389	566	42-109817	no
Kentucky Babe III	389		42-7553	no	Pot Luck	389	567	42-95071	yes
Knight of the Eighth	389	566	42-99982	no	Precious Jewell	389		42-110103	no
L. A. City Limits	389	567	42-63977	yes	Princess Konocti	389	565	42-100190	yes
L. A. City Limits	389	567	42-72833	no	Pugnacious Princess Pat	389	566	44-10579	yes
Lady Irene	389	564	42-40697	no	Puss N' Boots	389	567	42-95079	no

Name	Grp.	Sq.	Serial	Pic.
Raunch Rebel (The)	389		42-95063	no
Rhapsody in Junk	389		41-28733	yes
Round Trip Ticket	389	565	42-40171	yes
Ruptured Falcon	389	529	42-100215	yes
Sack Time Sally	389	565	42-40749	yes
Sack Warmer	389	566	41-28824	yes
Sad Sack (The)	389			no
Salvaged Sally	389	564	42-94964	yes
Sand Witch	389	566	42-40735	no
Satan's Mate	389	564	42-110074	no
Scheherezade	389	564	42-40772	yes
Screaming Mimi	389	565	42-40997	yes
Shack Time II	389		42-95250	no
Shady Lady	389	566	44-40439	yes
Shazam	389	564	42-110032	yes
Shoot Fritz, You're Faded	389	567	42-40768	yes
Skerby	389	567	44-40245	no
Sky Scorpions (The)	389	565	42-40629	yes
Sky Shark (The)	389	567	42-109915	yes
Sky Wolves	389	566	42-100281	no
Sleepy Time Gal	389			no
Southern Queen III	389	564		no
Southern Queen IV	389	564	42-63959	no
Stalky	389			no
Standby	389	567	42-50774	no
Stars & Stripes	389			no
Stinger	389			no
Stinkey	389	565	42-95088	no
Stinky	389	564	42-100085	yes
Stinky	389	565	42-95088	no
Stork Club	389		42-63967	yes
String of Pearls	389	567	42-94982	no
Su-Su	389			yes
Sunshine	389	564	41-28779	no
Susu	389			yes
Swamp Angel	389	565	42-100352	no
Swee Peaz	389	565	42-95085	no
Swee' Pea II	389			no
Sweet Adeline	389	565	41-23933	yes
Sweet and Lovely	389			no
Sweet and Lowdown	389	567	42-100428	no
Sweet Chariot	389		44-40087	no
Sweet Eloise	389		41-29511	yes
Sweet Pea	389	564	42-94822	no
T. S. Boys	389	566	42-73856	yes
Ten Hi Hit Parade	389		42-95570	no
Ten High	389	564	42-40665	yes
Tondelayo	389	566	42-40706	yes
Toonerville Trolley	389			yes
Topper	389			no
Torney	389	567	42-72833	no
Touch of Texas	389	567	42-40751	yes
Travelling Trollop	389	567	42-40784	no
Trouble N' Mind	389	566	42-41013	no
Tung Hoi	389		44-40230	no
Unstable Mable	389	564	42-63957	no
Vagabond King	389	565	42-40787	yes
Victory Ship	389		41-23813	no
Vivian	389		42-95063	no
War Champ	389	567	42-94951	yes
Weight Ship	389			yes
Wham Bam	389		41-23738	no
What's Cookin' Doc?	389	567	42-99977	no
Wicked Widget	389			no
Wicked Widget II	389			no
Win, Our Little Lady	389	565	42-95088	no
Wolf Waggin'	389	565	42-40775	yes
Wolf Waggin'	389	565	44-10510	no
Yankee Doodle Dandy	389	566	42-95588	no
Yankee Rebel Harmony	389	564	42-99975	no
You Cawn't Miss It	389	565	44-10510	yes
Yours Truly	389	565	42-40716	no
Yours Truly	389	566	42-100167	yes
Zombie	389			yes
Zoomin' Zombie	389	565	42-63961	yes

392ND BOMB GROUP

Name	Grp.	Sq.	Serial	Pic.
Able Mabel	392	578	42-52544	yes
Agony Wagon	392	578	44-50542	no
Alfred	392	578	42-7485	no
Alfred II	392	577	42-7546	yes
Alfred III	392			no
Alfred IV	392	579	42-94961	yes
Alfred V	392	577	42-95118	no
Amblin' Okie	392	577	41-29174	no
American Beauty	392	578	42-95293	no
Arsenal (The)	392	577	42-109826	no
Axis Grinder	392	577	42-7495	yes
B. T. O.	392	578	42-99981	yes
Bakadori	392	578	42-7502	yes
Berlin Bitch	392	579	42-95103	no
Big Ass Bird	392	578	42-7490	no
Big Dog	392	578	42-7483	no
Big Fat Mama	392	578	44-40067	yes
Big Time Operators	392	577	42-94897	yes
Birdie Schmidt ARC	392	576	42-50387	yes
Black Magic	392	576	42-7527	yes
Black Widow	392	576	42-7527	no
Black Widow II	392		42-94912	no
Blanid's Baby	392	576	42-7560	yes
Bomb Boogie	392	577	42-50792	no
Bronco Nagurski	392	579	41-29552	no
Bugs Bomby	392		42-72998	no
Bull Bat	392	578	42-7472	yes
Call Me Later	392	579	42-95035	yes
Carol Ann	392	578	42-7473	yes
Carol Ann II	392	579	41-29448	no
Chiefton (The)	392	577	42-51169	no
Cloud Hopper	392			no
Cloud Hopper II	392			no
Cloud Hopper III	392			no
Cloud Hopper IV	392	579	44-49886	yes

Name	Grp.	Sq.	Serial	Pic.	Name	Grp.	Sq.	Serial	Pic.
Coral Princess	392	576	42-7529	yes	Jawja Boy	392	578	42-52548	no
Crew Chief	392	576	42-7540	yes	Jay's Pool Hall	392	578	42-50446	no
Death Dealer	392		42-40611	yes	Jay's Poolhall	392	578	42-51121	no
Delayed Action	392	578	42-100117	no	Jinx (The)	392	577	42-7496	no
Dirty Gertie	392	578	42-50571	no	Jive Bomber	392	579	42-109814	yes
Dixie Dumper	392	576	42-99938	no	Jolly Duck	392	578	42-95241	no
Doodle Bug	392	576		no	Jungle Princess	392	576	42-7537	no
Double Trouble	392	578	42-100100	yes	Kathleen	392			yes
Dragon Lady	392	577	42-94906	yes	Kentucky Baby	392	578	42-99979	no
Drip (The)	392	579	42-7477	no	Knucklehead	392	578	41-29509	no
Drip (The)	392	579	42-7481	no	Lady Diana	392	579	42-50593	no
Dugan	392	578	44-50493	no	Lady Diana II	392	579	42-51459	no
El Capitan	392	578	41-28772	yes	Lady Eve	392	577	42-95164	yes
El Lobo	392	579	42-7510	yes	Lassie Come Home	392	578	42-51235	no
Eloise	392	578	41-29571	yes	Last Frontier	392	579	41-29135	no
Envy of 'em All	392	579	42-50279	no	Last Frontier	392	579	42-52605	no
Exterminator	392	579	41-29135	yes	Late Date	392	577	42-100346	yes
Exterminator	392	579	42-7470	yes	Late Date II (The)	392	577	42-109824	no
Exterminator II	392	577	42-7556	no	Late Date II (The)	392	577	42-109826	no
Fairy Belle	392		42-72998	no	Liberty Belle	392	576	42-50647	yes
Fairy Belle II	392	577	42-52415	no	Liberty Belle	392	578	42-7626	no
Fearless Fosdick	392	578	44-50568	yes	Lil' Gypsy	392	579	41-29127	yes
Filthy Annie	392	579	42-7471	no	Little Joe	392	576	42-7560	no
Flak Ducker (The)	392	576	42-7598	yes	Little Joe	392	577	42-51238	no
Flying Crusader/					Little Lulu	392	577	42-95223	no
My Diversion	392	578	42-7478	yes	Lonesome Polecat	392	577	42-52097	no
Flying Dutch	392		xx-xx131	no	Lyndy	392	577	42-110058	yes
Flying Patch	392	578	41-29131	no	Lyndy	392	578	42-7518	no
Flying Patch	392	578	41-29511	no	Lyndy II	392	577	42-110058	yes
Ford's Folly	392		42-94842	no	Mac's Sack	392	576	42-7471	yes
Ford's Folly	392	578	42-50466	yes	Mac's Sack II	392	579	42-7561	no
Fun House (The)	392			no	Mac's Sack III	392	579	42-7599	yes
Gallavantin' Gal	392	577	42-7509	no	Mah Ideal	392	578	42-7588	no
Gashouse Gus	392	578	41-29476	no	Mairsy Doats	392	579	42-94891	no
Gashouse Mouse	392	578	41-29476	no	Mairzy Doats	392	579	42-109789	yes
Georgia Belle	392	578	42-7543	no	Malfunction	392	577	42-7489	no
GI Jane Pallas Athene	392	578	42-100187	yes	Marion	392	577	42-94898	no
Good Conduct	392	577	42-110096	yes	Mary L.	392	576	42-95464	no
Gorgeous Gal	392			no	Mary Louise	392	576	42-95031	no
Green Hornet (The)	392	579	42-52504	yes	Million $ Baby	392	576	42-7487	yes
Gregory the Great	392	577	42-7493	no	Minerva	392	579	41-23689	yes
Gremlin's Roost (The)	392	579	44-49577	yes	Miss America	392	577	42-7503	no
Gypsy Queen	392	578	42-109896	no	Miss Minnie	392	578	42-95041	no
Half-Moon Trio (The)	392	576	41-28991	no	Miss Minnie II	392	578	42-78477	yes
Hap Hazard	392		42-7580	yes	Mistah Chick	392		42-100146	no
Hard To Get	392	578	42-7518	no	Model T	392	578	42-52517	no
Hazee	392	576	44-50527	yes	Monotonous Maggie	392	577	42-95151	yes
Heaven Can Wait	392	576	42-7507	no	My Diversion	392	578	42-7480	yes
Heaven Can Wait	392	576	44-50505	no	My Prayer	392	576	42-51194	no
Heavenly Body	392	577	41-28875	yes	Niagara Special	392	578	42-51121	no
Hell Cat (The)	392	576	42-7524	no	Night-Life-Nellie	392	579	42-52654	no
Hell Wagon (The)	392	576	42-7492	yes	No Feathered Injun	392	579	42-94886	no
Hellzadroppin'	392	579	42-7488	no	Old Daddy	392	577	42-7497	no
I Walk Alone	392	579	42-51150	no	Old Glory	392	579	41-28742	no
I'll Be Back	392	579	41-28788	no	Old Grey Wolf	392	576	42-51934	no
Idiot's Delight	392	578	42-50623	no	Old Man Boston Marclar	392	577	42-100005	no
J. C. Poolhall	392	578	42-50446	no	Old Stand By	392	576	42-50430	no

Name	Grp.	Sq.	Serial	Pic.
Ole War Horse	392	579	42-7479	no
Our Baby	392	578	42-7570	no
Our Gal	392	579	42-100308	yes
Out House Mouse	392	579	42-52083	no
P-Peter	392		42-95031	no
Pallas Athene...	392	576	44-50505	no
Peep Sight	392	579	42-7535	yes
Philly Filly (The)	392	577	41-28841	no
Pink Lady	392	578	42-99945	no
Pink Tub	392	579		no
Pleasant Surprise	392	578	42-50804	no
Pleasant Surprise	392	579	42-51268	yes
Pleasure Bent	392	578	42-50358	no
Pocatello Chief	392	576	42-99976	no
Poco Hero	392			no
Poco Loco	392	577	42-7658	yes
Poop Deck Pappy	392	577	42-7521	yes
Pregnant Peg	392			yes
Pregnant Peg	392	577	42-7491	no
Pregnant Peg II	392	577	42-52649	yes
Pretty Baby	392			no
Pursuit of Happiness	392	576	42-95272	no
Pursuit of Happiness	392	579	42-94886	no
Push Over	392	578	42-7518	no
Puss N Boots	392	577	42-95079	no
Queen of Peace (The)	392	577	42-7637	yes
Rap 'em Pappy	392	576	42-95070	no
Rap 'em Pappy	392	579	42-95229	yes
Rat Poison	392	579	41-29560	yes
Rebel Gal	392	578	42-94838	no
Ret by Ford	392		42-7465	no
Rose of Juarez	392	579	42-7469	yes
Royal Flush	392			no
Ruptured Duck (The)	392	576	42-52770	yes
Ruptured Falcon	392	576	42-52770	yes
Sack Happy	392	579		no
Sack Rat	392			no
Sally Ann	392	578	42-7484	yes
Satan's Flame	392	579	42-7474	no
Shack Rat	392	577	42-7482	yes
Shack Time II	392	578	42-95250	no
Shark (The)	392	578	42-7486	no
Sharp Character	392	577		yes
Sheila	392	578	42-7596	no
Shoo! Shoo! Baby	392	578	42-50284	yes
Short Round	392	577	42-52642	no
Short Round II	392	577	44-50753	yes
Short Snorter	392	579	42-99990	yes
Short Snorter II	392	578	44-10495	no
Silent Yokum	392	576	44-40297	no
Silver Chief	392	578	42-95033	no
Silver Streak	392	577	42-95040	yes
Ski-Nose	392	579	42-52160	yes
Sky Queen	392	576	42-7500	no
Slightly Dangerous	392	577	42-7556	no
Son of Satan	392	576	42-99989	no
Son of Satan II	392	577	42-52704	no
Southern Comfort	392	576	42-7506	no
Spirit of '46	392		41-29131	no
Star Swinger	392	578	42-51205	yes
Strippin' for Action	392			yes
Subconscious	392	579	41-28742	yes
Sweat N' Duck	392	578	42-51249	yes
Sweet Chariot	392	579	42-100261	yes
Sweet Eloise	392	578	41-29511	yes
Tail Wind	392	577	42-50792	no
Tar Heel Baby	392	577	41-29125	yes
Tempermental Duchess	392		42-6982	yes
Terri Ann	392	577	42-94898	no
Texas Refugees	392	576	42-100102	no
Tobapnwib	392			no
Tondelayo	392	577	42-50343	no
Tovarich	392			no
Trips Daily	392	577	42-95012	yes
Turnip Termite	392	578	42-7624	no
Umbriago	392	579	42-51126	yes
Umbriago II	392	578	42-50337	no
V for Victory	392	577	42-50813	no
Wabash Cannonball	392	578	42-50313	yes
We'll Get By	392	577	42-50697	yes
What's Up Doc?	392		44-40137	no
Whiskers	392	579	42-7477	no
Whiskers	392	579	42-7481	no
Wicked Wicket	392			no
Wicked Wicket II	392			no
Wild Hare (The)	392	579	44-49454	no
Willet Run?	392			no
Wimpy's Queen	392	577	42-50901	yes
Windy City Belle	392	578	42-51240	yes
Yankee Dood It	392			no
YMCA Flying Service	392	577	42-50758	no
YMCA Flying Service (The)	392	577	41-28700	yes
YMCA Flying Service II (The)	392	577	42-50901	no
Your Gal	392	579	42-52615	yes

406TH BOMB GROUP

Name	Grp.	Sq.	Serial	Pic.
Black Zombie	406		41-29602	no

445TH BOMB GROUP

Name	Grp.	Sq.	Serial	Pic.
$64 Question	445	701		no
Ann	445	701	42-7622	no
Arkansas Traveler	445		42-50618	no
Asbestos Alice	445			no
Axis Ex-Lax	445	702	42-94820	no
B. T. O.	445	702	42-7627	no
Bab King Kong	445			no
Bachelor's Delight	445		42-78481	no
Balls of Fire	445	700	42-109796	yes

Name	Grp.	Sq.	Serial	Pic.	Name	Grp.	Sq.	Serial	Pic.
Ballsafire	445	700	42-7643	no	Lead Poison	445	703	42-7532	no
Beast (The)	445		42-50743	no	Liberty Belle	445	703	42-7508	no
Betty	445	703	42-7562	no	Lillian Ann	445	700	42-7558	no
Big Joe	445	703	41-29123	no	Lillian Ann II	445	700	42-7571	yes
Billie Babe	445	703	42-7523	no	Little Audrey	445	701	42-50579	yes
Bit XX Big Joe	445	703	41-29123	no	Little Bill	445	702	42-7566	no
Black Jack	445			no	Little Milo	445	701	42-7586	no
Blasted Event	445			no	Little Orphan Annie	445			no
Bonnie D. or Dee	445	700	42-95128	no	Little Orphan Annie II	445	703	42-7571	no
Bonnie Vee	445	700	42-95128	no	Lizzy	445	701	42-7555	no
Boomerang	445			yes	Lonesome Lois	445	701	42-95020	yes
Boomerang the					Lucky	445			no
Sad Sack	445	703		yes	Lucky Gordon	445		41-24215	yes
Bubbling Lady	445	702	42-7597	no	Lyndy II	445		42-110058	yes
Bugs Bunny	445	700	42-95210	no	Mairzy Doats	445	703	42-109789	yes
Bullet Serenade	445	703	42-64439	no	Male Call	445			no
Bunnie	445		42-51349	no	Nine Yanks & a Jerk	445	703	41-29118	yes
Bunny	445			no	Old Baldy	445	701	42-94853	no
Bunny/Asbestos Alice	445	700	42-7619	no	Old Baldy	445	701	42-94863	no
Clay Pigeon	445	702	42-7604	no	Old Crow II	445	701	42-7509	no
Cockpit Trouble	445			no	Ole Baldy/Old Baldy	445	701	42-94863	no
Conquest Cavalier	445	703	41-29126	yes	Ole King Cole	445	700	42-50565	no
Consolidated Mess	445	701	42-7568	no	Our Gal	445	702	42-100308	yes
Count (The)	445	700	42-50639	no	Paper Doll	445	702	42-7579	no
Daisy Mae	445		42-51349	no	Paper Doll II	445	702	42-7590	no
Dixie Flyer	445	701	42-52247	no	Patches	445	700	42-110022	no
Dorothy	445	733	42-51707	yes	Patches	445	700	42-95015	yes
Dusty Deamons	445	701	42-64440	no	Patty Girl	445	703	42-50811	no
Eileen	445	702	42-50324	no	Pelton's Pissed Off	445	701		yes
Ellen	445	703	42-7602	no	Pistol Packin' Mama	445	702	42-7513	yes
Fearless Fosdick	445	702	41-29604	yes	Poco Moco	445			no
Flossye	445	701		yes	Q for Queenie	445	701	42-51015	no
Flyer's Fancy	445		42-94840	no	Ramblin' Wreck	445	700	42-64438	no
Fort Worth Maid	445	702	42-50321	no	Rough House Kate	445	702		no
Four (4)-Q-2	445	700	41-29149	no	Same Ole Crap	445		44-40466	yes
Fridget Bridget	445	703	42-51342	no	Scrap Drive	445	701	42-100426	no
Gallant Lady	445	700	42-7550	yes	Sharon D. (The)	445		42-94759	no
Georgia Peach	445	700	42-64434	no	Shoe Shoe Baby	445	700	42-64434	no
God Bless Our Ship	445	701	42-7586	no	Silver Streak	445	703	42-95192	yes
Good Nuff	445	700	42-7534	no	Sin Ship	445	702	42-7601	no
Green Gremlin	445	701	42-7515	no	Skipper's Clipper	445	701	42-95000	no
Green Hornet	445	702	41-29542	no	Sky Wolf	445	701	42-7569	yes
Green Hornet (The)	445	701	42-94940	yes	Slightly Dangerous	445	701	42-50618	no
Gremlin's Roost	445	703	42-7512	no	Slossie	445	701	44-40294	no
Hap Hazard	445	703	42-7580	yes	Snow Goose	445	700	42-7520	no
Head Wind Herky	445	702		no	Star Dust	445	700	42-7576	yes
Heavenly Body	445		42-94939	no	Stormy	445		42-50574	no
Helenbak	445		42-94921	no	Sunflower Sue	445	703	42-7617	no
Hell Cat	445	703	42-7585	no	Super Chief	445		42-95562	yes
Hell's Warrior	445	701	42-7563	no	Swamp Angel	445		42-51480	no
Hitler's Hearse	445			no	Sweatin' It Out	445	701	42-7541	no
Hot Rock	445	703	42-51532	no	Sweet Sue	445		42-95042	no
Kelly	445	703	42-7559	no	Sweet Sue	445	703	42-51480	no
King Kong	445	702	42-50340	no	Sweetest Rose of Texas	445	701	42-51105	yes
King Kong	445	702	42-50383	no	Tahelenbak	445	701	42-94921	yes
Lady Marie	445	702	41-29117	no	Tail End Charley	445	702	42-7554	no
Lady Shamrock	445	701	42-7614	yes	Ten Aces with a Queen	445			no

Name	Grp.	Sq.	Serial	Pic.
Ten Gun Dottie	445	700	42-50620	yes
Tennessee Dottie	445	703	41-28652	yes
Tenovus	445	703	41-29132	no
Terrible Terry's Terror	445	700	42-94810	yes
Texas Rose	445	701	41-28922	no
Thumper	445	703	42-95291	no
Too Tired	445	702	42-7517	no
Turd Bird	445	703	42-7565	no
Two Gun Flossie	445	701	42-64436	no
Varga Girl	445		42-52662	no
Wacky Donald	445	700	42-7567	no
Wallet A-Abel	445			no
Willer Run?	445	702	42-7526	no
Wind Haven	445		42-94853	no
Yellow Rose of Texas	445			no
You're Safe at Home	445		42-94828	no

446TH BOMB GROUP

Name	Grp.	Sq.	Serial	Pic.
A - Abel	446	707	44-48838	no
Attitude Adjustment	446			no
B. T. O.	446		44-40072	no
Bagin' Lulu	446			no
Banger	446	705	41-29140	yes
Bangi	446			no
Bangin' Lulu	446	707	44-48829	yes
Bar Fly	446	706		no
Bar Fly	446	707		yes
Barney's Buzz Wagon	446	705	42-50316	yes
Bastard	446	704	42-7628	yes
Battle Axe	446	706	42-51073	yes
Battle Dragon	446	705	42-50431	yes
Beach-Belle	446	705	44-50513	no
Beast (The)	446	704	42-7679	no
Big Drip (The)	446	705	41-29524	yes
Big Fat Mama	446		44-40067	no
Big Wheel	446	707	44-10529	yes
Black Magic	446	706	42-110093	yes
Black Widow	446	707	42-7542	no
Blackjack	446	707		no
Blunderbus	446	704	42-7593	no
Brown Knowser	446	704	42-99942	no
Brown Knowser	446	705	42-7659	yes
Buck Eye Belle	446			yes
Buckaroo (The)	446	706	42-95203	no
Buckshot	446	705	42-7625	yes
Bums Away	446	704	42-7494	no
Buzz Buggy	446	706	42-7577	no
Call Me Later	446			yes
Callipygia	446	704	42-94920	yes
Carolyn Sue	446	707	42-95190	no
Cherry	446	705	42-51184	no
Classy Chassy	446	704	42-95198	yes
Connie	446	707	41-29124	yes
Conquest Cavalier	446	704	41-29126	no
Corky Bergundy Bomber	446	706	42-52234	yes
Crippled Bitch (The)	446		41-29371	no
Daisy Mae Skraggs	446	704	42-109830	yes
Desperate Desmond	446	706	42-7498	yes
Dinky Duck	446	706	41-29142	yes
Dirty Deed (The)	446	707	42-50545	yes
Dissapated Duck	446	707	42-94994	no
Do-Jin-Don	446	706	disputed	yes
Dragon Lady	446	706	42-50306	yes
Dry Run	446	706	41-29137	yes
Eager Beaver	446		41-23737	no
El Toro, Bull of the Woods	446	707	41-29136	yes
Fearless Fosdick	446			no
Fearless Freddie	446		41-23737	yes
Fearless Freddie II	446	707	42-7654	no
Feather Injun	446		42-94886	no
Flak Bait	446	706	42-7581	no
Funny Face	446	704	42-95121	no
Gertie the Gremlin	446	707	42-7649	yes
Gertie the Gremlin II	446			no
Get Away Gertie	446			no
Ginge	446	706	41-29177	
Goin' My Way	446	707	44-10526	yes
Goin' My Way	446	707	44-10528	yes
Golden Girl	446			yes
Golden Girl	446			no
Guess What's Left	446	705	42-52598	no
Guess Who's Here	446	705	42-52598	no
Hap Hazard	446		42-7580	yes
Happy Go	446			no
Happy Go Lucky	446	705	42-7625	yes
Hard To Get	446	705	42-94988	no
Heine Hunter	446	704	42-95266	no
Hell's Belle	446	704	42-99937	yes
Henry's Pride	446	704	42-7574	yes
Hey Ride	446	704	44-49523	no
Home Breaker	446	706	42-52612	yes
Hot Rock	446	705	42-51532	no
Hot Shot Charlie	446	704	42-95126	yes
Hula Wahine	446	704	42-7578	yes
Hula Wahine II	446	704	42-52467	yes
I Hope So!	446	704	44-50523	yes
Jane	446			no
Jewel Sa	446			no
Jiggs	446	704	42-52733	yes
Joker	446	705	41-29151	no
Just One Time	446	704	41-29411	no
Kelly	446	704	42-7564	no
Kentucky Belle	446	706	44-40268	yes
Kentucky Colonel	446	706	44-40268	no
Kill-Joy	446	706	41-29141	yes
Laden Raider	446		42-52549	yes
Lady Barbara (The)	446	706	42-99978	no
Lady Luck	446	704	41-29128	yes
Lady Marian	446	703	42-50592	yes
Lassie Come Home	446	707	42-51356	yes

Name	Grp.	Sq.	Serial	Pic.	Name	Grp.	Sq.	Serial	Pic.
Lazy Lou	446	704	42-95198	no	Ronnie	446	704	41-29144	yes
Lazy Lou	446	706	42-7609	yes	Roost (The)	446	704	42-7679	no
Lil' Max	446	707	42-100347	no	Rough Buddy	446	707	42-95390	yes
Lil' Gypsy	446	704	41-29127	yes	Royal Screw	446	706	42-99983	no
Lil' Max	446	705	42-100347	yes	Rubber Check	446	705	42-95294	yes
Lil' Snooks	446	707	42-94936	yes	Rubber Check	446	706	42-99983	yes
Little King	446	706	42-50790	yes	Rumplestiltskin II	446		42-64452	no
Little Max	446	707	42-100347	yes	Sad Sack	446	707	41-29147	yes
Little Rollo	446	707	42-95289	yes	Satan's Little Sister	446	706	42-50318	yes
Luck and Stuff	446	706	41-28664	no	Satan's Little Sister	446	706	42-95180	yes
Luck and Stuff	446	706	42-100360	yes	Satan's Sister	446	706	42-7610	yes
Lucky Penny	446			no	Scotland Taxi	446	707	42-52583	yes
Major Hoople	446	707	42-100288	no	Shack (The)	446	704	41-29000	no
Mama's Angels	446			yes	Shack II (The)	446	704	41-29143	yes
Maximum Effort	446	706	42-95188	yes	Shack Rabbit	446	707	42-110043	no
Merle Lee	446	706	42-7584	yes	Shadie Sadie	446			no
Merle Lee II	446	706	42-99983	no	Shady Sadie	446	705	42-95059	yes
Merry Max (The)	446		42-7713	no	She's Mine	446	704	42-95105	no
Mi Akin Ass	446			no	Shif'lus Skonk	446	706	42-7595	yes
Mi-Akin-Ass	446	704	42-7613	no	Shoo Shoo Baby	446	707	42-52747	yes
Midge	446	704	42-7531	yes	Shoo Shoo Baby II	446	704	42-95197	yes
Mighty Mouse	446	704	44-50775	yes	Silver Dollar	446	704	42-7611	no
Mighty Warrior	446			no	Sittin' Bull	446	707	42-7575	no
Milk Run	446			no	Slightly Dangerous	446	704	42-50618	no
Minnie	446	706	41-28628	yes	Solid Comfort	446	705		yes
My Buddy	446	714	42-95083	yes	Spirit of '77 (The)	446	705	42-7607	yes
My Devotion	446	704	42-7587	no	Spirit of 77	446	705	42-7610	no
My Devotion	446	704	44-50734	yes	Star Dust	446	705	42-7576	yes
Nature's Nymphe	446	705		yes	Sterile Errol	446	707	42-7641	yes
Naughty Nan	446	705	42-51581	no	Super Chief	446		42-95562	yes
Naughty Nan II	446	705	42-52594	yes	Sure Shot	446			no
Neva Lorraine	446	704	42-50308	no	Susu	446	707	42-50365	yes
Nona Rhea	446	706	42-7612	yes	Sweet Moonbeam				
Norma Nan	446			no	McSwine	446	704	42-7592	yes
Nov Schmoz Ka Pop	446	704	41-29411	yes	Tail Wind	446	707	41-29550	yes
Oklahoma Gal	446	704	42-50567	yes	Tar Heel Baby	446	707	41-29125	yes
Old 933	446	706	42-51933	yes	Tarheel baby	446	707	41-29125	yes
Old Faithful	446	706	42-7605	yes	Temptation	446	705	42-50477	no
Old Hickory	446	707	42-110043	no	Thundermug	446			no
Old Thunder Mug (The)	446			no	Time's A Wastin'	446		42-50569	no
Pappy	446		41-24137	no	TS	446			no
Patriotic Patty	446	707	42-50734	yes	Umbriago	446		42-50280	no
Peg O' San Antone	446	706	42-50852	yes	Umbriago	446	705	42-50330	no
Pin Up Girl	446	705	42-94941	no	Wanda Lust	446	705		no
Pistol Packin' Bomma	446	707	42-7654	yes	War Goddess	446	706	42-100306	yes
Pistol Packin' Mama	446	707	42-7654	yes	Watch the Fords Go By	446	704	42-7574	no
Pistol Packin' Mama II	446	707	42-51278	no	Wedding Belle	446	704	42-95178	yes
Pistol Packing Bomma II	446	707	42-51278	yes	Wee Willie	446	707	42-7583	no
Princess (The)	446	706	42-7620	yes	Weiser Witch	446	707	42-95324	yes
Princess O'Rourke	446	705	42-7572	no	Wells Fargo	446	707	42-50365	yes
Queen of Angels	446	704	42-50735	no	Werewolf	446	705	42-7572	yes
Queenie	446	707	42-50773	yes	White Lit'nin'	446	705	42-95058	yes
Quivering Box	446	705	42-100315	yes	Wistful Vista	446	706	44-40104	yes
Red Ass	446	706	42-95203	yes	Wolf Patrol (The)	446	705	42-50882	yes
Red Butt	446	706	42-95203	yes	Worry Bird (The)	446	707	42-7616	yes
Ridge Runner	446	704	41-29411	no	Yankee Rebel	446			no
Rigor Mortis	446	705	42-7589	no	Ye Olde Thunder Mug	446	704	42-7539	yes

448TH BOMB GROUP

Name	Grp.	Sq.	Serial	Pic.	Name	Grp.	Sq.	Serial	Pic.
2nd Ave. El	448			no	Carol-N-Lick	448	712	42-7739	no
Abie's Irish Rose	448	714	41-28606	no	Carolyn Chick	448	712	41-29981	no
Abie's Irish Rose	448	714	42-7606	no	Carolyn Chick	448	712	42-63981	no
Achtung, Moon Balloon	448		44-50540	yes	Carry Me Back	448			no
Alabama Exterminator	448			no	Change-O-Luck	448			no
All American	448			no	Choo Choo Baby	448			no
B. T. O.	448		42-73193	no	Chubby Champ	448		42-7655	no
B. T. O.	448	714	42-50678	no	Classy Chassy	448			no
Baby Doll	448			no	Comanche (The)	448	714	42-64447	yes
Baby Shoes	448	712	41-28611	no	Come Along Boys	448	715	42-100322	no
Bachelor's Delight	448			no	Comfy N' Cozy	448			no
Back to the Sack	448	713	42-51288	yes	Commando	448	713	41-28602	no
Back to the Sack	448	713	42-51291	no	Consolidated Mess	448	715	42-64444	no
Bad Penny	448			no	Crazy Mary	448	715	41-28601	no
Bag O' Bolts	448	715	42-7746	no	Crud Wagon	448	712	42-52098	no
Bag-O-Bolts	448	715	42-7764	no	Cubby Champ	448			no
Bag-O-Bones	448			no	Daisy Mae	448	715	42-94972	yes
Ball of Fire	448			no	Dead End Kids	448	712	42-94992	yes
Banshee	448			no	Demon's Delight	448			no
Banshee II	448			no	Denver Zephyr	448	714	42-50357	no
Bar Fly	448		42-95055	no	Do Bunny	448	713	42-95185	yes
Bat Outa Hell	448			no	Doll Baby	448			no
Battlin' Baby	448	713	42-99971	yes	Don't Fence Me In	448	714	42-50525	yes
Berlin Box Car	448			no	Down and Go	448			no
Berlin Sleeper	448			no	Drop 'em N' Run	448	714		no
Betsy Jane	448		42-95169	no	Dual Sack	448	714	42-95089	yes
Betsy Jay	448			no	Duboney	448	713	42-95185	no
Big Ass Bird	448	713	42-64441	no	Duchess (The)	448			no
Big Bad Wolf	448	715	41-29479	no	Eager Beaver	448			no
Big Dick, Hard to Hit	448			no	Eager One	448		42-50326	no
Big Stuff	448			no	Eager One	448	712	44-10517	yes
Big Time Operator	448			no	Eagles Wrath	448			no
Bim Bam Bola	448	714	42-94735	no	El Korab	448			no
Birmingham Blitz Buggy	448			no	Eveless Eden	448	713	42-51123	yes
Black Widow	448	713	42-100109	yes	Exterminator	448	715	42-7717	no
Blake's Snakes	448			no	Fascinating Lady	448	713	42-72981	yes
Blues in the Night	448	713		no	Favorite Gal	448			no
Bold 75	448			no	Fearless Fosdick	448	714	42-50698	yes
Bomb Boogie	448	713	42-52120	no	Feather Merchant	448		42-73477	no
Boogie Joy	448			no	Feudin' Rebel	448			no
Boomerang	448	712	42-52132	no	Fightin' Pappy	448			no
Boomerang	448	714	42-52115	no	Fink's Jinks	448	713	42-7681	no
Boulder Buf	448			no	Flak Ducker (The)	448			no
Bring 'em Back Alive	448			no	Flak Happy	448			no
Broadway Bill	448			no	Flak Jack	448			no
Brooklyn-No Name Jive	448	714	41-29230	no	Flak Target	448			no
Brownie	448	714	42-50727	no	Flexible Flyer	448			no
BTO	448	712	44-50678	no	Flutter Duck	448			no
Bucket of Bolts	448			no	Flying Dragon	448			no
Buffalo Gal	448			no	Flying Sac (The)	448	712	42-110098	yes
Bugs Bunny	448			no	Forever Amber	448	714		no
Butcher Shop	448			no	Foul Ball	448		42-50290	no
Carol Marie	448	712	42-110040	yes	Four (4) F	448			no
Carol Marie	448	712	42-51079	no	Four Flusher	448			no
					Frenchy-N-More	448			no
					Frisco Frisky	448	715	42-51247	yes
					Frisco Trudy	448	714	42-95006	yes

Name	Grp.	Sq.	Serial	Pic.	Name	Grp.	Sq.	Serial	Pic.
Fuedin' Rebel	448			no	Lonesome Lou	448	714	42-50677	no
Full House	448			no	Luck O' the Irish	448			yes
Georgia Peach	448			no	Lucky 15	448			no
Gremlin's Roost	448			no	Lucky Thirteen	448			no
Gung Ho	448	712	44-10505	no	Maid of Orleans	448	715	42-7739	no
Gung Ho	448	713	42-50463	no	Maid of Tin	448	715	42-7709	no
Gypsy Queen	448		42-95197	no	Margaret L.	448			no
H for Helen	448			no	Mary Michele	448			no
Happy Hangover	448			no	Menace (The)	448	712	41-29232	no
Happy Warrior	448		42-94860	no	Merry Max (The)	448	715	42-7713	yes
Hard Times	448	714	42-7755	no	Misanthrope	448	715	42-94953	no
Harmful Lil' Armful	448	715	42-7754	no	Miss Behavin'	448			no
Heaven Can Wait	448	715	42-7758	no	Miss Carriage	448			no
Hell's Belle	448			no	Miss Happ	448	713	41-29523	no
Hell's Kitchen	448	713	41-24236	no	Miss-B-Haven	448			yes
Hell's Kitten	448	713	41-24236	yes	Monotonous Maggie	448		42-95151	yes
Hell's Natural	448	713	41-24236	no	Mother of Ten	448	713	44-10556	yes
Hello Natural	448	712	41-29191	yes	My Achin' Back	448			yes
Hello Natural II	448	712	42-50606	no	My Baby	448	713	42-95305	no
Hello Natural II	448	712	42-52606	yes	No Love, No Nothing	448	713	42-95138	no
Hellzadroppin'	448		41-23809	no	No Name Jive	448	714	41-29230	no
Hit Parade	448			no	No Nothing	448	714	41-28945	no
Hitler's V-4s	448			no	O-O-Nothing	448	713	42-50468	yes
Home Town	448			no	Oh, My Sufferin' Head	448			no
Honeybucket	448			no	Ol' Buddy	448		42-94774	yes
Hussy Lin	448			no	Ol' Soak	448	712	41-29358	no
Hydra	448			no	Old 75	448			no
Ice Cold Katie	448	713	41-28595	yes	Old Glory	448			no
Impatient Virgin (The)	448	714	41-29231	no	Old Pop	448			no
Incendiary Blonde	448		42-95158	no	Old Reliable	448			no
Ironbird	448			no	Old Swayback	448	714	42-7722	no
Ity Fad	448			no	Old Tom Cat	448	714	42-50699	no
Jonny Reb	448			no	Ole 76	448			no
Jumping Jive	448			no	Our Honey	448	713	42-50302	yes
Junior	448			no	Our Joy	448	713	42-51291	no
La Mamie	448			no	Patchie	448			no
Lady from Bristol	448	714	42-52100	no	Patricia Ann	448			no
Lady Godiva	448			no	Patrick Dempsey	448			no
Lady Halitosis	448			no	Peacemaker	448			no
Lady Lora	448	714	42-50799	no	Pete	448	714	42-95006	yes
Lady Luck	448	715	41-28578	yes	Piccadilly Commando	448			no
Lady Margaret	448	714	42-95134	no	Piccadilly Lady	448			no
Laki-Nuki	448	712	42-7733	no	Piccadilly Pat	448			no
Larrupin' Libby	448			no	Piccadilly Pete	448	712	42-52118	yes
Leading Lady	448			no	Piccidilly Lilly	448	715	42-50341	yes
Liberty Belle	448		42-94996	no	Pistol Packin' Mama	448			no
Lilly's Sister	448	715	44-50787	yes	Plane Sane	448			no
Limpin' Ol Sadie	448			no	Poo Tinky	448			no
Linda Mae	448	712	42-51075	no	Poop Deck Pappy	448			no
Little Audrey	448			no	Pop	448			yes
Little Gel	448			no	Princess Pat	448			no
Little Iodine	448		41-28941	yes	Problem Child	448			no
Little Iodine	448	714	44-10516	no	Prodigal Son (The)	448	712	41-28593	no
Little Jo	448	713	41-28958	yes	Purple Shaft Special	448			no
Little Jos	448			no	QQQQ	448			no
Little Sheppard	448	712	41-28711	yes	Queenie	448			no
Local Yokel	448			no	Quitcherbitchin	448			no

Name	Grp.	Sq.	Serial	Pic.	Name	Grp.	Sq.	Serial	Pic.
Rabduckit	448			yes	Tangerine	448			no
Raid of Terror	448			no	Tarbaby	448			yes
Rationed Passion	448			no	Tarfu	448	713	42-99993	yes
Rebel (The)	448			no	Tarfu II	448	714	42-100425	yes
Red Dog	448			no	Thanks A Lot	448			no
Red Hot Mama	448			no	Thar She Blows	448			no
Red Sox	448			no	Thirty Day Furlough	448	713	42-52123	yes
Reddy Teddy	448	715	42-51551	yes	Thirty Day Leave	448	713	42-51123	yes
Rome of New York	448			no	Thumbs Up	448			no
Rose's Rivets	448	712	42-95544	no	Time's A Wastin'	448			no
Rosie	448			no	To Hell N' Back	448			no
Rover Boys	448			no	Tondelayo	448	713	41-28240	no
Royal Flush	448			no	Tough Titty	448			no
Rugged But Right	448	715	42-94953	yes	Trouble N' Mind	448		44-50519	no
Rum Boogie	448			no	Trouble N' Mind	448	713	42-95298	no
Rum Runner	448	713	42-28583	yes	Twin Tails	448	715	42-100122	no
Ruth E.K. Allah					Umbriago	448			yes
Hassid (The)	448	714	41-29577	yes	Unholy Virgin	448	712	42-95544	no
Ruth-less	448			no	Urgin' Virgin	448			no
Sad Sack	448		42-94988	no	Vadie Raye	448	713	42-73497	yes
Screamin' Red Ass	448			no	Vicious Virgin	448			no
Sequina Girl	448	712	42-64451	no	Virgin Sturgeon	448			no
Shack Rabbit	448			no	Wabash Cannonball	448			no
Shady Lady	448	715	42-50759	yes	Wabbit Twacks	448			no
Shoo! Shoo! Baby	448	712	41-29208	yes	Wagon	448			no
Skeeter	448			no	Water Wagon	448			no
Skeeter II	448	714	42-52638	no	Wazzle Dazzle	448	715	42-50767	yes
Skid's Kids	448			no	We Dood It	448			no
Sky Queen (The)	448	713	41-28583	no	What A Cookie	448			no
Sky Queen (The)	448	713	42-110026	no	What Da Hell	448	715	44-50846	yes
Sky's the Limit	448			no	Willie's Sillies	448			no
Skylark	448		44-40224	no	Windhaven	448			no
Sleepy Time Gal	448			no	Windy Winnie	448		44-10599	no
Slick Chick	448	715	42-50460	yes	Windy Winnie	448	712	42-50676	no
Snow Queen	448			no	Wolf Pack	448	713	42-52121	yes
Snuffy's Delight	448			no	Wolfe Pack	448	712	42-51221	yes
Sonia	448			no	Yegg Beaters	448			no
Southern Comfort	448			no	You Cawn't Miss It	448		41-23809	yes
Spirit of '76	448			no	You're Safe At Home	448			no
Spirit of Colley H.S.	448	713	42-50777	no					
Spirit of Notre Dame	448			no					

449TH BOMB GROUP

Name	Grp.	Sq.	Serial	Pic.
Squat 'N' Droppit	448	712	41-28710	yes
St. Louis Woman	448	714	42-50459	no
Star Spangled Hell	448	712	42-7767	yes
Sturgeon (The)	448	715	42-110066	yes
Sullivan's Travellers	448			no
Sunshine	448			no
Sweat'er Out	448			no
Sweater Girl	448			no
Sweet Rose Marie	448			no
Sweet Sioux	448	714	42-7683	yes
Sweet Sioux Two	448	713	42-95013	no
Sweetheart of the				
Rockies	448		44-10544	yes
Taffy	448			no
Taffy II	448			no
Tail Heavy	448	715	42-52608	yes

Name	Grp.	Sq.	Serial	Pic.
Balls of Fire	449	718	42-109796	yes
Bestwedu	449	718		no
Betty Ann	449	719	41-29215	no
Betty Jean	449	719	41-28625	yes
Big Bill	449		42-64400	yes
Big Noise from Kentucky	449	718	42-52149	yes
Blind Date	449	716	41-29243	no
Bonnie's Boys	449	719	42-50307	no
Boom Boom	449	718		no
Born to Lose	449	719	41-29258	yes
Brady's Gang	449	716	42-7769	yes
Brass Monkey	449	717	41-28846	no
Bucket of Bolts	449	718	41-28600	yes
Butchie Darlin'	449	716	44-41049	yes
Buzzer (The)	449	719	41-29307	yes

Name	Grp.	Sq.	Serial	Pic.	Name	Grp.	Sq.	Serial	Pic.
By Fong Club	449	718		no	Lady Lightnin'	449	719	42-52760	no
Cinnsy's Margie	449	717	42-7723	yes	Lil' Butch	449	718	42-64363	no
City of Plainfield, NJ	449	719	42-51763	no	Lil' Jo Toddy	449	717	42-99856	yes
City of Waco	449	719		no	Little Beaver	449			yes
Classy Chassis	449	717	42-52157	yes	Lonesome Polecat	449			no
Collapsible Suzy	449	718		no	Lonesome?	449	719	42-7732	yes
Consolidated Mess	449	719	42-52159	yes	Lonesome? II	449	719	42-51652	yes
Coral Princess	449			no	Los Lobos	449	719	42-7761	yes
Cover Girl	449			yes	Lovely Heads	449	718		no
Daisy Mae	449	718	42-7726	no	Lurchin' Urchin	449	717	41-29233	no
Darling VI	449	719	44-10633	no	Lurchin' Urchin II	449	717	42-52092	no
Devil's Henchmen	449	716	42-52089	yes	Maui Maid	449	719	41-28623	yes
Dixie Belle	449	719	41-29193	yes	Maw Stricknine	449	716	42-52104	yes
Doodle Bug	449	718	41-23742	yes	Miasis Dragon	449	717	42-52172	yes
Double Trouble	449	717	42-50742	yes	Mighty Mouse	449	719	41-28594	no
Draggin' Waggin	449	716	42-99770	yes	Mis-Chief	449	717	42-64388	yes
Dragon Lady	449	717	42-52134	no	Miss Bad Penny	449	719		no
Dragon Lady #2	449	719	41-28647	yes	Miss Bea Haven	449	717	42-64394	no
Dry Run	449	717	42-78017	yes	Miss Behavin'	449	717	42-52086	no
Dumbo	449	716	42-7741	no	Miss De Flak	449	717	42-78125	yes
Dumbo	449	718	41-29217	no	Miss Judy	449	718	42-51639	no
Easy Maid	449	718	44-41119	yes	Miss Lee	449	716	42-7737	no
Easy Queen	449	716	42-95269	yes	Miss N' Moan	449	717	42-64394	yes
Eight Ball	449	718		no	Miss-I-Hope	449	718	42-78624	yes
Everybody's Baby	449	718	42-7756	yes	Miss-N-Moan	449	717		yes
Fearless Fosdick	449	716	42-51375	no	My Achin' Back	449	718	42-52434	yes
Fickle Finger	449	716	42-52550	yes	Nancy Jane	449	716	41-28833	no
Ghost of the Omar	449	716	42-52140	yes	Nancy Jane	449	716	41-29512	no
Gidi Gidi Boom Boom	449	717	41-28846	no	Nancy Jane II	449	719	41-28866	no
Great Iron Bird	449	717		no	Nobody	449	717	42-99856	no
Gremlin's Delite	449	719	42-64389	yes	Old Ironsides	449	717	42-52170	yes
Guardian Angel	449	719	42-7715	no	Old Sack	449	719	44-40321	yes
Gypsy Queen	449		42-95197	no	Olde Rugged Curse (Ye)	449	718	42-7762	yes
Harper's Ferry	449	718	41-28621	yes	Ole Faithful	449	717	42-64388	yes
Hassan the Assassin	449	719	41-29237	no	Ollies Trolley	449			no
Heading for Home	449	719	42-50406	yes	One Night Stand	449	717	41-29584	yes
Heavenly Body	449	716	42-7708	yes	Ore Shack	449			no
Hell's a-Poppin'	449	718	42-52166	yes	Our Babe	449	719	44-49752	no
Hey Mac	449	716	42-99803	yes	Our Baby	449	719	41-29428	yes
Hey Man	449			no	Our Baby, Too	449	719	44-49752	yes
High Life	449	719	41-28972	yes	Paper Doll	449	719	42-7691	yes
Hit Parader	449			no	Patches	449	719	42-52155	yes
Holy Joe	449	717	41-29225	yes	Patches II	449	719	41-29428	no
Holy Joe the 2nd	449	717	42-50282	no	Peerless Clipper	449	717	41-29216	yes
Honey Chile	449	717	42-78372	yes	Peerless Clipper II	449	716	42-64354	no
Hoppy	449	718		no	Peppy	449	717	41-28590	no
Hot Rock	449	718	41-29218	yes	Pistol Packin' Mama	449	716	42-52146	yes
Hot To Go	449	719	41-29003	yes	Pistol Packin' Mamma	449	718	41-28597	yes
Humpty Dumpty	449	716		no	Princess Helen	449	716	42-78479	yes
Inhoomin Critter (The)	449	718	42-78341	yes	Puggy II	449	719	42-7747	no
Instable	449	717	42-78195	no	Pugnacious Peggy	449	716	42-52269	yes
Irish Lass (The)	449			yes	Puss in Boots	449	718	44-49403	yes
Jinx (The)	449			yes	Queen Bee	449	719		no
Jonny Reb	449	716	42-7768	no	Queen of Hearts	449	716	42-64367	yes
Juanita	449	719	42-52126	yes	Queen of Hearts	449	717	42-64367	yes
Lady in the Dark	449		42-50665	no	Racy Tomato	449	718	42-78266	yes
Lady in the Dark	449	716	42-95286	yes	Rag-A-Das	449	717	42-51920	yes

Name	Grp.	Sq.	Serial	Pic.
Ramp Tramp	449	716	42-7700	yes
Red Hot Riding Hood	449	717	42-52086	no
Reluctant Liz	449	717	41-28596	yes
Sagittarius	449	716	41-29400	yes
Salty Dog	449	719	41-28864	yes
Shack (The)	449	718	42-94977	yes
Shack Happy	449	717	42-7744	yes
Shack? Wolf!	449	717	41-29194	yes
Shacking Stuff	449	716	42-50415	no
Shamrock	449	716	42-52243	yes
Shasta Shack	449	719	41-28833	no
Shasta Shack	449	719	42-64348	no
Shirley Jean	449	716	42-95397	yes
Silver Babe	449	716	44-40331	yes
Sinner's Dream	449	718	41-28605	no
Six O'Clock Joe	449	717	xx-xx061	yes
Skipper	449	719	42-78172	yes
Sleepy Time Gal	449	718	42-7745	yes
Sleepy Time Gal II	449	719	42-95271	no
Sleepytime Gal II	449	719	42-95271	no
Slick Chick	449	716	42-52110	no
Slick Chick II	449	716	42-52165	yes
Sophisticated Lady	449	716	41-29214	yes
Spirit of Illinois	449	716	42-51553	no
Spirit of Plainfield, NJ	449	719	42-51763	no
Star Dust	449	718	42-52188	yes
Star Eyes	449	719	41-29203	yes
Stinky the B.T.O.	449	716	42-64462	yes
Sunshine	449	719	42-52106	yes
Superstitious Aloysius	449	717	42-52136	yes
Suzan Jane	449	717	42-52396	yes
Sweet & Lovely	449	716		no
Sweet and Lovely	449	716		no
Sweet Mother	449	719	41-29309	yes
Sweet Sue	449	718		no
Tailwind	449			yes
Tarfu	449	719	42-72165	yes
Teepee Time Gal	449			no
Temptress (The)	449	717	42-52107	yes
Tepee Time Gal	449			yes
Things Is Rough	449	717	42-52091	yes
Thunder Bay Babe	449	717	42-7623	yes
Tigers Teeth	449			no
Touch Me Not	449	719	42-78510	yes
Troop Sleeper	449	716	41-29512	no
Truculent Turtle	449	717		no
Twinkletoes	449	719	42-95314	yes
Two Ton Tessie	449	717	42-52117	yes
Umbriago	449	717	41-28902	yes
Umbriago	449	719	41-28902	yes
Valiant Virgin-ia	449	716	41-29460	yes
Valiant Virgin-ia	449	716	42-78158	yes
Veni, Vidi, Vici	449	718	42-52150	yes
Virgin Vampire	449			no
Want-A-Play?	449	717		yes
Weary Willie	449	718	42-99816	yes
White Fang	449	718	41-28606	no

Name	Grp.	Sq.	Serial	Pic.
Wild Honey	449	717	42-52208	yes
Wine, Women & Song	449	718		no
Wise Virgin (The)	449	716	41-28616	yes
Wise Virgin II (The)	449	716	41-29274	yes
Woods Chopper	449	718	42-7750	yes
Worry Bird	449	719	42-78173	yes
Yankee Maid	449	716	42-94794	yes
Ye Olde Rugged Curse	449	718		yes

450TH BOMB GROUP

Name	Grp.	Sq.	Serial	Pic.
Augusta P.	450	721	42-78455	no
Babe in Arms	450	720	42-78234	yes
Bachelor's Bedlam	450	723		yes
Banana Boat	450	720	42-7742	no
Bottoms Up	450	721	42-64448	yes
Breezie Wheezie	450	723	42-78613	no
Buckeye Belle	450	720	42-7748	no
Buelah	450	723	41-29228	no
Daisy Mae	450	723	42-78404	no
Destiny's Deb	450	720	42-78170	no
Deuces Wild	450	721	41-29222	no
Dinah Might	450	723	42-52164	no
Dolly	450	720	42-50277	no
Dragonass	450	722	42-51848	no
Duchess	450	723	42-78311	no
Duchess II	450	723	44-50481	no
Ford's Folly	450	723	42-78412	no
Gadget	450	723	41-28620	no
Good Ship	450	722	42-78448	yes
Gremlin Gus	450	723	42-52161	no
Guardian Angel	450	722	41-29376	no
Hard To Get	450	720	42-78156	no
Heaven's Above	450	720	41-28757	yes
Hi Pockets	450	721	42-95385	no
Hubba Hubba	450	721	42-50776	yes
Hubba Hubba II	450	721	42-78506	no
I'll Get By	450	723	42-64339	no
Impatient Virgin	450	720	42-7697	no
Joint Venture	450	722	42-78194	no
Judy Lee	450	723	42-7752	yes
Kathleen	450	723	42-51603	no
Kitten	450	723	41-28821	no
Lady Lee	450	723		yes
Lady Luck	450	723	42-51777	yes
Leaky Tub	450	723	41-29226	no
Liberal Lady	450	720	42-52148	no
Little Beaver	450	721		no
Little Lady Joyce	450	723	42-52519	no
Little Stinker	450	723	42-52090	no
Long John Silver	450	721	41-28756	no
Long John Silver	450	723	42-78196	no
Louisiana Lady	450	723	42-78175	no
Madame Shoo Shoo	450	722	42-99805	yes
Maiden America	450	723	42-78356	yes
Marge	450	722	42-52122	no
Mary Jane	450	723	41-29338	no

Name	Grp.	Sq.	Serial	Pic.
Mi Akin Ass	450	722	44-40927	no
Miss Fortune	450	720	42-7728	no
MIss Fury	450	721	42-7746	no
Multi Bono	450	722	42-7714	no
My Akin' Ass	450	722	44-40927	no
Nita	450	723	42-51841	no
Paoli Local	450	723	44-41058	no
Pappy's Yokum	450	721	41-11933	yes
Pardon Me	450	723	44-50845	no
Passionate Pirate	450	720	44-41041	no
Passionate Witch	450	722	42-7731	no
Peekin' Thru	450	723	42-51159	no
Peelin' Off	450	723	41-28919	no
Peelin' Off	450	723	44-40949	no
Peg O' My Heart	450	720	42-7735	no
Penny	450	720	42-78405	no
Pistol Packin' Mama	450	720	42-52124	yes
Princess Pat	450	723	44-50245	no
Problem Child	450	723	42-7724	no
Queen Anne	450	722	42-95458	no
Queen of Hearts	450	723	44-50675	no
Rage in Heaven	450	721		no
Ramp Rat	450	721	42-78454	yes
Round Trip Rose	450	723	41-29213	no
Rowdy Dowdys	450	720	42-78184	yes
Sage Lady	450	723	41-28607	no
Satan's Gal II	450	720	42-78231	yes
Set 'em Up	450	723	42-94787	yes
Shady Lady	450	720	42-7743	no
Sleepytime Gal	450	720	42-78211	no
Snatch (The)	450	722	42-78197	no
Sonny Boy	450	723	44-50709	no
Stardust	450	721	42-64455	no
Stinky's Siren	450		42-52085	no
Strange Cargo	450	720	42-51153	no
Strange Cargo II	450	720	42-51623	yes
Strawberry Bitch	450	722	42-7753	no
Swamp Rat	450	721	42-78454	yes
Swashbuckler	450	723	42-95296	no
Sweet Chariot	450	723	42-78246	no
Takeoff Time	450	723	42-7710	no
Tanta Lisa	450	722	41-29281	no
Tanta Lisa	450	722	42-7740	no
Ten Fighting Cocks	450	720	42-52119	yes
Termite Chaser #1	450	722	42-52141	no
Tong Hoy	450	723	41-29345	no
Tough Ship	450	721	41-29244	no
Tung Hoy	450	723	41-29345	yes
Twin Tails	450	723	41-28579	no
Wells Cargo	450	723	42-52143	yes
Whiskey Kid	450	723	42-52163	no
Will Rogers Special	450	723	42-78593	no
Wolf Pack	450	723	42-64454	no
Yankee Fury	450	721	42-52109	yes
Yellow 28	450	723	44-41025	no

451ST BOMB GROUP

Name	Grp.	Sq.	Serial	Pic.
A Train (The)	451	726	42-52082	yes
Adolph and Tojo	451	724	42-7725	no
American Beauty	451	724	41-29530	no
American Maid	451	724	42-78276	no
Ape	451	727	42-95239	no
Babe	451	727	42-95359	no
Bachelor Bomber	451	725	42-52158	yes
Bad Penny (The)	451	726	42-51321	yes
Bat (The)	451	725	41-28740	no
Betty	451	727		yes
Betty Coed	451	725	44-41109	yes
Betty Jo	451	725	42-51682	no
Big Boober Girl	451	727	41-29199	yes
Big Fat Momma	451	726	42-52429	no
Big Idjit	451	724	42-52099	yes
Big Mogul	451	726	42-52078	yes
Bigger Boober Girl	451	727	41-28957	no
Bodacious Critter	451	727	42-64450	yes
Bodacious Critter II	451	727	42-78157	yes
Boomerang	451	725	41-29219	yes
Boot in the Ass	451	724	42-51369	yes
Boots and His Buddies	451	724	42-78414	no
Born to Lose	451	724	41-29258	yes
Bottom's Up	451	727	42-51674	no
Breezie Weesie	451	727	41-28806	yes
Bubble Trouble	451	725	42-51360	no
Bubble Trouble	451	726	42-78497	yes
Burma Bound	451	725	41-28861	no
Burma Bound	451	725	41-28897	yes
Calamity Jane	451	725	42-52440	yes
Cannon Fodder	451	726	42-78102	yes
Cave Girl	451	726	42-7687	no
Cherokee Strip	451	724	44-49585	no
Citadel (The)	451	725	42-52168	no
Cocky Crew	451	724	42-78274	yes
Con Job	451	727	42-78145	no
Consolidated Mess	451	727	42-64445	no
Crater Maker	451	727	41-28614	yes
Craven Raven	451	727	42-52103	no
Daisy Mae	451	726	42-50952	no
Damyankee	451	724	42-78414	yes
Deacon's Flivver	451	727		yes
Destiny's Tot	451	724	42-51590	no
Devil's Duchess	451	725	42-52094	yes
Diddlin' Dollie	451	724	42-52077	no
Diddlin' Dollie II	451	724	41-28786	no
Dirty Gertie	451	727	42-50298	yes
Double Trouble	451	725	41-29244	no
Drip (The)	451	726	44-49659	yes
Easy Does It	451	724	41-29253	yes
Eskimo Nell	451		42-78428	no
Extra Joker	451	725	41-29588	no
Extra Joker	451	725	42-95379	yes
Faye	451	725	41-29588	yes

Name	Grp.	Sq.	Serial	Pic.	Name	Grp.	Sq.	Serial	Pic.
Ferp Finesco	451	725	41-28933	yes	Lucky Ten	451	727	42-51409	no
Fertile Myrtle	451	724	42-78471	yes	Mac's Flop House	451	724	42-64465	no
Fickle Finger	451	727	42-51564	yes	Mairzy Doats	451	724	42-78188	yes
Flabbergasted Fanny	451	726	41-29242	yes	Male Box	451	725	44-49868	yes
Flying Ass (The)	451	727		yes	Merry Barbara	451	726	42-78484	no
Flying Wolf	451	727	42-78411	yes	Midnight Mistress	451	727	41-28897	no
Ford's Mistake	451	725	41-29590	no	Minnesota Mauler	451	724	42-50906	yes
Forty Two (42) - Kay	451	727	44-41056	yes	Miss America	451	727	42-52084	yes
Four (4) F	451	727	44-40418	yes	Miss Fire!!	451	724	42-51984	no
Full House	451	724	44-10621	no	Mugley Other	451	725	42-50730	no
Fur Wagon	451	727	42-50240	yes	My Gal	451	725	42-78227	no
Gang Bang	451	727	42-51750	yes	Nancy Lee	451	725	42-99754	no
Gas House	451	724	41-29195	no	Naughty But Nice	451	725		no
Gas House	451	724	42-52474	no	Nickel Plate Crate	451	727	41-28876	no
Gas House Jr.	451	724	42-78236	no	Nightmare	451	725	42-52079	yes
Gemini	451	727	41-29496	yes	Nitemare	451	727	42-52079	yes
Goosy Lucy	451	726	42-78250	yes	Oh Joy	451	725	42-52168	no
Gravel Gertie	451	727	42-73083	yes	Old Taylor	451	726	42-52111	yes
Hard To Get	451	724	42-78523	no	Old Tub	451	726	42-52151	yes
Hard To Get	451	725	42-7738	yes	Old Tub II	451	726	41-29229	no
Heat of the Night	451	727	42-52049	no	Ole Fur Wagon (Ye)	451	727	44-50240	yes
Hell's Hep Cats	451	724	42-51314	no	Our Gal	451	727	44-41152	yes
Hey, Moe	451	725	42-51090	yes	Ozark Upstart	451	726	41-29229	no
Hobo Queen	451	725	42-64353	no	Patches, the Tin-				
Honey Child	451	725	41-29220	no	Tappers Delight	451	726	42-78465	yes
Hop Scotch	451	727	41-29209	yes	Patsy Jack	451	727	42-64445	yes
Ice Cold Katie	451	726	42-7751	no	Peace Terms	451	726	41-29541	yes
Ice Cold Katie II	451	726	41-29541	no	Peace-Maker (The)	451	724	42-52101	no
Impatient Virgin	451	724	41-29251	no	Pistol Packin' Mama	451	724	41-29175	yes
In The Mood	451	725	42-51222	no	Politicians (The)	451	726	42-78478	no
Jane Lee (The)	451	727	42-94877	yes	Purple Shaft (The)	451	724	42-51880	yes
Janet Lee	451	725	41-28766	no	Rabbit Habit	451	725	42-51764	yes
Jeanie	451	724	44-41335	yes	Ready Betty	451	727	42-78254	yes
Jesse James	451	724	42-94808	no	Ready Teddy	451	726	42-52087	yes
Jolly Roger	451	727	42-52081	yes	Red Raider (The)	451	726		no
Jolly Roger	451	727	44-40425	yes	Red Ryder	451	726	42-52460	yes
Kayo	451	727	42-78576	yes	Rhoda	451	726	44-49866	yes
Klunker	451	726	41-28955	no	Roman's Candles/				
Knock It Off	451	724	42-7765	no	Thundermug II	451	726	42-52153	yes
Knockers Up	451	727	42-52054	no	Round Trip	451	726	42-50630	no
Lakanookie	451	725	42-7734	yes	Rover Boys (The)	451	726	42-78463	yes
Lakanookie II	451	725	42-52614	no	Royal Prod	451	727	41-29241	yes
Lamplighter (The)					Sack Time	451		44-40275	yes
(XC-109)	451	725	42-7721	no	Sad Sack	451	726	44-49456	yes
Lamplighter II (The)	451	725	42-52156	no	Sakin' Shack	451	724	41-29256	yes
Larrupin' Libby (The)	451	724	44-49460	no	Sakin' Shack II	451	724	44-50591	yes
Le Petite Fleur	451	727	42-51874	no	Sally D II	451	725	41-29426	yes
Leading Lady	451	727	42-95509	yes	Sally Lee	451	727	41-29239	no
Libby Raider	451	724	41-28642	no	Satan's Sister	451	724	41-29258	no
Lil' Butch II	451	727	42-50389	no	Screamin' Meemie	451	726	42-52082	yes
Little Butch	451	727	42-7465	no	Screamin' Meemie II	451	726	41-29850	yes
Little Butch	451	727	42-7759	yes	Seldom Available	451	725	42-7763	no
Little Butch	451	727	42-7765	no	Shack Time	451		44-40275	yes
Little De-Icer	451	725	41-28806	yes	Shack? Wolf!	451	725	41-29194	yes
Lo-An-Roy	451	727	44-50443	yes	Shsady Lady	451	727	42-78436	yes
Lonesome Polecat	451	726	42-52114	no	She Hasta	451	724	41-29251	no
Lucky Ducky	451	726	42-78208	no	Shilay-Lee	451	727	41-29239	yes

Name	Grp.	Sq.	Serial	Pic.	Name	Grp.	Sq.	Serial	Pic.
Short Stuff	451		44-49043	yes	Cabin in the Sky	453	735	42-64478	yes
Skylark	451	726	42-51677	yes	Cee Cee	453	735	42-52186	no
Sloppy But Safe	451	727	44-41008	yes	Cee Cee II	453	735	42-64490	yes
Small Fry	451	726	42-52429	no	Century Queen	453	735	42-95166	no
Sod Buster (The)	451	727	41-29233	yes	Channel Shy	453			no
Special Delivery	451	726	41-28760	no	Choo Choo Baby	453	734	42-52298	no
Special Mission II	451	727	41-28804	no	Consolidated Mess	453			no
St. Peter's Ferry	451	727	42-7720	no	Consolidated Mess II	453			no
Stinky Poo	451	725	42-52452	no	Cooter	453	732		no
Stork (The)	451	726	42-7687	yes	Corky Bergundy Bomber	453	733	42-52234	yes
Super Moose	451	727	42-64442	no	Crow's Nest	453			yes
Sure Thing	451	727	42-51680	no	Curly	453			no
Susan Diane	451	727	41-29238	no	Dizzy E. Easy	453	734	42-50317	yes
Sweatty Betty	451	727	42-78254	yes	Dizzy R. Roger	453	734	44-50577	yes
T'ings Is Tough	451	727	41-28931	yes	Dolly's Sister	453	734	41-29005	yes
T. S. the Chaplain	451	726	41-28860	no	Draggin' Lady	453			no
Three Feathers	451	726	42-7636	yes	Dugan	453		44-51276	no
Thundermug	451	726	42-7475	no	Dumbo	453	735	41-28943	no
Toddlin' Trollop	451	724	42-78445	yes	Dumbo the Pistol				
Urgent Virgin	451	726		yes	Packin' Pachyderm	453	735	41-28943	no
Waco Wench	451	727	42-51680	no	El Flako	453	735	42-64469	yes
Weary Willie	451	727	42-99816	yes	Fearless Fosdick	453			no
Wee Willie	451	725	42-52167	yes	Fertile Myrtle	453			no
Weesie	451	727	44-41056	yes	Flak Hack	453		42-110100	yes
Wet Dream	451	726	42-51300	yes	Flak Happy	453	735	42-110100	no
Whistling Annie	451	724	44-49747	no	Flamin' Mamie	453			yes
Windy City	451	724	42-7757	no	Foil Proof	453	735	42-94805	yes
Windy City #2	451	724	42-52378	no	Ford's Folly	453	732	42-50296	yes
Wolf Wagon	451	724	42-64449	yes	Galloping Ghost	453			no
Wolf Wagon II	451	724	41-28950	no	Ginnie	453	733	41-28615	no

453RD BOMB GROUP

Name	Grp.	Sq.	Serial	Pic.	Name	Grp.	Sq.	Serial	Pic.
					Golden Gaboon	453	733	41-28645	yes
					Green Dragon	453			no
663	453	735	42-52240	no	Green Dragon	453		41-23683	no
Archibald	453	735	41-28591	no	Gypsy Queen	453		42-109896	no
Arrowhead	453	734	42-51108	yes	Gypsy Queen	453	735	42-50327	no
Barrelhouse Bess	453			no	Hattie Belle	453	735	44-40292	yes
Bastard	453	734	42-50720	no	Hazee	453	733	44-50527	yes
Battle Package	453	732	42-52201	no	Heavenly Body	453		41-29210	yes
Becky	453		42-51216	no	Hell for Hitler	453			no
Becky	453	735	42-94850	no	Hell Wagon	453		42-7492	no
Becoming Back	453	735	44-10575	yes	Her Man	453			no
Begin the Beguine	453	732	41-28619	no	Hollywood & Vine	453	734	41-28610	no
Betty Jane	453	733	xx-x3387	yes	Hoo Jive	453	734	42-52174	yes
Betty Jean	453	733	xx-x3387	no	Hot Stuff	453			no
Big Axe	453	732	41-29250	yes	Humpshot	453	732		no
Billie Mae	453			no	Hustlin' Hussy	453	734		no
Billy Mae	453			no	Inspector's Squak	453			no
Black Jed 654	453	735	42-52244	yes	Jabberwock	453	732	41-28641	no
Blasted Event	453			no	Jake	453		xx-xx219	no
Blondes Away	453			no	Je Revien	453	735		no
Blood and Guts	453	733	44-50671	no	Jug Head	453	732	42-51102	no
Boise Babe	453	735	42-50715	yes	Ken-O-Kay	453	732	42-52302	yes
Borsuk's Bitch	453	735	42-64496	yes	Ken-O-Kay II	453	732	42-52301	no
Briney Marlin	453	733	42-52139	no	Ken-O-Kay III	453	732	42-94990	no
Buffalo	453			no	Lace	453	732	42-95076	yes
Butch	453			no	Lacey	453			no
					Larry	453	735	41-29259	no

Name	Grp.	Sq.	Serial	Pic.
Leading Lady	453			no
Libby Raider	453	734	41-28642	no
Liberty Run	453	733	42-110078	yes
Lil Mike	453	734	41-29257	no
Lil Nemo	453	732	42-50471	no
Lil' Eight Ball	453	734	42-52180	no
Lillie Belle	453	735	42-52191	no
Linda Lou	453	735	42-50764	no
Little Agnes	453	735	42-52178	no
Little Angus	453			no
Little Bryan	453	733	41-28649	no
Little Joe	453	732	42-52185	yes
Little Nancy	453	732	42-52472	yes
Lonesome Polecat	453	734	41-29249	yes
Lover's Lane	453	735	42-64473	no
Lucky Penny	453	734	42-52169	yes
Lucky Penny	453	734	42-7734	no
Lucky Penny II	453	734	42-52169	yes
Maid of Fury	453	733	41-28613	no
Maid of Fury II	453	732	42-50337	no
Male Call	453	734	42-52154	yes
Mary Harriet	453		42-110049	no
Melody Lane	453			no
My Babs	453	733	42-95276	yes
Never Mrs.	453	734	42-95167	yes
Never Mrs. Too	453	734	44-50477	no
Nokish	453			no
Ohio Silver	453	732	42-95206	yes
Old Butch	453	735	41-29250	no
Our Baby	453	735	41-29259	no
Paper Doll	453	734	42-52237	no
Partial Payment	453	732	42-50333	no
Patsy	453	735		no
Patsy	453	735	xx-xx282	no
Pay Day	453	732		no
Pistol Packin' Mama	453			no
Porky	453	733	42-95111	no
Portland Annie	453	735	42-52175	no
Pug	453	732	42-52147	no
Purple Shaft	453	734	42-52296	yes
Queenie	453	735	41-28631	no
Rainbow Goddess	453	735	42-64469	no
Reluctant Dragon	453		41-xx286	yes
Rip Tide	453	732	41-28627	no
Rooster	453	735	41-28650	no
Rum Collins	453	733	44-49972	no
Rumplestiltskin	453	735	42-52182	yes
Rumplestiltskin II	453	735	42-64452	no
Ruth Marie	453	734	42-51301	yes
S for Sugar	453	735		no
Sack Happy	453	734		no
Sad Sack	453	733		no
Shack Happy	453	734	42-95252	no
Shack II (The)	453			no
Shack Rabbit	453	733	42-64460	no
Shamrock	453	735	42-50510	no
Silent Yokum	453	735	44-40297	yes
Sky Chief	453	734	42-95173	no
Sleepy Time Gal	453	735	42-50426	yes
Son of a Beach	453	732	42-52185	no
Spare Parts	453	732	41-28654	yes
Spirit of Notre Dame	453	734	41-29257	yes
Spirit of Notre Dame	453	734	42-95102	yes
Squee-Gee	453	735	42-50379	no
Squee-Gee	453	735	42-95086	no
Star Dust	453	733	42-51009	no
Star Eyes	453	735	42-51089	yes
Stardust	453	735	42-52627	yes
Stinky	453	733	42-110138	no
Stolen Moment	453			no
Strictly Business	453			no
Sunshine	453	735	42-52186	no
Swed (The)	453			no
Sweet Sue	453		44-10563	no
Sweet Sue	453	735	42-50301	no
Toonerville Trolley	453	733		no
Valkyrie	453	734	42-52176	no
Vampin' Vera	453	733	42-52176	yes
Wandering Wanda	453	735	42-95214	yes
Wangering Winds	453	735		no
War Bride	453	734	42-52196	no
We Go	453	731		no
We Go II	453	731	xx-xx243	no
Wham Bam	453	735	41-23738	yes
What Da Hell	453	733	41-28591	no
Whiskey Jingles	453	733	42-51114	yes
Wishing Jingles	453			no
Wiskey Jingles	453	735	42-51114	yes
Yankee Doll	453	734	41-28644	yes
Youthful Rocket	453	732	42-50898	no
Yuvadit	453	735	42-64472	yes
Zeus	453	735	42-95353	no

454TH BOMB GROUP

Name	Grp.	Sq.	Serial	Pic.
Amacraw Lou	454	737	42-78395	no
Ancient and Honorable Artillery Company of Massachussetts	454	737	42-52264	yes
B. T. O.	454	738	42-78504	yes
Bama Baby	454	739	42-52205	no
Beast (The)	454	736	42-99758	no
Betty Coed	454	739	41-28656	no
Big Dog & Nine Old Men	454	739	41-28815	no
Borrowed Time	454	739	42-64474	no
Bright Eyes	454	739	41-28790	no
Bruise Cruiser	454	736	42-52324	no
Buffalo Gal	454	738	42-52297	no
Buttercup	454	737	42-52193	no
Buzz Job	454	738	42-52252	yes
Buzz Job Two	454	738	42-94967	no
Cherokee	454	737	42-52323	no
Cherrie	454	737	42-52075	yes
Chicken Ship	454	738	44-49406	no

151

Name	Grp.	Sq.	Serial	Pic.	Name	Grp.	Sq.	Serial	Pic.
Chief's Delight	454	736	44-49370	yes	Laura Sue	454	736	42-99802	no
Chief's Flight	454	739	42-52314	no	Lonesome Polecat	454	738	42-64467	no
Chuck-A-Lug	454	737	42-99801	no	Lotta Laffs	454	738	44-41341	yes
Chuck-O-Luck	454	737	42-52236	yes	Maggie	454			no
Club 400	454	736	41-28808	yes	Maid in the U.S.A.	454		42-64372	no
Daisy Mae	454			no	Massachusetts	454			no
Delayed Action	454	736	42-52242	no	Mickey Finn	454	738	42-64485	yes
Dinah Might	454	737	42-64359	yes	Miss America 1944	454	739	42-52312	yes
Dorothy K	454	738	41-29310	no	Miss Dorothy	454	739	42-78169	yes
Dragon Lady	454	737	42-94978	yes	Miss Edna	454	738	42-51542	no
Easy Takeoff	454	738	42-78377	yes	Miss Ginnie	454	736	42-78244	no
Fart Sack Phyllis	454		42-78638	no	Miss I Hope	454	736	42-78213	no
Final Approach	454	736	42-78432	yes	Miss Maggie	454	738	42-52207	no
Final Approach II	454	736	42-78489	no	Miss Marie	454	738	42-50416	no
Flak Happy	454	736	42-78324	no	Miss Minuki	454	736	42-52027	no
Flak Happy	454	739	42-50910	no	Miss Polly	454	738	41-29246	no
Flying Home	454	736	41-28914	no	Miss-U	454	738	42-64493	no
Free and Easy	454	736	42-78503	yes	Mohawk Chief	454	736	42-78451	no
Frightful Old Pig (The)	454		42-64364	no	Mohawk Chief	454	738	42-51415	no
Full Boost	454	736	42-52311	yes	Moo Juice	454	737	42-52209	no
Gang Bang	454			no	Moonbeam McSwine	454	736	42-50315	no
Genii	454	737	42-52203	no	Mrs. Lucky	454	738	44-10571	yes
Gentleman Jim	454	737	42-52263	no	My Nell	454		44-50791	no
Ghost (The)	454	738	44-40483	yes	Natchely	454	736	42-52255	no
Ginny	454	738	44-41009	no	Ophelia Bumps	454	736	41-28660	no
Girl Crazy	454	736	42-78668	yes	Ophelia Bumps	454	736	42-51413	no
Good Heavens	454	736	44-41059	no	Ophelia Bumps	454	736	42-78213	no
Good Heavens	454	739	41-29592	yes	Our Baby	454	736	42-52173	yes
Gravel Gertie	454	737	42-78278	no	Our Lady and				
Guardian Angel	454			no	Her Knights	454	738	42-99773	no
Hair Power	454	736		no	Our Little Guy	454	738		no
Hairless Joe	454	738	42-52228	yes	Our Mom	454			no
Hard To Get	454	736	42-78450	yes	Patches	454	737	42-51978	no
Hare Power	454	738	42-51959	no	Penny C.	454	738	42-64488	no
Hare Power	454	739	41-29325	no	Pied Piper (The)	454	739	42-52245	yes
Hawk (The)	454	736	42-52266	no	Pink Panties	454	737	42-64466	no
Hawk (The)	454	736	44-49341	no	Pisces	454	739	42-52179	no
Hell's Angels	454			no	Pistol Packin' Parson	454	737	42-78150	no
Hell's Bell's	454	739	42-52310	yes	Pittsburgh Babe	454	739	42-78264	yes
Henry's Ford	454	738	42-52313	no	Powder Room	454	737	42-78297	yes
Homesick Angel	454	736	42-52125	no	Pregnant Duck	454	739	44-49264	no
Hot Rock	454	737	42-52225	yes	Pretty Mickey	454	736	42-50423	no
Hot Shotsie	454	739	42-78214	yes	Pug Nose Annie	454			no
Hotcha Baby	454	736	42-50285	yes	Purple Shaft	454	736	42-78256	yes
Into the Blue	454	738	42-78079	yes	Purple Shaft	454	738	41-28811	no
It Had To Be You	454	738	41-28608	no	Puss 'N Boots	454	739	42-51905	no
Jap-A-Nazi Jinx	454	738		no	Queen of Hearts	454	738	42-78074	yes
Jodey	454	736	42-52261	yes	R-Baby	454	736		no
Jodey	454	736	42-78503	no	Ragged But Right	454	736	41-28914	no
Joker	454	737	41-28993	no	Ragged But Right	454	737	42-52265	no
Katie Did	454	738	44-41163	no	Rebel Raigh	454	736	44-50876	yes
Knockout	454	736	42-78288	no	Revenge	454	736	42-52272	no
Ladies Delight	454	736	42-78204	no	Rosie	454	737		yes
Lady in the Dark	454	739	42-50570	no	Rough Cobb	454	737	42-78458	yes
Lady Katherine	454	736	41-28873	no	Rough Rid'er	454	739	42-78182	no
Lady Katherine	454	736	42-51398	no	Sad Sack	454	736	44-49703	yes
Lady of Loretto	454	739	42-52262	no	Salvo Sal	454	738	42-64471	no

Name	Grp.	Sq.	Serial	Pic.
San Antonio Rose	454	737	42-95009	yes
Sassy Lassie	454	737	41-29265	no
Shack Date	454			no
Shackup	454	737	42-51323	no
Shadow (The)	454	737	42-100198	no
Silver Fleet	454	737	42-52256	no
Silver Shark	454	736	42-51370	yes
Silver Shark II	454	739	42-78230	no
Slipstream	454	738	42-64459	yes
St. Louis Belle	454	738	42-64392	no
Stand-by	454	738	42-52248	no
Star Dust	454	737	42-78601	no
Stardust	454	737	42-64495	no
Sub-Depot Susy	454	737	44-49392	yes
Sweet Sue	454	736	42-78461	no
Tailwind	454			yes
Teepee Time Gal	454	737	42-95380	no
Terrible Terry	454	739	42-95522	no
Texas Hellcat	454	738	42-50312	no
Thunder Mist	454	739	41-28927	no
Thunder Mist	454	739	44-41165	no
Thundermug	454	739	44-41165	yes
TNT	454	736	44-41059	no
Tuff Nut Tessie	454	738	41-29426	no
Turd Bird	454	739	42-52197	no
Vicious Vixen	454	738	41-29263	no
Victoria Vixen	454	737	42-52171	no
Virgin Annie	454	738	41-28659	no
Virgin Sturgeon	454	736	42-52254	no
Wa-Hoo	454	739	44-41074	no
War Weary Wanda	454	736	42-52229	no
Warrior Maiden	454	738	41-29304	yes
Wench (The)	454	737	42-78387	yes
Who Nose	454	739	41-28699	no
Willie Joe	454	738	42-50987	no
Willie the Wolf	454	737	42-51417	no
Winged Victory	454	739	42-52300	yes
Wolf's Gang	454	737	42-52264	no
Yakamaw	454	737	42-78367	no
You Speak	454	737	42-51366	yes
Zoot Suiter (The)	454	737	42-94978	no

455TH BOMB GROUP

Name	Grp.	Sq.	Serial	Pic.
Arkansas Joe	455	741	42-64456	no
B. T. O.	455			yes
Balls O' Fire	455	740	44-41115	yes
Barumska	455	742	42-51990	no
Bestwedu	455	741	42-52257	yes
Big Gas Bird	455	743	42-78081	yes
Blasted Event	455		42-95334	yes
Blockbuster Bernard	455	742	41-29570	no
Blonde Bombshell (The)	455	742	42-52230	yes
Blonde Bombshell II	455	740	42-78620	no
Bucket of Bolts II	455	740	42-50400	no
Buzz Job	455	741	42-78435	yes
Censored	455		42-52271	yes

Name	Grp.	Sq.	Serial	Pic.
Chattanooga Choo Choo	455	740	41-28994	yes
Cowtown Blonde	455	742	42-52282	no
Dakota Queen	455		42-50892	no
Dakota Queen	455		42-78166	no
Dazzlin' Duchess & the Ten Dukes	455	743	42-64500	yes
Dinah Mite	455		42-64481	no
Double Trouble	455	740	41-29282	yes
Dragon Lady	455	740	42-52223	no
Dragon Lady	455	742	42-51290	no
Easy Maid	455	742		no
Evelyn E.	455	740	44-49366	no
Five Grand	455	742	44-10560	yes
Flak Alley Sally	455	742	41-28815	yes
Ford's Folly	455	741	42-52224	no
Ford's Folly	455	741	42-52249	no
Ford's Other Folly	455	741	42-52249	no
Full House	455	741	42-94949	no
Gargantua	455	742		no
Glammer Gal	455	742	41-29296	no
Good Heavens	455			no
Gray Goose	455	743	41-29583	no
Gremlin's Gripe	455	743	42-52271	no
Gremlin's Gripe II	455	741	42-52281	yes
Heaven Can Wait	455	740	42-52210	no
Heavenly Body	455	741	42-94938	no
Home James	455	743	41-28952	no
Irish Lassie	455	741	44-40517	yes
King of the Pack	455	741	42-52280	no
Knockout	455	741	41-29290	no
Knockout	455	741	42-52260	no
Larry	455	742		no
Late Frate	455	740	42-99748	no
Leakin' Deacon	455	743	41-29271	yes
Liberty's Belle	455	741	42-50425	no
Lincoln Heights	455	742	42-52238	no
Lucky Babe	455	743	41-28658	no
Lucky Lois	455	743	42-78470	yes
Menacing Messalina	455	742	42-64482	no
Minnie Ha-Cha	455	740	42-64497	no
Miss U	455		42-52278	no
Miss Fit	455	742	42-78292	no
Miss I Hope	455	740	42-51624	no
Miss Lincoln Heights	455	742	42-52238	no
Miss Marjorie	455	743	44-41055	no
Moby Dick	455	741	41-29266	no
Moonbeam McSwine	455	743	44-49625	yes
Multa Bona	455	742	42-51332	yes
Omiakinbak	455	741	42-64481	no
Organized Confusion	455	741	42-78397	yes
Our Love	455	742	42-78240	no
Peace Maker	455	743	41-28982	no
Peacemaker (The)	455	743	41-28982	no
Peel Off	455	741	42-64476	yes
Penny C.	455		42-64498	no
Pin Down Girl	455	741	42-52241	no

Name	Grp.	Sq.	Serial	Pic.	Name	Grp.	Sq.	Serial	Pic.
Pindown Girl	455	741	42-52260	yes	Baby Boots	456	746	42-51688	yes
Pistol Packin' Parson	455	741	42-52216	no	Baby Jane	456	745	42-78239	no
Pithonu	455		42-52271	no	Barbara Jane	456	745	42-52304	yes
Pittsburgh Babe	455	742	42-78453	yes	Barbara Jane II	456	744	44-40592	no
Ramp Rooster	455	742	41-28640	no	Bear Baby	456	747	42-64470	no
Red Hot Ridin' Hood	455	743	42-52204	yes	Belle of the Brawl	456	746		no
Reddy Teddy Too	455	742	41-28989	yes	Big Burn	456			no
Roger the Lodger	455	742	42-64482	no	Bonnie	456			no
Rosalie Mae	455	741	42-78166	no	Cancelled Leave (T.S.)	456		42-78673	yes
Rubber Check (The)	455	743	41-29271	no	Cecilia	456	746	44-41092	no
Rusty Dusty	455	742	42-99771	yes	Cheryl Kay	456	747	44-10573	yes
San Antonio Rose	455	742	42-52230	no	Curly Top	456	746	42-64492	no
Sassy Lassy	455	740	41-29282	yes	Der Flittermouse	456		41-29606	no
Satan's Siren	455	740	42-52239	no	Deuces Wild	456	746	42-52222	yes
Secret Weapon (The)	455	740	42-52190	no	Diana Lynn	456	745		yes
Seldom Miss	455		42-51341	no	Draga	456			no
Shoo Shoo Baby	455	742	41-29407	no	Ellen Ann	456	746		yes
Sissy	455	743	44-48760	no	Fatass	456	747	42-52287	no
Sissy Lee	455	741	42-51974	yes	Flak Happy	456	747	42-78328	no
Skeeter	455	742	41-28640	no	Gallopin' Ghost	456	744	41-28934	no
Sky Queen	455	741	42-52216	no	George	456		42-51955	no
Sky Wolf	455	740	41-29264	yes	Gin Rae	456	746	41-28643	yes
Slim Chance	455	742	42-51645	no	Hairless Joe	456		42-51284	no
Smoothie	455		42-99771	yes	Heavenly Body	456	746	41-28768	yes
Snuffy Smith	455	743		yes	Homeward Angel	456			no
Squat N' Drop	455	740	42-95462	no	Ice Cold Katie	456	746	42-64477	no
Star Dust	455		41-29267	no	Imp (The)	456	745	41-29297	no
Star Dust II	455	743	42-52283	no	Irma Kay	456	746		yes
Star Duster	455	740	42-64497	no	J-Bird	456	747	42-52345	no
Star Duster II	455	742	42-50497	yes	Jacob's Ladder	456	744	44-10628	no
Stardust II	455	792	42-50497	yes	Jean	456	744	42-99799	no
Stinky	455	742	42-78609	yes	Jennie Ann	456	747		no
Swamp Angel	455	741	44-40499	no	Judy Ann	456	744	41-29501	no
Swamp Angel	455	742	44-10569	no	Lady Corinne	456	747	44-40485	yes
Sweatin' It Out	455	743	42-52278	no	Lady Patricia (The)	456	745	42-51672	no
Sweet Sue	455		42-51480	no	Lassie Come Home	456	746	42-52215	yes
Sweet Sue	455		42-95042	no	Lassie Come Home	456	746	42-64480	no
Tailwind	455	741	42-64456	no	Linda Kay	456	746		no
Teepee Time Gal	455	743		yes	Little Moe the				
Ten Hits & A Miss	455	741	42-78359	yes	Peacemaker	456	746	42-64486	yes
Tepee Time Gal	455	741	42-94790	yes	Lonesome Polecat	456	747	42-78098	yes
Turbo-Culosis	455	743	41-28879	no	Man-O-War	456	746	41-28831	yes
Twin Tails	455	742	42-52259	no	Marilyn	456	745		no
Virginia Princess (The)	455	742		no	Miss Behave	456	746	42-52232	no
Watta Crok	455			no	Miss Conduct	456	746	42-51548	yes
What's Cookin' Doc?	455	742		no	Miss Laid	456	746	42-51678	yes
Windy Clipper	455	742		no	Miss Minerva II	456		41-29294	no
Wotta Crock	455			no	Miss Ourlovin'	456	746	42-99853	yes
Yo-Yo	455	740	44-41199	yes	Miss Yourlovin'	456	746	42-99853	yes
					Miss Zeke	456			no

456TH BOMB GROUP

Name	Grp.	Sq.	Serial	Pic.
Nancy Anne (The)	456		41-29311	no
Naughty 40	456	745	42-99807	yes
O'Reilly's Datter	456	745	42-78598	yes
Agony Wagon	456	746	44-50436	no
Paper Doll	456			no
Alice	456	747	42-94777	no
Phoney Express II	456	744	42-78403	yes
Anita Lynn (The)	456	744	42-52276	no
Piece Maker (The)	456	746	42-64486	yes
Arkansas Joe	456	746	42-78594	no
Baby (The)	456	746	42-51855	yes
Plum Lake	456	745	42-52334	yes

Name	Grp.	Sq.	Serial	Pic.
Porky	456	746		yes
Preg-Peg	456	747	41-29283	no
Racken Jumper	456			no
Ran Dee Dan	456	747	42-64470	yes
Red Hot Riding Hood	456	747	42-94886	yes
Reddy Maid	456	746	44-50382	yes
Reluctant Beaver	456	745	42-78329	no
Savanna Sue	456	745	44-49478	no
Second Hand Rose	456	746	44-40487	no
Sky Grazer	456	745	42-52309	no
Spunky Punky	456	746	42-51637	yes
Sugar	456	745	42-51715	no
Sugar Baby	456	746		yes
Sweet Sue	456	745	44-10563	yes
Texas Ranger	456			no
Thundermug No. 2	456	745	42-64475	yes
Virgin Wolf	456	746	42-52227	no
Wait for Me, Mary	456	744	42-52290	no
Windy Clipper	456	746		no
Wolf Wagon 2	456	745	42-99749	yes
Worry Bird	456	745	42-51293	no
Yo Yo	456	746		no

458TH BOMB GROUP

Name	Grp.	Sq.	Serial	Pic.
A & G Fish Shoppe	458			yes
Admirable Character	458			no
Admirable Little Character	458	754	42-52335	yes
Al's Youth	458			no
Arise My Love and Come With Me	458	754	42-50768	yes
Baby Shoes	458	753	42-50555	yes
Bachelor's Bedlam	458	753	44-40287	yes
Bad Girl	458	753	44-40288	yes
Beast (The)	458	755	42-50743	yes
Becky	458	752	42-95216	no
Belle of Boston	458	754	41-29299	yes
Belle of Boston	458	754	42-52404	yes
Betty	458	755		yes
Biff Bam	458	752	41-28718	no
Big Chief Lil' Beaver	458		42-51514	yes
Big Dick, Hard to Hit	458	754	41-28682	yes
Big Time Operator	458	753	41-29288	yes
Bird (The)	458	752	42-100425	yes
Blondie's Folly	458	755	41-29331	yes
Bo / Bif Bam	458	752	41-28718	yes
Bo 41	458		42-7718	yes
Bo II	458			no
Bomb Totin' Mama	458	754	41-29295	yes
Bomb-Ah-Dear	458	755	41-29342	yes
Bombs Away	458	753	42-95096	yes
Breezy Lady	458	755	42-110141	yes
Briney Marlin	458	755	42-95183	yes
Bugs Bunny	458	754	42-50640	no
Cancer	458		42-52650	no
Cat's Ass (The)	458	752	42-94946	yes
Chicago Shirl	458	755	42-110184	no
Consolidated Mess	458			no
Cookie	458	752	42-95165	yes
Cookie	458	755	42-50499	no
Daisy Mae	458	754	42-100362	no
Dear Mom	458		41-29277	yes
Dinky Duck	458		41-29142	no
Dixie Belle	458			no
Dixie Belle II	458	754	42-95163	yes
Donna Mia	458		42-40939	yes
Down Wind	458	786	42-52566	no
Downwind Leg	458	755	41-29331	yes
Dreamboat	458	753	41-28706	yes
Elmer	458	753	42-100070	no
Elmer	458	755	42-110141	no
Envy of 'em All	458	754	42-50279	no
Envy of 'em All II	458	754	42-95108	yes
ETO Playhouse	458	752	42-50314	yes
Fat Stuff II	458	712	42-7591	yes
Filthy McNaughty	458	755	42-50608	no
Final Approach	458	752	42-52457	yes
First Sergeant	458	754	42-40127	yes
Flak Magnet	458	753	41-29373	yes
Flak Magnet II	458	753	41-28962	yes
Ford's Follies	458	754	42-52515	no
Ford's Folly	458			no
Fritzi	458	752	41-29329	yes
G.I. Jill	458	754	42-51170	no
Gas House Mouse	458	752	42-95050	yes
Gashouse Mouse	458	752	41-29329	no
Gator	458	755	42-7516	yes
Ginny	458	754	41-28669	no
Ginny	458	754	41-28682	no
Grim Reaper (The)	458		42-100404	no
Gus' Ball of Fire	458	753	42-52392	yes
Gwen	458	755	42-110184	yes
Gypsy Queen	458	754	42-95196	no
Hard T' Find	458		42-50373	yes
Heavenly Hideaway	458	753	44-40277	yes
Hell's Angels	458	754	41-29596	no
Here I Come Again	458			no
Here I Go Again	458	752	42-95179	yes
Holiday Raiders	458	753		no
Hookem Cow	458	755	42-95120	yes
Hot Box	458	753	42-100431	no
Howling Banshee	458	753	44-40207	no
Howling Banshee	458	753	44-40273	yes
Hypochondriac	458			no
I'll Be Back	458	754	41-29305	yes
I'll Be Back	458	754	42-52305	no
Iron Duke	458	754	44-10491	no
It's A Dog's Life	458	753	44-40281	yes
Jayhawker	458	752	41-28667	yes
Jolly Roger	458	752	44-40475	yes
Jolly Roger	458	755	42-50864	no
Judy Sue	458			no

Name	Grp.	Sq.	Serial	Pic.	Name	Grp.	Sq.	Serial	Pic.
Judy's Buggy	458		42-52293	no	Satan's Mate	458	753	42-100341	yes
Junior	458	754	42-95116	no	Satan's Playmate	458	753	42-100341	no
Just Around the Corner	458			no	Shack (The)	458	753	44-40298	yes
Kiss Me Baby	458	753	44-40264	yes	Shack Time	458	753	44-40275	yes
Lady Jane	458	753	42-95133	no	Shazam	458			no
Lady Luck	458	754	42-110070	yes	She Devil	458		44-40123	no
Lady Luck	458	755	42-110141	no	Shicago Shirl	458	755	42-110184	no
Lassie Come Home	458	753	44-40283	yes	Shoo Shoo Baby	458	754	44-51095	no
Last Card Louie	458	755	42-52441	yes	Ski-Nose	458		42-52160	no
Laurippin' Laura	458	755	42-50502	no	Sky Room	458	754	42-50578	yes
Liberty Belle (The)	458	754	42-95199	no	Sleepy Time Gal	458			no
Liberty Lib	458	752	41-29303	yes	Spare Parts	458	753	41-28706	yes
Lily Marlene	458	752	42-95117	yes	Spittin' Kitten	458	754	44-40126	no
Little Joe	458			no	Spotted Ass Ape	458	754	41-28967	yes
Little Lambsy					Squat 'N' Droppit	458		41-28710	no
Divey	458	752	42-100407	yes	Stardust	458	754	42-50516	yes
Little Shepherd	458		41-29359	no	Stinky	458	755	42-95120	yes
Lorelei	458	755	41-29300	yes	Sweet Lorraine	458	754	42-110172	yes
Louie	458			no	Table Stuff	458	753	44-40285	yes
Lucky Strike	458	755	41-28709	yes	Tailwind	458	755	41-29359	yes
Man From Down Under	458			no	Thar She Blows	458	754	42-40127	no
Marez-EE-Doates	458			yes	That's Jayhawker	458	752	41-28667	no
Marie	458	753	42-110163	no	Time's A Wastin'	458	753	42-110163	no
Martha R.	458			no	Top O' the Mark	458	752	42-95110	yes
Mary Lee	458			no	Travlin' Bag (The)	458	753	42-50912	yes
McNamara's Band	458	752	42-52353	no	Vampin' Vera	458	752	41-29302	no
Minnie	458	755	41-28628	yes	Wabbit Twacks	458	753	41-29276	yes
Mispah	458	754	42-100366	no	Wolf's Lair	458	755	44-40470	yes
Miss Carriage	458			no	Wolfgang	458	755	42-52423	yes
Miss Pat	458	754	42-95106	no	Wolves Lair	458	755	41-29352	yes
Miss Used	458	753	44-40277	yes	Wolves, Inc.	458		41-28981	no
Mizpah	458	754	42-100366	yes	Worry Bird	458		44-40470	no
Mona	458	754		yes	Worry Bird	458	755	42-7516	no
My Bunnie	458	752	41-29567	yes	Wurf'less	458	753	42-52382	yes
My Bunnie II	458	752	42-51270	yes	Yankee Buzz Bomb	458	752	41-29340	yes
Nellie	458			yes	Yokum Boy	458	752	42-109812	no
Nokkish	458	752	41-29302	yes	You Bet	458	755	44-10602	yes
Oh, Mona	458	755	44-49544	yes	You Can't Take It				
Old Doc's Yacht	458	754	42-95018	yes	With You	458		42-51097	yes
Olde Hellgate (Ye)	458	753	41-28705	yes					
Ole Satan	458	755	42-52432	yes					
Open Post	458	753	42-50449	yes					
Our Burma	458	755	42-50740	yes					
Our Burma	458	755	42-50864	no					
Paddlefoot	458	755	41-28719	yes					
Pappy Yokum	458	755	42-110059	no					
Pappy's Yokum	458	755	42-110159	no					
Patchie	458	752	42-95219	yes					
Patdue	458			no					
Pied Piper (The)	458	752	42-51206	yes					
Playhouse	458			no					
Plutocrat	458		42-52455	yes					
Princess Pat	458	752	42-95316	yes					
Rhapsody in Junk	458	753	41-28733	yes					
Rough Riders	458	755	41-29342	yes					
Royal Flush	458	753	44-40291	yes					
S. O. L.	458	753	44-40066	yes					

459TH BOMB GROUP

Name	Grp.	Sq.	Serial	Pic.
Azza	459	757		no
B. T. O.	459	758	42-52326	yes
Beautiful Takeoff	459	756	44-49732	yes
Bestwedu	459	756		yes
Bet's Bet	459	759	42-52257	yes
Betty	459	756		yes
Betty Anne	459	758	42-51262	no
Beverly Ann	459	759		no
Black Magic	459	757		no
Blushing Virgin	459			no
Boardwalk Flyer	459			no
Bomb Jockier	459			no
Broken Dollar	459	759		no
Bugs Bunny	459	757		no
California Rocket	459	757	42-51714	yes

Name	Grp.	Sq.	Serial	Pic.	Name	Grp.	Sq.	Serial	Pic.
Cherokee Maiden	459	756	42-52427	yes	Merle	459	759	42-51627	no
Cherry	459	758	42-78106	yes	Mickey Mouse	459	756		yes
Cherry II	459	758	42-78106	no	Miss Annie	459	758		no
Consolidated Miss					Miss Behavin'	459	757	42-52007	yes
Carriage	459	756		yes	Miss Carriage	459	756	42-78427	yes
Corsica Kid	459	759	42-78269	no	Miss Marcia	459	758	42-52322	yes
Countess Inn	459	758		no	Moron (The)	459			no
Cryin' Lion (The)	459			yes	My Prayer	459	756	42-78388	no
Delayed Action	459	757	42-52187	no	Naughty Angel	459	757	42-52341	yes
Devil's Delight	459			no	Nightmare	459			no
Devil's Mistress (The)	459	758	42-51367	no	Norma	459	756		no
Dogpatch Express	459	756	44-10626	yes	O'Riley's Daughter	459	757	42-50432	yes
Dogpatch Express	459	756	44-49750	yes	Old Dutch Cleanser	459	757	42-52500	yes
Early Delivery	459	757	42-52319	no	Old Grey Wolf	459	756	42-51934	yes
Edith	459	759	44-48789	no	Ole Worry	459	756	42-52007	yes
Eightball	459	759	42-95265	no	Our Baby	459	756	42-51265	yes
Elmer's Blitz	459	756		yes	Our Devotion	459	758		no
Exasperatin'					Our Sweetheart	459	756		yes
Gazaborator	459	756	42-78221	yes	Paper Doll	459	756	42-52316	yes
Fearless Fosdick	459	756	41-29438	yes	Patches	459	756	42-51978	no
Fighting Mudcat	459	756	42-42342	yes	Peace Maker	459	757		yes
Ford's Folly	459	757	42-51911	no	Peacemaker (The)	459	757		yes
Frisco Kid Alias					Pluto	459	756		no
The Whip	459	756	42-95265	yes	Ragged But Right	459		42-78490	yes
Gen	459	759	42-51772	no	Rubber Check	459			yes
Generator Kid	459	758		no	Ruff Stuff	459			yes
Ginnie	459	736		yes	Sad Sack	459			yes
Goofy	459	756	42-52400	yes	Sam Sent Me	459			no
Great Speckled Bird	459	757	42-50299	yes	Satan's Shuttlebus	459	756	41-28802	yes
Grim Reaper	459	759		no	Satan's Shuttlebus	459	756	42-52351	no
Hairless Joe	459	758	42-52228	no	Slightly Eager	459	759	42-78177	no
Hard Way (The)	459	758	44-40877	yes	Smokey	459	756	42-52406	yes
Hassan the Assassin	459	757	41-29237	no	So Round, So Firm				
Heaven Can Wait	459	758		no	So Fully Stacked	459	759	42-51701	yes
Heavenly Body	459	757	44-42417	no	Stinky Avenger	459	759	41-28996	no
Hell's Belle	459	756	42-52358	yes	Stinky-The Hot Rock	459	759		no
Hell's Belle	459	756	44-40926	yes	Swiss Itch	459		41-29316	yes
Homesick Moe	459			no	Tall, Torrid & Texas	459	757	44-50418	yes
Hot & Bothered	459	758	42-52295	yes	Tamerlane	459	757	42-52328	no
Hot Sketch	459	756	42-52356	no	Teasin' but Pleasin'	459	758	41-28727	yes
Irish Lassie	459	757		yes	Ten Hits & A Miss	459	758	42-78160	yes
It Had To Be You	459			no	Texarkana Hussy	459			yes
Jackie Boy	459	756	42-52717	no	Texas Lassie II	459	756	42-52373	no
Juanita	459	756		yes	Too-Hot-To-Handle	459	756	42-52307	no
Judith Ann	459	756	44-49771	yes	Totem Pole	459	756		yes
La Borracha	459	756	42-52319	no	Unfinished Business	459	757	42-52046	yes
Lady Katherine	459	756		no	Virgin Annie	459		41-28659	no
Leila Bell	459	759	42-52317	yes	Waddlin' Warrior	459	756		yes
Lethal Louise	459	759	41-28646	no	What's Up Doc?	459	757	41-29457	yes
Linda Ann	459	758	44-49789	no	Who Nose	459		41-28699	no
Little Butch	459	759		no	Why Bother	459	759		no
Lucky 13	459	757	42-52413	no	Wickie (The)	459	759	42-78207	yes
Lucky Lady	459	757	42-51344	no	Yankee Rebel	459	756	44-48763	yes
Marcia	459	758	42-52322	yes					
Mazie	459	757	42-51601	yes					
Mazie	459	758	42-51601	yes					
Meat Around the Corner	459	754	41-28738	yes					

460TH BOMB GROUP

Name	Grp.	Sq.	Serial	Pic.
Agony Wagon	460	763	42-52355	yes

157

Name	Grp.	Sq.	Serial	Pic.
Alexander's Rag Time Band	460	763	41-29320	no
Angel of the Sky	460		42-52365	yes
Ashcan Charlie	460	763	42-99798	no
Avenger of Agony Wagon	460	763	42-78301	no
Barbara Ann	460			yes
Belle Ringer	460	762	42-52347	yes
Betty Jane	460			no
Big Time Operator	460	763	42-94923	no
Blue M for Mike	460	760	44-41252	no
Boomerang	460			yes
Bottoms Up	460	760	42-51926	yes
Cajun Kate	460		42-52401	yes
Chris' Crate II	460		42-110160	no
Cuddles	460	763	42-52337	yes
Dinah Might	460			yes
Ditney Hill	460	760	42-78678	yes
Flyin' Fool	460		42-52408	no
Flying Fool	460		42-78408	no
Gal 'O Mine II	460	763	42-78270	yes
Go-Ta-Hay-It	460	760	42-51285	no
Hangar Queen	460	763	42-51084	yes
Helen	460	760		yes
Honey Chile	460	760	42-52538	no
Jane	460	760	42-78413	no
Junior	460	763	42-99763	no
Junior II	460	763	44-41014	no
K - King	460	762	41-28883	no
Mary Dinah	460	762	42-51602	no
Maxwell House	460	761	41-28702	yes
May Bell	460		44-48769	yes
Mexicali Rose	460	760	44-40514	no
Miss Fortune	460	760	41-29291	yes
Mixed Nuts	460			no
My Arkansas Sweetheart	460			yes
N - Nan	460	762	44-41233	no
Nancy	460	761	41-28997	yes
Naughty Nan	460	761	41-28997	yes
No Love, No Nothing	460	762		no
Ole Repulsive	460	763	42-52363	yes
Our Hobby II	460			yes
P - Peter	460	762	42-51845	no
Pappy's Pride	460	760		yes
Patricia Ann	460	761	42-51536	yes
Pleasant Bent	460	762	44-49693	no
Pretty Baby	460			no
Rattlesnake Hank	460	763	42-52367	yes
Roger's Rangers	460	763	41-28698	no
Roseanna from Indiana	460			yes
Rough Rider	460	470		yes
Sandy	460			yes
Seldom Available	460	760	44-40495	yes
Silver Satan	460			yes
Sky Wolves	460	760	42-78429	yes
Slick Chick With a Hot Lick	460	761	42-50746	no
Southern Belle	460			yes
Stork Club	460	762	42-52333	no
Straight Shot	460	761	42-52385	yes
Sweet Sue	460			no
T. S. Express	460			yes
Target for Tonight	460		44-48977	yes
This Love of Mine	460	760	42-78071	yes
Thumper	460			yes
Thumper II	460			yes
Tondelayo	460			yes
White Mike	460			no
Yakima Kid (The)	460			yes

461ST BOMB GROUP

Name	Grp.	Sq.	Serial	Pic.
All American	461	765	42-78444	yes
Alma-Mi-Amor	461	765		yes
Arsenic & Old Lace	461	765	42-52025	no
Battle Crate	461	764	41-29289	yes
Big Stinky	461	765	41-28717	no
Billie K.	461	765	44-49038	yes
Bingo	461	764	44-49897	yes
Boise Belle	461	766	42-52398	no
Boobie Trap	461	767	41-29332	yes
Bubble Trouble	461	764	42-78437	no
Cherokee	461	766	42-52389	yes
Chippie Doll	461	764	42-52458	yes
Dry Run	461	767	42-52395	yes
Dwatted Wabbit	461	766	41-29337	no
Dwatted Wabbit	461	766	42-50827	no
El Pagliaccio	461	764	42-51925	yes
Evil Weevil	461	764	41-29335	yes
Evil Weevil Too	461	764	42-51816	no
Fearless Fosdick	461	765	42-52438	yes
Fertile Myrtle	461	764	42-78123	yes
Flak Finder	461	767	42-52399	yes
Flying Finger (The)	461	765	42-50953	no
Gene's Hare Power	461	765	44-48993	yes
Hard Guy	461	765	41-28681	no
Hare Power	461	765	41-29325	no
Heaven Can Wait	461	765	42-51971	no
Heaven Can Wait	461	766	41-28679	yes
Hi Ho Silver	461		42-51778	no
Hi Ho Silver	461	766	41-29336	no
Hottest ??? in Town	461	766	41-29313	no
Iggy	461		42-51xxx	no
Invictus	461	765	41-28725	no
Irish Angel II	461	765	42-52486	yes
Jake's Nabor	461	765	42-51346	no
Jizzy Outch	461	767	41-28724	no
Kissed Off Kids	461	766	42-52408	no
Lady Edith	461	765	41-29284	no
Lazy Lady	461	764	42-51762	no
Leading Lady	461	765	41-28685	yes
Lucky Lady	461	764	42-50970	no
Lucky Seven (The)	461	764	41-29362	yes
Mailbox	461	764	44-41039	no

Name	Grp.	Sq.	Serial	Pic.
Malfunction Sired By Ford	461	767	41-28670	yes
Marjorie H.	461	765	42-51610	no
Miss Kay	461	764	42-78103	yes
Miss Lace	461	764	44-49511	yes
Mister Period	461	764	41-28726	yes
Nov Schmoz Ka Pop	461	764	41-28734	no
Old Bird	461	764	41-29334	no
Olde Hellgate (Ye)	461	765	41-28705	no
One Eyed Jack (The)	461	764	42-52390	yes
One-Eyed Jack (The)	461	764	42-52393	yes
Our Baby	461	767	42-52388	yes
Our Hobby	461			no
Paulette	461	764	42-51324	no
Piece Maker	461	765	42-51599	yes
Piece Maker	461	765	42-52368	no
Plastered Bastard (The)	461			no
Red Head	461	767	44-49501	no
Red Ryder	461	764	42-52460	no
Rhoda	461	765	41-28740	no
Rhode Island Red	461	765	41-28737	no
Rhode Island Red II	461	765		yes
Scrounch	461	764	41-29338	no
Shack Wagon	461	765	42-78616	yes
Shady Lady	461	766	41-29268	no
Stinky	461	764	41-29333	yes
Strange Cargo	461	765	42-51967	yes
Strictly GI	461	766	42-95287	no
Stumpy Joe	461	765	44-41162	no
Sub Depot Sue	461	767	42-64361	yes
Swee Pea	461	764	41-28732	yes
Sweet Chariot	461	766	41-28689	no
Tail Dragon	461	767	42-94732	yes
Thundermug	461	765	42-51474	no
Tulsa-American (The)	461	765	42-51430	no
Upstairs Maid	461	765	42-52371	yes
Urgent Virgin	461	766	42-78446	no
War Eagle	461	764	41-28693	yes
What Next?	461	765	42-51783	yes
What's Next?	461	765	42-51783	yes
Windy City II	461	767	42-52378	no
Zombie of 69	461		42-51501	yes

464TH BOMB GROUP

Name	Grp.	Sq.	Serial	Pic.
Ain't Misbehavin' Minnie	464	776	42-52540	no
Alice of Dallas	464			no
All Meat, No Potatoes	464	777	42-78318	yes
Bachelor's Roost	464	776	41-29453	yes
Bad Penny (The)	464	779	42-78488	yes
Be Comin' Back	464	778	44-41043	no
Belle Ringer	464			no
Belzebub	464	777	41-29444	no
Big Fat Mama	464	779	44-41213	yes
Big Wheeler Dealer	464	778	42-78374	no
Black Fox (The)	464	779	41-29398	no
Black Fox (The)	464	779	42-78618	no
Black Hal	464	779	42-51083	no
Black Item	464	779	42-51663	no
Black Jig	464	779	42-78671	no
Black Mike	464	779	44-41053	no
Black Nan	464	779	44-49710	yes
Black Oboe	464	779	42-51129	no
Black Roger	464	779	44-49028	no
Black Widow	464	779	42-95336	yes
Black Zebra	464	779	42-50867	no
Blonde Bomber	464	777	42-78333	no
Blonde Bomber (The)	464	776	42-78431	no
Bonnie-Annie-Laurie	464	778	42-51760	yes
Boozin' Susan	464	779	42-52502	yes
Brown Nose	464	778	42-52485	yes
Brown Nose 2	464	778	42-52485	no
Butch-My-Love	464	778	42-78340	yes
Cherry	464	778	42-64441	no
Chick	464	777	42-95340	no
Com-Bat	464	778	42-78091	yes
Combatty	464	776	42-52520	no
Crack Up	464	778		no
Death of Me Yet	464	777	42-78241	no
Dollar Ride	464	777	42-78257	no
Duration +	464		42-78093	yes
Easy Maid	464			no
Fast Number	464	779	42-52469	yes
Fertile Turtle (The)	464	777		yes
Flakman (The)	464	779	42-95332	yes
Flamin' Mamie	464	776	44-41337	yes
Flyin' Duchess (The)	464			no
Flyin' Patches	464	778	42-52522	no
Flying Duchess (The)	464			no
Flying Phartsac (The)	464	779	41-28999	no
Flying Potty	464			no
Flying Zebra	464	779	42-50867	no
Free Delivery	464	776	42-52484	no
Fuel Cell Fanny	464		42-52453	yes
Fun House	464	776	42-78248	no
Ginee	464			yes
Green Hornet (The)	464	778	42-52504	no
Guardian Angel	464		42-78115	no
Gum Drop	464		42-52449	no
Hard Hearted Hannah	464	778	41-28755	yes
Heaven's Above	464			yes
Hell's Bells	464	776	42-51953	yes
Hell's Bells II	464	778	44-41227	no
Home for Christmas	464	778	42-52437	yes
Hoosier Pete	464	779	44-49713	no
Jack & Charlie's '21'	464			yes
Kiwi Bird	464	779	42-50920	yes
Lady Duzz	464			yes
Lady Esther	464	776		yes
Lakanooky	464			yes

Name	Grp.	Sq.	Serial	Pic.
Libby Raider	464	779		no
Little Gizmo	464	776	42-78133	yes
Little Gizmo II	464	776	42-78376	no
Little Lulu	464	776	42-52479	yes
Little Miss Muff-It	464		42-78131	yes
Little Rocket	464	778	42-50962	yes
Little Willie	464	776	42-51178	yes
Lively Lady	464	777	44-41070	no
Lucky Strike	464	777	42-52487	yes
Maiden USA	464	776	42-78392	yes
Mary O	464	776	42-51423	no
Mickey	464	779	42-52526	yes
Military Secret	464	778	42-52446	yes
Milk Run	464			no
Mismyshaktime	464	779	41-29361	no
Miss Vicky	464	778		yes
Miss-B-Havin' Minnie	464	776	42-52540	yes
Monster (The)	464	778	41-29394	yes
Nancy	464	779	41-28998	no
No Excuse	464	778	42-51840	no
Off Limits	464	776	42-73432	yes
Old Gran-Dad	464	777		yes
Old Grandad's Dream	464	777	42-78092	yes
Old Iron Ass	464	777	42-52462	no
Paper Doll	464	779	41-29351	yes
Pappy's Pride	464	776		no
Pappy's Puss	464	776	41-29410	no
Patches	464		42-52449	no
Pistol Packin' Mama	464	776	42-52563	yes
Portland Rose	464	778	42-78431	yes
Princess Pat	464	779	42-78350	no
Rat Race	464	776	42-78128	no
Ready	464	776	42-52402	yes
Red Hot Riding Hood	464			no
Red J - Jig	464			yes
Red Victor	464	776	41-28969	no
Repulsive Raider	464	777	42-95382	no
Repulsive Raider II	464	777	42-78365	no
Ritz	464	776	44-49073	no
Roger the 2nd	464	779	44-49028	no
Ruthie the Raider	464	778	42-52537	yes
Shoo Shoo Baby	464	779	41-29458	yes
Short, Fat & 4F	464			yes
Skirt Patrol (The)	464	778	42-78096	yes
Sleeping Time Gal	464			no
Sleepy Time Gal	464	776	42-99813	yes
Sleepy Time Gal II	464	776	44-99813	yes
Southern Comfort	464	777	41-29441	yes
Sparky's Hot Box	464	779	44-40928	yes
Stevenovich	464	779	44-49710	yes
Stevonovich	464	776	42-51625	no
Stinky	464	779		no
Strawberry Butch	464	776		yes
Strictly from Hunger	464	778	41-29412	yes
Strictly from Hunger	464	778	42-94785	no
Sultan II	464	778	42-95348	no
Sweet Gen	464			no
Table Stuff	464	779	42-52463	yes
Target for Tonite	464	777	41-28748	yes
Ten Hits and a Miss	464			yes
That's Us	464	778	42-52522	yes
Three Cornered Kid (A)	464	776		no
Toggle Annie	464		42-52357	yes
Toonerville Trolley (The)	464	776		no
Ugly Duckling (The)	464	716	42-524xx	yes
Uninvited (The)	464	776		no
Victor	464	779	42-78434	no
Victory Gal	464	778		yes
Wheel N' Deal	464	778	42-95364	yes
Whirling Dervish	464		41-28741	yes
Whiskey Straight	464			yes
White J	464	778	42-78682	no
Willie	464		42-78473	no
Willy	464	777	42-51903	no
Yellow How	464	777	44-41231	no
Yellow L	464	777	44-49328	no
Yellow Mike	464	777	44-10566	no

465TH BOMB GROUP

Name	Grp.	Sq.	Serial	Pic.
Agony Wagon	465	780	42-52376	no
Agony Wagon	465	780	42-52726	no
Alley Oop	465	780		yes
Angel of the Sky	465	781	42-51254	yes
Angel of the Sky	465	781	42-52365	yes
Angel of the Sky	465	781	42-52365	yes
Belle Ringer	465	781	42-52503	no
Belzebub	465		41-29444	no
Blitz Buggy	465		44-40632	no
Blue 1	465	783	41-28853	yes
Blue N	465	783	44-41106	no
Bugs	465	780	42-78259	no
Chief Jo-Jon	465	781	41-29414	yes
Come-N'-Get-Me-You-Bastards	465	781	41-29414	no
Crescent of the Half Moon	465	781	41-29415	no
Custer's Folly	465	781	41-29356	no
Dragonass	465	781	42-51858	no
Easy Maid	465	781	42-78352	yes
Fertile Turtle	465	781		no
Flamin' Mame	465	781	42-51631	no
Flying Box Car	465	781		no
Guardian Angel	465	781	41-29376	yes
Guardian Angel II	465	781	41-28959	no
Hell's Belle	465	781	42-52505	no
Horrible Bastard	465		42-51583	no
Hot Mathilda	465	781	44-41122	yes
Jack Pine Joe	465	780	42-52466	yes
Joe-gia Wolf	465	781	42-52321	yes
Joker	465	782	42-78287	no
Little Lulu	465		42-52479	no
Long John Silver	465	781	41-28915	no

Name	Grp.	Sq.	Serial	Pic.	Name	Grp.	Sq.	Serial	Pic.
Lovey's Dovies	465	781	42-51628	yes	Big Fat Mama	466	786	44-40067	no
Madcap Margie	465	781	41-28756	no	Bird Dog	466	784	42-95084	yes
Margie the Magnificent	465	783	44-48990	no	Black Cat	466	784	42-95592	yes
Mickey	465		42-52526	no	Black Jack	466			no
Mission Belle	465	780	42-51421	no	Blockbuster	466	787	42-110164	no
Moby Dick	465	783	42-52589	no	Bonnie	466	784	41-29459	yes
Nite Mare	465	781		no	Boys from Hell	466			no
No Love, No Nothin	465	782	42-52533	yes	Brainchild of Warchant	466	784	42-94915	no
Nobody's Baby	465	783	42-52403	yes	Brute (The)(Lft. side)	466	784	41-29419	yes
Old Dutch Cleanser	465	780		yes	Carioca Bev	466			no
Our Baby	465	781	42-50723	yes	Chicago Red	466	787	41-29370	no
Paper Doll	465	781	42-52521	yes	Chief (The)	466	784	44-49850	no
Patches	465	781	42-52449	no	Chris' Crate	466	785		no
Perry & the Pirates	465	780	41-28761	no	Chris' Crate II	466	784	42-110160	yes
Pith and Moan	465	783	42-52473	yes	Cindy	466	784	44-49529	no
Pleasure Bent	465	781	41-29357	yes	Connie	466	785	42-7682	no
Porky	465	783	44-41137	no	Consolidated Mess	466	785	44-10545	yes
Princess Pat	465	781	42-51894	no	Crippled Bitch (The)	466	786	41-29371	no
Quanta Costa	465	782	42-78391	no	Crow's Nest	466	786	42-95010	yes
Red F	465	780	42-52994	no	Damifino	466	784	42-50465	yes
Red O	465	780	42-51421	no	Dark Rhapsody	466	785	41-29466	no
Red Y	465	780	44-48861	no	Delores Jean	466	787	42-50368	yes
Reddy Maid	465	746	44-50387	yes	Desperate Virgin	466	785	41-28747	no
Reputation Cloudy	465	782	41-28906	yes	Dirty Gertie	466	786	41-29366	no
Ruff 'N Ready	465	783	42-52464	no	Dixie	466	785	44-10499	yes
Rum Dum	465	780		no	Dogpatch Clipper	466	785	41-28949	yes
Sacajawea	465	781	42-52558	no	Duffy's Tavern	466	784	42-51699	yes
Sans Souci	465	783	41-29424	no	E Pluribus Aluminum	466	784	42-52590	yes
Scorpia (The)	465	781	42-52762	yes	Eager Beaver	466			no
Section Eight	465	783	42-52585	no	Earthquake McGoon	466	787	42-50448	yes
Shack Queen	465	783	41-28736	yes	Eastern Beast	466	785	41-28743	yes
Shoo Shoo Baby	465		41-29458	no	Easy Queen	466		44-40456	no
Short Stuff	465		42-78538	no	Eephus	466	784	42-95254	no
Silver Buck (The)	465	781		no	Eophus	466	784	42-95108	no
Skin Wagon	465	781	44-49380	no	Eophus	466	784	42-95254	no
Southern Gal	465	783	42-52539	yes	Ernie's Beavers	466	786	44-40173	no
Super Natural	465	781	42-52470	yes	Falcon (The)	466	785	42-95248	yes
Table Stuff	465	783	41-29360	no	Fan Dancer (The)	466	787	41-29423	no
TS	465	783	42-52478	no	Fay Day	466	787	41-28938	no
Umbriago	465	783	41-29377	yes	Fearless Fosdick	466		42-50698	no
V Grand	465	783	44-41064	yes	Fearless Freddie	466			no
What's Up Doc?	465	781		no	Feudin Wagon (The)	466			no
Whiskey Jim	465	780		no	Flying Dutchman (The)	466			no
White U.	465	782	44-49085	no	Flying Witch (The)	466	787	42-95194	no
White X	465	782		no	Fran	466	784	44-49582	yes
Yellow H	465	781		no	French Dressing	466			no
					Gallopin' Ghost	466	787	41-29439	yes

466TH BOMB GROUP

Name	Grp.	Sq.	Serial	Pic.
Ain't Misbehavin'	466	784	42-52509	yes
Assole	466	787	42-52518	no
B. T. O.	466		44-40072	no
Belle	466	785	42-51099	yes
Berlin Bound	466	784	42-50717	no
Betta Duck	466	785	44-40454	yes
Bif Bam	466	785	42-95283	yes
Big Brute	466	784	42-29419	yes

Name	Grp.	Sq.	Serial	Pic.
General Ike	466			no
Generator Jenny	466	785	44-40320	no
Ghost, Too	466	784	42-95609	yes
Glad To See Ya	466	787	42-95361	yes
Gran Slam	466	784	42-51094	yes
Green Dragon	466	784	42-51094	no
Gruesome Goose	466	787	41-28747	yes
Guess Who's Here	466	787	42-52598	yes
Hard Luck	466	787	44-40253	yes
Hard T' Find	466	786	42-50373	yes

Name	Grp.	Sq.	Serial	Pic.	Name	Grp.	Sq.	Serial	Pic.
Heine Hunter	466		42-95266	no	Ol' Tom Cat	466	785	42-52555	no
Hell's Belle	466			no	Old Tom Cat	466	785	42-50699	no
Homesick Angel	466	784	41-29395	no	Ole Goat (The)	466	784	41-28910	yes
Homeward Angel	466	784	41-29395	no	Our Baby	466	784	41-29413	no
Honey Gal	466	787	42-95246	yes	Our Honey	466	786	42-52480	yes
Hookem Cow	466			no	Out of Season,				
Hot Box	466	785	41-29374	yes	Don't Shoot	466	785	42-52574	no
Hull's Angels	466	787	42-50581	yes	Pale Ale	466	784	42-50336	yes
Is This Trip Necessary	466			no	Paper Doll	466	786	42-94799	yes
Jamaica?	466	785	41-28746	yes	Parson's Chariot	466	784	42-110162	no
Jennie	466	784	42-95617	no	Parson's Chariot	466	784	44-40699	yes
Joker (The)	466	787	42-51317	yes	Pay Day	466	787	41-28938	no
Judy Sue	466	787	42-50791	yes	Peck's Bad Boys	466	785	42-51353	yes
Just for You	466	784		yes	Peck's Bad Boys II	466	785	42-51353	yes
Laden Maid	466	786	42-52560	yes	Pegasus the				
Laden Maid	466	786	44-10521	no	Flying Horse	466	784	42-51141	yes
Laden Maid Again	466	786	44-10521	no	Peggy Ann	466	787	42-50666	no
Laden Maiden	466	786	44-48781	yes	Peggy Ann	466	787	42-51185	no
Lady	466	787	42-95255	no	Pelican (The)	466	785	42-52574	yes
Lady Jane	466	785	44-50484	no	Penthouse for Ten	466	785	42-95268	yes
Lady Lightning	466	784	42-52597	yes	Piccadilly Commando	466	787	42-50305	yes
Lady Peace	466	784	42-95557	no	Piccadilly Lily	466	784	44-49553	yes
Lady Peach	466	784	42-95557	no	Piece Maker	466	784	42-51599	yes
Lady Too (The)	466	784	42-95511	no	Playboy	466	784	41-29399	yes
Lemon (The)	466	785	42-52524	yes	Pluto Crate	466	784	42-50670	no
Let 'er Rip	466	785	44-50548	yes	Polaris II	466	784	42-50488	no
Liberty Belle	466	784	42-51134	yes	Polaris, the				
Lil Snooks	466			no	Heavenly Body	466	787	41-29384	yes
Little Behind	466			yes	Predominant Yankee	466	787	42-50516	no
Little Eva	466			no	Pretty Little Lass	466	785	42-95202	no
Little Lulu	466	787	41-29391	yes	Pub Hound	466	786	42-95211	yes
Little Rebel	466	786	41-29593	no	Purple Shaft	466			no
Lovely Lady	466	786	42-52569	no	Queenie	466	785	44-10518	no
Lovely Lady	466	786	xx-xx567	no	Rabbit Habit	466			no
Lovely Lady's Avenger	466	786	44-40093	yes	Ramblin' Wreck	466	787	41-28932	yes
Mad Monk (The)	466	786	41-29402	yes	Ready and Waiting	466	787	41-28971	yes
Madame (The)	466	787	42-52610	no	Ready and Willing	466	784	41-24109	no
Madame II (The)	466	787	41-29392	yes	Rebel Yell	466	784	41-29422	no
Makin' Believe	466			yes	Rebel Yell	466	786	41-29416	no
Mama's Lil' Angel	466	785	44-10558	yes	Red Hot Riding Hood	466	786	42-52442	no
Mammy Yokum	466	784	42-52596	no	Reliable Babe	466	786	42-52527	yes
Merchant of Venice	466	785	41-28664	yes	Rosebalm	466	786	42-52511	yes
Milk Run	466			no	Sack Happy	466	786	42-52570	yes
Miss Minooky	466	786	42-50438	yes	Salty Dog (Rt. Side)	466	784	41-29419	yes
Mist'er Chance	466	785	41-28691	yes	Shack (The)	466	786	41-29000	yes
Moonlight Marge	466	787	44-40325	no	Shack Date	466	786	42-52566	yes
Moonshine Express	466	784	44-48807	yes	Shack II (The)	466			no
Murphy's Mighty Mob	466	787	42-52609	no	Shady Sadie	466	786	42-95059	yes
Murphy's Motley Mob	466	787	42-52609	no	Shamrock	466	784	42-95109	no
Nature's Nymphe	466	785		yes	Shoo Shoo Baby	466	785	42-52587	yes
Near Miss	466		44-40795	no	Shoo-Shoo Baby	466	785	41-28752	yes
No Feathered Injun	466	787	42-94886	yes	Shy Ann	466			no
Nobody's Baby	466	787	42-52518	yes	Silent Yokum	466	787	42-50581	no
Nobody's Baby II	466	785	42-95283	no	Silver Dollar	466	784	42-51154	yes
Off Limits Again	466	786	42-94974	yes	Silver Eagle	466	786	42-50362	yes
Oh, Mona	466	787	42-52343	no	Slick Chick	466	785	42-94979	yes
Ol' Soak	466	785	41-29358	yes	Small Change	466	786	42-50585	no

Name	Grp.	Sq.	Serial	Pic.
Snafu Snark	466	785	41-29387	yes
Spare Parts	466	785	41-29350	yes
Splash	466	785	42-52510	yes
Stardust	466	784	42-50364	no
Stardust	466	784	42-94902	no
Stardust	466	787	41-29439	no
Stardust	466	787	42-50516	no
Stormy	466	787	41-29392	no
Sully's Saloon	466	786	42-52529	yes
Sunshine Jane	466	787	42-52600	yes
Sweater Girl	466			no
Tail End Charlie	466			yes
Tell Me More	466	787	41-28754	no
Terry & the Pirates	466	786	41-29434	no
Terry & the Pirates	466	786	42-50438	no
That Red Headed Gal	466	784	42-95569	yes
This Above All	466	786	44-40328	yes
This Is It!	466	785	42-50364	yes
This Is It!	466		44-40328	yes
Throbbing Monster	466	786	42-52570	no
Trouble Maker	466	787	42-95067	yes
True Love	466	786	41-29449	yes
Virgin Sturgeon	466	784	42-52516	no
War Champ	466	784	42-94915	no
What's Cookin' Doc?	466	786	42-110157	yes
White Duck	466	785	42-52574	no
White Elephant (The)	466	784	44-49626	yes
Wild Princess	466	786	42-52529	no
Wild Pussy	466	786	42-52529	yes
Winged Victory	466	784	42-50765	yes
Worry Bird (The)	466	787	42-52582	no
Worry Bird II	466	787	42-52584	no

467TH BOMB GROUP

Name	Grp.	Sq.	Serial	Pic.
Ace of Spades	467		41-28976	no
Alice	467		44-40140	no
Also Ran	467	790	41-29445	no
Angel	467	790	42-95057	yes
Aye's Dynamiters	467	789	42-50515	no
Baffling Brat	467	789	42-52512	no
Battlin' Baby	467	791	42-99971	no
Belle of the East	467	789	42-110187	no
Bleeding Heart	467	791	42-51227	no
Blonde Bomber	467		42-50471	yes
Bold Venture III	467	788	42-50675	no
Bomb Boogie	467	789	42-50792	no
Broad and High	467	788	42-50439	no
Bugs Bunny	467	791	42-52530	yes
Cherub (The)	467		42-94943	no
Chicago Red	467		41-29370	no
Crippled Bitch (The)	467		41-29371	no
Devil's Hostess	467	790	42-51531	yes
Double Trouble	467	791	41-29385	yes
Dugar	467	788	42-50641	no
Dye's Dynamiters	467	789	42-50515	no

Name	Grp.	Sq.	Serial	Pic.
E Pluribus Aluminum	467	789	42-52590	no
Eli Swof, Jr.	467	790	42-51171	no
Everything's Jake	467		42-95234	no
Fearless Fosdick	467	791	42-50698	no
Feudin Wagon	467		44-40155	no
Fickle Finger of Fate	467	790	42-50354	no
Flak Magnet	467	788	41-29373	no
Flak Magnet II	467	790	41-28962	no
Flying Home	467	789	42-95073	no
Gallopin' Ghost	467		41-29439	no
Gerocko	467	791	41-29386	yes
Gerocko	467	791	42-50484	no
Ginnie	467		44-48816	no
Go Better	467	789	41-28744	no
Go Better	467	789	42-50479	no
Happy Warrior	467	791	42-50621	no
Hard To Get	467		42-94988	no
Homeward Bound	467	790	41-29378	yes
Jack the Ripper	467			no
Jack the Ripper II	467	791	42-52424	yes
Jerilyne Sue	467	789	42-52499	yes
Katy	467	789	42-52535	no
Leading Lady	467		xx-xx201	no
Leading Lady	467	790	42-95094	no
Lil Peach	467	788	41-29373	yes
Lil Peach	467	791	41-29375	yes
Little Chum	467	790	42-51180	no
Little Chum	467	790	42-51280	no
Little Pete	467			no
Lonely Heart	467	791	42-95224	yes
Lucky Ieven, Always a Winner	467	791	44-48820	yes
Mademoiselle Zig-Zig	467	790	44-40070	yes
Massachusetts Girl	467	788	42-50614	no
Massilon Tiger	467	789	44-10488	yes
Messie Bessie	467	790	42-50354	no
Miss Fortune	467	790	42-52559	yes
Miss Judy	467	788	42-50641	no
Miss Judy	467	789	42-52507	no
Miss-B-Haven	467	788	42-94811	no
Monster	467	788	44-40166	no
Monster (The)	467		42-50720	yes
My Wild Irish Rose	467	790	41-29270	no
Normandy Queen	467	790	44-50250	no
Normandy Queen	467	791	42-95237	no
Old Iron Pants	467	789	42-110168	no
Osage Express	467	790	42-52497	no
P'Noach	467	791	44-50668	no
Packet for Hitler	467			no
Palace Meat Market	467	791	42-52394	yes
Pappy's Yokum	467		42-50624	no
Party Girl	467	788	42-94811	no
Perfect Lady (The)	467	789	42-110168	no
Perils of Pauline	467	790	42-95162	yes
Pete the POM Inspector	467		41-29393	no

Name	Grp.	Sq.	Serial	Pic.
Pete the POM Inspector II	467		42-40370	yes
Piccadilly Commando	467	788	44-10600	no
Plow Jockey	467	789	42-50309	no
Rangoon Rambler	467			yes
Rangoon Rambler II	467	790	42-52554	no
Ready, Willing & Able	467	790	42-29427	no
Rheinmacher	467	790	42-52556	no
Rosalyn	467	788	44-10601	yes
Rose Marie	467	790	41-28695	yes
Ruptured Duck	467			no
Ruth Marie	467	790	41-28695	no
Sack Time	467		42-110173	no
Sacktime	467	789	42-94931	no
Salty Dog	467		41-29419	no
Saucy Pants	467	790	42-95201	no
School Daze	467	791	42-51832	yes
Scrapper	467	788	41-29397	no
Scrapper	467	790	42-52394	no
Screwball	467			no
Shady Lady	467		xx-xx791	no
Shoo Shoo Baby	467	791	41-29393	yes
Silver Chief	467	790	42-95032	yes
Six Bits	467	789	42-52525	no
Slick Chick	467	788	41-29380	no
Slick Chick	467	791	41-29388	yes
Slugger, Jr.	467	788	41-29397	yes
Snappe	467		xx-xx394	no
Snooper	467			no
Snooper	467		xx-xx731	no
Snooper	467	790	42-52571	yes
Southern Clipper	467	788	42-50684	yes
Southern Clipper	467	788	42-52546	no
Southern Cross	467	790	42-52565	no
Squitch	467	788	42-52561	no
Stardust	467		41-29439	no
Stinger?	467	788	42-52542	no
Stinker	467		42-95201	no
Super Wolf	467	791	42-95080	yes
Tailwind	467	789	41-29368	yes
Tailwind II	467	789	42-50792	no
Tangerine	467	790	41-29446	yes
Tender Comrade	467	791	41-29369	no
Tenofus	467	789	42-50309	no
That's All Brother	467		44-40120	no
Three (III) Special	467	788	42-94986	no
Thundermug	467	789	41-28750	yes
Tommy Thumper	467	788	42-94811	no
Topper	467	791	42-52303	no
Umbriago	467	788	44-40068	no
Up In Arms	467	791	42-50621	no
Valiant Lady	467	790	41-29408	no
Wabbit	467	789	42-52663	yes
Wabbit	467	789	42-62663	no
Wallowing Wilbert	467	791	41-29421	yes
We'll Get By	467		42-50697	no

Name	Grp.	Sq.	Serial	Pic.
Witchcraft	467	790	42-52534	yes
Witchcraft II	467	790	42-28631	yes
Wolves, Inc.	467	791	41-28981	yes

479TH BOMB GROUP

Name	Grp.	Sq.	Serial	Pic.
Jug Haid	479			no
Night Mission	479		42-40891	yes
Tidewater Tillie	479			no
White Savage	479		42-40921	yes
Worry Bird (The)	479		42-40927	yes

480TH BOMB GROUP

Name	Grp.	Sq.	Serial	Pic.
Davy Jones' Helper	480	1	41-24002	yes
Eager Beaver	480		41-24196	no
Frivolous Sal	480	1	41-23984	yes
Nitemare	480	2	42-40328	yes
Skeezix	480	2		yes
Subconscious II	480	2	42-40100	yes
Tiger Lil	480	1	41-24261	yes
Varga Girl	480		41-24196	no
Varga Virgin	480	2	41-24196	yes
Beast of Bourbon	482	36	42-50385	yes
Berlin First	482		42-32002	no
Boots	482	36	41-29599	no
Eagle	482		44-42344	no
Feudin' Wagon	482			no
Lil' Pudge	482		44-42344	yes
Little Audrey	482			no
Miss-B-Haven	482	36	42-50844	no
Paper Doll	482	812	42-3492	no
Peace Offering	482	814	42-7672	no
Ramp Rooster	482	36	42-50671	yes
Stinky	482		42-5793	no
Tiger's Revenge	482	814	42-7646	no
White Savage	482	814	42-40921	yes

484TH BOMB GROUP

Name	Grp.	Sq.	Serial	Pic.
A-Broad Abroad	484	827	42-51993	yes
American Beauty	484	827	41-29530	no
Awkward Angel	484	825	41-29502	yes
Bells of St. Jo	484	826	44-49828	no
Big Dick	484	825	42-94740	yes
Big Drip	484	824	42-52708	no
Black Jack II	484	824	44-40941	yes
Bona Venture	484	825	44-49580	no
Buzz Job #2	484	825	42-78268	no
Century Limited (The)	484	824	42-52641	yes
Collapsible Susie	484	824	42-94758	no
Damned Yankee	484	825	42-52438	no
Darling Darlene	484	826	42-52633	yes
Demaio's Delinquents	484	824	42-51988	no
Duck (The)	484	827	42-94737	no
Dwatted Wabbit	484		42-52658	no

Name	Grp.	Sq.	Serial	Pic.
El Pagliaccio	484	824	42-51925	yes
Everybody's Baby	484			no
Fargo Express	484	825	42-78289	no
Feather Merchants (The)	484	824	42-94733	no
Fertile Myrtle	484	824	42-52371	no
Flak Strainer	484	824	42-99851	yes
Flying Dutchman (The)	484	826	42-52775	yes
Generator Joe	484	827	42-52700	yes
Great Speckled Bird (The)	484	825	44-48988	yes
Guardian Angel	484	824	42-52687	no
Hangar Annie	484	825	42-50394	yes
Heaven Can Wait	484			no
Hell's Hangover	484	827	44-49936	no
Hot Rocks	484	827	42-52683	yes
Hotcha Babe	484	824	42-51694	no
Hustlin' Hussy	484	827	42-52677	no
Imagine	484	826	44-49738	yes
Knockout	484	827	42-94738	yes
Kuuipo's	484		44-40xx3	no
Lady Luck	484	826	42-52774	yes
Lakanookie II	484	824	42-52614	no
Leading Lady	484	824	42-52647	no
Little Joe	484	824	42-50934	yes
Little Mac	484	825	42-50642	yes
Malfunction Sired by Ford	484	826	42-52668	yes
Maximum Effort	484		44-50450	no
Me Worry?	484	824	41-28935	no
Miss Fire	484	826	42-52675	yes
Miss Snow Job	484	827	42-94751	no
Moe's Meteor	484	825	44-50557	yes
Ol' 45	484	825	42-52635	no
Our Hobby II	484	826	44-50364	yes
Painted Lady	484	824	44-49988	no
Patient Kitten	484			no
Peggy Ann	484	827	44-50476	yes
Pontiac Squaw (The)	484	826	42-52774	yes
Pot Luck	484	825	42-51851	no
Pouting Squaw (The)	484	825	42-94753	yes
Puss in Boots	484	826	41-28835	yes
Ramp Rooster	484	824	42-52576	yes
Red-Hot Riden-Hood II	484			no
Roll Me Over	484	827	44-49939	no
Rum Hound	484	825	42-52690	no
Rum Runner	484	824	42-52660	no
Sa Wrong Gal	484	826	42-52671	yes
Sally	484			no
Sally D II	484		41-29426	no
Salvo Sally II	484	826	42-52697	yes
Sinful Cynthia	484	827	42-52661	no
Sleepless Nights	484	825	42-52653	no
Sleepy Time Gal	484	826	42-94734	yes
Snuffie's Pubing Mission	484	825	44-50319	no
Stew Bum	484	826	42-52602	no
Strange Cargo	484	826	42-51967	no
Stud Horse	484	825	42-52658	yes

Name	Grp.	Sq.	Serial	Pic.
Superchick	484			no
Sweet Ginny Lee	484	826	44-10484	yes
Sweet Revenge	484	827	42-52648	yes
Tail Dragon	484		42-94732	yes
Tailenders	484	824	41-29539	yes
Toggle Annie	484	826	42-52357	yes
Toretto Taxi	484		44-41110	no
Trouble Maker	484	827	42-52667	yes
TS-Chaplain (The)	484	824	41-28860	no
Uninvited (The)	484	827	42-52683	yes
Vicious Virgin	484	826	42-52715	no
Vicious Virgin	484	826	42-94746	yes
Victory	484	825	42-52715	no
Vivacious Lady	484	826	42-94741	yes
War Weary	484	827	42-95360	yes
Weary Willie	484	825	42-94755	no
What's Up, Doc?	484	825	42-78351	no

485TH BOMB GROUP

Name	Grp.	Sq.	Serial	Pic.
Better Late than Never	485	828	42-78446	no
Big Alice from Dallas	485	829	42-52730	no
Big Stoop	485	830	41-28842	no
Bizzy Bitch	485	830	42-51166	yes
Black Swan	485			yes
Boozer	485	830	42-52702	no
Butch	485	831	42-50486	no
Buzz Job	485	830	42-52724	yes
Buzz Job	485	830	42-95203	no
Character	485	831	42-52727	no
Dottie the New Hampshire Troubadour	485	829	44-41144	no
Dotty Do	485	831	42-51872	no
Double Trouble	485	829	42-78149	no
Dwatted Wabbit	485		42-50827	no
Flak Shack	485	831	41-29534	no
Flak Shack II	485	831	44-49899	no
Flak Shack III	485	831	42-78501	no
Gawgia Peach	485	831	42-52709	no
Gunga Din	485	835	41-29505	no
Heat's On (The)	485	828	42-78474	no
Hell from Heaven	485	830	42-52722	no
Hell's Angels	485	831	41-29494	no
Hitler's Egg Men	485	831	42-52601	no
Homeward Angel	485	829	44-41157	no
Hot Pants	485	831	42-51872	no
Hottest ??? in Town (The)	485	831	42-78139	yes
Jerrie Ann (The)	485	828	42-78116	no
Lady (The)	485	828	42-52725	no
Lazy Eight	485	828	42-52674	no
Life	485	830	42-52728	yes
Little Emma	485	829	42-78136	no
Miss Fitz	485	829	41-29503	no
Miss Myloven	485	830	42-50921	no
Miss Tit	485	829	42-78141	no
Miz-pah	485	830	42-52713	no

Name	Grp.	Sq.	Serial	Pic.
My Briney Marlin	485	831	42-78134	no
My Brother and I	485	828	42-52703	no
Nudist Kay	485	829	42-78147	no
Nudist Kay III	485	830	42-51992	no
Our Kay	485	830	44-41157	no
Outcast	485	830	42-78089	no
Piccadilly Tilly	485	828	44-40458	no
Pick Up	485	830	42-94750	no
Princess Marie	485	830	42-52694	no
Rape Shape	485	829	42-78137	no
Roll Me Over	485		44-49939	no
Rough Deal Lucille	485	828	42-94791	no
Rough House Annie	485	831	42-50819	no
Sick Call	485	828	41-29491	no
Slic Chick	485	830	42-95460	no
Stardust	485	831	44-50819	no
Tailwind II	485	829	42-78416	no
Texas Star	485	828	41-29477	no
Virginia Lee	485			no
Winona Belle	485	828	42-50827	no
Yankee Doodle Dandy	485	828	42-52718	no

486TH BOMB GROUP

Name	Grp.	Sq.	Serial	Pic.
American Beauty	486	834	42-98008	no
Andy's Angels	486	833	42-52732	no
Aquaria	486	834	42-52545	yes
Aquarius	486	834	xx-xx650	no
Aries	486	834	xx-xx545	yes
Aries II	486	834	42-52693	yes
Aries the 1st	486	834	42-52765	yes
Baby Shoe (The)	486	833		no
Baby Shoe II (The)	486	833		no
Bad Boy	486	835	41-29472	no
Brown Nose	486		42-94821	no
California's Golden Bare	486	832	42-52691	no
Cancer	486	834	42-52650	yes
Cancer	486	834	42-52665	no
Cancer	486	834	xx-xx500	no
Capricorn	486	834	42-52744	no
Capricorn	486	834	xx-xx605	yes
Chief Oshkosh	486	833	41-29510	no
Classy Chassy	486			no
Consolidated Mess	486	833		no
Ding Dong Daddy from Dixie	486	834	42-52765	yes
Flying Commode (The)	486	832		no
Flying Pin-Up Girl	486		42-52714	no
Gemini	486		42-52639	no
Gemini	486		xx-xx762	no
Gemini	486	834	41-29496	yes
Gemini II	486	834	xx-xx762	no
Gin Mill Jill	486	835	42-52758	no
Gremlin's Roost	486	832	xx-xx601	no
Gunga Din	486	835	41-29505	no
Hard T' Get	486		41-29486	no
Hard T' Get	486	835	42-52753	yes

Name	Grp.	Sq.	Serial	Pic.
Hard To Get	486			no
I Wanted Wings	486	833	42-52740	yes
In God We Trust	486	833	42-52475	no
In The Mood	486	838	42-52664	no
Jeva	486	833	42-50651	no
Junior	486	833		no
Lady from Hell	486	835	42-52573	yes
Lady Lightnin'	486	832	42-52760	no
Late Again 4F	486	834		no
Leo	486	834	41-29605	yes
Leo	486	834	42-52768	yes
Libra	486	834	42-52508	yes
Libra	486	834	xx-xx693	no
Mike, Spirit of LSU	486	832	42-52731	no
Mike, Spirit of LSU	486	832	42-52764	no
Monty	486	835	41-29461	yes
Monty's Return	486	835	41-29461	yes
Ole Baldy	486			no
Pandora's Box	486	832	xx-xx714	no
Paper Doll (The)	486		42-52688	yes
Pisces	486	834	41-29517	yes
Pisces	486	834	xx-xx490	no
Ramblin' Reck	486	835		no
Rodney the Rocks	486	835	xx-xx500	no
Rum Runner	486		42-52496	no
Sagittarius	486	834	41-29400	yes
Sagittarius	486	834	xx-xx744	no
Scorpia (The)	486	834	42-52762	yes
Shack Date	486			no
Short Round II	486		42-52753	no
Silver Dollar	486			no
Slammin' Spammy	486	833	42-52637	yes
Swingtime in the Rockies	486	833		no
Swingtime in the Rockies	486	835	42-52681	yes
Swingtime in the Rockies	486	835	42-52758	no
Taurus	486	834		yes
Tiger's Revenge	486	832		no
Tommy Thumper	486	833	41-28838	no
Turnip Termite	486	832	41-29418	no
Twentieth Century Wolf	486	835	42-52483	no
Up In Arms	486		42-52621	no
Virgo	486	834	42-52508	no
Virgo	486	834	42-52532	yes
Winged Virgin	486	834		no
Winnie	486	834		no
Wolfel Bear	486	833	xx-xx908	no

487TH BOMB GROUP

Name	Grp.	Sq.	Serial	Pic.
Apocalypse	487	836	41-23879	no
Bashful Bessie	487			no
Beelzebub's Babe	487		42-52745	yes
Betsie	487		42-52736	no
Big Ast Bird	487	836	41-29520	no

Name	Grp.	Sq.	Serial	Pic.
Big Bad Wolf	487	836	41-29479	no
Big Drip	487	836	41-29524	yes
Big Drip, Jr. (The)	487		42-52636	no
Black Widow	487			no
Blasted Event	487	837	42-52487	no
Blow Job	487	839	41-28837	yes
Box Car Babe	487		42-52646	no
Bug Drip	487			no
Buzz Tail	487		42-52669	no
Buzz Tail II	487		42-52653	yes
Buzz Trail	487		42-52669	no
Buzzin' Bessie	487		42-52736	no
Caught in the Draft	487		42-52776	no
Chief Wapello	487	839	42-52618	yes
Cold Turkey	487		42-52425	no
Cover Girl	487	839	44-10576	yes
Cubby	487		42-52766	no
D'nif Annie	487		42-52640	no
Dreamboat	487		42-52657	no
Eager Beaver II	487			no
Eager Edgar	487		42-52592	no
Eager Edgar II	487		42-52592	no
Flak Happy Pappy	487		42-52666	no
Flutterbye	487	838	42-52577	no
Fluxuation Kate	487			no
Foxy Phoebe	487	839	41-29527	yes
Gas House Gus	487	839	41-29483	yes
Gas House Mouse	487	839	41-29476	no
GI Wife	487	836	41-29483	yes
Goin' Up, Doc?	487			no
Hard T' Find	487	839	42-50373	yes
Hard T' Get	487			no
Hell's Belle	487			no
Hell's Belle Peggy	487			no
High Hopes	487		42-52581	no
High Hopes	487		42-52592	no
Honorable Patches	487			no
Jane and Sharon Ann	487			no
Judy	487	836	41-29478	no
Just F/O 20%	487			no
Lady Marion	487	837	41-29466	no
Lazy Lady	487	838	42-52444	no
Leacherous Lou	487	838	41-29528	no
Lumberin' Liz	487		42-52578	no
Luscious Lady	487			no
Mac's Mighty Midgets	487		42-52625	no
Mean Widdle Kid	487	838	42-52763	no
Midnight Mistress	487		42-52461	no
Midnite Mistress	487		42-94756	no
Mis Bea Havin'	487		42-52761	no
Miss Happ	487	836	41-29523	no
Mission Belle	487	839	41-29514	no
Mountin Time	487		42-52619	yes
Murphy's Mighty Mob	487	836	42-52609	no
My Baby	487		42-52771	no
My Gal Eileen	487		42-52767	no
My Homely Chum	487	837	41-29469	no
Naughty Mariette	487		42-52739	no
Off Limits	487			no
Old Grey Gull	487		42-52748	no
Ole Andy of Kansas	487			no
Paddlefoot	487			no
Passionate Witch	487			no
Peg O My Heart	487	838	41-29468	no
Problem Child	487	838	41-28813	no
Rackem' Back	487	837	41-29525	no
Ready Betty	487		41-29524	yes
Reluctant Dragon	487			no
Reluctant Lady	487		42-52561	no
Reluctant Lady	487		42-52769	no
Rhapsody in Rivets	487		42-52622	no
Rough Raiders	487			no
Sammy's Niece	487	838	42-52629	no
Satan's Lady	487			no
Satchel Lass	487	838	41-29482	no
Shack (The)	487		44-40298	yes
Shoo Shoo Baby II	487			no
Silver Fox	487			no
Sky Master	487		42-52746	no
Sleepless Knight	487		42-52653	no
Sleepless Knights	487	837	41-29487	no
Sleepy Time Gal	487			no
Smokey Joe	487		42-52620	no
Solid Sender	487		42-52431	no
Spirit of '76	487			no
Spook (The)	487	837	41-29553	no
Star Duster	487		42-52769	no
Star Duster	487	837	42-52651	yes
Stinky Poo	487		42-52452	no
Sweat Box	487			no
Sweatin' It Out	487	839	41-29488	no
Tailwind	487	859	41-29481	no
Texas Rose	487	839	41-29554	no
This Above All	487		44-40328	yes
Trade Winds	487			yes
Twecherous Wabbit (The)	487		42-52652	yes
Varga Girl	487		42-52662	no
VirginVampire	487	839	42-52745	yes
Weary Wolfe (The)	487	837	42-52656	yes
Worry Bird	487			no
Yankee Maid	487	838	41-29537	no

489TH BOMB GROUP

Name	Grp.	Sq.	Serial	Pic.
Ace of Spades	489	844	41-28976	no
Agony Wagon	489	846	42-94914	yes
Alda M.	489	844	42-50320	yes
American Lady	489		42-50384	yes
Appassionata	489	846	42-50437	yes
B. T. O.	489	846	44-40072	yes
Baby Doll (The)	489	844	42-52698	yes
Battling Betsy	489			no
Beautiful Takeoff	489	844	42-50451	yes

Name	Grp.	Sq.	Serial	Pic.
Betty-Jim (The)	489	847	42-94947	yes
Black Magic	489	846	42-52737	yes
Blackie's Bastards	489	846	42-52288	no
Bomb Baby	489	847	42-94829	yes
Bomber's Moon	489	844	42-94903	yes
Buck Shot	489	846	42-94761	no
Buckshot Annie	489	846	42-94819	yes
Bugs Bunny	489			no
Callipygia	489	847	42-94920	yes
Captain & the Kids	489			no
Censored	489	846	42-94905	yes
Consolidated Mess	489		42-100429	yes
Corrine	489	815	42-94793	yes
Cover Girl	489	845	42-94945	yes
Cyclone	489			yes
Don't Fence Me In	489	847	42-50525	no
ETO	489			no
Fay Day	489	844	42-94874	yes
Flak Shak III	489		42-51501	no
Ford's Folly	489	844	42-94842	no
Four or Five Times	489		41-28820	no
Fox (The)	489			no
Frannie Belle	489			no
Frivolous Freddie	489			no
Happy Warrior	489		42-50587	yes
Happy Warrior	489	846	42-94860	no
Heaven Can Wait	489	845	41-28832	yes
Heaven Can Wait II	489	845	42-94786	no
Hit Parade (The)	489		42-94883	no
Homesick Lass	489	845	42-94906	yes
Honey Bucket	489			no
Ike and Monty	489	845	42-94855	no
Jewel	489			no
Jo	489	847	42-94783	yes
Joe E. Brown	489	847	42-94783	no
Johnny Reb	489	844	42-94826	no
Johnson's Jalopy	489	844	42-94788	no
Lethal Linda	489	845	42-94776	yes
Liberator (The)	489			no
Lid's ON - Lid's OFF	489			no
Lil' Cookie	489		42-7552	yes
Little Audrey	489		44-10615	yes
Little Iodine	489	847	41-28941	yes
Lonesome Polecat (The)	489	846	42-94857	yes
Lusty Lib	489			no
Lynda Lee	489		41-28976	no
Malfunction Junction	489	847	42-94825	no
Malignant Lady	489			no
Manistee	489	847	41-28870	yes
Marion	489	845	42-94898	no
Matchless Jeep	489	846	42-94817	yes
Misfit	489			yes
Mispah	489	845	42-94788	no
Miss Gus	489			yes
Miss Pam	489			no
Mizpah	489	845	42-94778	no
Moonshine Express	489			no
Mother's Boy	489			no
Myasis Draggin'	489			no
Nightmare	489			no
No Nook Ee Now	489	846	42-94909	yes
No Nookie Now	489	846	42-94854	yes
Ol' Buddy	489			yes
Old Blister Butt	489		42-40776	yes
Paper Doll	489	846	42-52688	no
Paper Doll	489	846	42-94932	yes
Phoney Express	489	844	42-94833	yes
Piccadilly Commando	489	847	42-51128	yes
Pin Up Girl	489	844	42-94941	yes
Plate's Date	489	847	42-94830	yes
Plucky Lucky	489	844	42-94820	yes
Pregnant Peggy	489	847	42-94913	yes
Rebel Gal	489	845	42-94838	yes
Ripper (The)	489	846	42-50360	yes
Ripper's Clipper	489	846	42-50360	yes
Royal Carriage	489	847	42-94925	no
Rugged Cross	489			no
Rum Dum	489	845	42-50280	yes
Rum Runner	489	845	42-94900	yes
Ruth E-K Allah Hassid	489	845	41-29577	yes
Sack (The)	489	846	42-94857	no
Sack (The)	489	847	41-29603	no
Sack Happy	489			no
Sad Sack	489	844	42-94831	no
Safu	489	846	42-94909	yes
Satan's Sister	489	844	42-50541	yes
Shaft (The)	489	846	42-52737	yes
Sharon D. (The)	489	847	42-94759	yes
Shoo! Shoo! Baby	489	578	42-50284	no
Silver Queen	489	846	42-95267	yes
Sing Bing	489			no
Sky Wolf	489	844	41-29547	no
Sky Wolves	489			yes
Slick Chick	489	846	42-50388	yes
Small Change	489			no
Snafu	489	846	42-94909	no
Snow White	489	847	42-94834	yes
Southern Cross	489			no
Special Delivery	489	845	42-94896	yes
Special Delivery II	489	844	42-94888	no
Squee-Gee	489	846	42-95086	no
St. Louis Woman	489			no
Stinker	489			no
Stinky	489	846	42-94864	yes
Struggle Buggy	489	845	42-94785	yes
Struggle Buggy	489	847	42-94836	no
Stubby Gal	489	847	42-94836	yes
Stubby Gal II	489	846	42-94933	no
Stubby Gal III	489	847	42-94888	no
Su Su	489			no
Sweater Girl	489			no
Tahelenbak	489			no
Tarfu	489			no
Teaser	489	845	42-95249	no

Name	Grp.	Sq.	Serial	Pic.
Terri Ann	489	845	42-94898	yes
Tiger's Revenge	489	846	42-94816	yes
Unholy Virgin	489			yes
Urgin' Virgin	489			no
Virginia	489			no
War Bride	489	847	42-94924	yes

490TH BOMB GROUP

Name	Grp.	Sq.	Serial	Pic.
Axis Ex-Lax	490	848	42-94820	no
Axis ExLax	490	848	41-28870	no
Baby Bug	490	850	42-94865	yes
Bad Penny Always Comes Back	490			no
Bolicat	490	851	41-29473	no
Booby Trap	490	850	42-94802	yes
Boots	490	850	41-29599	yes
Brown Nose	490	849	42-94821	no
Cal'donia	490	850	41-28882	no
Call Me Savage	490	849	42-94937	yes
Carolina Moon	490	851	42-94944	no
Cherub (The)	490	851	42-94943	no
Classy Chassis	490	849		no
Classy Chassis II	490	849	42-50291	no
Dee Luck	490			no
Destiny's Tot	490	849	42-97875	no
Devil's Stepchild	490	851	41-28868	no
Duchess	490	849	42-94821	no
E for Easy	490		44-40424	no
Edie	490	849	42-94958	no
Extra Joker	490			no
Flyer's Fancy	490	849	42-94840	no
Flying Boxcar (The)	490	848	41-29587	yes
Flying Ginny	490	849	42-94894	no
Foul Ball	490		42-50290	no
Gag 'N Vomit	490	850	41-29544	no
Generator Jenny	490		44-40320	no
Going My Way	490	850		no
Gremlin's Roost	490	848	41-29601	no
Heavenly Body	490	849	42-94939	no
Homesick Angel	490	850		no
Idiot's Delight	490	848	42-94839	yes
Jinx (The)	490	848	42-94837	yes
Lady Kessler	490	850	42-94856	yes
Leave Me Be	490	851	42-94844	no
Lee Mee Bee	490	850		no
Lee Mee Bee II	490	850		no
Lee Mee Bee III	490	850		no
Leevus Bee	490	851	42-50490	yes
Len Dee Luck	490	848	42-94922	yes
Li'l Edie	490	850		no
Little Eva	490	849	41-28869	no
Little Iron Pants	490	849	42-94781	yes
Little Lackassaky	490	850	42-94812	no
Little Rebel	490	851		no
Little Warrior	490	850	42-94812	yes
Lizzy Belle	490	848	42-94884	yes
Loretta Ann (The)	490	850	41-29602	no
Lotta Stern	490	850	42-94876	no
Lotta Stern	490	850	xx-xx851	no
Love 'em All	490	851	41-28946	no
Lucy Quipment	490	851	41-29545	yes
Mairzy Doats	490	848	42-94891	yes
Mandy J.	490			no
Mandy J. II	490	850		no
Mandy J. III	490	850		no
Maxwell House	490	849	42-94885	no
Miakinback	490			no
Misanthrope	490	851	42-94953	no
Mischief Maker	490	850		no
Miss Hotcha	490	849	42-94862	no
Miss Me	490	848	42-94847	no
Miss Minookie	490	851	42-94798	no
Missouri Mule	490	848	42-51281	no
Mizry Merchant	490	850	41-29561	no
Moby Dick	490	851	42-94789	no
My Mama Done Told Me	490	849	42-94955	no
Myakinback	490	850	42-94918	no
Noble Effort	490	850	42-94981	no
Old Baldy	490	849	42-94853	no
Old Fud	490	850	42-94928	no
Ole Baldy	490	851	42-94863	yes
Ole Irish	490	851	42-94863	no
Pappy's Pill	490	850	42-94792	no
Pennsy Belle	490	850	42-2882	no
Pete	490			yes
Pete the Pelican	490	848	42-94821	no
Philly Filly (The)	490	848	41-28841	no
Plenty on the Ball	490			no
Queenie	490	851		no
Quit Shovin'	490	851	42-94916	no
Raiden Maiden	490	849	42-94763	no
Red Hot Riding Hood	490	849	42-52086	yes
Rugged But Right	490	851	42-94953	no
Sack Time	490	849	42-94841	no
Shady Lady	490	850		no
Shoo! Shoo! Baby	490	849	42-50284	yes
Silver Wolf (The)	490	848	42-94882	no
Sky Pirate	490	848	42-94823	no
Snafuperman	490	848	42-94784	no
Snootie Cutie	490	848	41-29597	yes
Snottie Dottie	490	851	42-94803	yes
Sweet Job	490	849	42-94927	yes
Swivel Chair	490	850	42-94843	no
Ten High	490	849	42-50292	no
Thumper	490			no
Thumper II	490	848	42-94848	no
Troublesome Twins	490	851	42-94743	no
Whatzit?	490	851	42-94912	no
Why Worry?	490	850	41-29568	no
Wind Haven	490	849	42-94853	no
Wishbone	490	850	41-29594	no
Wishbone	490	850	42-94797	no

Name	Grp.	Sq.	Serial	Pic.	Name	Grp.	Sq.	Serial	Pic.
Yankee Maid	490	849	42-94794	yes	Grease Ball	491	854	44-40172	yes
You're Safe at Home	490	851	42-94828	yes	Green Hornet (The)	491	852	44-40286	yes
Yuk-Yuk	490	848	42-94899	no	Hare Power	491	854	44-40117	yes
					Heavenly Body	491	852	42-110135	no
					Heine Headache	491	855	44-40203	no
					Homing Pigeon (The)	491			no

491ST BOMB GROUP

Name	Grp.	Sq.	Serial	Pic.	Name	Grp.	Sq.	Serial	Pic.
Ain't Bluffin'	491	854	44-40246	no	Hot Rock	491	855	44-40162	no
Airborn Angel	491	852	42-51294	no	House of Rumor	491	854	44-40271	yes
Ark Angel	491	853	44-40073	yes	I'll Be Around?	491		44-40132	no
Ark Angel	491	854	44-40271	no	I'll Be Seeing You	491	854	44-40210	no
B. T. O.	491	855	42-50678	no	Idiot's Delight	491	853	42-51530	no
Back to the Sack	491	854	44-40249	yes	Ike & Monty	491	852	42-94855	no
Ballot Baker	491	853	42-110186	no	Is This Trip Necessary?	491	853	42-50532	yes
Batter Bam	491			no	Jail Bait	491	853	42-110161	yes
Beautiful Takeoff	491	854	42-50451	no	Jezabelle	491	852	44-40213	yes
Becomin' Back	491	855	44-10575	no	Jigg's Up!	491			yes
Belle of the East	491	854	42-110187	yes	Jinny	491			no
Belle Ringer	491	852	42-52347	no	Johnny Come Lately	491	855	42-110154	yes
Belle Ringer	491	855	42-51296	yes	King Bird	491			no
Betsy	491	854	42-50610	yes	La Chiquitae	491			no
Betty-Jim (The)	491	954	42-94947	no	Lady Luck II	491	852	42-40722	no
Bi-U Baby	491	855	42-95619	yes	Lambsy Divey	491	853	44-40170	yes
Big 'Un	491	855	42-50680	yes	Latrine Rumor (The)	491	854	44-40271	no
Big Sugar	491	855	42-110170	no	Leacherous Lou	491		41-29528	no
Bill Flap and Gear Specialist	491			no	Lil' Gramper	491	852	42-40722	no
Bird Dog	491	854	42-110187	no	Little Beaver	491	855	44-40194	yes
Blockbuster	491	853	42-110164	yes	Little Gramper (The)	491		42-40722	yes
Blue Circle	491	854	44-40242	no	Little Joe	491	854	44-40084	yes
Blue Circle	491	855	44-40108	no	Lookin' Good	491	852	42-50918	no
Bronx Express (The)	491	854	44-40248	yes	Lucky Buck	491	852	42-110158	yes
By the Numbers	491	854	44-40121	yes	Ma's Little Angel	491			no
Cabin in the Sky	491			no	Mad Madeleine	491			no
Carousin' Cock	491	855	44-40202	yes	Mah Aikin Back	491	853	44-40226	yes
Cheec Hako	491	852	44-50884	yes	Maiden America	491			no
Chris' Crate II	491	853	42-110160	no	Mama's Lil' Angel	491	852	44-10558	yes
Cokey Flo	491	854	44-40486	no	Mary Harriett	491	854	42-110149	no
D'nif	491	852	44-40100	yes	Maxie's Nightmare	491	854	44-40459	yes
Daisy Mae	491			no	Merchant of Menace	491	855	44-40089	no
Delirious Delores	491	853	44-40200	yes	Milkrun Betty	491			yes
Dirty Tale	491			yes	Miss Alda Flak	491			no
Dorty Treek	491	852	44-10485	yes	Miss Francia	491	854	42-51267	no
Dual Sack	491	855	42-110168	no	Modest Maiden	491	853	42-95264	yes
Easy Way (The)	491	853		yes	Moose (The)	491	853	44-40205	yes
Elie	491			no	Mr. Invader	491	852	42-110038	yes
Fearless Fosdick	491			no	Old Iron Pants	491	855	42-110168	yes
Fightin' Gremlin	491			no	Ole Buckshot	491		42-50739	no
Firebird	491	852	42-110167	yes	Ole Buddy	491	855	42-51120	no
Flamin' Mamie	491			no	Paddy's Wagon	491	855	44-40114	no
Flying Ass (The)	491			no	Pancho	491			yes
Flying Bull	491	852	42-110138	no	Pappy's Persuaders	491	852	44-40144	yes
Flying Jackass (The)	491	853	44-40239	yes	Pappy's Yokum	491	853	41-110159	yes
Flying Sheriffs	491	854	44-40240	yes	Parson's Chariot	491	853	42-110162	yes
Four-Five Time	491	855	44-40232	no	Payday	491	855	41-28938	no
Four-Five-Time	491	854	41-28820	no	Pegasus	491	854	44-40164	no
French Dressing	491	853	44-50299	yes	Phantom Revegada Le Simulacre Renegat	491	852	42-110185	no
Going My Way	491			no					

Name	Grp.	Sq.	Serial	Pic.
Piccadilly Lily	491			no
Plenty on the Ball	491			no
Ponderous Pachyderm	491	853	42-94753	yes
Prowler (The)	491	854	42-110171	yes
Puss 'n Boots	491	853	44-50340	yes
Rage in Heaven	491	852	44-40165	yes
Ragged But Right	491		44-10622	no
Reddy Maid	491			no
Reluctant Dragon	491		42-95610	no
Reluctant Dragon	491	853	42-51088	yes
Renegade (The)	491	852	42-110186	no
Rumplestiltskin II	491		42-64452	no
Ruthless Ruthie	491	854	44-40317	yes
Sack Rat	491	852	44-40206	no
Sack Time	491	855	42-110173	yes
Satan's Sister	491	854	42-50541	no
Scarface	491	855	42-95007	no
Section 8	491	853	42-50365	yes
She Devil	491	852	44-40123	yes
Silver Queen	491	852	42-95267	yes
Slo Freight	491	852	44-40111	yes
So Round, So Firm, So Fully Packed	491	854	42-95123	yes
Sparky's Hot Box	491			no
Stinky	491	852	42-110138	no
Sweet Eloise	491			no
Tally Ho	491	854	42-110165	yes
Tender Foot	491	853	44-40243	yes
Thunderbird	491	852	44-40238	yes
Time's A Wastin'	491	855	44-40234	yes
Tubarao	491	854	44-40101	yes
Tung Hoi	491	852	44-40230	yes
Tung Hoi II	491	852	42-95622	yes
Twang	491			no
Unconditional Surrender	491	855	42-110146	yes
Uninvited	491	853	44-40124	no
United...In God We Trust	491			no
Unlimited (The)	491	853	41-29464	no
Wham Bam, Thank You, Maam	491	854	42-110107	yes
What's Cookin' Doc?	491	855	42-110157	yes
Workin' for the Yankee Dollar	491	852	42-51113	yes
Yankee Doll-ah (The)	491			no

492ND BOMB GROUP

Name	Grp.	Sq.	Serial	Pic.
Alice	492	857	44-40140	yes
B. T. O.	492	857	44-40072	yes
Baby Shoes	492		42-50555	no
Battling Boops	492	858	44-40159	no
Benutz Joy	492			no
Beverly Joy	492	857	42-50492	yes
Big Brown Jug (The)	492	856	42-110148	no
Big Fat Mama	492	856	44-40067	no
Black Magic	492			no
Bold Venture III	492	859	42-50675	no
Boomerang	492	857	44-40171	no
Boop	492	858	44-40159	no
Bootling Boop	492	858	44-40159	yes
Bottle Baby	492	858	44-40169	yes
Boulder Buff	492	857	44-40195	yes
Breezy Lady	492	859	42-110141	no
Broad and High	492		42-50439	no
Buzz Tail II	492	859	42-50447	yes
Classy Chassis	492		42-51291	no
Classy Chassy	492		42-95198	no
Daisy Mae	492	856	xx-xx581	no
Daisy Mae	492	858	44-40135	no
Elmer	492	859	42-110141	no
Envy of 'em All	492		42-50279	no
Ernie's Beavers	492	857	44-40173	no
Everything's Jake	492		42-95234	no
Feudin' Wagon	492	859	44-40155	no
Flying Rumor	492	859	42-50447	yes
Four Beers	492	856	44-40227	no
G.I. Joe	492	857	42-110151	no
Gambling Lady	492	857	44-40113	no
Gas House Mouse	492			no
Gwen	492	857	42-110184	yes
Herk's Jerks	492	858	44-40125	yes
I'll Be Around	492	859	44-40132	no
Irishman's Shanty	492	857	44-40166	yes
Jane's Wittle Wabbit	492		42-52757	no
Lady Grace	492	858	42-95011	yes
Larrupin' Linda	492	857	44-40118	yes
Laura Jo	492	858	44-40086	no
Little Lulu	492	856	42-110143	yes
Lucky 1	492	856	44-40134	yes
Lucky Lass	492	857	44-40157	yes
Lucky Strike	492	856	42-110148	yes
Massachusetts Girl	492		42-50614	no
Merchant (of Menace)	492			yes
Midnight Mistress	492	857	42-50483	yes
Militant Mistress	492	858	44-40115	no
Miss Irene	492	859	44-40211	no
Mojalajab	492	859	44-40132	no
Moonshine Express	492		42-95215	no
My Aiken Back	492		44-40226	no
Night Knight	492	858	44-40119	no
Oma Akin Bak	492	857	42-51555	no
Our Gal	492		42-100308	no
Playmate	492	856		no
Pursuit of Happiness	492		42-95272	no
Ruptured Duck	492	856	44-40150	no
S. O. L.	492	858	44-40066	yes
Sack Time	492	857	42-110184	no
Say When	492	858	44-40103	yes
Screwball	492	859	42-52711	yes
Sierra Blanca	492	858	44-40167	no
Silver Chief	492	857	44-40201	yes
Silver Witch	492	857	44-40136	yes
Sknappy	492	856	44-40142	yes

Name	Grp.	Sq.	Serial	Pic.	Name	Grp.	Sq.	Serial	Pic.
Southern Comfort	492			no	Generator Jenny	493		44-40320	no
Spirit of Colley H.S.	492		42-50777	no	GI Wife	493		44-40477	no
Spittin' Kitten	492	858	44-40126	yes	Green Hornet (The)	493		44-40286	yes
Star Spangled Hell	492		42-72873	yes	Hairless Joe	493	860	44-40437	yes
Strange Cargo	492			no	Hell and Back	493		42-95170	yes
Super Wolf	492	859	44-40050	yes	Hell and Back	493		44-42951	no
Sweat Box	492	857	44-40071	yes	Henry	493		44-40279	no
Sweat'er Gal	492	859	44-40053	yes	Huckle De Buck	493		44-40235	no
Sweet Chariot	492	856	44-40087	yes	Jane's Wittle Wabbit	493	861	42-52751	no
Tequila Daisy	492	857	44-40168	yes	Jeannie with the				
Thar She Blows III	492	857	44-40168	yes	Light Brown Hair	493			no
That's All Brother	492	859	44-40120	yes	Jerk's Berserks	493		44-40443	no
Tiger's Revenge	492	858	42-94816	no	Joker (The)	493		44-40472	yes
Tinker Belle	492	857	44-40158	yes	Jolly Roger	493		44-40475	yes
Umbriago	492	859	44-40068	yes	Just One More Time	493		44-40464	no
Wabash Cannonball	492		42-50313	no	Katrinka	493	863	42-51197	yes
What's Next Doc?	492	857	44-40167	yes	Kentucky Belle	493		44-40268	no
What's Up Doc	492	857	44-40167	no	Kitrinka	493			no
What's Up Doc?	492	858	44-40167	no	Leo	493		42-52768	yes
					Little Lackassaky	493	862	42-94812	no

493RD BOMB GROUP

Name	Grp.	Sq.	Serial	Pic.
'Lil Hoot	493		44-40140	yes
'Lil Hoot	493		44-40440	no
Baby Bug	493		42-94865	no
Baby Doll	493		42-50554	yes
Bad Penny II	493		44-40267	no
Betta Duck	493		44-40454	no
Betty Jane	493		42-94768	no
Big Dealer	493	862	42-52759	yes
Bold Sea Rover (The)	493	861	42-94745	no
Bolicat	493	861	41-29473	no
Bomble Bee	493	860	44-40414	yes
Bonnie B.	493		42-51195	no
Boomerang	493		44-40957	no
Call Me Savage	493		42-94937	no
Capricorn	493			no
Chief Oshkosh	493		41-29510	no
Cock of the Sky	493	861	41-29569	no
Collapsible Susie	493	861	42-94745	no
Dangerous Dance	493	860	44-40361	yes
Dugan Wagon	493			no
Dugan Wagon II	493		42-94757	no
Easy Queen	493		44-40456	no
European Clipper	493	863	44-40049	yes
Feather Merchant	493			yes
Fifinella	493		42-110102	yes
Fightin' Rebel	493		41-28849	no
Floogie Boo	493		44-40441	no
Flossie	493	862	42-50762	no
Flying Boxcar (The)	493		41-29587	no
Flying Devil (The)	493	862	41-29548	no
Four (4) F	493		44-40418	yes
Four (IV) F	493		44-40380	no
Foxy Phoebe	493		41-29527	no
G.I. Wife	493		44-40477	no
Gag N' Vomit	493		41-29544	no

Name	Grp.	Sq.	Serial	Pic.
Little Lulu	493		44-40233	no
Little Warrior	493	862	42-94812	yes
Lizzy Belle	493			no
Maxie's Nightmare	493		44-40459	yes
Mean Kid	493		44-40468	no
Merchant	493	862	42-94789	yes
Mickey Mouse	493		42-94851	no
Mizry Merchant	493	863	41-29561	no
Moonlight Marge	493		44-40325	no
Myakinback	493		42-94918	no
Nancy	493		44-40436	yes
No Love, No Nothin'	493		44-40471	no
Old Sack	493		44-40425	no
Ole Baldy	493		42-94863	no
Ole Irish	493		42-94863	no
Ole Sack	493		44-40421	no
Piccadilly Lucy	493		41-29518	no
Piccadilly Tilly	493	861	44-40458	yes
Purty Baby	493		44-40299	yes
Quit Shovin'	493		42-94916	no
Randy Dandy	493		44-40477	no
Rat Poison	493		41-29560	no
Rat Poison	493		44-40477	no
Rose Marie	493		44-40207	no
Rum Runner	493		42-52496	yes
Ruptured Duck (The)	493		42-52770	yes
Ruthless Ruthie	493		44-40317	no
Sack Time Sally	493	863	42-110094	yes
Same Ole Crap	493		44-40466	yes
Savage	493			no
Shack (The)	493		44-40298	no
Shady Lady	493		44-40439	no
Short Bier	493		44-40442	no
Spirit of '76	493	860	41-29473	no
Sunshine Rose	493		44-40323	no
Sweetheart of the South	493		44-40469	no
Ten High	493		42-50292	no

Name	Grp.	Sq.	Serial	Pic.
This Above All	493		44-40328	yes
Tondelayo	493			no
Troublesome Twins	493		42-94743	no
Turgo Joe	493		44-40303	no
Wild Hare (The)	493		42-52695	yes
Won Long Hop	493	861	44-40460	no
Worry Bird	493		44-40470	no
Zippo	493			no
Armed Venus	494	867	44-40740	yes

494TH BOMB GROUP

Name	Grp.	Sq.	Serial	Pic.
Belle (The)	494			no
Big Time Operator	494	864	44-40757	yes
Black Cat	494	864	44-40704	yes
Black Sheep	494	867	44-40760	yes
Blunderin' Ben	494	864	44-40746	yes
Bomb Babe	494	866	44-40709	yes
Brief	494	867	44-42058	yes
Bugs Buggy	494	864	44-40707	yes
Bugs Bunny Jr.	494	865	44-40654	no
Bull II (The)	494	865	44-40688	yes
Bull Snooker (The)	494	864	42-40405	yes
Contrary Mary	494	864	44-40739	yes
Cowbird	494	867	44-40790	yes
Crash Kids	494	865	44-40756	yes
Double Trouble	494	865	44-40563	yes
Duchess (The)	494	867	44-40567	yes
Duchess (The) II	494	867	44-40754	no
Eagle (The)	494	865	44-40751	no
Early Bird (The)	494	865	44-40748	yes
Eight Ball	494		44-40744	yes
Final Objective	494	864	44-41945	yes
Flyin' Pay	494	865	44-40732	yes
Flying Boxcar	494	867	44-40749	yes
Flying Fay	494	865	44-40732	yes
Flying Fifer	494	865	44-40742	yes
Flying Pay	494	865	44-40732	yes
Glidin' Home	494		44-41238	no
Hawaiian Woman	494	867	44-40754	no
Hay Maker	494	867	44-40729	yes
Heaven Can Wait II	494	866	44-42061	yes
Hell's Belle	494	864	44-40715	yes
Horrible Monster	494	864	44-40690	yes
I'll Be Around	494			no
I'll Get By	494	864	44-40743	yes
Innocence A-Broad	494	865	44-40733	yes
Kuuipo's	494	864	44-40559	yes
Lady Duzz	494			no
Lady Kaye	494	867	44-40647	yes
Lady Leone	494	864	44-40736	yes
Lady Luck II	494	865	44-42131	yes
Les Miserables	494	866	44-40666	yes
Liquidator	494	866	44-42052	yes
Little Red	494	866	44-40693	yes
Lonesome Lady	494	866	44-40680	yes
Minnehaha	494	864	44-41578	yes
Minniehaha	494	864	44-41578	yes
Missouri Mule (The)	494	864	44-40717	yes
Near Miss	494	867	44-40795	yes
Norman S. Mackie (The)	494	864	44-42055	yes
Old George	494	866	44-40747	yes
Our Baby	494	867	44-40689	yes
Over Loaded	494	864		yes
Pacific Passion	494			yes
Pacific Vamp	494	867	41-24168	no
Park N' Strip Patty	494		42-109948	no
Pathfinder	494	866	44-40684	no
Pilot Error	494	865	44-40738	no
Pious Plunderer	494	867	44-40668	yes
Play Boy	494	867	44-40791	yes
Playboy's Friend	494	867	44-40791	yes
Playmate (R. Side)				no
Playboy (L. Side)	494	867	44-40791	yes
Plunderbus	494	864	44-40712	yes
Queen of Hearts	494	866	44-40685	yes
Riot Call	494	864	44-40755	yes
Rip Snorter (The)	494	866	44-40684	yes
Round Trip Ticket	494			yes
Rover Boys' Baby	494	865	44-40752	yes
Sack Time Sal	494	866	44-40741	no
Sack Time Sal II	494	866	44-40796	yes
Screaming Meemie	494		44-42055	no
Senator (The)	494	864	44-40713	yes
Shack Bunny	494	867	44-40759	yes
Short Run	494	867	44-40686	yes
Sittin' Pretty	494	865	44-40711	yes
Sluggin' Sal	494	865	44-40750	yes
Sniffin' Griffin	494	865	44-40705	yes
Star Dust	494	867	44-41610	yes
Super Chick	494	865	44-40761	yes
Taloa	494	866	44-40716	yes
Texas Termite	494			yes
Til Then	494	866	44-40731	yes
Tiny Mac	494	866	44-40672	yes
Tropical Dream	494			no
Well Developed	494			no
Wolf	494	867	44-40737	yes

801ST BOMB GROUP

Name	Grp.	Sq.	Serial	Pic.
Betty Jane	801		42-94768	no
Br'er Rabbit	801		42-63798	yes
Chief	801		41-28781	no
Cookie	801		42-40549	no
Dark Eyes	801	406	42-50652	no
Feather Merchant	801			no
Hell and Back	801		42-95170	no
Lazy Lou	801	36	42-7609	no
Mag Drop	801	859	42-95131	no
Margie/Ready N' Able	801	36	42-95221	no
Mickey Mouse	801	406	42-94851	no
Midnight Mistress II	801	36	42-50750	no
Miss-B-Haven	801	36	42-94811	no

Name	Grp.	Sq.	Serial	Pic.
Miz-Pah	801		42-94845	no
Plate's Date	801		42-94830	no
Playmate	801		42-63980	yes
Shack II (The)	801	36	41-29143	no
Snootie Cutie	801		41-29597	no
Varga Belle	801	859	42-95262	no
Kentucky Kloudhopper	803		44-40380	yes

2641ST BOMB GROUP

Name	Grp.	Sq.	Serial	Pic.
Dallas Lady	2641	885	42-78243	no
Mag Drop	2641	859	42-95731	no
Miss Charlotte	2641	885		yes
Screwball	2641		42-52711	yes

11TH AIR FORCE

Name	Grp.	Sq.	Serial	Pic.
Ground Hog	11AF	404	41-23892	no
Iggy	11AF	404	41-1104	no
Lil De-Icer	11AF	404		no

15TH AIR FORCE

Name	Grp.	Sq.	Serial	Pic.
Baby	15AF			yes
Betsy	15AF		42-50610	yes
Kajun Kate	15AF			yes
Patches	15AF			yes
Short Snorter	15AF			yes
Snow White	15AF			yes
Takin' Off	15AF			yes
Upstairs Maid	15AF			yes

2ND AIR DIVISION DEPOT

Name	Grp.	Sq.	Serial	Pic.
Alamagordo	2AD			no
Belligerent Bess	2AD			no
Billy the Kid	2AD			no
Bunnie	2AD			no
Clam Winkle	2AD			no
Courageous	2AD			no
Gabe's Angels	2AD			no
Ju Ju	2AD			no
My Sugar	2AD			no
My Sugar II	2AD			no
Silly Filly	2AD			no

6TH AIR FORCE

Name	Grp.	Sq.	Serial	Pic.
Boston Deb	6AF			yes
Fifinella	6AF			yes
Groundhog	6AF			yes
It's For You	6AF			yes
Old Bessie	6AF	29	41-23681	yes
Tail Wind	6AF			yes

6TH PHOTO RECON GROUP

Name	Grp.	Sq.	Serial	Pic.
American Beauty	6PR	20CM	42-73045	yes
Blue Dragon	6PR	24CM	44-41680	yes
Bourbon Boxcar	6PR	20CM	42-73048	yes
Cherokee Strip	6PR	20CM	44-40198	yes
Cyclone	6PR	24CM	42-64103	yes
Dodo	6PR	24CM	44-42687	yes
Flying Anvil (The)	6PR	24CM	42-64158	no
Hangover Haven II	6PR	20CM	42-64053	yes
Idle Curiosity	6PR	20CM	44-40423	yes
Kay-18	6PR	20CM	44-40656	yes
Little Joe (F-7)	6PR	20CM	42-64054	yes
Mary Lou	6PR	20CM	44-42239	yes
My Assam Dragon	6PR	24CM	42-64055	no
My Assam Wagon	6PR	24CM	42-64170	no
Nasty 'Lil	6PR	24CM	42-64055	no
Nosie Josie	6PR	24CM	42-64258	yes
Nosie Rosie	6PR	24CM	42-64102	yes
Patched Up Piece	6PR	20CM	42-64047	yes
Photo Queen (F-7)	6PR	20CM	42-73049	yes
Queen Mae	6PR	20CM	44-40337	yes
Rice Pattie Hattie	6PR	24CM	42-73038	yes
Rip Snorter	6PR	20CM	42-73047	yes
Smooth Sue	6PR	24CM	42-64168	yes
St. Louis Blues	6PR	20CM	42-64172	yes
T S	6PR	20CM	42-64051	yes
Under Exposed	6PR	20CM	42-73052	yes
Wango Wango Bird (The)	6PR	20CM	42-64048	yes

7TH AIR FORCE

Name	Grp.	Sq.	Serial	Pic.
Sad Sack	7AF			yes
Sad Sack	7AF		FP-685	yes
Pacific Tramp III	7AHQ		42-109936	yes
Sad Sack	7AHQ		FP-685	yes
Seventh Heaven	7AHQ		AL633	yes

AIR TRANSPORT COMMAND

Name	Grp.	Sq.	Serial	Pic.
Dysentery Special	ATC		42-107267	yes
Florida Cracker	ATC		42-107255	yes
Gulliver	ATC	PW	41-11608	yes
Gulliver II	ATC			yes
Kongo Kutie	ATC		41-11709	yes
Murphy's Mother-in-Law	ATC		44-49017	yes

ANTI-SUBMARINE GROUPS

Name	Grp.	Sq.	Serial	Pic.
Junior Miss	479	6		yes
Air Tramp	479		42-40618	yes
Biscay Belle	479			yes
Blind Bat (The)	479		42-40750	yes
De Boid	479		42-40499	no

Name	Grp.	Sq.	Serial	Pic.
Hoopee	479		42-63779	no
Ash Can Annie	480		41-24021	no
Charlotte the Harlot	480		42-40339	yes
En-Diving	480		42-40333	no
Off Limits	480		41-24263	no
Sad Sack (The)	480		41-23992	no
Sad Sack (The)	480		42-40376	yes
Sub-Mission	480		41-24007	no
Tidewater Tillie	480		42-40334	yes

ARMY AIRWAYS COMMUNICATION

Name	Grp.	Sq.	Serial	Pic.
Kilocycle Kitty	AACS			yes

AUSTRALIAN AIR FORCE

Name	Grp.	Sq.	Serial	Pic.
Jini	Austr.			no
Kangaroo Kate	Austr.			yes

STEERABLE BOMB PROJECT

Name	Grp.	Sq.	Serial	Pic.
Bachelor's Bedlam	AZON		44-40287	no
Bad Girl	AZON		44-40288	yes
Heavenly Hideaway	AZON		44-40277	no
Howling Banshee	AZON		44-40273	no
Kiss Me Baby	AZON		44-40264	yes
Lassie Come Home	AZON		44-40283	no
Miss Used	AZON		44-40277	no
Royal Flush	AZON		44-40291	no
Table Stuff	AZON		44-40285	no

ORIGINAL PLOESTI RAIDERS

Name	Grp.	Sq.	Serial	Pic.
Ball of Fire	HALP		41-11624	no
Blue Goose	HALP		41-11597	no
Brooklyn Rambler	HALP		41-11596	yes
Draggin' Lady	HALP		41-11592	no
Eager Beaver	HALP		41-11600	no
Edna Elizabeth	HALP		41-11620	yes
Florine Jo-Jo	HALP		41-11613	no
Jap Trap	HALP		41-11629	no
Little Eva	HALP		41-11609	no
Mona the Lame Duck	HALP		41-11615	no
Ole Rock	HALP		41-11618	yes
Town Hall	HALP		41-11622	yes

NIGHT LEAFLET SQUADRON

Name	Grp.	Sq.	Serial	Pic.
Mickey Mouse	NLS		42-94851	no
Night Night (The)	NLS			no
Shady Lady	NLS		42-37726	no
Snafu	NLS		41-24614	no
Swing Shift	NLS			no
Target for Tonite	NLS		41-24615	no

RAF – RCAF

Name	Grp.	Sq.	Serial	Pic.
Canadian Cutie	RAF	159		yes
Clarence	RAF	356		yes
Lucifer	RAF	335		yes
Magic Carpet	RAF	231	41-11741	yes
Marco Polo	RAF	231	AL 578	yes
Trader Horn	RAF			yes
Wandering Witch	RAF	355		yes
Yvonne, Yippee	RAF	159		yes
Algy	RCAF			yes
Basterpiece	RCAF		3704	yes
Battlin' Bitch	RCAF		42-64224	yes
Carioca Joe	RCAF			yes
Cloo-Lus	RCAF			yes
Dumbo Delivers	RCAF			yes
Earthquake McGoon	RCAF			yes
Gasoline Alley	RCAF			yes
Goofy	RCAF			yes
Karioka Joe	RCAF			yes
Lady X	RCAF			yes
Mabel	RCAF		42-64182	yes
Peace Persuader	RCAF		44-10286	yes
Pistol Packin' Mama	RCAF			yes
Ready and Willing	RCAF			yes
Rockcliffe Ice Wagon	RCAF			yes
Rogue's Retreat	RCAF			yes
Top Pull	RCAF			yes
Woodcutter	RCAF			yes

RADIO COUNTER MEASURES

Name	Grp.	Sq.	Serial	Pic.
21 Special	RCM	36	44-10609	no
Bama Bound- Lovely Libby	RCM	36	42-50622	no
Beast of Bourbon	RCM	36	42-50385	yes
Gravy Train (The)	RCM	36	42-51546	no
Gypsy Jane (The)	RCM	36	44-50502	no
I Walk Alone	RCM	36	42-51546	no
Jig's Up (The)	RCM	36	42-51232	no
Just Jeanne	RCM	36	42-51307	no
Lady Doris	RCM	36	42-95507	yes
Lazy Lou	RCM		42-7609	no
Liberty Belle	RCM		42-30039	no
Lil' Pudge	RCM	36	42-51230	no
Margie	RCM	36	42-95221	no
Miss B-Haven	RCM	36	42-50844	yes
Miss-B-Haven	RCM		42-94811	no
Modest Maid	RCM	36	42-51308	yes
Peck's Bad Boys	RCM	36	44-50576	no
Playmate	RCM		52-51685	no
Ramp Rooster	RCM	36	42-50671	no
Ready N' Able	RCM		42-95221	yes
Ready-N-Able	RCM	36	42-95221	no
Rum Dum	RCM	36	42-51230	no

Name	Grp.	Sq.	Serial	Pic.
Shack (The)	RCM	36	41-29143	no
Slick Chick	RCM			no
Spirit of '77 (The)	RCM	36	42-7607	no
Strange Cargo	RCM			no
Tar Baby	RCM	36	42-51311	no
This Is It, Men!	RCM	36	42-50622	no
Uninvited	RCM	36	42-51239	no
Worry Bird	RCM			no

ROYAL NAVY

Name	Grp.	Sq.	Serial	Pic.
Piccadilly Pam	RNavy			yes

SECRET OPERATIONS

Name	Grp.	Sq.	Serial	Pic.
Benutz Joy	SOP			no
Betty Jane	SOP		42-94768	no
Beverly Joy	SOP			no
Blasted Event	SOP		41-23682	yes
Chief	SOP		41-28781	no
Classy Chassis	SOP		42-51291	no
Cookie	SOP		42-40549	no
Daisy Mae	SOP		xx-xx581	no
Feather Merchant	SOP			no
Gas House Mouse	SOP			no
Hell and Back	SOP		42-95170	no
Lady Grace	SOP			yes
Malfunction Junction	SOP		42-94825	no
Miz-Pah	SOP		42-94845	no
Plate's Date	SOP		42-94830	no
Playmate	SOP			no
Ramp Rooster	SOP			no
Screwball	SOP		42-52711	no
Shack II (The)	SOP		41-29143	no
Snootie Cutie	SOP		41-29597	no
Tondelayo	SOP			no
Wind Haven	SOP		42-94853	no

SOUTHERN CROSS AIRWAYS

Name	Grp.	Sq.	Serial	Pic.
Fast Freight/Samoa			AL626	Yes
Flight Chief/Australia			AL617	No
Old Failtful/Seveth Heaven			AL633	Yes
Southern Cross #4			FP685	No
Trader Horn/ComAirFwd			AL617	Yes

US NAVY – VB, VP & VD SQUADRONS

Name	Grp.	Sq.	Serial	Pic.
Blue Bell	VD	5		yes
Bozo	VB	103	Bu32039	no
Bulldog	VD	3	Bu31986	no
Chick's Chick	VP	106		yes
Easy Maid	VB	102	Bu32323	no
Galloping Ghost	VB	102	Bu31977	no
Lemon (The)	VD	1		yes

Name	Grp.	Sq.	Serial	Pic.
Macahyba Maiden	VP	107		yes
Mark's Farts	VB	104	44-40313	yes
Mitzi-Bishi	VB	106		yes
Muck's Mauler	VB	103	Bu32035	no
Pistol Packin' Mama	VB	101	Bu31973	yes
Pistol Packin' Mama	VB	102		yes
Pistol Packin' Mama	VB	102		yes
Rovin Redhead	VD	5	Bu65299	yes
Sears Steers	VB	104	Bu32079	no
Sweet Marie	VB	115		yes
Thunder Mug	VB	109	Bu32108	no
Thundermug	VB	108		yes
Unapproachable	VB	106		yes
Urge Me	VB	109		yes
Whitsshits	VB	104	Bu32081	yes

US NAVY – VPB SQUADRONS

Name	Grp.	Sq.	Serial	Pic.
Abroad for Action	VPB	121	Bu59450	yes
Accentuate the Positive	VPB	108	Bu59441	yes
Anchors Away	VPB	121	Bu59483	yes
Black Sheep	VPB	120	Bu59745	yes
Blue Diamond	VPB	106	Bu59396	yes
Buccaneer Bunny	VPB	121	Bu59478	yes
Come N' Get It	VPB	121		yes
Cover Girl	VPB	121		yes
Doc's Delight	VPB	111	Bu38746	yes
Els-Notcho	VPB	108	Bu59460	yes
Flying Dutchman (The)	VPB	108		no
Indian Maid/ Redwing	VPB	106	Bu59586	yes
Lady Luck II	VPB	108	Bu59446	yes
Lady Luck III	VPB	116	Bu59459	yes
Lotta Tayle	VPB	121		yes
Louisiana Lil	VPB	121	Bu59475	yes
Lucky Puss	VPB	111	Bu38896	yes
Mad Frenchman (The)	VPB	121	Bu59566	yes
Miller's Reluctant Raiders	VPB	109		no
Miss Behavin'	VPB	118	Bu59392	yes
Miss Milovin'	VPB	116	Bu59617	yes
Miss Sea Ducer	VPB	121	Bu59582	yes
Missile Packin' Mama	VPB	121		yes
Modest Miss	VPB	111		yes
Modest Miss	VPB	116	Bu38733	yes
Mr. Kip	VPB	121	Bu38733	yes
Muckalone	VPB	111	Bu38895	no
Naval Body	VPB	121	Bu59406	yes
Nippo Nippin' Kitten	VPB	109		no
Nobody Else's Butt	VPB	116	Bu59520	yes
Ol' Blunderbus	VPB	121	Bu59564	yes
Open Bottom	VPB	104		no
Our Baby	VPB	106		yes
Pastime	VPB	121	Bu59504	yes
Peace Feeler	VPB	116	Bu59755	yes
Photo Sailor	VPB	121	Bu59406	yes
Pirate Princess	VPB	121	Bu59492	yes

Name	Grp.	Sq.	Serial	Pic.
Pistol Packin' Mama	VPB	108		no
Pistol Packin' Mama II	VPB	121		yes
Redwing	VPB	121	Bu59505	yes
Rugged Beloved	VPB	111	44-41308	yes
Sugar	VPB	108		yes
Superchief (The)	VPB	106		yes
Tail Chaser	VPB	121	Bu59491	yes
Tortilla Flat	VPB	197	Bu59398	yes
Twitchy Bitch	VPB	118	Bu59430	yes
Wabbit Twacks	VPB	108		no
Willie's Wild Cat II	VPB	116		yes
Worrybird	VPB	116		yes

US NAVY – MISCELLANEOUS

Name	Grp.	Sq.	Serial	Pic.
A-Tease	Navy			yes
Berlin Express	Navy			yes
Blunderbus	Navy			yes
Bouncin' Betty	Navy		Bu59741	no
Brown Bagger's Retreat	Navy		Bu65385	yes
Bull of the Woods Bulld	Navy			yes
Comair Wolfpack II	Navy			yes
Dazy May	Navy			yes
Easy Maid	Navy		Bu38923	yes
Easy Maid	Navy		44-40096	yes
Easy Maid (PB4Y-1)	Navy		44-41328	no
Fearless Fosdick	Navy			yes
Flying Seadog (The)	Navy		Bu32161	yes
Flying Tail	Navy			yes
I'll Get By	Navy			yes
Joy Rider	Navy			yes
Kamikaze Miss (The)	Navy			yes
Lady Luck	VPB	1	Bu38892	no
Lady of Leisure	Navy			yes
Lucky-Leven	Navy			yes
Miss Pandemonium	Navy			yes
Miss You	Navy			yes
Modest O'Miss	Navy			yes
Mon Cheri	Navy			yes
No Strain	Navy			yes
Packy's Packrat	Navy			yes
Patches	Navy			yes
Patuxent River Wart Hog	Navy		Bu32096	no
Pay Day	Navy			yes
Pistol Packin' Mama	Navy			yes
Pistol Packin' Mama III	Navy			no
Sleepy Time Gal	Navy			yes
Tarfu	Navy			yes
Torchy Lena	Navy			yes
Umbriago	Navy		Bu59390	yes
Wild Cherry II	Navy			yes

ZONE OF THE INTERIOR

Name	Grp.	Sq.	Serial	Pic.
4F	ZI			yes
All American	ZI	rest.		yes
B-23 1/2	ZI			yes
Bat (The)	ZI			yes
Blythe's Old Maid	ZI		42-41185	yes
Boobie Trap	ZI			yes
Flying Coffin	ZI			yes
Gangrene Gerty	ZI		42-100052	yes
Lil' Texas Filley	ZI		44-40848	yes
Old 99 Proof	ZI		44-49001	yes
Ramp Rat	ZI			yes
Storm Cloud	ZI			yes

MISCELLANEOUS

Name	Grp.	Sq.	Serial	Pic.
4-F	4PC			no
A Drupe				no
A Run on Sugar				yes
A Tisket A Tasket...			41-23757	yes
A Token for Tokio				yes
A-vailable			42-40980	yes
Able Mabel				yes
Adorable Angie				yes
After Hours				yes
Agony Wagon				yes
Agony Wagon				yes
Agony Wagon				yes
Ain't Miss Behavin'				no
Ain't She Sweet				no
Air Wac (The)				yes
Ali Baba and His Nine Wolves				no
All 'er Nothin'			42-98017	no
All Mine				no
Angel				yes
Angel				yes
Arabian Nights			40-2370	no
Aries				no
Arkansas Bobo				no
Assender				no
Avenger				yes
B. O. II			42-95177	no
Baby				yes
Baby (C-109)			44-48999	yes
Baby Bug II				yes
Baby Ruth			41-24292	no
Baby Shoe III (The)			44-6202	no
Baby's Shoes			41-28611	no
Back Sheesh Bessie				no
Back to the Sack			42-7563	no
Bad Penny				yes
Bad Penny (The)				no
Balls 'n All(C-87)				yes
Balls of Fire				yes

Name	Grp.	Sq.	Serial	Pic.	Name	Grp.	Sq.	Serial	Pic.
Bama Bound-					Bomb Wacky				
Lovely Libby		801	42-50622	no	Wabbit				yes
Banger			41-29567	no	Bombat			xx-xx134	yes
Bar Que				no	Bomerang Jr.				no
Barber Pole (The)				no	Bonnie				no
Bashful Marion			41-28820	no	Bonnie B.			44-40378	no
Basil				yes	Bonnie's Pride				no
Battin' Lady				no	Booby Trap				no
Beast of Bourbon		801	42-50385	yes	Boomerang				yes
Beaufort Belle		WEA		yes	Boomerang				no
Before (and After)				yes	Boomerang			42-52215	no
Bell Hotel				no	Boston				no
Belle				no	Bottoms Up			44-40487	yes
Belle				yes	Bottoms Up			44-40489	yes
Belle of the Brawl				yes	Bottoms Up				yes
Belle Wringer				yes	Bottoms Up (F-7)				yes
Berlin Express				no	Bowen's Banshee			44-40773	no
Bess				yes	Boy's Howdy			41-29138	no
Bessie				no	Broganelle Fireball			AL57	no
Bessie May Mucho				no	Bucket O' Bolts				yes
Beth				no	Buffalo Bill				no
Betta Duck				no	Bugs Bunny				no
Betta Duck			41-23783	no	Bulltoria				no
Betty	AD4			no	Bums Away		868	42-40812	yes
Betty J				yes	Burgundy Bombers				no
Big Ass Bird				no	Burma Babe from				
Big Ass Bird				yes	Birmingham				no
Big Big				yes	Burma Roadster				yes
Big Dear				no	Burma Virgin				yes
Big Fat Butterfly			42-99939	no	Buzzzz Job				yes
Big Gas Bird				yes	Call House Madam				yes
Big Noise				no	Capt. Eddie				
Big Noise III				yes	Rickenbacker				yes
Big Operator				yes	Capt. Tom's Cabin				yes
Big Operator's					Captain Gene (The)			42-7085	yes
Scoreboard				yes	Careeme Back				no
Big Stud				yes	Carol Ann				yes
Biggest Boid			42-51233	no	Carol-N-Chick				no
Bird Dog				no	Carolina Lick				no
Black Jack				no	Carter's Kids				no
Black M			42-100093	yes	Censored				yes
Black Magic				yes	Chariot				no
Black Widow				yes	Chattanooga				
Blasted Event				yes	Choo Choo				yes
Blind Date				yes	Chief Manhattan				no
Blind Date				yes	China Doll			41-24066	no
Blonde Bomb					Chubby Champ				no
Baby				no	Cindy				yes
Blondes Away				yes	Classy Chassy				yes
Blubber Butt		2PCS	42-64254	yes	Classy Chassy				no
Blunderbus				yes	Clique and				
Bob Alfred				no	Shudder (F-7)		4PCS	44-42710	yes
Bob Alfred II				no	Cock o' the North				yes
Bobbie				no	Cokey Flo				no
Bobbit				yes	Colorado Rose				no
Bomb Babe				no	Coming Home				
Bomb Em Baby				no	Soon				yes

Name	Grp.	Sq.	Serial	Pic.	Name	Grp.	Sq.	Serial	Pic.
Commando	AL504			yes	Eight Ball				no
Contrary Mary				yes	Eight Ball				yes
Copenhagen Kid			44-40289	no	El Diablo				no
Coral Princess			42-72977	yes	El Sluggo				no
Courtin'				no	Elusive Elcy				no
Crater Maker				yes	Elusive Elcy II				no
Culham's Yardbirds				no	Elusive Elcy III				no
Daddie's Ray				no	Elusive Elsie				no
Daddy's Boy				no	Elusive Elsie 2nd				no
Daisy Mae				yes	Envy of 'em All			42-49180	no
Damsel Easy				yes	Esky Special				yes
Danny Boy			42-50441	no	Estelle of Fort				
Daring Dame			44-40222	yes	Smith				no
De-Imp				no	Evasive Ann				no
Dead End Kids				no	Evelyn				no
Dear Duchess				yes	F for Freddie			41-23770	no
Defiance				no	Fairy Belle			42-73505	no
Destination Tokio				yes	False Alarm				no
Destiny's Digit				yes	Fearless Fosdick				no
Detail			xx-xx098	yes	Fearless Fosdick				yes
Devil's Own				no	Feather Merchant				no
Diamond Lil	CAF	rest.	LB-30	yes	Fertile Myrtle				yes
Dic's Delight				yes	Feudin' Wagon				no
Dick's Dixie				yes	Feudin; Rebel				no
Dina-Mite				no	Fifinella				yes
Dina-Mite				yes	Fighting Mudcat			42-52392	no
Dinah Mite				yes	Finito Combatt				yes
Ding Hao				yes	Finnigan's Female				no
Ding Hou				yes	Firefly				no
Dirty Gertie				yes	Flak Magnet II				no
Dirty Shame				no	Flak-Shy				yes
Dixie Dew Cup				no	Flame of the				
Dog Fight				no	Squadron				yes
Dogpatch Raider			41-24215	no	Flamin' Mamie				yes
Donna D Wanna				yes	Flap and Gear				
Donna K.				yes	Specialist				yes
Doodlebug				no	Floogie!				yes
Dottie's Double				yes	Floogie, Jr.				yes
Double Shot Nell				yes	Flying (Outhouse)				yes
Double Trouble				yes	Flying Boxcar				yes
Double Trouble				yes	Flying Cloud (The)				no
Dragon Fly				no	Flying Duchess (The)				yes
Dragon Lady				yes	Flying Dutchman (The)				yes
Dragon Lady				yes	Flying Fool				no
Dream Girl				no	Flying Ginny			42-51296	no
Dronkie		SAAF	34	yes	Flying Goose				no
Droopy Drawers				yes	Flying Home				no
Drunk Skunk				no	Flying Patches				no
Drunkard Dram				no	Flying Redhead				no
Duchess				yes	Flying Squaw				no
Duration Baby				no	Flying Submarine				yes
Dwatted Wabbit				yes	Flying Wolves (The)				no
Eager Beaver				yes	Four-Five Time				no
Earthquake McGoon	India		R385	yes	Foxy Lady	AD4			no
Eastern Queen				no	Foxy Lady				no
Easy Movement				yes	Frances Fury				no
Eephus			42-95108	no	Frankie C.				no

Name	Grp.	Sq.	Serial	Pic.	Name	Grp.	Sq.	Serial	Pic.
Freckle Face			42-7608	no	Hell and Back			44-48288	no
French Dressing				yes	Hell Wagon				yes
Friday's Cat			41-29513	yes	Hell's Belle				yes
Frowning Flossie				no	Hell's Belles				yes
Fubar				no	Heller B. Happy				no
Fun, Wasn't It?				yes	Hellno				no
G.I. Joe				no	Hellsadroppin'				no
Galloping Ghost of					Her Baroness			42-40252	yes
the English Coast				no	Hi-Priority Stuff		2 PCS	44-40967	yes
Gambler's Luck				yes	Holiday Inn				no
Georgia				no	Home Alive in '45				yes
Georgia Peach				yes	Homesick Angel				yes
Georgia Piece				no	Homesick Susie				no
Gerenime				no	Homing Pigeon			44-40247	no
Glamouras'		4 PCS	44-40616	yes	Honey Lulu				yes
Glass House				no	Hornet's Nest				no
Glo Girl			44-41138	no	Hot and Available				yes
Glorious Lady				no	Hot Dish				no
Godfather's Inc.			42-97266	no	Hot Rock				no
Goin' Home-					Hot To Go				yes
Tennessee				yes	Hotcha Baby				no
Gol Walloper				no	I Walk Alone Also			42-51546	no
Goose's Garbage					I Yam Wot I Yam				yes
Wagon				yes	I'll Be Around				yes
Gracie (Fields)				yes	Impatient Lady				no
Gran Slam				no	Innocence Abroad				yes
Granpappy (XB-24)			39-680	yes	Is This Trip Necessary?				yes
Gravel Gertie				yes	Island Dream				yes
Green Eyes				no	Island Queen				yes
Gremlin (The)				no	IV F Sack Time Sally			44-40380	yes
Gremlin's Delight			41-23858	yes	J.F.Whiggles Delivery				
Gremlin's Haven		868	42-40653	no	Service				yes
Ground Happy				no	Jamey				yes
Guardian Angel				yes	Jay Bird (The)				no
Guiding Light (The)				yes	Jazz Ax Blues (The)		2PC		no
Gus			42-40255	yes	Jean B				no
Gussie				yes	Jersey the Gremlin				no
Gypsy from					Jest for Laughs				no
Pokipsie				yes	Jester				no
Half & Half				no	Jig's Up (The)		801	42-51232	yes
Half & Half			44-49577	yes	Jigs Up (The)				no
Hamtramch Mama				yes	Jilted Joker				no
Hangar Queen				yes	Jinx (The)				yes
Hangover				yes	Jive Bomber - Hilarious Hell				no
Happy				no	Joe				yes
Happy Go-Lucky			42-52772	yes	Joker				yes
Hard Luck				no	Joker (The)				yes
Hard Luck				no	Joker's Wild (The)			42-40772	yes
Hard T' Get			42-52299	yes	Jokers (The)				no
Hard To Get				yes	Jose				yes
Hard To Hit				yes	Jose Carioca			42-100078	yes
Hare Force			42-97948	yes	Jose's "El Diablo"	5AF			yes
Harry S. Truman (The)				yes	Juarez				no
Hart's Ease				no	Judith Ann				no
Heaven Can Wait				no	Judy Sue				no
Heaven Can Wait				yes	Jukie L. Lynn				no
Heaven's Above				yes	Jungle Queen			AL640	no

Name	Grp.	Sq.	Serial	Pic.	Name	Grp.	Sq.	Serial	Pic.
K for King			41-23811	no	Little Joe				yes
Katy-Did				no	Little Joe Buffalo				no
Kay Bar				yes	Little Lulu			44-40147	no
KO! Kidde		55W	44-49527	yes	Little Queen II	SAAF			yes
Krachy Kourier				yes	Lonesome Polecat				no
L'il Peach				no	Lonesome				
Laden Maiden				no	Polecat, Jr.				yes
Lady from Hades				no	Long Distance			xx-x0640	yes
Lady in the Dark		36	42-50665	no	Long Island Belle		2REC	42-64327	no
Lady Irene		885	42-40697	no	Look Who's Here				no
Lady Jane		36	42-51188	no	Lovable Lorena				yes
Lady Jane II		868	44-41464	yes	Lovell's Air Force				no
Lady Luck				yes	Lovely Louise				yes
Lady Luck			42-40778	no	Luck's Stuff				no
Lady Luck II		868	44-42131	no	Lucky ____				yes
Lady Margaret (The)		868	42-40639	no	Lucky 7 (The)				yes
Lady Mary		885	44-49336	no	Lucky Lass II			42-95023	no
Lady Penny				no	Lucky Penny			42-40169	no
Lady Pete			42-109969	yes	Lucky Strike				yes
Lady Will (The)				yes	Lucky Strike			44-40146	no
Lady X	India	45		yes	Lucky Thirty				no
Lakanookie			42-50789	yes	Lucy Quipment				no
Lambsy Divey				no	Lus Shus Lay Dee				yes
Lamsy Divey				no	M for Mike				no
Land's End				no	Mabel			42-64182	yes
Lane Tech of Chicago				no	Mad Mis Fit				no
Lascivious Lil				yes	Madson's Madhouse				no
Last Roundup (The)			xx-xx927	no	Maggie - The War Horse				no
Latest Rumor (The)				no	Maggie-Nut (The)				yes
Laude End				no	Magic Carpet				no
Leading Lady (The)		406	41-28871	no	Maid in U.S.A.			44-40776	yes
Leakin' Deakom				yes	Maiden America				yes
Leaking Lucy			41-23736	yes	Makin' Believe				no
Left Out				yes	Mal Function				no
Li'l Cookie			42-7461	no	Male				no
Li'l Pudge/Rum Dum		36	42-51230	no	Male Call				yes
Liberator			42-52117	yes	Male Call				yes
Liberator Express			AHYB	yes	Male Call				yes
Liberty Belle			xx-xx656	yes	Mama's Kids Bombs Away				no
Liberty Run				yes	Mamma's Kids				yes
Lil De-Icer				yes	Mammy Yokum				yes
Lil' Cookie			42-94842	no	Man-O-War				no
Lil' De-Icer				yes	Margie Ann				no
Lil' De-Icer				yes	Margie Ann III				no
Lily Marlene				yes	Marizy Doats				no
Linda Ann & Her Wee R			44-40492	no	Marlene				yes
Lingering Lil				yes	Mary				yes
Little Audrey			41-29522	no	Mary - Big Wheels				yes
Little Bold				no	Maternity Ward				yes
Little Brother				yes	Max Sack				no
Little Clamwinkle			44-8424	no	McSwine's Flying Comet				yes
Little Darling				no	Meddlesome				
Little Davey			44-40459	no	Maggie				yes
Little Fellow				no	Men from Mars				no
Little Flower		406		no	Midnight Mistress		406		no
Little Joe			42-40532	yes	Mighty Seven/				
Little Joe			42-40533	yes	Tojo's Doom Gal				yes

181

Name	Grp.	Sq.	Serial	Pic.	Name	Grp.	Sq.	Serial	Pic.
Milk Run Mamie				no	No Name				no
Milk Wagon Express				yes	No Name Baby				no
Miller High Life				yes	Nobody's Baby				no
Million $ Baby				yes	Nocturnal Mission			44-41263	yes
Million Dollar Baby			42-97268	no	Nocturnal Nemesis				yes
Misbehavin'				yes	Not Hard To Take				yes
Miss America			44-10554	yes	O'Riley's Daughter				yes
Miss Ann		55W	44-49555	yes	O-Bar				no
Miss B-Haven		801	42-50844	yes	Oakland County, Mich.				yes
Miss Bubbles		868	42-40836	no	Octane Ozzie				no
Miss Dede Belle				yes	Odessa				yes
Miss Dorothy				yes	Off Limits				yes
Miss Gay				no	Off We Go		2PCS	42-64185	yes
Miss Giving				yes	Oklahoma				no
Miss Irish			42-97998	no	Ol' Witch				yes
Miss Led				yes	Old 26				no
Miss Liberty				yes	Old Bag of Bolts			40-2376	no
Miss Mandy				yes	Old Baldy				yes
Miss Manookie				yes	Old Big Sugah				no
Miss McKrachin				yes	Old Consistent			40-2375	no
Miss Minooky				no	Old Flak Alley				no
Miss Possum				yes	Old George				no
Miss Possum /My Texas				yes	Old Goat (The)				no
Miss Stardust			41-29522	no	Old Mutual (The)				yes
Miss Stardust		406	42-37522	no	Old Patches (F-7)		4PR		yes
Miss Temptation				yes	Old Yard Dog (The)			42-98006	no
Miss-Ma-Nookie				no	Olde Mother Hubbard				yes
Mission Complete				yes	Ole Buckshot			42-50139	yes
Mission Maid				yes	Ole Herringbone				yes
Mister. (period)				yes	One More Time			44-50702	no
Mites Pet				no	Our Baby			41-29289	no
Mizpah				yes	Our Gal			42-100508	no
Modest O'Miss				yes	Our Honey				no
Monster			44-40474	no	Our Kissin' Cousin			40-2369	no
Mouse (The)				no	Our Last Hope				no
Mrs. Lucky				yes	Outa This World				yes
Muscle Bound				no	Over Exposed				yes
Muscle Bound II				no	Over Exposed		2PC	42-73020	yes
Mutzie B			42-98014	no	Over Loaded		55W	44-49520	yes
Mutzie B			42-98019	no	Pacific Passion		4PC	44-40147	yes
My Beloved Norma				no	Paddlin' Madelin				yes
My Bill				yes	Pancho				yes
My Boy Jerry				yes	Paper Doll				no
My Buddy				no	Patricia Ann				yes
My Dying Ass			44-40088	no	Pay Day			41-28938	yes
My Heart Belongs to Daddy			44-41696	yes	Payload Patty				no
My Tuffy				no	Pecker Red				yes
Nancy			44-41498	yes	Peggy				no
Nancy Girl				no	Peggy			42-40502	no
Naughty Nan			52-51581	no	Peggy Jo			42-94744	no
Nella			42-94940	no	Peggy Rose				yes
Nelly Fly				yes	Pepsodent Kid				no
Nemsis		86CMS	42-73032	yes	Pepsodent Maid				yes
Nightmare				yes	Perils of Pauline				no
Nipponese Nipper			AL570	no	Pete				yes
Nita			41-29146	no	Photo Fanny (F-7)		2PCS	42-73157	yes
					Piccadilly Commando				no

Name	Grp.	Sq.	Serial	Pic.	Name	Grp.	Sq.	Serial	Pic.
Pickled Peach				yes	Returner (The)				yes
Pidgeon Coop				yes	Rice Paddy Hattie				yes
Pig Dealer			42-94851	no	Rim Runner				no
Pima Paisano			44-44175	yes	Road Back (The)				yes
Pinocchio			42-40355	yes	Rob				yes
Pirate Princess		86CM	42-64174	no	Ronny				no
Pistol Packin' Mama				yes	Roost (The)				no
Pistol Packin' Mama				yes	Rose O'Day				yes
Pistol Packin' Mama				yes	Rough and ...				yes
Pittsburgh Babe				yes	Rough Rid'er				yes
Plastered Bastard				no	Rovin' Lady				yes
Play Boy				yes	Royal Screw!				yes
Playmate		36	42-51685	no	Run on Sugar (A)				yes
Pleasure Cruise				no	Ruptured Duck (The)				no
Pleasure Cruise II				no	Rusty				no
Pleasure Cruise III				no	S-S-Sylvia				yes
Polaris the					Sac Rat				no
Heavenly Body				yes	Sack Rat				no
Pom Pom Express			44-50459	yes	Sad Sack				yes
Powers Girl (The)				yes	Sad Sack (The)			42-99988	no
Pretty Kitty				yes	Saipanda				yes
Pretty Mickey				yes	Sally				no
Pretty Petty				yes	Sally Ann				yes
Pretty Prairie Special				yes	Salvo Sally			42-52757	no
Princess Carol		3	44-41331	yes	Sassy Lassy				yes
Princess Pat				yes	Satan's Baby				yes
Problem Child				yes	Satan's Baby				yes
Problem Child				yes	Schooner (The)				yes
Pudgy				no	Scorpion				yes
Pug				yes	Scorpion (drawing)				yes
Punkie				yes	Screaming (Out) House				yes
Purple Shaft				no	Seed-of-Satan			42-40745	no
Purple Shaft				yes	Semi Eager				no
Pursuit of Happiness				yes	Sentimental Journey-Am				yes
Que Pasa?				yes	Seven Up				no
Queen of Hearts				yes	Shack (The)			44-40398	no
Question Mark (The)				no	Shack Rabbit II			42-30372	yes
Rabbit Habit				no	Shack Time II			42-94841	no
Rag Doll			42-95099	no	Shackin' Stuff		2PCS	42-73033	yes
Rage in Heaven			44-40186	no	Shady Character III				yes
Rainbow Virgin				yes	Shady Lady				no
Ramblin Rocket				no	Shady Lady			44-41916	no
Ramblin Wreck II				no	Shady Sadie				yes
Ramblin' Wreck				yes	Shake				no
Ramp Champ		3PRS	44-41996	yes	Shake II				no
Ramp Rooster				yes	Shake III				no
Razzle Dazzle				yes	Shaknstuff		2PCS	42-73033	yes
Ready and Waiting				no	Shanghai Lil				yes
Ready for Let				no	Sharpy				no
Ready, Willing and Able			42-95427	no	She Wolf				yes
Rebel (The)				yes	She Wolf	AD4			no
Red Ace				no	Shirley Ann				yes
Red Arrow (The)				yes	Shiverless				yes
Redding's Rummies				yes	Shoo Shoo Baby			42-95183	no
Reddy Teddy				yes	Shoo! Shoo Baby				no
Redwing				yes	Shoo! Shoo! Baby			42-50201	no
Repulser			41-28843	no	Shoo! Shoo! Baby			42-50204	yes

Name	Grp.	Sq.	Serial	Pic.	Name	Grp.	Sq.	Serial	Pic.
Shoo-Shoo Baby				no	Spain			41-23740	no
Shoo-Shoo Baby				no	Spare Parts				no
Shoot, You're					Spike and Pickles Pub				yes
Faded				yes	Spirit of '44				yes
Short Arm				yes	Spirit of '76				yes
Short Snorter				yes	Spirit of Jackson Heights				yes
Shot Load				yes	Spirit of London	EW620		44-39237	no
Shy Ann				yes	St. Louis Woman				yes
Shy Daddy				no	St. Teresa of Little Flower	406			no
Shy Shark				no	Star Dust			41-29364	no
Siapanda				yes	Stardust				no
Sierra Blanca			44-40152	no	Stardust				yes
Silver Dollar				yes	Stardust			41-29634	no
Silver Dollar			xx-xx631	no	State of New York				no
Silver Shark				yes	Stella				yes
Sittin' Pretty				no	Sterile Errol	India			yes
Sitting Pretty				yes	Stingeroo				yes
Skipper				yes	Stinky				no
Skipper Junior				no	Stinky				yes
Skippy				yes	Stinky				yes
Sky Lady				yes	Stinky				yes
Sky Watch				yes	Stork Club				yes
Sky Witch				yes	Strange Cargo				no
Sky Wolf Avenger				yes	Stud Duck			44-40538	no
Sky's the Limit (The)			44-28276	yes	Subdued				no
Slammin' Spammy				no	Subtractor				no
Sleepless Nights			41-29487	no	Sugar Baby			42-51091	yes
Sleepy Time Gal				yes	Sunday Punch				no
Sleepy Time Gal				yes	Sunrise				no
Sleepy Time Gal				yes	Sunsetter				yes
Sleepytime Gal				yes	Sunshine Jane			42-94801	no
Sleepytime Gal				yes	Supercan				yes
Sleepytime Gal			42-98007	yes	Superstitious Aloysius				no
Sleepytime Gal			44-41503	yes	Swea Pea II				no
Slick Chick				no	Sweat Box				yes
Slightly Virgin				yes	Sweat Box			44-50471	yes
Slip Stream				yes	Sweating Betty				no
Slo Freight			42-50793	no	Sweet Job		868	42-94927	yes
Small Change				yes	Sweet N Bitter				no
Smooth Sailing				yes	Sweet Revenge				yes
Smooth Takeoff				yes	Sweet Sue				no
Snafu				yes	Swing Shift				no
Snag On				yes	T-Bar				no
Snark			41-29347	yes	Tail Wind		868	44-40467	yes
Sneezy				yes	Tailwind				yes
Snicklefritz				no	Tain't What You Do...				yes
Snow White				yes	Tally Ho			42-110173	no
So Round So Firm					Tangerine				yes
So Fully Packed				yes	Tantalizing Tillie				no
So Velly Solly			41-23985	no	Tar Baby				yes
Solid				yes	Tarfu				yes
Sooner Queen				no	Ten-O-K				no
Sorry Bird				no	Ten-O-K II				no
Southern Belle			44-51082	no	Texas Termite				yes
Southern Belle				yes	Texas Twister				no
Southern Comfort III			42-50895	yes	Thai Times				yes
Southern Queen II			42-63959	yes	This Above All		4PCS	44-40316	yes

Name	Grp.	Sq.	Serial	Pic.	Name	Grp.	Sq.	Serial	Pic.
This Is It Men/ Bama Bound- Lovely Libba		36	42-50622	no	Weather Witch II		55W	44-49522	yes
					Weaver's Beavers				yes
This Is It!				no	Well Developed		4PCS	44-40209	yes
Three Dreams and a Drink				yes	Whaler (The)				no
Thumper II				yes	What's Cookin'				yes
Thunder Bird				yes	What's Cookin' Doc?			42-110102	yes
Thuper Wabbit				yes	What's Up Doc?				yes
Tiger			42-51100	no	Whee				yes
Tiger Bell				no	Wheels of Justice				no
Time Wounds All Heels				yes	White Angel(C-109)				yes
Tobasco Keeds				no	Why Daddy?				no
Tojo				no	Wicked Widget III			42-109792	no
Toni-7				yes	Wild Bill				no
Tropical Trollop				no	Willie's Folly				yes
Trouble				yes	Win With Page				no
Trouble Maker				yes	Wind Haven			42-51903	no
True Love		55W	44-49502	yes	Wing Man				no
Trula Marie				yes	Winged Fury				yes
Tuff Ship				yes	Winged Victory				yes
Tug				no	Witch (The)				yes
Tulsa Joe				yes	Wokkish				yes
Twin Nifties II				yes	Wolf Gang II				no
Twin Tail				yes	Wolf Pack			42-100268	no
Two Pair				yes	Wolf Patrol				yes
Typhoon				yes	Wolf Patrol				yes
U Name It, We'll Fly It				yes	Wolfgang				no
U.S.A.F.I.				yes	Worry Bird (The)				no
Umbriago				yes	Worth Fighting For				yes
Uncle Jim		3	44-41315	yes	Yankee Maid				yes
Uncle's Fury		868		no	Yard Bird			AL515	no
Uninvited		36	42-51239	no	You Name It				no
Union Jack				no	ZZGGAAKK (The)				yes
Up Late				no					
Urgin' Virgin				yes					
Urgin' Virgin			42-40608	yes					
US Express (The)				yes					
USAFI				yes					
V8			44-51251	yes					
Vampin' Vera			41-29301	no					
Velma				yes					
Vinegar Joe				yes					
Virgin on the Verge				yes					
Virgin's Vampire				no					
Vulture (The)				yes					
Vulture (The)				yes					
Wacky Wabbit				yes					
Waddy's Wagon				yes					
Wajid Trouble				yes					
Walden Belle				yes					
Wapello Belle				yes					
Warm Front		55W	44-49524	yes					
We The People				yes					
We'll Get By			44-40118	no					
Weary Wolf (The)			41-29478	no					
Weary Wolf II (The)				yes					
Weather Witch		55W	44-49506	yes					

B-24s Worldwide in World War II

Eighth Air Force, May, 1945
(England)

B-24

2nd Wing	14th Wing	20th Wing	96th Wing
389th BG	44th BG	93rd BG	458th BG
445th BG	392nd BG	446th BG	466th BG
453rd BG	491st BG	448th BG	467th BG

Fifteenth Air Force May, 1945
(Italy)

47th Wing	304th Wing	55th Wing	49th Wing
98th BG	454th BG	460th BG	451st BG
376th BG	455th BG	464th BG	461st BG
449th BG	456th BG	465th BG	484th BG
450th BG	459th BG	485th BG	

Pacific Air Forces, Summer 1945
(Asia-Pacific-Alaska)

5th AF	7th AF	10th AF	11th AF	13th AF	14th AF
22 BG	11 BG	7 BG	28 BG	5 BG	308 BG
43 BG	30 BG			307 BG	
90 BG	494 BG				
380 BG					

All Pacific B-17 units eventually converted to B-24s except the 19 BG,
   which became a B-29 outfit.

8th AF organization is shown after 6 bomb groups converted from
   B-24s to B-17s. Most of those B-24s went to the 15th AF.

8th AF Heavy Bomber Org. -- May, 1945

1st Division

1st Wing		40th Wing		41st Wing		94th Wing	
91	A	92	B	303	C	351	J
322	LG	325	NV	358	VK	508	YB
323	OR	326	JW	359	BN	509	RQ
324	DF	327	UX	360	PU	510	TU
401	LL	407	PY	427	GN	511	DS
381	L	305	G	379	K	401	S
532	VE	364	WF	524	WA	612	SC
533	VP	365	XK	525	FR	613	IN
534	GD	366	KY	526	LF	614	IW
535	MS	422	JJ	527	FO	615	IY
398	W	306	H	384	P	457	U
600	N8	367	GY	544	SU	748	--
601	3O	368	BO	545	JD	749	--
602	K8	369	W	546	BK	750	--
603	N7	423	RD	547	SO	751	--

3rd Division

13th Wing		45th Wing		4th Wing		93rd Wing	
95	B	96	C	94	A	34	S
334	BG	337	QJ	331	QE	4	Q6
335	OE	338	BX	332	XM	7	R2
336	ET	339	AW	333	TS	18	8I
412	QW	413	MZ	410	GL	391	3L
100	D	388	H	447	K	385	G
349	XR	560	--	708	CQ	548	GK
350	LN	561	--	709	IE	549	XA
351	EP	562	--	710	IJ	550	SG
418	LD	563	--	711	IR	551	HR
390	J	452	L	486	W	490	T
568	BI	728	9Z	832	3R	848	7W
569	CC	729	M3	833	4N	849	W8
570	DI	730	6K	834	2S	850	7Q
571	FC	731	7D	835	H8	851	S3
				487	P	493	X
				836	2G	860	NG
				837	4F	861	Q4
				838	2C	862	8M
				839	R5	863	G6

2nd Division

2nd Wing		14th Wing		20th Wing		96th Wing	
389	C	44	A	93	B	458	K
564	YO	66	WQ	328	GO	752	7V
565	EE	67	NB	329	RE	753	J4
566	RR	68	GJ	330	AG	754	Z5
567	HP	506	QK	409	YM	755	J3
445	F	392	D	446	H	466	L
700	RN	576	CI	704	FL	784	T9
701	MK	577	DC	705	HM	785	2U
702	WV	578	EC	706	RT	786	U8
453	J	491	Z	448	I	467	P
732	E3	852	3Q	712	CT	788	X7
733	E8	853	T8	713	IG	789	6A
734	F8	854	6X	714	EI	790	QZ
735	R6	855	V2	715	IO	791	4Z

489 BG not shown
(last mission 10 Nov 44)
844 - 4R
845 - S4
846 - 8R
847 - T4

492 BG not shown
(last mission 7 Aug 44)
856 - 5Z
857 - 9H
858 - 9A
859 - X4

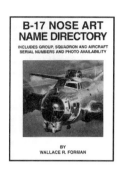

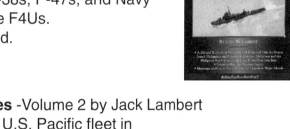
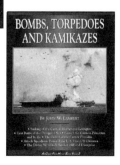